I0032681

The Rise of the House of Rothschild

Ancestral Home of the Rothschild Family
at Frankfort-on-the-Main

The Rise of the House of Rothschild

COUNT EGON CAESAR CORTI

Translated from the German by
Brian and Beatrix Lunn

Books for Business
New York-Hong Kong

The Rise of the House of Rothschild

by
Count Egon Caesar Corti

ISBN: 0-89499-058-6

Copyright © 2001 by Books for Business

Reprinted from the 1928 edition

Books for Business
New York - Hong Kong
http://www.BusinessBooksInternational.com

All rights reserved, including the right to reproduce this book, or portions thereof, in any form.

In order to make original editions of historical works available to scholars at an economical price, this facsimile of the original edition of 1928 is reproduced from the best available copy and has been digitally enhanced to improve legibility, but the text remains unaltered to retain historical authenticity.

FOREWORD

Historians, in interpreting the nineteenth century, have laid stress on many and various aspects of the period under study; and descriptions of isolated periods, single episodes, and individuals are scattered amongst hundreds and even thousands of books. On the other hand, certain special features of the period under consideration have been, for various reasons, entirely neglected.

An example of such neglect is the ignoring by historians of the rôle played by the Rothschild family in the history of the nineteenth century, and the object of this work is to appraise the important influence of this family on the politics of the period, not only in Europe but throughout the world. For, strangely enough, the influence of the Rothschilds is barely mentioned, or at the most casually referred to, in otherwise comprehensive and painstaking historical treatises.

Special literature dealing with the House of Rothschild usually falls into one of two groups, either fulsome pæans of praise commissioned by the House itself, or scurrilous pamphlets inspired by hatred—both equally unpleasant. There are, however, two works of serious value in existence, which are partially compiled from legal documents, but they are of small scope. One is by an employee of the Rothschilds, Christian Wilhelm Berghoeffer, and the other is the impartial work of Dr. Richard Ehrenberg; but these treat only of isolated incidents in the history of the House, and throw no light on its pan-European importance.

The object of the present work, which deals with the period 1770-1830, is to trace the rise of the House of Rothschild from its small beginnings to the great position it attained, culminating in the year of its great crisis.

In the course of my researches I found that references to the name of Rothschild in official documents and in books of memoirs were as common as they are rare in contemporary textbooks. I made a point of collecting all available data until my drawers were literally crammed with letters, deeds, and documents containing the name of Rothschild, and bearing dates of almost every year of the nineteenth century. My next step was to visit the various European capitals which had been the scene of the family activities, in order to enrich my store of references with all the relevant literature. The subject is indeed inexhaustible, but the material I had amassed encouraged me to essay a complete picture.

The subject required the most delicate treatment, but my determination to undertake the work was accompanied by the definite intention of according it complete impartiality, for I was convinced from the beginning that a prejudiced outlook would render the work utterly valueless.

The House of Rothschild, as will be readily understood, did not throw open its archives to my inspection, for it is particularly careful in guarding its more important business secrets. But this was not entirely without its advantage, for it left me completely free from political considerations and uninfluenced by racial, national, and religious predilections or antipathies. I was thus enabled, in accordance with my wish, to begin an independent historical research into the part played by this House in the nineteenth century, which I knew to be far more important than is commonly thought.

The general scheme of this work will be built upon facts alone, in a practical way such as will help us to form our own judgment on individuals and the part they played in world events.

I should like to take this opportunity of expressing my special sense of gratitude toward all those whose advice and assistance have been so valuable to me in my work.

Above all I have to thank Dr. Bittner, Director of the State Archives at Vienna, as well as his exceedingly helpful staff, Professors Gross, Antonius, Reinoehl, Schmidt, Wolkan, and his Chief Clerk, Herr Marek. I should also like to thank Lieutenant-Colonel von Carlshausen, grandnephew of the man who helped the Rothschilds up the first rung of the ladder, and the Director of the Prussian Secret State Archives at Berlin, Geheimrat Klinkenborg. My thanks are also due to Dr. Losch of the Prussian State Library in Berlin, Dr. A. Richel at Frankfort and the staff of the Municipal Museum in that city who, together with the Director of the Portrait Collection in the Vienna National Library, Hofrat Dr. Rottinger and Dr. Wilhelm Beetz, who so kindly assisted me with the illustrations.

The material was collected for over a period of three and a half years, and only after much care has been spent on it do I now offer it to the public. It is submitted in the hope that it will be judged in accordance with its intentions. It is inspired by an intense love of truth, and it relates the story of an unseen but infinitely powerful driving force which permeated the whole of the nineteenth century.

The Author

Vienna, July, 1927.

CONTENTS

ILLUSTRATIONS

The Rise of the House of Rothschild

The Rise of the House of Rothschild

CHAPTER I

The Origins and the Early Activities of the Frankfort Family Rothschild

FRANKFORT-ON-THE-MAIN, seat of the Imperial Elections since the Golden Bull of 1356, acquired a dominating position amongst the great cities of Germany during the second half of the eighteenth century. Formerly the capital of the kingdom of the East Franks, it had become subject to the empire alone as early as 1245, and in spite of many vicissitudes it had maintained its leading position throughout the centuries. It expanded considerably during the last few centuries before the French Revolution and now numbered some 35,000 inhabitants, of whom one-tenth were Jews. By virtue of its natural position, lying so close to the great waterway of the Rhine and to the frontiers of France and Holland, it had become the gateway for the trade of Germany with the western states. Trade with England too constituted an important element in the activities of its inhabitants.

It was natural that members of the Jewish race, with their special gifts for trade and finance, should be particularly attracted to this city. Moreover, towards the end of the Middle Ages the Jews in Frankfort enjoyed a great measure of freedom, and at first no difficulties were placed in the way of their settlement. It was not until the non-Jewish members of the business community at Worms saw that they were suffering from the competition of these enterprising people that the Christian citizens combined in their superior numbers.

Now began a period of harsh oppression for the Jewish inhabitants. In order that they might be removed from the neighborhood of the most important church in the town, they were ordered by a law passed in the year 1462 to leave the houses they had been living in and to settle in a quarter set aside for the purpose—the so-called Jewish City.[1] This, however, consisted only of a single dark alley, about twelve feet broad, and lay, as described by Goethe, between the city wall and a trench. For more than three hundred years this continued to be the sole residence of the Frankfort Jews, whose continuance in the city became more and more unpopular with the other inhabitants. As early as the second decade of the seventeenth century a rising broke out under one Fettmilch, one of the objects of which was to drive the Jews out of Frankfort. This object was indeed achieved through murder and pillage. Although the Jews soon returned to the city, they had to submit to innumerable restrictions and regulations embodied in a special law dealing with the so-called "Status of Jews." They were made subject to a poll-tax, and were compelled, as being a foreign element in the town, to purchase the "protection" of their persons and property. Hence they came to be called "protected Jews." The number of their families was to be limited to five hundred and only twelve marriages a year were allowed, although this number might be increased if a family died out. The Jews were not allowed to acquire land, or to practice farming or handicrafts. They were also forbidden to trade in various commodities, such as fruit, weapons and silk. Moreover, except during fairs, they were forbidden to offer their wares anywhere except outside the Jewish quarter. They were forbidden to leave the space within the ghetto walls by night, or on Sundays or holy days. If a Jew crossed a bridge he had to pay a fee for doing so. They were not allowed to visit public taverns and were excluded from the more attractive walks in the city. The Jews accordingly did not stand high in public esteem. When they appeared in public, they were often greeted with shouts of contempt and stones were sometimes thrown at them. Boerne has stated that any street urchin could say to a passing Jew, "Jew, do your duty," and the Jew then had to step aside and take off his hat. However that may be, the oppressed condition of the Jews and the bent of many of them to usury, combined with the natural hostility of the Christians and their feeling that they were not as sharp in business, created an atmosphere of mutual hatred that can scarcely have been more painful anywhere than in Frankfort.

The progenitors of the House of Rothschild lived under conditions such as those in the ghetto of Frankfort. The earlier ancestors of Meyer Amschel Rothschild, who laid the foundations of the future greatness of the house, existed in the middle of the sixteenth century; we know their names, and their tombs have been preserved in the old Jewish cemetery at Frankfort. Formerly the houses in the Jewish quarter were not numbered, each house being distinguished by a shield of a particular color or by a sign. The house in which the members of the Rothschild family lived bore a small red shield. There is no doubt that it is to this fact that they owe their family name; it is first mentioned in 1585 in the name "Isaak Elchanan [2] at the Red Shield," his father's tombstone simply bearing the name Elchanan. About a century later Naftali Hirz at the Red Shield left the ruinous old building from which the family had derived its name, and occupied the so-called Haus zur Hinterpfann, in which the Rothschilds were now domiciled as protected Jews.

Until the time when Meyer Amschel Rothschild—who

was born in the year 1743, six years before Goethe—reached manhood, the family were principally engaged in various kinds of retail trade. At the beginning of the eighteenth century they had become money-changers in a small way. From the occasional records of their tax payments which have been preserved, it would appear that they were not a poor Jewish family, but that they were only reasonably well off.

In any case it is clear that Meyer Amschel came into some small inheritance when, in 1755, in his twelfth year, he lost his father and mother, of whom he was the eldest son; this gave him the incentive to throw himself into the battle of life with that vigor and industry which his parents had implanted in him in his early childhood. In the conditions of those times the struggle was certainly much more severe for a young Jew than for his more fortunate Christian neighbors.

When he was a boy of ten Meyer Amschel had been employed by his father in changing coins of every kind, that is, in exchanging gold and silver for the appropriate amount of copper known as coarse money. In the chaotic conditions prevailing in Germany—divided as the country was into innumerable small principalities, cities and spiritual jurisdictions, all of which had their own currency systems—the business of money-changing offered magnificent opportunities of profit, since everybody was compelled, before undertaking even the shortest journey, to call for the assistance of the exchange merchant. As the boy grew up, an important side interest developed out of this occupation, as he occasionally became possessed of rare and historically valuable coins, which awoke in him the instincts of the coin collector.

After leaving the school at Fürth, where he was educated in the Jewish faith, Meyer Amschel entered the firm of Oppenheim at Hanover. While there he happened to make the acquaintance of the Hanoverian General von Estorff, an ardent coin collector, who employed him to obtain many valuable coins for his collection. As the general was connected with the ruling house in Hesse, this acquaintance was to have fruitful results. In his spare time Meyer Amschel now devoted himself more and more to numismatics. He got hold of any papers about the subject that he could, and in course of time became an expert in his subject, although his general education left a very great deal to be desired. At a comparatively early age he returned to his native city of Frankfort, in order to take possession of his inheritance, and having done so, to lay the foundations of a business of his own. For this he had received a practical education from his earliest youth, both at home and at Hanover.

About the same time General von Estorff left Hanover for the court of Prince William of Hesse, the grandson of the old Landgrave William VIII, who resided at Hesse; he proceeded to the small town of Hanau, which lies quite close to Frankfort. The prince's father Frederick II of Hesse had married a daughter of King George III of England of the House of Hanover, and the two rulers used their family relationships to consolidate their dynastic and political interests. The sale of soldiers for service under foreign governments, practiced by so many German princes at this time, was an important part of their activities; England, being particularly accustomed to carrying on wars with foreign mercenaries, was an exceedingly good customer.

Unfortunately Frederick II fell out with his wife, his father, and his father-in-law, because he changed over from the Protestant to the Catholic faith. In order to protect his grandson from his father's influence the old landgrave decided that William was to be kept away from Cassel, and allotted the county of Hanau to him. Until he should be able to assume the rulership of that province he was sent to King Frederick V of Denmark, who had married the second daughter of the King of England, and whose daughter was destined to be the future bride of young William.

The relations of the ruling House of Hesse with England and Denmark were to be fraught with the most important consequences for the rise of the House of Rothschild, which was enabled to make use of the close business connection that it succeeded in establishing with the ruling House of Hesse, to get into touch with the courts and the leading statesmen of Denmark and England.

The old Landgrave William VIII died in 1760. Frederick assumed the government at Cassel, and William became crown prince; and as the bridegroom of the Danish princess he became, in accordance with the will of his grandfather, independent ruler of the small county of Hanau with its 50,000 inhabitants, to whose interests he devoted himself with the greatest zeal. William was a thoroughly active person, and was never idle for a moment. He read a great deal, and actually wrote some essays on matters of local historical interest. He also tried his hand, though without any great success, at etching, modeling and carpentering, and he had a very definite flair for collecting.

It would appear that General von Estorff aroused his ruler's interest in coin-collecting; in 1763 William adopted this hobby with great enthusiasm, and it afforded him much pleasure and satisfaction. Estorff spoke to him about Meyer Amschel Rothschild, who had bought coins for him in Hanover in former days, as being a great expert in that line.[3] On the strength of this introduction Rothschild selected some of his finest medals and rarest coins, and went to Hanau to offer them to the young prince. He did not succeed in seeing him personally, but he managed to hand them to someone in the prince's immediate entourage. This offer proved to be the starting-point of a lasting business connection, even though at first it was of a quite loose and impersonal nature.

At that time a large number of foreigners used to visit Frankfort every spring. The town fairs were widely famous. The latest products of the whole world were on view there, and young William of Hanau, who had a talent for business, took a special interest in these fairs and constantly attended them. Meyer Amschel always managed to get advance information about these journeys from the prince's servants, and profited by these occasions to offer William while he was in Frankfort not only rare coins but also precious stones and antiques. Although this was principally done through the prince's retinue, he sometimes managed to conduct these transactions personally, and in any case he managed to establish a regular business relationship. He was fortunate in that the prince did not share the general aversion to Jews, and appreciated anyone who seemed intelligent and good at business, and whom he thought he could use in his own interests.

At that time titles and honors were of far greater practical importance than they are today; unless a person had some kind of prefix or suffix all doors were closed to him, and everyone who did not have a title of nobility by the accident of birth would endeavor to obtain an office, or at any rate an official title, from some one of the innumerable counts or princelings who in that day still enjoyed sovereign rights. Meyer Amschel Rothschild, being a shrewd man with an astonishing knowledge of human nature for his years—he was only twenty-five—concentrated on using his connection with the Prince of Hanau to obtain a court title. He hoped thereby not merely to raise his prestige generally, but more particularly to advance his relations with other princes interested in coins.

In 1769 he wrote a most humble petition [4] to the Prince of Hanau, in which, after referring to various goods delivered to the prince to his Highness's most gracious satisfaction, he begged that he might "most graciously be granted the advantage of being appointed court agent." Meyer Amschel promised always to devote all his energy and property to the prince's service, and he concluded his letter with a perfectly sincere statement that if he received the designation in question he hoped thereby to gain business esteem, and that it would otherwise enable him to make his fortune in the city of Frankfort.

This letter, which was written in a style expressive of extreme humility, was the first of an almost endless series of petitions which the various members of the House of Rothschild were to address in the course of the nineteenth century to those occupying the seats of the mighty. Many of these were favorably considered, and assisted no little in establishing the fortunes of that House. This, the first of the series, was granted, and the nomination was duly carried into effect on September 21, 1769. Henceforth to the name of Rothschild was attached the decorative suffix "Crown Agent to the Principality of Hesse-Hanau."

This more or less corresponded with the present-day practice under which a tradesman may display the royal coat-of-arms with the legend "By special appointment," etc. It was a mere designation carrying no obligation, and although it gave expression to the fact that a business man enjoyed the patronage of a customer in the highest circles, it did not imply any official status whatever. Nevertheless this first success gave much joy to Meyer Amschel, since it not only enabled him to make great profits in his old coin business, but gave his firm a special prestige with the world at large, as even the smallest prince shed a certain glamour upon all who came anywhere near his magic circle; and the Prince of Hanau was grandson of the King of England, husband of the daughter of the King of Denmark, and destined to be the ruler of Hesse-Cassel.

Frankfort at the End of the Eighteenth Century
From a painting by F. J. Elmant in the Frankfort Historical Museum

At the age of twenty-five Meyer Amschel was a tall, impressive-looking man of pronounced Hebraic type; his expression, if rather sly, was good-natured. In accordance with the custom of those times he wore a wig, although, as he was a Jew, he was not allowed to have it powdered, and in accordance with the customs of his race he wore a small, pointed black beard. When he took stock of his business and his little property, he could say to himself with justice that he had not merely administered his inheritance intelligently, but substantially increased it. Although he could certainly not be classed amongst the wealthy men of Frankfort, or even amongst the wealthy Jews of that city, he could assuredly be described as well off, and was in a position to think of founding a family.

He had been attracted for some time by the youthful daughter of a tradesman called Wolf Solomon Schnapper, who lived not far from the Rothschilds' house in the Jewish quarter. She was seventeen years old when Meyer Amschel courted her, had been brought up in all the domestic virtues, was simple and modest, and exceedingly industrious, and brought a dowry with her which, though small, was in solid cash. Meyer Amschel's marriage was celebrated on August 29, 1770. After his marriage he would have liked to move from the house *zur Hinterpfann,* which he rented, into a house of his own, but he could not yet afford to do so. The young couple's first child, a daughter, was born as early as 1771, after which followed three boys in the years 1773, 1774, 1775, who were given the names Amschel, Solomon, and Nathan.

While his wife was fully occupied in bringing up the children and running the house, Meyer Amschel developed his business, in which his invalid brother Kalman was a partner until he died in 1782. Without neglecting his ordinary business of money-changing, he bought several collections of coins from needy aristocratic collectors in the district, and he had an antique coin catalogue of his own printed, which he circulated widely, especially among such princes as were interested in numismatics. He sent such catalogues to Goethe's patron Duke Karl August of Weimar, to Duke Karl Theodore of the Palatinate, and of course always to his own benefactor at Hanau,[5] Prince William.

The prince's mother still kept him away from his father, Landgrave Frederick, who was ruling at Cassel, and who made several unsuccessful attempts to get into touch with his son. William had married Princess Caroline of Denmark six years before Meyer Amschel's marriage; but from the first moment of their union they had realized that they were not suited [6] to one another. Indeed so little physical or spiritual harmony was there between the young couple that their marriage might be regarded as an absolute affliction. It finally led to William's entirely neglecting his wife and living with numerous favorites, who bore him children. The families Haynau, Heimrod, and Hessenstein are the descendants of such unions, it being William's practice to obtain titles for his illegitimate children from the Emperor of Austria, in return for the moneys he lent to him. It is difficult to verify the fantastic figures [7] given as to the total number of his illegitimate children; but there is no doubt they were very numerous.

When he assumed the government of his small territory, William of Hanau was in a position to play the rôle of absolute ruler, and his highly marked individuality immediately made itself felt. He was insolent even with the nobility, and often observed that he did not like them to take advantage of any marks of familiar "condescension" [8] that he showed them. On the other hand he did not show any pride in dealing with persons who he thought would serve his interests. He was exceedingly suspicious, quick to see a point, and easily made angry, especially if his divine right was questioned.

He held broad views in religious matters, associated much with Freemasons and practiced complete religious tolerance. Under his rule the Jews enjoyed all kinds of liberties; they did not, for instance, have to display in the market signs to distinguish them from Christian tradespeople. Indeed William took pleasure in their marked talent for business, for in this matter he felt himself to be a kindred spirit. Business considerations governed him even when he was specifically considering the welfare of his soldiers. He would concern himself with the smallest details of their equipment; would pass the new recruits, and would give precise instructions as to the length of the pigtail to be worn. He was particularly fond of parades, and tortured his men with drill and button-polishing. One reason he was particularly anxious that his troops should look smart was that he could make a great deal of money by following the example of his father and grandfather in selling his men to England.

His father Landgrave Frederick had in this way gradually transferred to England 12,000 Hessians, and amassed an enormous fortune in the process. In the same way William sold to England in 1776 the small Hanau regiment, which he had just formed. The conditions of such "subsidy-contracts" were exceedingly oppressive to the customer, as he had to pay substantial compensation for any man who was killed or wounded. The crown prince also increased his property considerably by this means. After deducting all expenses he realized a net profit of about 3,500,000 marks from this business, and there being no distinction between the public and the private purse of a prince, this money was at his absolute personal disposal.

In spite of his princely origin, such were the business instincts of this talented young man that this financial success simply whetted his appetite for amassing greater riches. Had William not been destined to succeed to the throne of Hesse, he would have been an outstandingly successful man of business. As it was he found such outlet as he could for his commercial instincts within the sphere of his princely dignity. Father and son continued to accumulate large capital sums, and they refrained from bringing over to the Continent substantial proportions of the subsidy moneys, which they invested in England itself. The management of these funds was entrusted to the Amsterdam financial house Van der Notten. England did not always pay in cash, but often in bills of exchange that had to be discounted. For this purpose the prince and his officials had to employ suitable middlemen in large commercial centers like Frankfort; although the middlemen had to get their profit out of the business they could not be dispensed with in view of the restricted means of transport and communication at that time. Purchases and sales had to be carefully regulated to prevent the market from being suddenly flooded with bills, the rate of exchange being consequently depressed.

This work fell to the various crown agents and factors; of these the Jew Veidel David was the principal one attached to the landgrave at Cassel, Rothschild being employed only by the crown prince at Hanau, and only in exchange business and to a limited extent in conjunction with several others. His personal relation with the prince was at first exceedingly slender, for, however enlightened he might be, a ruling prince did not easily associate with a Jew, and only long years of useful service, acting upon a temperament such as William's, could break down such natural obstacles. In the first instance men of business had to deal with the crown prince's officials; to get on good terms with them was a primary essential for anybody who wanted to do business with the prince.

One of the most influential members of the crown prince's civil service was an official at the treasury called Carl Frederick Buderus.[9] He was the son of a Hanau schoolmaster, and had shown a special aptitude for the duties of a careful and accurate treasury clerk. His father had been writing- and music-master to the children of the crown prince's mistress Frau von Ritter-Lindenthal, ancestress of the Haynaus, and this had given him the opportunity of bringing to the crown prince's attention a plan of his son's for increasing the milk profits from one of the prince's dairies by the simple expedient of forbidding the practice, adopted by the office concerned, of omitting fractions of a heller in the accounts. Young Buderus showed that this would increase the revenue by 120 thalers. This discovery appealed so strongly to the avaricious prince, who counted every halfpenny, that he entrusted Buderus with the accounts of his private purse, in addition to his normal duties.

Buderus henceforth displayed the greatest zeal in looking after the financial interests of the crown prince. He is generally credited with having been responsible for the introduction of the Salt Tax when the problem of providing for the prince's innumerable natural children became pressing. The resulting increase in the cost of this important article of diet was heavily felt, especially by the poorest inhabitants of Hesse-Cassel. There being no distinction between the public treasury and the private purse we can readily imagine how great this man's influence was. Moreover, the officials of that period were always personally interested on a percentage basis in the financial dealings which they carried through in their official capacity. By arrangement with amenable crown agents with whom they had to deal they could, without any suggestion of bribery, or of acting against the influence of their master, easily so arrange matters that their personal interests would be better served by a clever agent than by one who was less adaptable.

Meyer Amschel brought to his work a certain natural flair for psychology, and he always endeavored to create personal links wherever he possibly could. He naturally made a special point of being on good terms with the

Hanau Treasury officials, and especially with Buderus. They, however, had not as yet sufficient confidence in the financial resources of the Frankfort Jew Rothschild to entrust to him anything except the smaller transactions.

Through the death of Landgrave Frederick, the crown prince suddenly succeeded to the throne of Hesse-Cassel, and to the most extensive property of any German prince of that period. On October 31, 1785, his father Frederick II had suddenly had a stroke during his midday meal and had fallen off his chair, dying a few minutes later. This news came as a complete surprise to the crown prince, as his father had latterly scarcely ever been ill. William of Hanau accordingly succeeded to the throne of Hesse-Cassel as Landgrave William IX. On reading his father's will he learned with pleasure that the country was free of debt, and that he had come into an enormous property. The subsidies received for the sale of mercenaries had been most profitably invested, and estimates the value of the inheritance varied between twenty [10] and sixty [11] million thalers—unparalleled sums for those times.

The new landgrave united his private property at Hanau with his inherited posssessions, and now found himself disposing of an amount of money which conferred far greater power on him than his new dignity. He moved his residence from Hanau, which was close to Frankfort, to Cassel, which lay much farther north, with the result that Meyer Amschel Rothschild's relations with the Hessian court at first suffered from the greater distance which separated him from his patron. But the Jewish tradesman was determined not to lose such a useful connection without a struggle. In order to remind the new landgrave of his existence he visited Cassel again in 1787, bringing with him a remarkably beautiful collection of coins, medals, and jeweled gold chains, and offered these wares to the landgrave at exceptionally low prices. The prince at once appreciated the real value of the articles, and eagerly did business with Meyer Amschel, who took advantage of the opportunity to submit the humble request that he should not be forgotten if any future bills of exchange required discounting, or the prince wanted to purchase English coins.

Rothschild had deliberately made a loss on these small deals in order to secure the chance of much more profitable business in the future, and his valuable articles were readily purchased from him because they were cheap, promises being freely made with regard to the future. But two years passed without his services being asked for. He stood by enviously, seeing other agents getting bills to discount, and being asked to pay interest only after six or eight months, or else to pay over the money in instalments, an arrangement equivalent to allowing the firms concerned substantial free credits. Rothschild had closely followed the business dealings of these firms, and had thought out a very useful way of transacting such matters if he should be entrusted with them.

He decided to pay another call at Cassel. During the summer of 1789 he wrote a letter to the landgrave [12] in which he referred to the services that he had rendered during a long course of years as Hesse-Hanau crown agent, and asked to be considered in connection with the bills-of-exchange business on a credit basis. In order to put himself on a level with his rivals he promised always to do business at a price at least as high as that offered by any banker in Cassel.

The petition—which shows that Rothschild already had control of considerable sums of money—was submitted to the landgrave by Buderus, but William decided that he must first obtain further information about Rothschild's business. His inquiries all produced satisfactory results; Meyer Amschel was described as being punctual in his payments, and as being an energetic and honorable man, who therefore deserved to be granted credit, even if precise figures regarding the extent of his possessions could not be obtained. Nevertheless, Rothschild received only a comparatively small credit transaction to carry out, whilst simultaneously a transaction thirty times as great was entrusted to Veidel David; but, though modest, it was a beginning. Buderus, whose position in the meantime had been steadily increasing in importance, often had occassion to travel between Cassel and Frankfort on business matters. We have evidence of the fact that as early as 1790 he had business dealings with Rothschild's father-in-law Wolf Solomon Schnapper, and it was Schnapper who brought him and Meyer Amschel together.

Rothschild would often get advance information of Buderus's journeys to Frankfort so that he could go and see him when he came. The Hessian official heard from other sources in Frankfort of the clever Jew's rising reputation, and of how he always met his obligations punctually. Buderus was also gradually influenced by Rothschild's own persuasive powers. As early as November, 1790, Buderus's accounts contain an entry regarding a "draft of 2,000 *Laubtaler* to the order of the crown agent Meyer Amschel Rothschild." [13]

Rothschild now urged Buderus, if occasion should arise, to recommend him to the landgrave for substantial dealings also. In 1794 an opportunity for this occurred. The capital sums invested by Hesse in England had grown to a very considerable amount, and the landgrave gave instructions that a portion of them should be brought over to Cassel. In addition to the Christian banking firm of Simon Moritz von Bethmann, which had been established in Frankfort for centuries, and four other firms, Buderus put forward the name of the crown agent Rothschild as suitable for carrying through this transaction. The landgrave, however, attached far too much importance to his old connection with Bethmann, at that time the outstanding banking firm in Germany, and with the other old established firms. and on this occa-

The Ghetto in Frankfort

From a painting by Wilhelm von Hanno
in the Frankfort Historical Museum

sion too Rothschild was left out. But it did not occur again. In the end Buderus's efforts were successful in overcoming the landgrave's aversion, and henceforward Rothschild also was employed to an increasing extent in discounting bills and in other business.

His dealings with the court at Cassel soon became very active, and as Meyer Amschel carried through the matters entrusted to him, not merely conscientiously but with a shrewd eye to gain, the profits which he derived from them increased considerably. It was necessary for the young household that business should be brisk, for in 1788 another son, Carl Meyer, was born, and in 1792 a fifth son Jacob, called James, and Meyer Amschel's marriage had also been blessed with five daughters. There was the large family of twelve persons to feed; however, Meyer Amschel's flourishing business was not merely adequate to support his family, but there was a considerable and constantly increasing surplus available for increasing his business capital. In 1785, as an outward and visible sign of his increasing prosperity, he bought a handsome residence, the house known as *zum grünen Schild,* while he transferred to a relative the house *zur Hinterpfann* in which he had lived hitherto, and which he had partially purchased since being nominated crown agent.

The house into which the Rothschild family now moved is still standing almost as it was then; it is the right half of a building comprising two quite small family dwellings, typical of the straitened circumstances of the Jewish quarter. Only the three left windows of the house front belonged to the Rothschilds, and above the first door was a small, scarcely noticeable five-sided convex green shield.[14] The right half of the building, known as the house *zur Arche,* belonged to the Jewish family Schiffe, who kept a second-hand shop in it; over the door was a small carved ship representing the boat of Columbus.[15]

As the door of the Rothschild house was opened, an ancient bell was set ringing, sending its warning notes right through the house. Every step one took revealed the painful congestion in which the Jews of that period were compelled to exist, the only quarters where they were allowed to live being comprised within the small and narrow Jews' street. Everything in the house was very narrow, and each particle of space was turned to account. A creaking wooden staircase, underneath which cupboards had been built in, led to the upper floor, and to the little "green room" of Gudula, the mistress of the house, so called because the modest furniture in it was upholstered in green. In a glass case on the table was the withered bridal wreath of Meyer Amschel's wife. Let into the left wall was a small secret cupboard, concealed by a mirror hanging in front of it. In this matter, too, space was carefully utilized, there being cupboards built into the wall wherever possible, such as are now coming into use again.

On the ground floor was the parents' small bedroom, while the numerous children had to share one other little room. A narrow passage led to a kind of roof terrace—a tiny roof garden with a few plants. As the Jews were not allowed in the public gardens this roof garden furnished a modest substitute, and served as the family recreation ground. As it is laid down that the Feast of the Tabernacle must be celebrated in the open air, and there was no other place available, the little roof garden was used for this purpose.

Behind the house, and overlooking the narrow courtyard, was a room about nine feet square, which was actually the first banking house of the Rothschilds. Its most important article of furniture was a large iron chest with an enormous padlock. However, the lock was so contrived that the chest could not be opened on the side where the lock was, but only by lifting the lid from the back. In this room, too, there were secret shelves cleverly concealed in the walls. The kitchen of the house was very modest, the room being about twelve feet long and only about five feet broad; a tiny hearth, which could accommodate only one cooking pot, a chest, and a bench were about all that it contained. There was one fixture that constituted a great luxury for those times, a primitive pump which conveyed drinking water direct to the kitchen.

Such was the scene of the early activities of Meyer Amschel and his sons, whose energy and enterprise laid the foundations for the future development of their House.

Berghoeffer's researches indicate that the annual income of the House of Rothschild, before the war period of the 1790's, may be estimated at between 2,000 and 3,000 gulden.[16] We are better able to realize what this meant when we consider that the expenditure of Goethe's family, who were people of position, was about 2,400 gulden a year. On such an income it was possible to live quite comfortably at Frankfort at that time, although the political disturbances which were developing soon began to produce their effect. Events profoundly affecting the course of all future history had taken place.

The repercussions of the French Revolution were felt throughout Europe. There was no one, whether prince or peasant, who did not directly or indirectly feel its influence. The principle of equality which it proclaimed aroused emotions of hope or dismay throughout the world, according to the social position of each individual. On the standards of the revolutionary armies was inscribed their determination to extend the benefits of their achievements throughout the world, and those who had seized the reins of power were soon to aim at world dominion. This fact constituted a special menace to the German princes whose territories bordered on France. The refugees of the French nobility flooded Germany, and many of them arrived at the Cassel court.

Landgrave William had occasion to hear many of the terrible stories told by the emigrants who had lost their nearest relatives under the guillotine, and had been forced to go abroad as homeless refugees reduced to absolute poverty. The impression gained from the sufferers themselves, the news regarding the threatened execution of the king and his consort, and the reports of the cruel treatment meted out to all who enjoyed princely or noble privileges caused him to tremble for his crown, as all the princes of Europe were trembling. He was also concerned about his enormous wealth, a special source of danger at such a time; and he therefore did not require much pressing to join the great coalition of princes against revolutionary France.

At the head of this coalition was Francis of Austria, who was shortly to be elected emperor, and who had been the first to ally himself with Prussia against France. Landgrave William attached particular importance to his relations with the man who was shortly to be emperor, and in a letter [17] to the "Most Excellent, Most Puissant King and highly honored cousin" he hastened to promise his military help as a proof of his "most special devotion to your high wishes." Francis of Austria expressed his gratitude and observed that this should serve as an example to others, especially as "not only every territorial prince and government of whatever kind they may be, but also every private person possessed of any property, or who has been blessed by God with any possessions or rights acquired by inheritance or otherwise must realize with ever growing conviction . . . that the war is a universal war declared upon all states, all forms of government, and even upon all forms of private property, and any orderly regulation of human society, as is clearly proved by the chaotic condition and internal desolation of France and her raging determination to spread similar conditions throughout the world." [18]

But the union of princes had much underrated the offensive of revolutionary France. Under the handicap of bad leadership and lack of unity the Allies were unable to prevail against the revolutionary armies, inspired by the ideals of liberty and nationalism. Prussia and Hesse were forced to retire; and the French General de Custine actually succeeded in crossing the Rhine in 1792 and reaching Frankfort, with the result that William retired in a panic to Cassel, greatly concerned about his crown treasures. With rage and indignation he read the French manifesto to the Hessian soldiers which urged them to forsake the "tyrant and tiger who sold their blood in order to fill his chest." The landgrave finally succeeded in driving the small French force out of Frankfort. This cost him a considerable sum of money but his loss was made good by a new subsidy contract under which he delivered 8,000 Hessian soldiers to England, which had joined the Coalition against France. Meyer Amschel Rothschild and his rivals were kept fully occupied in discounting the bills received from England in connection with this transaction.

When, in 1795, Prussia withdrew from the war against the French Republic, the Landgrave of Hesse followed her example. His ambition now was to have the comparatively modest title of landgrave changed, and to attain electoral rank. In the meantime he had been created a field-marshal of Prussia, and in 1796, when Napoleon's star was in the ascendant, relations between the two countries were particularly cordial. In spite, however, of the secession of Prussia and Hesse, England and Austria continued to carry on the war of the coalition with varying success. Whilst Bonaparte was victorious in Italy, the Archduke Karl gained a series of successes in the south of Germany. Frankfort had to suffer again from the vicissitudes of war; on July 13, 1796, it was actually bombarded by the French with the result that some of the houses in the Jewish quarter—156 buildings including the synagogue, most of which were inferior wooden structures—were set on fire.

The Rothschild house, which was one of the best-constructed buildings in the street, suffered only slight damage. In view of the time required to rebuild these houses a departure had to be made from the ghetto precinct, and the Jews had to be allowed to reside and trade outside the strictly defined boundary. The Rothschilds were among those who took advantage of this favorable opportunity, and transferred their merchandise business—they were dealing increasingly in war requirements such as cloth, foodstuffs, and wine—to the Schnur Gasse which lay near the center of the town, renting accommodation at a leather dealer's.

The military developments of the first coalition war, in which Meyer Amschel's princely customer at Cassel was actively engaged with varying fortunes, entailed considerably increased activity on the part of the various crown agents in the landgrave's service. Although the war had caused not a little damage to Frankfort[19] it had brought the town certain indirect advantages. The Frankfort Bourse benefited by the decline of the Amsterdam Bourse, which had hitherto held a dominating position, and which almost completely collapsed when the French conquered Holland in 1795. The result was that much more business came the way of the Frankfort bankers, and Meyer Amschel Rothschild's financial and trading business, which was closely associated with war requirements, increased by leaps and bounds.

The war profits realized at that time formed the real foundation of the enormous fortune that was later built up by the House of Rothschild. It was of course impossible any longer completely to conceal such large profits. Until 1794 the family property had for twenty years been assessed at the constant figure of only 2,000 gulden, and they had paid taxes in accordance with this "assessment," amounting to about thirteen gulden annually. Suddenly in the year 1795 this amount was doubled, and in the year after that Rothschild was included amongst those whose property was worth 15,000 gulden or more, that being the highest figure adopted for assessment purposes.

Meanwhile the three eldest sons had grown up, and after the age of twenty were associated with their father in the business to an increasing extent. Like their two eldest sisters they were placed in responsible positions and rendered active assistance to their father. A large family, which to so many people is a cause of worry and anxiety, was in this case a positive blessing as there was abundance of work for everybody. It made it unnecessary for Meyer Amschel to take strangers into his business and let them into the various secret and subtle moves of the game. Since the number of available children increased in proportion as the business expanded, it was possible to keep all the confidential positions in the family. The strong traditional community and family sense of the Jews, reenforced by persecution from outside, compelling them to unite in their own defense, did wonders. The two eldest sons had been zealously engaged in the business from boyhood, and their father wisely encouraged them by letting them share personally in the business, apart from the general family interest in its prosperity.

When the eldest daughter married, in 1795, the son-in-law Moses Worms was not employed in the business, but when the eldest son Amschel Meyer married in 1796, the daughter-in-law Eva Hanau was given a post.

In spite of the growing number of available members of the family, Meyer Amschel found it necessary also to engage bookkeepers with a knowledge of languages, as the Rothschild family at that time were all quite uneducated, speaking and writing only a bad kind of Frankfort Yiddish German, apart from Hebrew; and in view of their expanding connections with persons in the highest circles they had to pay particular attention to matters of epistolary style. As the only person he could find capable of carrying out this work was a Christian girl, Rothschild did not hesitate to take her into the business.

It was at this period that Meyer Amschel entered into a highly elaborate deed of partnership with his two eldest sons, which provided that profits and losses should be divided between the three partners according to a definite scheme.

The growing demands upon the treasury arising out of the war served to develop the relations with the Landgrave of Hesse. After the separate Peace of Basel William of Hesse adopted the attitude of an impartial observer of the warlike activities in Europe, and occupied himself principally in the profitable administration of his extensive possessions. He was no stranger to the authentic delights of avarice. Great though his wealth was, his appetite for increasing it remained keen. He showed the greatest ingenuity in effecting savings of every kind, and spent all his spare time thinking out schemes for the profitable investment of the large cash resources which were accumulating in his treasury.

The ruling landgrave gradually became a banker to the whole world, advancing his money not only to princes and nobles, but also to small shopkeepers and Jews, and even to artizans, where he could get good interest. The amounts lent ranged from hundreds of thousands to a few thalers, according to the financial repute of his customers. Cobblers and tailors paid the same rate of interest for small advances as princes for heavy ones. The debts were all accurately registered in account books, making up an enormous number of volumes. If a banker wanted to borrow from him he had to deposit government securities with the landgrave. Thus his enormous fortune consisted of cash, jewels, art treasures and coins,

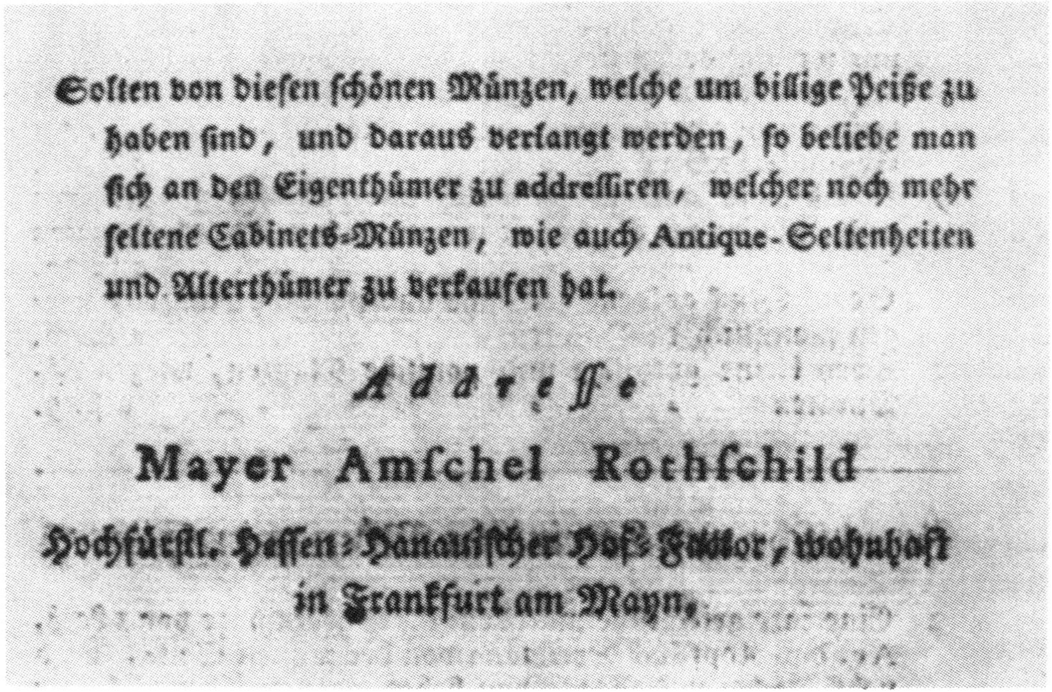
Solten von diesen schönen Münzen, welche um billige Preiße zu haben sind, und daraus verlangt werden, so beliebe man sich an den Eigenthümer zu addressiren, welcher noch mehr seltene Cabinets-Münzen, wie auch Antique-Seltenheiten und Alterthümer zu verkaufen hat.

Addresse

Mayer Amschel Rothschild

Hochfürstl. Hessen-Hanauischer Hof-Factor, wohnhaft in Frankfurt am Mayn.

Title-page of a Rothschild Coin Catalogue, 1770-1780
In the possession of the Frankfort Library

as well as acknowledgments of sums lent and debenture certificates deposited as security.

The withdrawal in 1795 of Prussia and Hesse from the war against France had resulted in the temporary estrangement of the Austrian Emperor Francis; but he and the landgrave soon reestablished cordial relations, for each of them had need of the other. William desired support in the acquisition of territory, and in his efforts to attain the dignity of elector, while the emperor was sadly in lack of funds owing to the long war with France. The landgrave therefore asked the emperor's support in his aims; the emperor wrote on September 8, 1797,[20] to say that he appreciated the efforts which his cousin was making on his behalf, and was grateful to learn that the landgrave was sympathetic to his need for a loan. "I also believe," he wrote, "as it is my duty to do, in your sentiments of loyalty to me and to my house, of which I have received special proof in the matter of the loan that is being negotiated by Herr Kornrumpf. I flatter myself that your Highness will carry this through to my complete satisfaction. Your Highness may rest assured that for my part I sincerely wish to be of service to you also."

The details of such transactions were generally negotiated by Jewish agents, and although Meyer Amschel was not employed on this occasion, he was soon to serve as the middleman between the landgrave and the emperor.

This was made possible by the fact that Rothschild's wealth had increased rapidly during the last years of the war. Towards the end of the eighteenth century it cannot have been far short of a million gulden. The transfer of bills of exchange, cash payments, and the consignments of merchandise from England, the principal supply of the Frankfurter Platz, which in its turn, supplied the whole of Germany, made it necessary to appoint a representative on the other side of the Channel. As it was essential that any such representative should be a trustworthy person, the obvious thing was to appoint one of the five sons.

The two eldest, Amschel [21] and Solomon, who, in 1798, were twenty-five and twenty-four years old respectively, were thoroughly initiated into the Frankfort business. The third son, Nathan, a highly gifted young man of twenty-one, intensely industrious and with a very independent spirit, felt that his elder brothers did not give him sufficient scope. In spite of his youth, he too benefited by the wise arrangements of his father, and had his own personal share in the business and in the family property.

As the continental states, owing to war and revolution, produced much less, but consumed a great deal more than in normal times, English commercial travelers swarmed over the Continent of Europe and in 1798, one of them called at the Rothschilds' house of business, and was received by Nathan. English commercial travelers of that period were exceedingly conscious of the commercial and political supremacy of their country, and they were wont to adopt an arrogant manner, as they felt that the Continent was dependent upon their goods. The Englishman's manner annoyed Nathan Rothschild; and he met his arrogance with brusqueness, whereupon the foreigner took his departure.

This incident was the immediate cause that decided Nathan to propose to his father that he should go to England himself, in order to become a merchant there on his own account and also to represent the firm of Rothschild generally. His father and brothers did not show any opposition to the enterprising young man and supported his decision in every way. Nathan took as much ready money with him as was practicable and the rest he had sent on after him; the capital which he brought with him to England amounted altogether to a sum of about twenty thousand pounds or a quarter of a million gulden. About a fifth of this sum was his own money; the rest belonged to the business. The action of his father and brothers showed great confidence in this young man who did not even know the language of the country he was about to enter as a complete stranger. Their confidence was to be justified, for Nathan was destined to become the outstanding figure in the Rothschild business.

This first branch establishment of the House of Rothschild resulted from the family relationships and the requirements of the trade with England, without any preconceived plan, and without the remotest idea of the importance of this step for the future of the business.

The Napoleonic epoch, which followed upon the French Revolution, was to be the occasion for the foundation of a second branch in Paris and for the first collaboration between the brothers Rothschild in Frankfort, London, and Paris.

CHAPTER II

The Rothschild Family During the Napoleonic Era

THE turn of the century coincided with an important part of the wars against the French Republic, arising out of the revolution. The Peace of Lunéville, concluded in 1801, had set the seal on the brilliant Bonaparte's territorial victories, thereby giving France the leadership on land, while, however, England's preeminence at sea was confirmed. Although Bonaparte had overcome all his other enemies, he was bound to admit that sea-girt England had maintained its position. The Treaty of Amiens, which followed upon that of Lunéville, merely marked a transition stage, and was bound to lead to a resumption of the struggle, until one of the two great opponents should lie bleeding on the ground.

This struggle was the predominant feature of the next fifteen years, and converted almost the whole of the mainland of Europe into a theater of war. The result was that innumerable substantial firms, banks, and private persons lost their property, while on the other hand persons possessing industry, energy, and resource, with a flair for turning opportunity to account, were enabled to gain riches and power.

At any rate within their own caste, the Rothschild family had at that time achieved a position in which their future was bound to be profoundly affected by political developments. As early as 1800 their father Meyer Amschel had been the tenth richest Jew in Frankfort; the only question was as to the attitude that the head of the business house and his sons would take in the stormy times that were to follow.

Numerous competitors were richer than they, or as rich, had better and older connections, and some had been received into the Christian Church and no longer suffered from the stigma of Judaism. The Rothschilds, on the other hand, had the advantage of a chief who was industrious, energetic, and reliable, and a man of intelligence. He had to help him four hard-working sons who were developing into first-rate business men under the guidance of their father. One of these, Solomon, had just married Caroline Stern, herself the prosperous daughter of a Frankfort tradesman, and had thus been enabled to found a home of his own. The third son Nathan was living in the camp of Napoleon's great enemy England.

In that country with its sea-power and its world-wide commerce, his undertakings were far better protected against Napoleonic interference than those of his father and brothers on the Continent. He was able to form a much more dispassionate judgment of the great events which followed so rapidly upon one another during those years, and was in a better position to turn them to account. Moreover, Nathan was the most enterprising of the five sons, of which fact his decision to go to England was itself an indication.

The commercial activities of the House of Rothschild in Frankfort itself were not limited to one branch of business. It took any chance of earning a profit, whether as commission or forwarding agents, or in the trade of wine and textiles, which had recently been declared free, and in silk and muslin, not to mention coins and antiquities. The wine business in particular expanded greatly; and Meyer Amschel did not fail to use every opportunity for extending his connections with princes and potentates even beyond the sphere of the Duke of Hesse.

One of the most important connections established at Frankfort was that with the princely House of Thurn and Taxis, the head of which, Prince Karl Anselm, held the important position of hereditary postmaster in the Holy Roman Empire.

This family was of Milanese extraction; in Italy it was known as della Torre, in France as de la Tour. It had invented the idea of a post, and had introduced a postal system in the Tyrol, toward the end of the fifteenth century. In 1516 it was commissioned by the Emperor Maximilian I to inaugurate a mounted postal service between Vienna and Brussels. Even at that early date the dignified rank of postmaster general was conferred upon one of its members.

That was the starting point of the impressive development of the Thurn and Taxis postal system, which came to embrace the whole of Central Europe. The head offices of the system were at Frankfort, but the family were not satisfied with the normal development of their undertaking. They turned the information obtainable from the letters entrusted to their charge to profit.

The end of the eighteenth and the beginning of the nineteenth centuries saw the development of the practice of opening letters, noting the contents and then sending them on to their destinations. In order to retain the postal monopoly, the House of Thurn and Taxis offered to place the emperor in possession of the information derived from the so-called secret manipulation of letters. If, therefore, one were on good terms with the House one could easily and swiftly obtain news, and also dispatch it.

In the course of time Meyer Amschel had come to realize that it is of the greatest importance to the banker and merchant to have early and accurate information of important events, especially in time of war. As his native town was the headquarters of the postal and information service, he had had the foresight to get into touch with the House of Thurn and Taxis, and had transacted various financial matters to their great satisfaction. It was on this fact that he relied when he appealed to the fountainhead of the Imperial Postal Service at Frankfort, his Imperial Majesty himself.

In a petition to his Majesty that he and his sons should

be granted the title of crown agent, Meyer Amschel brought forward precisely those matters from which he had derived the greatest profit, namely, his financial and commercial transactions in the war against France, and the services which he had rendered to the House of Thurn and Taxis. He had been honest and punctual in his business dealings, as those witnesses would testify who indorsed his petition.

The Roman-German Emperor, whose power at this time was practically limited to the granting of honors, did actually consent to grant Meyer Amschel the title of imperial crown agent by a patent dated January 29, 1800. Not only was this a passport to him throughout the whole of the Roman Empire in Germany; it also carried the right to bear arms, and liberated him from several of the taxes and obligations laid upon the Jews of that period. The patent and the title were signed and granted by Francis II, simply as Roman-German Emperor, and had nothing to do with Austria or Austrian Government departments. It was not until much later that the brothers Rothschild entered into actual relations with Austria and her statesmen. Even as late as 1795, when the Landgrave of Hesse lent the Emperor Francis a million gulden, and in 1798 when he lent him an additional half-million, other bankers conducted the transaction, the Rothschilds having nothing whatever to do with it.

The dispensations enumerated in the imperial patent were more or less paper ones, since most of the smaller or greater territorial princes, of whom there was such a plenitude in Germany in 1800, applied their own laws and regulations. This, however, was a minor consideration with Meyer Amschel; the important point was that the new title "imperial crown agent" sounded much better than Hessian Landgraviate, and was likely to attract a number of other titles. Prince von Ysenburg and the German Order of St. John both conferred upon him court titles in recognition of loans of money from the principality, negotiated by Meyer Amschel. In 1804 Rothschild requested the Prince of Thurn and Taxis to bestow a similar favor upon one of his sons, in view of the fact that he himself bore the title of imperial crown agent.

It was characteristic that when asking the emperor for a title he should mention the services rendered to the House of Taxis, and that when he applied for a favor to that house he should have based his claim on the fact that his services had been recognized by the emperor. Such promotions were necessarily of service to him, too, in his relations with his old patron the Landgrave of Hesse, who in spite of everything was still inclined to be suspicious.

William of Hesse was in every way a most important person to Meyer Amschel, for he was colossally rich, richer than the emperor himself, and—a much more important point in those days than now—he was close at hand. Moreover, he had family ties with England, where Nathan was living, and with chronically penurious Denmark, by lending money to which the firm of Rüppell and Harnier, as well as that of Bethmann, had made great profits.

Meyer Amschel advised the landgrave to participate in this loan by buying stock. He did purchase a small amount, Rothschild being commissioned to carry through the transaction. This was done to the landgrave's satisfaction; but Meyer Amschel required a considerable sum of ready money in order to take advantage of a favorable opportunity for purchasing goods and bills of exchange. Knowing that the landgrave, whose investments in England as well as in Germany brought in very good returns, had spare cash available, he asked, and obtained from him on two occasions—in November, 1801, and July, 1802—160,000 thalers and 200,000 gulden as a guaranteed loan, the securities being Danish and Frankfort debentures.

Although the security offered was exceptionally good,

William of Hesse was persuaded to lend the money only after pressure had been brought to bear, and on the special recommendation of his principal financial administrator Buderus. The transaction certainly marked a distinct advance in Rothschild's confidential relations with the landgrave.

The second amount was wanted, not merely for Meyer Amschel himself, but also to assist his two eldest sons, who were already beginning to acquire the titles of court appointments wherever they could. As early as 1801 they were appointed official agents for making war payments on behalf of the State of Hesse.

Meyer Amschel had been enviously observing Rüppell and Harnier's financial transactions with Denmark. It was his ambition to do similar business with Denmark, with landgraviate moneys, on his own account, independently of any other firm. He still lacked any large capital sum, such as others had available, but he was accurately informed by Buderus of the large amount of ready money in the possession of the ruler of Hesse, which was seeking investment. He was determined to put his competitors out of the field by offering the prince better terms.

The Frankfort firms were accustomed to wait until orders came to them, but he meant to get in and negotiate personally. He had put through the secured loans at Cassel personally; and he decided to go there again in order to secure the cooperation of William's counselors with Buderus at their head, so that they might make the landgrave disinclined to negotiate direct with Denmark.

An important point was that Denmark was not to know where the money came from, because William did not wish to be regarded as wealthy in his family circle, as he was afraid that some of them might ask for special favors. For this reason it was decided that a go-between who had relations with Buderus, and through him with Rothschild too, and who lived in Hamburg, which was conveniently near to Denmark, and far enough away from

Hesse to allay suspicion, should be the first person to make approaches to that country. This was a Jewish banker called Lawaetz.

Moreover, on Rothschild's own suggestion, and contrary to the usual practice, the loan was to run over a long period. Notice for repayment was not to be given for ten years or more, and after that period payment could be demanded only in quite small instalments, over a period of twenty or thirty years. They did actually succeed in securing William of Hesse's consent to granting such a loan; and no sooner were the conditions agreed than Lawaetz showed his hand to the extent of making the interest payable to Meyer Amschel Rothschild at Frankfort.

"The lender," the Hamburg banker wrote to Denmark, "is an exceedingly rich capitalist, and exceptionally friendly to the Danish Court. It is possible that even greater sums and better conditions may be obtainable from him." [1] It is true that Lawaetz did not know Rothschild personally at this time.

The successful conclusion in September, 1803, of this, the first loan which he had carried through privately, not only brought Meyer Amschel financial profit, but also resulted in his obtaining the title of crown agent to the Court of Hesse. His rivals had been highly displeased to hear of this loan, and kept making representations of a nature calculated to damage Rothschild, to the landgrave. Rüppell and Harnier were particularly assiduous. They drew attention to the fact that the last Danish loan had been issued in the form of debentures, in the name of Rothschild; and in order to rouse Danish national vanity they stressed the idea that this suggested that "it was not the national credit of Denmark but merely the Jewish name of Rothschild that had got these obligations accepted in Hesse." [2]

Rothschild's fight with his rivals involved the officials entrusted with the financial administration of the land-

Verzeichniß von raren Thalern

nach des Herrn von Madai vollständigen Thaler Cabinet numeriret, wie auch einigen Goldgulden, nach Herrn Köhlers Ducaten-Cabinet verzeichnet, und um beygesetzte Preise zu haben, bey M. A. Rothschild.

No.	Röm. Kayserliche.	fl.	kr.	No.		fl.	kr.
2414	von 1645	3	20	401	von 1627	5	–
40	von 1658	3	– –	2825	von 1638	3	[illegible]
43	von 1683	3	10	2528	von 1642	1	–
	Rußisch-Kayserl.			404	½ von 1642 . . .	1	[illegible]
55	von 1725	2	45	2829	ohne Jahrzahl .	1	[illegible]
	Kön. Spanische.			407	Doppelthl. von 1674.	8	–
82	von 1622	3	—	409	Doppelthl. von 1679.	10	–
93	von 1689	3	—	410	ohne Jahrzahl . .	1	[illegible]
99	von 1702	3	30	413	von 1696	1	–
	Kön. Französische			2832	von 1697	1	[illegible]
2554	von 1610	10	– –		Chur-Trierische.		
	Kön. Schwedische.			424	von 1624	3	[illegible]
292	½ von 1559 . . .	1	30	425	Einfach von 1657	4	[illegible]
206	von 1603	3	30	426	von 1659	3	[illegible]
2629	von 1632	1	—	2841	ohne Jahrzahl . .	3	[illegible]
217	von 1632	3	—	2845	von 1702	1	[illegible]
219	von 1633	3	—		Chur-Cöllnische.		
225	von 1641	3	—	431	von 1549	1	–
227	von 1645	3	—	435	von 1558	2	[illegible]
232	von 1657	1	—	437	von 1568	1	–
251	von 1718	3	—	438	von 1572	1	–
	Kön. Dänische.			2855	ohne Jahrzahl . .	4	–
277	von 1640	3	—		Chur Pfälzische.		
2665	von 1624	2	40	467	von 1662	1	–
280	von 1650	1	—	5657	von 1679	1	[illegible]
2676	von 1666	3	—		Chur-Bayrische.		
2684	von 1685	3	—	2892	von 1626	1	–
307	von 1711	3	—	481	von 1740	3	[illegible]
	Böhmische.				Chur-Sächsische.		
342	½ von 1620 . . .	1	30	2916	Doppelthl. von 1534.	8	–
	Kön. Preußische.			502	Doppelthl. von 1539.	6	[illegible]
381	von 1704	4	30	504	von 1542	1	[illegible]
382	von 1707	3	—	517	von 1659	3	–
2805	½ von 1714 . . .	1	30	2958	Doppelthl. von 1661.	7	[illegible]
	Chur-Mayntzische.			581	von 1671	1	–
2821	Doppelthl. von 1593.	6	30	544	von 1680	1	[illegible]
2823	von 1627	7	30	550	Klippe von 1693 .	1	–

A Page of the Rothschild Catalogue of Rare Coins
In the possession of the Frankfort Library

graviate in the struggle. Buderus became increasingly a partizan of Rothschild, whereas Lennep of the War Office took the side of Rüppell and Harnier. Rothschild and Buderus, however, had the upper hand for the time being, and by 1806 no less than seven landgraviate loans were issued. The profit realized from this transaction served to key up still further the hatred and enmity of the rival firms and of Lennep, and led to awkward developments.

Rothschild had shown the greatest energy in these undertakings. He did not even spare himself the journey to Hamburg, an exceedingly difficult one at that time, in order to get into personal touch with the banker, Lawaetz, and to see that the Danish business was carried on as energetically as possible.

A letter [3] from the Hamburg banker to Buderus contains the following statement: "The Crown Agent Rothschild is coming to see me tomorrow in order to settle up our remaining accounts, and he intends to return the day after. It has been a pleasure to me to make the acquaintance of this man, and I shall be glad to be able to do him any service in future."

The intrigues of the rivals, however, did not wholly fail of their effect upon William of Hesse. His attitude continued to be suspicious, and he several times refused to have anything to do with other business propositions suggested by Rothschild, agreeing to them only as the result of much pleading and persuasion. Besides the Danish loans, loans were issued for Hesse-Darmstadt and the Order of St. John, these also being subscribed by landgraviate funds through the intermediary of Rothschild. The sums involved were already considerable, running into hundreds of thousands.

The larger they were, the better pleased was Meyer Amschel, because his percentage profit rose in proportion, while the risk was borne, not by him but by the landgrave, whose favorite occupation had always been the careful administration and development of his property. The sums invested in England called for particular attention. Since the Peace of Basel, relations between Hesse and England had been rather strained, although they were not likely to become critical, as the landgrave had cleverly succeeded in enlisting the interests of responsible people on his side. He had lent the Prince of Wales, afterwards King George IV, about £200,000 in two instalments. The dukes of York and Clarence were guarantors of this loan, but they also borrowed money from the landgrave. In addition to this, William of Hesse had put out £640,000 at interest in London in various ways, a fact which was to prove exceedingly useful to him.

The example of their patron was a lesson to the House of Rothschild, and they soon learned to copy his wise practice of lending money by preference to persons in the highest position. Even though William of Hesse remained neutral in the second War of the Coalition, he secretly wished success to the enemies of France for he eagerly hoped for the resumption of his profitable subsidy contracts with England.

The Peace of Lunéville, which extended France's boundaries to the Rhine, also conferred on William the dignity of elector, which he had so much desired, and which was duly proclaimed in 1803; but the meteoric rise of Bonaparte and revolutionary France's position in the world seemed to him to be unnatural and menacing. His friendship with Prussia was rather shattered, because that state had succeeded in annexing considerable territory, but had left the Hessian prince in the cold.

The peace between France and England did not last long. As early as May, 1803, the Island Kingdom again declared war upon the usurper in Paris. It was not long before William of Hesse was forced to take an attitude toward the new world situation. In October, 1803, the French, having invaded English Hanover, tried to get money from the elector in exchange for Hanoverian territory. His fear of offending England caused him to refuse this offer, and thus the elector first gave offense to the Corsican.

He had no true idea at the time how dangerous the Corsican might be. The quiet times for Frankfort and Hesse were now at an end. Stirred up by Napoleon's powerful genius Europe passed from one crisis to another, and in such circumstances it was exceedingly difficult for William of Hesse to administer his enormous property with foresight and wisdom. He felt the need more and more of Meyer Amschel's advice, so that Rothschild's journeys to Cassel became more and more frequent. His eldest son had for some months been residing permanently in that town.

The preference shown to the Frankfort family aroused the envy and hatred of the Cassel Jews against this outsider. They complained that not merely did he steal their best business, but he was not even subject to the night-rate and poll-tax which other Jews had to pay. Meyer Amschel did his utmost to evade such payments as far as possible, but in the end he was forced to pay some of these taxes.

In August, 1803, he found it necessary to apply to the elector for a letter of protection in Cassel for himself and his sons, so that, although resident in Frankfort, he should enjoy the same rights as the protected Jews of Cassel. This would certainly entail obligations as well. His request was granted on payment of 400 reichsthaler, but the document was not completed, possibly in accordance with Meyer Amschel's own wishes, for he would then have been liable to pay taxes in Cassel also.

The Cassel Jews, however, soon got wind of this maneuver, and in the end Meyer Amschel was required to state in whose name he wished the letter of protection made out, whereupon he wrote the following letter to the elector: [4]

Most gracious Elector, most excellent Prince and Lord!

Your Excellency has most graciously deigned to grant that in return for the payment of 100 florins I should be exempt from night-rate, and that on the payment of 400 florins one of my sons or I should be admitted to protection.

I am now required to state in whose name the letter of protection should be made out, and this is causing me great difficulty, since the son for whom I had intended taking it out has been settled for some time with another of my sons in London, and is engaged in doing business with him there.

I have therefore decided to take out the protection for myself, if I may be most graciously permitted to pay an annual amount similar to that paid by other Jews not residing in the town . . . as I only do business here, and could do most of it quite as well from another place; as I have now held the office of Crown Agent for over forty years, your Electoral Highness having even in my youth shown me such gracious condescension, so I hope now, too, to receive your most gracious consent, and remain with deepest respect, your Electoral Highness

My most gracious Prince and Lord's

most obedient servant,

MEYER AMSCHEL ROTHSCHILD.

Cassel, 21st April 1805.

This personal request, sent in by Meyer Rothschild in rather inferior German, provoked a certain amount of amusement at the electoral court. Meyer Amschel was informed that his request could not be granted unless he moved to Cassel with all his property; and that naturally he was not prepared to do. In the end the letter of protection was made out in the name of Amschel Meyer Rothschild, his eldest son.

Although Meyer Amschel had to fight for his position in Cassel, his prestige at Frankfort rose, on account of his connection with the Hessian ruler, which was now becoming generally known. This was made manifest in various ways. When shops were put up to auction in the electoral courtyard, to which Jews, even resident Jews, were not admitted, an exception was made in favor of Meyer Amschel. One of the shops was definitely excluded from the auction and reserved for Rothschild. It is possible that ready money was a factor, as well as his prestige in this matter.

This period saw the conclusion of the two last, and by far the most substantial Danish loans, of 700,000 and 600,000 thalers. In these transactions too, Lawaetz played a part of some importance. In spite of very friendly business relations, he was still somewhat reserved in his attitude toward the Rothschild family. Whilst in talking to his friends he often declared that he had found [5] "Herr Rothschild always to be exceedingly prompt and businesslike and worthy of the most complete confidence," yet he felt that where such large amounts were at stake, one ought to be very cautious, even in dealing with Rothschild. The atmosphere then was full of suspicion, all the more so because the political barometer in Europe pointed to stormy times, and the capitalists were exceedingly uneasy as to the possible fate of their wealth.

Bonaparte had already cast aside his mask and was boldly grasping at the imperial purple; toward the end of the summer of 1804 the whole of France was echoing with the shout *"Vive l'Empereur!"* The prestige of the German imperial system was suffering a corresponding decline, an obvious symptom of which was the proclamation on August 10, 1804, of Francis II as Emperor of Austria.

Moreover, September, 1804, already saw Napoleon touring the newly won Rhine provinces. He appeared in full splendor and magnificence at Aix-la-Chapelle and Mainz as if he were indeed the successor of Charles the

Great. It was on this occasion that, with the assistance of the Mainz Electoral High Chancellor, Dalberg, he laid the foundations of that union of German princes which was to be known as the Confederation of the Rhine.

Napoleon was already adopting the rôle of their protector, and invited William of Hesse, too, to Mainz, an invitation which was exceedingly suggestive of a command to come and do homage. The elector pleaded a sudden attack of gout. Napoleon replied coldly; he was still polite, but he swore that William should pay for having failed immediately to adhere to the confederation which was being formed under Napoleon's protection. The French ambassador at Cassel had uttered the menacing words, when he heard that the prince was not going to Mainz, *"On n'oublie pas, on n'oublie rien!"* [6]

The Elector of Hesse was left feeling rather uncomfortable, and he secretly threw out cautious feelers toward England and Austria—Austria was already showing a marked inclination to side against France. The occasion of the Emperor Francis' assuming the imperial title connected with his Austrian hereditary territories, afforded him an opportunity of expressing his most sincere and devoted good wishes to the "most excellent, puissant, and invincible Roman Emperor and most gracious Lord [7] for the continuous welfare of the sacred person of his Imperial Majesty and for the ever-increasing glory of the all-highest Imperial House."

His pen was jogged by the need he felt for powerful support, and incidentally the letter was to serve the purpose of reminding the emperor of a request which the writer had made on November 22, 1804, and which so far had not been granted. The elector's first favorite, the apothecary's daughter Ritter, whom the emperor had raised to the rank of Frau von Lindenthal, and who was ancestress of the Haynaus, was now out of favor, since she had preferred a young subaltern to the aged landgrave. For over a year her place had been occupied by Caroline von Schlotheim, the beautiful daughter of a Russian officer whom the emperor had been asked to create Countess von Hessenstein.

In May, 1805, Austria finally joined the coalition against Napoleon. Napoleon gave up his idea of landing in the British Isles, and concentrated on Austria. This resulted in great shortage of money, for the Austrian Treasury had heavy burdens to bear from former wars; coin was scarce and paper money much depreciated. It was therefore decided that the interest on loans should not, as had hitherto been the practice, be payable in hard cash in all the principal exchanges in Europe, but should be payable in paper in Vienna only. This was hard for the elector personally, as he had advanced a million and a half gulden to the Emperor Francis; and he at once begged that an exception might be made in his favor since "ill-disposed persons had suggested to him that the Austrian state was going to go bankrupt, as far as all external debts were concerned." [8]

The imperial ambassador Baron von Wessenberg, naturally wishing to turn the general situation to account, sent this request forward under cover of a private dispatch of his own in which he wrote:

"Since avarice is the elector's great weakness, it might be possible, should you wish to do so, to obtain a still greater loan from him if you agreed that interest in future should be payable in cash. He would be more likely to fall in with such a suggestion if his Imperial Majesty would grant Frau von Schlotheim the title of Countess of Hessenstein, without payment. The granting of this request would particularly delight the elector." [9]

In the second particular his wishes were granted, but it was not possible to make an exception in the matter of the interest charges. However, both Vienna and London endeavored to secure the elector's accession to the confederation, and he replied to these overtures with demands for subsidies. Yet he was hard put to it to find investments for all the money that he had at his disposal, and as late as December 2, 1805, he had lent ten million thalers to Prussia. He had hoped that the Austro-Russo-English war against Napoleon would end in victory; but Austerlitz put a speedy end to such hopes.

During the war, England sent financial assistance to Austria in the shape of a monthly payment of a third of a million pounds in cash, which was sent to Austria by the most difficult and circuitous routes. The Rothschild method of transferring large sums of money was as yet unknown, and the only method in use was the dangerous one of sending actual bullion by road. A consignment of money was actually on the way when Austerlitz was being fought, and, in fear of a defeat, orders were issued from imperial headquarters instructing this consignment to be diverted in a wide circuit through Galicia and the Carpathians.

The war complications in which Europe was involved forced almost all states, whether they wished to or not, to take sides. The Elector of Hesse characteristically wished to attach himself to that party out of which he could make the greatest profit. As Prussia was now also being drawn into conflict with Napoleon, she attempted to draw the elector in on her side. On the other hand, the French Court gave him to understand that substantial advantages would be gained by the electorate if he kept himself completely free from Prussian influence. This suggestion was unpleasantly underlined by the gathering of bodies of French troops in the neighborhood of Hesse.

The elector bargained with everybody and secured from Paris accessions of territory and the incorporation of the town of Frankfort within his domains. The only awkward point was that Napoleon demanded that the British ambassador, through whom the subsidy arrangements were carried on, should be sent home; and when the elector delayed about doing this, Napoleon expressed his displeasure in no uncertain language, until the elector gave way, and sent the ambassador away.

Annoyed at France's threatening attitude the Hessian ruler again endeavored to attach himself to Prussia. Then, on July 12, 1806, the document regarding the Confederation of the Rhine was published, through which Napoleon, with the assistance of Prince Theodor von Dalberg, Electoral High Chancellor, won sixteen German states by promising them separation from the German Empire.

As a counterblast to this, Prussia attempted to bring about a union of the princes of Northern Germany, and to gain the support of the Elector of Hesse by offering him the prospect of an accession of territory and the dignity of kingship which he so much desired. These moves were followed by threats and promises on the side of France. The attitude of the elector remained undefined. He now thought it best to preserve the appearance of neutrality until the actual outbreak of war, and then simply to join the side which was winning, although a signed, if not ratified, treaty with Prussia was in existence.

He had, however, not reckoned sufficiently with the forceful personality of Napoleon. It was impossible to conduct a nebulous diplomacy with such a man. He had long been tired of the vacillating attitude of Hesse. A state of war was declared in early October, 1806. On the 14th of that month, Prussia was decisively beaten through Napoleon's lightning advance at Jena and Auerstedt. Napoleon now scorned Hessian "neutrality." He ordered that Cassel and Hesse should be occupied, and that unless the elector and the crown prince left they should be made prisoners of war as Prussian field-marshals.

"You will," commanded Napoleon, "seal up all treasuries and stores and appoint General Lagrange as governor of the country. You will raise taxes and pronounce judgments in my name. Secrecy and speed will be the means through which you will insure complete success. My object is to remove the House of Hesse-Cassel from rulership and to strike it out of the list of powers." [10]

At Frankfort, Meyer Amschel Rothschild had been watching the precipitate development of events with terror; and his son Amschel, at Cassel, as well as he himself at Frankfort, took all possible measures to prevent themselves and the elector from suffering too great financial loss. Business had just been going so exceedingly well. The firm of Bethmann, which had felt that it was being driven into the background, and had just been making strenuous efforts to get a share in the elector's loan business with Denmark, was forced to withdraw from the contest, on account of the political conditions and the resulting shortage of money, and thereby left the way open to Rothschild, who still had resources available.

In the meantime Lawaetz in Hamburg had definitely decided in Rothschild's favor. On July 2, 1806, he wrote himself to Buderus [11] to say that he would stand by their good friend Rothschild as far as he could, saying: "I hope that in the end people will realize that he is a good fellow who deserves to be respected; the envious may say what they like against him."

In spite of all that Rothschild had hitherto done in the service of the elector, he had not won his confidence to the extent of being called in in a matter which had become pressing on account of the developing military situation; for although the elector continued to hope that the notices naïvely posted on the roads leading to Hesse, bearing the words *"Pays Neutre"* would be respected, he was sufficiently concerned for the safety of his treasures to send away and conceal his more valuable possessions. But it was no light task to deal with the extensive banking accounts of the electoral loan office, and with his vast accumulations of treasure, and after several months the work was still far from complete.

There being no distinction between the treasury and

the prince's private purse, it was necessary to get out of the way, not only his own valuables, but also the cabinet, war and chancery cash records, for a period covering several decades; for so the books of his financial administration were called, in order to make it impossible to examine into the state of his affairs. There were large volumes of these records, representing vast sums; in the war chest alone there was over twenty-one million thalers, sixteen millions of which were out on loan in various places, and bringing in interest to the tune of many thousands of thalers. All this had to be concealed as far as possible, and this business was done by trusty officials, under the guidance of Buderus. But there is nothing to show that any of the Rothschilds were employed in the long-continued work of transport and concealment.

Time was pressing; some of the things were sent to Denmark; but it was impossible to get everything out of the country, and to have done so would have attracted too much attention. So the elector, who gave the closest personal attention to the plans for insuring the safety of his possessions, decided that the most precious articles should be buried within the walls of three of his castles. Under the stairs of the castle of Wilhelmshöhe were hidden twenty-four chests, containing silver and mortgage documents to the value of one and a half million gulden, amongst which were certain Rothschild debentures, while twenty-four chests with cash vouchers and certain valuable volumes from the library were concealed in the walls under the roof. A similar number of chests were concealed in the picturesque castle of Löwenburg, built in the Wilhelmshöhe park, while further treasures were conveyed in forty-seven chests to the Sababurg, situated in a remote forest.

The elector had originally intended to send the last consignment down the Weser to England, but he and the shipowner disagreed over a matter of fifty thalers and so they were not sent away. It was impossible to carry through such measures in secrecy, as too many persons were involved in the transaction; and long before the French invaded the country, there was general alarm throughout the district, because the elector was said to be hiding all his treasures.

Meanwhile Napoleon's commands were being carried out. French troops, coming from Frankfort, were already encamped on the night of October 31 on the heights surrounding Cassel. The elector gazed anxiously from the windows of his castle at the enemy's camp-fires, and sent adjutant after adjutant to Mortier, the French marshal. In due course the French envoy was announced, and brought an ultimatum from Napoleon, significantly addressed: "To the Elector of Hesse-Cassel, Field-Marshal in the service of Prussia."

In short, biting sentences William's double game was exposed, and the occupation of the country and the disarmament of its inhabitants was proclaimed. The elector immediately decided to throw in his lot with Napoleon and to join the Confederation of the Rhine. But it was too late; Marshal Mortier would no longer listen to the elector's messengers. The elector realized that there was nothing for him but flight.

In the few hours before the French entered the country he would have to move as many of his remaining possessions as he could, and make the more urgent dispositions regarding outstanding accounts. William gave Buderus power of attorney to receive the interest payments due from the Emperor Francis in Vienna; and Buderus transferred this power of attorney to Rothschild, who proceeded to collect these payments for the elector, through a business friend in Vienna, the banker Frank.

Besides this, Buderus that night brought two chests containing securities and statements of accounts to the house of the Austrian ambassador at Cassel, Baron von Wessenberg, and begged him to take charge of them. In addition, a member of the elector's bodyguard roused the ambassador in the middle of the night[12] to give him five envelops containing one and a half million thalers in valid bills of exchange and coupons, as well as the elector's compromising correspondence with Prussia and England. He also gave him a casket of jewels, requesting that the ambassador deal with these things as he would for a friend.

Baron von Wessenberg felt extremely uncomfortable; his position as ambassador of a neutral power was being seriously compromised, but he was fortunately able to entrust the money to a chamberlain of his acquaintance, who was traveling to Hanover that night. The letters, however, were of such a compromising nature that he burned them in terror. He had dealt with everything excepting the jewels, when the trumpets and marching songs of the French invading troops were heard in the morning. A few minutes earlier the elector had left the town with his son in a traveling coach and six. After having been held up by French troops at one gate, he escaped by another, and drove without stopping through Hameln and Altona, to Rendsburg in Schleswig.

Having entered Cassel, Marshal Mortier immediately began to carry out all Napoleon's instructions, and also commandeered all the electoral moneys and possessions, even including the stables and the court furniture. He took over the electoral rooms in the castle for his own personal use, and the electoral flunkeys as his personal servants. He did not molest the elector's consort, and Wessenberg succeeded in sending her the jewels, which she sewed into her garments and those of her servants.

Buderus felt that things might get rather warm for him, and he left Cassel disguised as an apprentice, with a knapsack on his back, to follow his master into exile.[13] His despairing family stayed behind.

While these events were taking place, neither Meyer Amschel Rothschild nor either of his sons seems to have been at Cassel.[14] They had long realized that the attitude of the French toward the elector was critical, and that their relations with him might get them into trouble. Frankfort, too, had been occupied by the French, and the headquarters of the firm, their house and their whole property, were at the mercy of the enemy.

In his heart Meyer Amschel remained loyal to the elector, and saw that the position arising out of the French invasion and the flight of the elector was one in which he could still be of great service to him. He presumably came quite rightly to the conclusion, that it was in the elector's own interest that he should stay away at this critical period, so that he might, if possible, carry on the elector's business behind the backs of the French. In following his natural inclinations, and not compromising himself in the eyes of the French, and in keeping out of the way of these dangerous companions as far as possible, he was also following the course of the greatest practical utility.

Even if Meyer Amschel or one of his sons had actually been in Cassel, the moneys entrusted to Baron von Wessenberg would not have been placed in their keeping. They were, as yet, far from enjoying such a degree of confidence; indeed, the ambassador actually stated in his report to Vienna at the time that the elector had sent the things to him "because of lack of confidence in his business agents."

The French immediately instituted investigations to discover where the elector had hidden his wealth. Napoleon had received news at Berlin of the occurrences at Cassel. At four o'clock on the morning of November 5, 1806, he sent the following orders to Lagrange: "Have all the artillery, ordnance stores, furniture, statues and other articles in the palace of the court brought to Mainz. Proclaim that this prince may no longer rule. I shall not continue to suffer a hostile prince on my boundaries, especially one who is practically a Prussian, not to say an Englishman, and who sells his subjects. You must completely disarm the inhabitants, and authorize an intendant to seize the prince's revenue. In general you may treat the country mercifully, but if there is any sign of insurrection anywhere, you must make a terrible example. . . . Let yourself be guided by the principle that I wish to see the House of Hesse, whose existence on the Rhine cannot be reconciled with the safety of France, permanently removed from power."[15]

Such were Napoleon's feelings toward the elector. The latter sent messenger after messenger, and letter upon letter to Napoleon, but the emperor refused to answer. On the 1st of November, 1806, William of Hesse arrived at his destination, the castle at Gottorp, near Schleswig, belonging to his brother, who had also married a Danish princess. A whole crowd of exile princelings from small German states was gathered there. They had all been suddenly wrenched from a comfortable and careless existence, and were suffering acutely, especially from financial distress.

"We are in the greatest misery here," wrote Buderus to London,[16] on November 17, 1806. "Please help us to get some money soon, because we do not know what we shall do otherwise, as we are not getting a farthing from Cassel. God, how things have changed!"

Meanwhile the French occupied Hamburg and advanced unpleasantly close to the elector's place of refuge. He became exceedingly nervous and excited, and feared that he might yet fall into the hands of the French, with all the belongings that he had rescued; his possessions were all packed in chests, ready for further transport. He once got into such a state of panic that he wanted to send Buderus straight off into the blue with as many valuables and securities as possible, leaving it to him to make such provision as he could for their safe custody. However, the outlook became less menacing; the French did not come to Schleswig for the time being, and the elector gradually recovered his composure.

Meanwhile Lagrange was ruthlessly executing Napoleon's severe commands at Cassel. Even Wessenberg, suspected of concealing electoral treasure, was placed temporarily under arrest. Gradually all the treasures that had been concealed in the castle, including the gold and silver plate, the antiques, the whole collection of coins and medals to which Rothschild had contributed so many valuable specimens, and also the innumerable chests containing deeds and securities, were discovered. The elector might well regret that for the sake of fifty thalers, he had failed to have the silver carried down the river. All his splendid silver was sent to Mainz to be melted down.

Dazzled by the vast extent of the riches that were being brought to light, Lagrange was moved to take steps to feather his own nest. Although his imperial master well knew that the elector was rich, he could hardly expect his wealth to be as extensive as actually proved to be the case.

Lagrange reported to Napoleon that the property discovered was only worth eleven million thalers, which of course was not remotely in accordance with the facts; and in return for a *douceur* of 260,000 francs in cash, he returned to the Hessian officials forty-two of the chests, including almost all those that contained securities and title-deeds. Running great dangers, a brave electoral captain brought the chests into safety, and conveyed nineteen of them to Frankfort, where they were stored, not with Meyer Amschel Rothschild, but in the warehouse of Preye and Jordis, in whose extensive vaults they could be concealed without attracting attention.

For an additional 800,000 livres * paid to himself and the intendant, the dishonest governor promised to return other papers too, and not to carry out any further investigation. Thereby countless chests were released, which were distributed amongst various trusted persons, for safe-

* One livre equaled one franc; four francs were the equivalent of one thaler.

keeping. Four of these chests, containing papers of the Privy Council, found their way to Meyer Amschel Rothschild's house with the green shield in the Jewish quarter, during the Spring Fair of 1807. This was the only part played by the House of Rothschild in the actual saving of the electoral treasures.

Meyer Amschel Rothschild hid these chests, having left one of them for a time with his son-in-law Moses Worms, in the cellar of his house. In case of emergency he could have recourse to a separate cellar behind the house and under the courtyard, the approach to this cellar from the house cellar being very easy to conceal. The courtyard cellar, too, was connected by a secret passage with the neighboring house. The persecution of the Frankfort Jews in earlier times, had led to many such secret refuges being constructed. In this case it was therefore reasonable to assume that if the house were searched by foreigners like the French, the cellar under the courtyard would not be discovered at all, and that even if it were discovered there was a good chance of getting its contents into the next house.

In the meantime political changes had occurred which put an end to the political independence of Frankfort. Karl von Dalberg, who had collaborated with Talleyrand in the creation of the Confederation of the Rhine, was nominated Primate of the Confederation on June 12, 1806, and by a decree of Napoleon was granted the city of Frankfort and the surrounding territory as his residence.

This was a fact of much importance, both to the elector and to his devoted servants the Rothschild family, for Dalberg was particularly well-disposed to the elector and to his administrator Buderus, on account of his business dealings with them in earlier times; and, although he was an archbishop and a strict Catholic, he was known to be tolerant in his religious views. The incorporation of Frankfort in the Confederation of the Rhine put an end to its constitution as a state of the empire; and the Jews, who had hitherto been subjected to oppression by the hostile patrician families who had controlled the senate, now hoped for the abolition of all those restrictions, prohibitions and special laws under which they had suffered for centuries.

Under the new régime life in the great commercial city took on an entirely different complexion. It had to be ordered in accordance with the wishes, or rather the commands, of the French. This was especially the case when Napoleon, in order to deal a deadly blow at the arch enemy England, declared the continental blockade whereby all commerce and communication by letter or otherwise with England was prohibited. As that country was practically the only emporium for such indispensable colonial produce as coffee, sugar, and tobacco, the prices of these articles rose enormously, and a clever merchant could make large profits through timely purchases or by smuggling goods through Holland and the harbors of North Germany.

In spite of the control exercised by France over the trade of Frankfort, Meyer Amschel and his son contrived, with the assistance of Nathan in England, to make a good deal of money in this way. There were certainly risks attached to this form of commerce, for under Article 5 of the continental blockade, all goods of English origin were declared lawful prize. With the passage of time this kind of business became more restricted, for as Napoleon's power increased he was able to make the control more effective.

Meyer Amschel well knew that in spite of his flight and the loss of property which he had suffered at the hands of the French, the elector was still in possession of very considerable resources. There was, moreover, always the possibility of a sudden change in Napoleon's fantastic career, and such an event would immediately alter the whole situation. He therefore adhered to his policy of ingratiating himself to the best of his ability with Napoleon's nominee, the new lord of Frankfort, while he continued faithfully to serve the elector in secret. For this purpose it was necessary that he should remain in constant communication with him.

On the 15th of December, 1806, Meyer Amschel sent an account [17] to Schleswig of his earlier sales of London bills of exchange, and reported that the other bills which he held were unsalable at the moment. Although the "servile script" was full of protestations of groveling humility, and was composed in the illiterate style and full of the spelling mistakes of the old Meyer Amschel, it revealed a certain pride, for Father Rothschild made considerable play with the good relations which he had established with Dalberg.

Rothschild reported with pride that he had influenced Dalberg in favor of the elector, and had induced the new lord of Frankfort to intercede with the Emperor and Empress of France on the elector's behalf. He begged to state, however, that Dalberg advised that the elector should not stand so much upon his rights, but should adopt towards Napoleon the attitude of a "humble petitioner." Meyer Amschel concluded by assuring the elector of his unswerving loyalty and devotion, and declared that he hoped, through his influence with Dalberg, substantially to reduce the war contribution of one million, three hundred thousand thalers imposed by Napoleon upon the elector personally. He also asserted that Dalberg had commended him to all the French marshals and ministers.

Although this letter of Meyer Amschel's was written in a boastful vein, and although he exaggerated his influence, as in point of fact he did not succeed in getting the levy reduced (incidentally, the elector got the levy transferred to the estates of the realm of Hesse), yet the report contained an element of truth. It was certainly most remarkable that the Archbishop and Lord of the

Confederation of the Rhine, who ruled over sixteen German princes, and stood so high in Napoleon's favor, should have shown so much good-will to the Jew Meyer Amschel Rothschild of Frankfort, who, although now a rich man, had no claim to move in high and influential circles. There appear to have been financial reasons for this relationship, and it no doubt originated in loans granted by Rothschild.

When the elector had come to feel reasonably secure in his new place of refuge in Schleswig, he devoted himself again to his favorite hobby, and tried to set in order his chaotic possessions. Buderus had control of this work at every point. He had left Schleswig some time before and returned to Hanau, where he was occupied in calling in debts due to the elector, before they could accrue to the French. There was, for instance, the claim on Prince von Zeil-Wurzach, which was in great danger of being lost. Buderus, however, succeeded in saving this item, and in his report he referred with emphasis to the assistance granted by Rothschild, mentioning his name repeatedly.

"I owe it entirely to the efforts of the Crown Agent Rothschild," he wrote to his master on March 8, 1807, "that I am still not entirely without hope; and he has undertaken to arrange an interview between myself and the Wurzach chancellor in a place which he will select." [18]

The eldest son of the princely debtor attended this conference himself, and it resulted in the repayment to Buderus of the outstanding amount, which Buderus ascribed to the fact that Rothschild had used his influence to such good effect with the advisers and officials of the prince. He added, as especially illustrating Rothschild's trustworthiness, that the French in Cassel had offered to pay Rothschild twenty to twenty-five per cent of the amount at issue, if he would assist in diverting this debt of nine thousand gulden in accordance with Napoleon's orders.

"Your Electoral Highness," the letter continued, "may certainly deign most graciously to realize, the labor involved in saving this amount in the most dangerous circumstances." Besides Buderus, Lennep at Cassel, Lawaetz at Hamburg, and the war commissioners, paymasters and crown agents such as Meyer Amschel and his sons were looking after the financial interests of the elector. "Frankfort is the center point of all my business," Buderus, who directed all the operations, wrote to the elector.[19]

To an ever-increasing degree Buderus was entrusting the elector's business to the Rothschild family; indeed he was now employing them almost exclusively. They looked after the correspondence with Cassel, with the elector, and with Lawaetz at Hamburg, pseudonyms being employed for the more important persons and transactions. Thus the elector was known as "the principal" or "Herr von Goldstein." The stocks in England were known as "stockfish";[20] Rothschild himself was called "Arnoldi" in these letters.

Meyer Amschel was often sent to the elector by Buderus to convey accounts or other information. These seven-day journeys in bad coaches over rough roads, with the constant risk of falling into the hands of the enemy, with the letters with which he had been entrusted, came to be felt as exceedingly burdensome by Meyer Amschel in the course of time. He was not more than sixty-four years old, but his health had latterly suffered from the extraordinary demands made upon the chief of the extensive business house. Henceforward he generally left these journeys to the north to his son Kallmann (or Carl), as his two eldest sons, Amschel and Solomon, were fully occupied at the head office in Frankfort.

These journeys had now to be very frequently undertaken, because Napoleon had entered upon a definite offensive against the elector's property; and this called for counter-measures of all kinds, from the elector's loyal adherents. In accordance with Napoleon's instructions, the French attempted, as they had already done in the case of Prince von Zeil-Wurzach, to divert the moneys lent by the elector in his own country to the French Treasury, by offering substantial discounts on the amount due.

It is true that Lagrange had valued these amounts at only four million thalers, the equivalent of sixteen million francs, but actually they amounted to about sixteen million thalers. One can therefore readily imagine the dismay which the action of the French occasioned the elector. A large number of princes belonging to the Confederation of the Rhine, who owed him money, took advantage of the opportunity of settling their debts at a reduction. On Rothschild's advice, the elector implored the Emperor Francis at Vienna on no account to pay to the French either the capital sum or the interest due in respect of the million and a half gulden which he had borrowed from the elector.

All the efforts to cause Napoleon to change his attitude failed; and meanwhile the situation at Gottorp had become impossible. The elector had arranged for his favorite mistress Schlotheim to join him, and his host's wife, who was a sister of the elector's consort, was afraid of causing pain to the latter if she associated with the Schlotheim. Also the collapse of a rising in Hesse deprived him of a last hope.

"Fools!" exclaimed Lagrange in a proclamation to the Hessians on the 18th of February, 1807. "Count no longer upon your prince; he and his house have ceased to rule. Whoever resists will be shot."

William in the meantime had migrated to Rendsburg, and later to Schloss Itzehoe. In moving language he wrote to the King of Prussia and to the Emperor of Austria.

To the former he wrote: "I have now been living here for four months, groaning under the weight of intolerable grief, and filled with deep concern for the many bitter experiences through which your Majesty is passing, and which . . . affect me even more than my own misfortunes. I have had to watch the land of my fathers suffering an arbitrary rule, and my private property being squandered, and to see my loyal subjects suffering and being gradually reduced to beggary, if they are not speedily succored. It is indeed hard, your Royal Majesty, to have to endure such experiences, and doubly hard when one is conscious that one has always acted in a manner which one could justify before God and men." [21]

His letter to the Emperor of Austria was written in exactly the same vein.[22] In the opening sentence the epithet "most invincible" was on this occasion, in view of the battle of Austerlitz, not added to those of "most excellent" and "most powerful." He begged in the strongest terms, for the emperor's help and support.

These letters were written after the elector's efforts to conciliate Napoleon had merely resulted in the Emperor of France showing his personal contempt and aversion more clearly than ever. William of Hesse's attitude continued to be completely unreliable and vacillating as far as everybody was concerned. At the same time that he was overwhelming Napoleon with supplications, he was negotiating with England for landing on the coast for combined action against the French. But in England, his overtures to Napoleon were known. He was no longer trusted, and the electoral funds invested in that country were sequestrated, so that although he received the interest, he had no power to dispose of the capital.

All these things had not helped to improve the elector's temper. Prince Wittgenstein, who frequently had occasion to visit him in exile on behalf of the Prussian government, wrote: "Personal association with him is indescribably unpleasant; the greatest patience is required in order to put up with his endless complaints and sudden outbursts."[23]

Buderus and Meyer Amschel Rothschild were soon to suffer in the same way. Rothschild had latterly been collecting and accounting for the interest on the English and Danish loans due to the elector. As this had not been settled by the elector personally, he complained of the arrangement. He again became suspicious, and suddenly required that Buderus should not allow this money to pass through Rothschild's hands, but that it should be paid direct into the reserve treasury at Itzehoe, an arrangement which was more difficult to carry out. This was galling, both for Buderus and for Meyer Amschel Rothschild, who was just endeavoring through Dalberg's good offices to buy back the elector's coin collection, containing so many gold and silver specimens of priceless value, which had been carried off to Paris. The following events did not improve the elector's temper.

By offering the tsar the prospect of sharing the world dominion with himself, Napoleon had in the Treaty of Tilsit reaped the fruits of his campaign against Prussia. The result was that Hesse was allotted to the newly created kingdom of Westphalia, and Napoleon's brother Jerome pitched his tent in William's residence at Cassel. The exiled elector was filled with rage and indignation, and his tendency to behave unjustly to those about him became more marked. When Buderus was again staying with his master at Itzehoe, and spoke of Rothschild and the services that he had rendered, the elector indicated that he noted the special favor shown to Rothschild with surprise, as after all, he was a Jew of very obscure antecedents, and expressed his concern to find Buderus employing him, as he had lately been doing, to the exclusion of almost everybody else, in the most important financial transactions. Buderus declared himself strongly in reply. He pointed out how promptly Rothschild had always paid, especially in the case of the moneys from London, and emphasized the skill with which Rothschild had succeeded in concealing from the French his English dealings on behalf of the elector. He related how French officials in Frankfort had recently been instructed to carry out investigations at Meyer Amschel Rothschild's, in order to ascertain whether he did not collect English moneys for the elector; and how Meyer Amschel had immediately produced his books, an inspection of which had revealed absolutely nothing of this matter.[24]

This fact proved that even then Meyer Amschel was keeping two sets of books, one of which was suitable for inspection by the various authorities and tax collectors, the other containing the record of the more secret and profitable transactions.

Buderus pointed out that Bethmann, in view of his standing as a Frankfort patrician, and as the head of a firm that was centuries old, could not so suitably be employed in transactions which in the difficult political conditions of the time could not bear the light of day. He added that Bethmann's financial resources had given out in connection with the Danish loan in 1806, and that Rothschild far surpassed him in determination and energy. He also suggested that Rothschild had given greater proof of loyalty, for they had hardly heard anything of Bethmann since the elector had gone into exile, whereas Meyer Amschel was constantly concerning himself with the elector's interests, and also, when necessary, coming personally to Schleswig, or sending one of his sons.

Buderus's representations succeeded finally in allaying this bout of suspicion against the Rothschild family, with whom he had now established very close personal relations. Through the efforts of the administrator of the elector's estates, all the other bankers were gradually forced into the background, Rothschild taking their place.[25] From this time onwards he enjoyed the elector's confidence as far as such a thing was possible, and we find Meyer Amschel becoming, not only William's principal banker, but also his confidential adviser in various difficult matters.

As his health no longer permitted him to do full justice to the strenuous requirements of the elector's service, he placed one of his sons at the elector's disposal when necessary. Up to this time the elector had turned down the various proposals regarding the collection of interest and the investment of capital that Nathan had made to him from London. As late as June, 1807, he actually instructed his chargé d'affaires in London to vouchsafe no reply whatever if Nathan should venture again to inquire as to the elector's financial affairs.[26] In this matter too, he was slowly and completely to change his attitude, without any disadvantage to himself. Everybody who possibly could was borrowing money from the elector, for the German sovereigns, and not least, the King of Prussia, were suffering from extreme shortage of money after Napoleon's victorious march through their country, owing to the heavy war expenses and the subsidies which he imposed.

Prince Wittgenstein repeatedly urged the King of Prussia to be very cordial to the elector, and as soon as it should be practicable to invite him to live in Berlin, because it might then perhaps be possible to persuade him to grant a loan. The invitation was actually sent, but the king had then himself been obliged to flee from his capital, and was suffering the most grievous misfortunes, so that Berlin was out of the question. Meanwhile Denmark had also been forced by Napoleon to give up her neutrality. The French invaded the dukedoms and the Danish royal house found the presence of the elector, who was such a thorn in Napoleon's side, most embarrassing.

In these circumstances, the refugee was in constant danger of being discovered and taken prisoner. Jerome was ruling in Hesse, and it was of little use to the elector that Lagrange's double-dealing was brought to light, and

William, Elector of Hesse
From a portrait by W. Böttner in the Vienna National Library

the general dismissed. In spite of an invitation from the Prince of Wales, William did not wish to go to England, since that would have meant a final breach with the powerful usurper, for the elector continued to cherish an unreasonable hope of Napoleon's forgiveness.

There was still Austria. In his last letter[27] the Emperor Francis had expressed his "most heartfelt sympathy in these sad circumstances," with the hope that he might be of assistance to him. The elector accordingly asked for asylum in Austrian territory, and decided to continue his flight to Bohemia, stopping first at Carlsbad.

He did not part with his treasures, but took with him all the valuables and papers which had been saved, including a chest full of deeds which Meyer Amschel had proposed to bring on afterwards from Hamburg. The travelers were carefully disguised on their journey. In one place where there were French troops they nearly lost their most valuable belongings, as the wheels of the carriage in which they were packed broke in the marketplace, and they were forced to transfer them to another vehicle. Fortunately nobody guessed what the bales contained; the journey proceeded without further mishap; and on July 28, 1808, the elector arrived at Carlsbad, where he awaited the emperor's decision as to his final place of abode.

Meanwhile Meyer Amschel and his son were carrying on their business at Frankfort and developing the trading as well as the purely financial side of it. All the members of the family were actively engaged in it, and Rothschild's unmarried daughter sat at the cash desk, assisted by the wives of Solomon and Amschel. Meanwhile the fifth son, Jacob, generally called James, had reached the age of sixteen, and like his elder brothers had begun to take an active part in the business. This had made it possible for the eldest son Amschel also to leave Frankfort fairly often, in order, like Carl, who was the firm's "traveler," to visit the elector in Bohemia.

Buderus in the meantime had arranged that the elector's cash income, which it was really his duty to administer, should be collected by Rothschild and remain in his hands at four per cent interest. Thus, during the summer of 1808 [28] he received 223,800 gulden against bills at four per cent—a very respectable sum at a time when ready money was so scarce, and the elector was reluctant to leave it all with him. However he found in due course that Rothschild accounted with extreme accuracy for every penny of it.

In accordance with the wishes of Emperor Francis, the elector moved to Prague toward the end of August, 1808. That monarch knew well what he was doing in welcoming the elector to his territories. Austria was chronically in need of money; nevertheless plans were being made to avenge her defeat. Count Stadion especially was the prime mover in the idea of waging a new war against the insolent Emperor of the French.

Financial affairs in Austria were in a state of chaos, as revealed by the Vienna Bourse of the period. A confidential friend of Emperor Francis had sent him a report on the subject in which he did not mince his words. "I feel it my duty to observe," he wrote,[29] "that the Bourse at the present time seems more like a jumble sale than an Imperial Bourse. The dregs and scourings of the population invade it, and decent business men, capable of handling such matters, are pushed into the background and shouted down, so that reasonable discussion becomes impossible. Closer investigation will reveal the fact that many of these people are paid by stock-jobbers, systematically to create disorder at the Bourse." The collapse in the value of the paper currency, the violent fluctuations in all quotations, the fear of war and the general unrest all contributed to this state of affairs. It was in vain for Emperor Francis to "resolve that measures must be taken to prevent the Bourse from degenerating into a rowdy collection of persons of no position who sacrifice all considerations to the basest greed for profit."[30] The fundamental cause of these conditions remained unaltered.

The Austrian state hoped for some financial assistance from the elector at Prague. He was living a retired life at the Palace Liechtenstein, and Vienna set itself to discover the state of the elector's purse. All kinds of confidential persons and secret agents of the police, some of them disguised under titles of nobility and wearing officers' uniforms, were sent to Prague. One of them reported[31] that the Elector of Hesse had large sums at his disposal, and was in communication with *"particuliers"* through middlemen, regarding the purchase of state obligations. He stated that it was not at all unlikely that a loan to the imperial court could be obtained under favorable conditions, and suggested that it might be worth while to make inquiries on this matter through confidential bankers and exchange merchants.

Immediately on receipt of this report, the emperor with quite unwonted promptitude instructed the chancellor of the exchequer Count O'Donnell to let him have his opinion as speedily as possible on this report received "from a trustworthy source."[32]

We now for the first time find the name of Rothschild mentioned in connection with the Austrian court. Count O'Donnell reported that there was no doubt that the elector had rescued considerable sums and also had large amounts to his credit in England, and that it was therefore worth attempting to induce him to subscribe to a loan, either in "solid gold" or in "reliable bills of exchange on places abroad." The count emphasized that "in order to achieve this object the best method would probably be to approach the middlemen to whom the elector entrusts his financial affairs, and this can best be done through a reliable exchange office in Vienna or Prague."

O'Donnell recommended that such middlemen should

receive one, two, or three per cent commission, this being in any case customary in such proceedings, and they would then have an interest in stimulating the elector to carry through the transaction. "The papers of the Credits Commission reveal," the count's report continued, "that the persons who appeared on behalf of the elector, then landgrave, in connection with the negotiation of the loan of one million, two hundred thousand gulden in 1796 were the Frankfort firm Rüppell and Harnier, and Privy Councilor Buderus. At that time the interest on these loans . . . was collected by the local firm Frank and Company, on behalf of the Jewish firm at Frankfort of Meyer Amschel Rothschild, who were authorized to collect them by a power of attorney executed by Privy Councilor Buderus, and it appears to me abundantly evident that this privy councilor is the principal person who should be moved, through some advantage, to smooth our path." [33]

It was decided to put up to the intermediaries two proposals: either that they should obtain a five per cent loan on mortgage security, or that they should persuade the elector to invest a considerable sum, at least one or two million, in the lottery loan. Hereupon the following resolution was issued by his Imperial Majesty: "In view of the indubitable necessity for providing if possible for the collection in hard cash of an adequate supply of money I approve of an attempt being made to obtain a cash loan from the Elector of Hesse. . . . The important thing is to make use of a reliable and intelligent mediator who may be relied upon to carry through the negotiations cautiously and skilfully, so as to achieve the desired end on the most favorable terms possible." [34]

In accordance with these instructions Buderus and Rothschild were confidentially approached as mediators, and they promised that they would do their best, but they emphasized the fact that the ultimate decision lay solely with the elector. They at once duly informed the elector of the wishes of Austria, but he showed a reluctance to meet them, and then war broke out and the negotiations were postponed.

During the period which followed the elector, regarding whose avarice and enormous wealth the most varied stories were spread at Prague, was closely watched by secret police specially sent from Vienna. He took an active interest in current affairs, and closely followed the powerful movement which was developing in Germany, particularly in Prussia, its aim being to shake off the foreign yoke. This movement could not as yet come into the open, but in Königsberg, where the king and the government of Prussia were residing, the "Tugendbund" was formed, a league which ostensibly pursued moral-scientific aims, but the ultimate object of which was deliverance of Germany.

The principal protector of the league was the minister Baron von Stein; and William of Hesse held an important position in it. Its membership was so wide that it also included Jews, and the Rothschilds appear to have become members. At any rate they acted as go-betweens for the elector's correspondence on this matter, and made payments in favor of the Tugendbund.

Through an intercepted letter from Stein which mentioned the elector,[35] Napoleon learned of the desire for a war of revenge, and of the plans for a rising in Hesse. Stein had to flee, and Napoleon's distrust of the elector and of his servants was very much increased. The emperor saw clearly that the elector was implicated, that is, was financing it. Further intercepted letters confirmed this view.[36] As a result several business men mentioned in them by the elector were arrested; it was desired through them to obtain further information regarding the apparently inexhaustible resources of the elector.

Amongst these men of business Buderus was prominent, and it was particularly desired to ascertain his precise connection with the bankers. One of these was

Meyer Amschel Rothschild, whose relations with Buderus had long been no secret to the French officials. The Frankfort banker was accordingly cited to appear before the Chancery of the Urban and District of Frankfort on August 13, 1808; but he could not obey his summons since he was confined to his bed.

He had fallen seriously ill in June, 1808, had been operated on by a professor from Mainz, and, fearing that his days were numbered, he had made his will. He therefore sent his son Solomon to appear in his place, telling him not to let himself be drawn, and to make only such statements as were not likely to furnish the French with any clue, or else to provide false clues. Solomon carried out his mission with great skill. The French were but little enlightened by the cross-examination, and in the end they dismissed the young Jew with the order that he should immediately hand over to the court any letter from Buderus to the firm of Rothschild.[37]

Buderus and Lennep were themselves arrested in September, 1808, and minutely examined for several days at Mainz, this being only natural in view of the fact that these men, who were the elector's tools, were in the power of the French at Frankfort, whereas their chief was living in Prague, out of Napoleon's reach.

Napoleon's mistrust of William was fully justified, for in October, 1808, the elector was carrying on negotiations at Prague for promoting insurrections throughout the whole of the northwest of Germany, with the view that they should spread to the south as well. This matter was certainly carried on with great secrecy; even the Austrian secret police agents knew only in a general way that something was in the wind. It is amusing to note the naïve manner in which they arrived at the conclusions contained in their reports.

"The Elector of Hesse," says one of these reports, "has forty-one natural sons, all of whom he has decently provided for, but as the fall of the elector has disappointed their hopes of a brilliant career, they are endeavoring to reinstate their father. As the defeat of Prussia has deprived them of all chance of achieving their object by force, they have had recourse to a secret association which is intended to extend its activities throughout the whole of Germany under the protection of the English Masonic Lodge at Hanover. This league will take a suitable opportunity to reveal itself in a public conspiracy in order to attain its final object. . . . The probability of another war has aroused fresh expectations of making proselytes. In small confidential circles something is occasionally said about the possibility of putting an end to the miseries of the country by putting Napoleon and his brothers out of the way." [38]

Vienna, however, was not merely interested in the elector's high politics. Further information was also desired as to his financial advisers, particularly as to Rothschild, mentioned by O'Donnell. Urgent instructions were therefore sent to the chief of police of the city of Prague to obtain as accurate information as possible regarding that man's activities.

The chief of police reported: [39]

> Amsel Mayer Rotschild, living under the registered number 184 in the third main district, is agent for war payments to the Elector of Hesse, and in that capacity he has achieved mention, together with his brother, Moses Mayer Rotschild, in the electoral almanac for the year 1806. The father of these two men appears in the almanac as a war paymaster. According to information supplied by Major von Thümmel, Amsel Mayer Rotschild, has come here from Frankfort, where he has been living hitherto, in order to look after the elector's financial affairs, which were formerly entrusted to Ballabom, who seems to have shown a certain lack of diligence. Be that as it may, we may assume that Amsel Mayer Rotschild renders the elector important services in

> other matters too, and it is not entirely improbable that this Jew is at the head of an important propaganda system in favor of the elector, whose branches extend throughout the former Hessian territories.
>
> I have reasons for this opinion. These suppositions are based on the following fact: whenever I enter the elector's quarters, I always find Rotschild there, and generally in the company of Army Councilor Schminke and War Secretary Knatz, and they go into their own rooms, and Rotschild generally has papers with him. We may assume that their aims are in no sense hostile to Austria, since the elector is exceedingly anxious to recover the possession of his electorate, so that it is scarcely open to question that the organizations and associations, whose guiding spirit Rotschild probably is, are entirely concerned with the popular reactions and the other measures to be adopted, if Austria should have the good fortune to make any progress against France and Germany. Owing to his extensive business connections it is probable that he can ascertain this more easily than anybody else, and can also conceal his machinations under the cloak of business.

This report was more or less in accordance with the facts; for Rothschild was the connecting link between Buderus, who lived in Hesse and could never come to Prague, and the elector. Rothschild was also constantly busy with the elector's financial affairs, and these were of a particularly wide scope at the beginning of 1809, since with the passage of time the accumulations of money in England, by way of interest and otherwise, had grown so large that their supervision required particular care. Buderus proposed that his master should acquire British securities at three per cent,[40] and suggested that Meyer Amschel should be commissioned to effect the purchase of them. Rothschild had naturally made this proposal to Buderus in the first instance, and Buderus had duly put it forward as his own suggestion.

The close relations between Buderus and Rothschild had at that time actually been embodied in a written agreement between them which virtually made the electoral official a secret partner in the firm of Rothschild. This highly important document runs as follows:

"The following confidential agreement has today been concluded between the Privy War Councilor Buderus von Carlshausen, and the business house of Meyer Amschel Rothschild at Frankfort: Whereas Buderus has handed over to the banking firm of Meyer Amschel Rothschild the capital sum of 20,000 gulden, 24 florins, and has promised to advise that firm in all business matters to the best of his ability and to advance its interests as far as he may find practicable, the firm of Meyer Amschel Rothschild promises to render Buderus a true account of the profits made in respect of the above-mentioned capital sum of 20,000 gulden, and to allow him access to all books at any time so that he may satisfy himself with regard to this provision." [41]

The agreement contained a provision for its termination on either side by giving six months' notice.

Buderus now had a personal interest in securing for Meyer Amschel Rothschild a monopoly in the conduct of the elector's business. What he had done had been in the best interests of all concerned. His experience of a period of years had proved to him the reliability and the skill of the House of Rothschild; he harbored no prejudices against the Jews; and he was firmly convinced that the elector, his master, was bound to gain by placing his financial affairs in the hands of one firm, especially of such an able firm as the House of Rothschild.

The Rothschilds on the other hand needed the support of a man who could gain for them the confidence of the suspicious and avaricious elector, who was an exceedingly difficult person to handle. They had achieved this object through Buderus, but they wanted to secure the relationship for the future, and therefore gave him a personal interest in the continued prosperity of the business. Finally Buderus himself profited by this arrangement as he fully deserved to do after the persevering and self-sacrificing efforts that he had made; and he could never hope that he would be regarded in accordance with his deserts by the rapacious elector. Moreover, he was far too scrupulous and honorable spontaneously to appropriate money in the course of his administration of the elector's property; but he had a very large family, and by becoming a secret partner in the firm of Rothschild he was enabled to meet its requirements.

Buderus's efforts with his master were successful. The elector acted upon Rothschild's recommendations regarding British stocks, and he then actually ordered that £150,000 of the stocks should be purchased on his account, which in fact exceeded the amount that Buderus had suggested. The investment itself was entrusted to Rothschild.

Up to this time the financial transactions in England had been the most reliable as far as interest payments were concerned; but the payments in respect of interest due from members of the English royal house came in at most irregular intervals and were often outstanding for very long periods. The elector, however, did not agitate to get these payments in, for he regarded the money laid out in this direction less as an investment than as a means of putting the members of the ruling house under an obligation to himself.

The brothers Rothschild noted this practice of the elector with important personages; they had practical evidence, from the experience of their princely client, of the fact that transactions involving temporary loss may ultimately result in very good business. The debtors' uneasy feeling on failing to make payments at the date when they fell due sometimes led them to try to make amends in other ways, through furnishing valuable information or through political services, and such favors often produced cash results far exceeding the amount actually owing.

At this time the bond between the House of Rothschild and the elector had become a very close one; and this was not due to Buderus only, but also to their loyalty; although this quality resulted to their advantage, they incurred the risks that loyalty involved. The only really unpleasant circumstance in this connection was the fact that the frivolous heir to the elector, who was always in need of money, exploited the situation and at every possible opportunity borrowed from his father's faithful Jewish servant. In any case that could not be a very serious matter, as Rothschild was morally certain to get his money back, the prince being the heir to the enormous fortune which his father had amassed.

These large financial transactions did not put an end to the dealings in small antiques between the elector and Rothschild, which had been the starting-point of their business relations. However, there was a difference: their rôles were reversed; the elector now sold to Rothschild vases, jewels and antique boxes, etc. more often than he bought them. These dealings constituted a peculiar bond of sympathy between the elector and his Jewish crown agent, and the elector enjoyed showing his talent in this field, as far as was consistent with his high birth.

Meanwhile the relations between Austria and France had become more acute. The Emperor Napoleon had returned from Spain, and a new war between Napoleon and the Emperor Francis was imminent. The elector offered the emperor a legion of four thousand men, this offer being coupled with a touching appeal that the emperor should secure his reinstatement in the rulership of his territories.[42] The offer was thankfully accepted.

On April 9, 1809, the Austrians crossed the Inn; thereupon Napoleon ceased to be a factor in the treatment accorded to the elector at Prague. The elector was granted the honors due to a sovereign, and society was commanded to call on his favorite at Prague, who until then had been very much slighted. They wanted to "get on the right side of him" in order to get as much money and as many troops from him as possible. The elector, however, put only one half of the promised forces in the field. That cost him 600,000 gulden; and it was Rothschild who saw to the collection and distribution of this sum.

This work was full of danger for the Rothschilds as they were at the mercy of the French in Frankfort. In spite of the great scarcity of money at the time it was Rothschild who from his own resources advanced to the elector the cash amount of several hundred thousand gulden required on short loan. The elector already saw himself in possession of his states. "I come," he wrote somewhat prematurely in a proclamation of April, 1809, "to loose your bonds; Austria's exalted monarch protects me and protects you. Let us hail the brave Austrians; they are our true friends, and it is in their midst and with their assistance that I come to you."

It was with eloquence rather than with cash that he called upon his Hessians to rise. When one of the local leaders wanted to seize Cassel and take King Jerome prisoner, he applied to the elector in the first instance for financial support. All that he received, however, was a piece of paper, representing an order for 30,000 thalers, "payable only in the event of the rising being successful." When the attempt failed, the elector laid the blame, "upon the premature and unprepared nature of the attack."

The immediate result of the attempt was that the elector's servants in Hessian territory were subjected to more stringent regulations. Notwithstanding that Buderus and Rothschild were on such exceedingly good terms with the Primate of the Confederation at Frankfort, the fact that King Jerome's position in Westphalia had been seriously threatened caused the police at Cassel to watch the movements of Buderus and Rothschild with renewed assiduity, as they suspected them, not unjustly, of having financed the rising.

This favorable opportunity was exploited by jealous rivals at Cassel, who supplied the police and their notorious chief, Savagner, with information. Moreover, Baron Bacher, the accredited Westphalian ambassador to Dalberg at Frankfort, was a bitter enemy of Rothschild, and felt particular displeasure at the favor shown by Dalberg to the Jew, since he had long been convinced that Rothschild was in the elector's confidence in all the activities undertaken against the French. Savagner, who thought that a prosecution of the rich Jew might accrue to the benefit of his own pocket, concentrated all his efforts on inducing King Jerome of Westphalia to authorize the issue of a warrant against Meyer Amschel Rothschild on the ground that he had been a channel through whom the elector's money had passed to the rebels.

In this dangerous situation Rothschild appealed to Dalberg to intervene on his behalf; Dalberg did what he could, and it was only with great difficulty that the French police in Cassel managed to obtain the warrant. A certain Levy, the son-in-law of a rival of Rothschild, informed Savagner as to the lines on which Rothschild should be examined regarding his business dealings with the elector.

On May 9, 1809, Buderus was again arrested at Hanau, submitted to searching cross-examinations, and was let out on substantial bail only after an interval of several days. On May 10 Savagner set out for Frankfort with the warrant which he had at last succeeded in obtaining, but which authorized only a domiciliary search and a close examination of all members of the House of Rothschild.

They had been warned in good time; the prevailing sentiment amongst the local inhabitants, both at Cassel and at Frankfort, was one of solidarity against the foreign invader. It was only rarely that this feeling was subordinated to commercial rivalry. Meyer Amschel was also given a hint by Dalberg. He was particularly concerned about the elector's four chests containing account books which were under his care; they were in his house cellar, and he did not even know what they contained. As the cellar would naturally be searched, he would have to do his best to rescue the elector's property as speedily as possible in the general excitement arising out of the sudden menace.

Old Meyer Amschel and his wife, Solomon and James, and the wives of the two eldest sons were at home. Amschel, the eldest son, was staying with the elector at Prague, and Carl was traveling on other business. Those members of the family who were at home now tried to get the compromising chests through the connecting passage to the yard cellar at the back, but they found that the passage was too narrow for the chests. These were therefore emptied, and their contents placed in other cases, together with some coupons representing unrealized obligations due to the firm itself. The family then set about the work of hiding the compromising account books and the secret records of the elector's intimate affairs, as well as certain embarrassing correspondence.

When the Westphalian commissioner of police arrived on the 10th of May, 1809, furnished with his exceedingly limited warrant for summoning the Rothschild family and searching their house at Frankfort, the most important documents had already been well concealed, and the individual members of the family had arranged between themselves what they would say when they were examined, so that they would not get involved in contradictory statements.

Dalberg, the sovereign at Frankfort, had been watching the activities directed from Cassel with a certain resentment; they constituted an infringement of his sovereign rights, and they affected a valued financier to whom he would soon want to apply again for a personal loan; on the other hand he felt that it would be exceedingly unwise for him to oppose the wishes of King Jerome's great brother. At the same time, for financial reasons it was only with reluctance that the King of Westphalia himself had consented to the issue of the warrant. It was therefore a foregone conclusion that the Rothschild family would not suffer any serious harm. Dalberg also gave orders that one of his own police officials should accompany Savagner. The two commissioners accordingly betook themselves to Rothschild's business house in the Jewish quarter where the whole family were expecting them.

Old Meyer Amschel, who on this occasion too was unwell, was placed under arrest in his own room, while Solomon and James were placed under arrest in the office below, under the guard of police constables. In the meantime all cupboards containing papers and business correspondence were sealed, and a systematic search of the whole house was instituted. Simultaneously the home of Solomon, who also lived in the town, was submitted to a similar search. Thanks to the advance warnings and to the well-concealed duplicate books, not much incriminating matter was discovered.

The next step was to investigate the individual members of the family. Meyer Amschel had to answer the questions drafted by the Jew Levy on the instructions of his rival, the banker Simon, at Cassel—questions affecting the details of Rothschild's financial dealings with the elector. In many cases he replied that he had no recollection of the matters referred to, pointing out that he had suffered a severe illness and undergone an operation in 1808; he stated that this had had serious aftereffects, and more particularly, that it had affected his memory. By this method of evasion he succeeded in avoiding making statements which the commissioner of police could have used as incriminating material.

In these circumstances recourse had to be had to an examination of the other members of the family, including Meyer Amschel's wife. The old mother replied [43] that she knew nothing at all, as she only concerned herself with the house, never went out from one year's end to another, and had nothing whatever to do with the business. The two sons made the statements which they had previously arranged with their father, and in general said as little as possible.

The examination of such books as were discovered yielded very slight result, as the incriminating documents had been removed. Meyer Amschel cleverly used an opportunity which proffered itself, of lending Savagner three hundred thalers, and this helped considerably to expedite the conclusion of the official investigation. In any case, Savagner's authority was of a limited kind, and Dalberg's commissioner, who was himself a Jew, was well-disposed toward Rothschild, and used his influence to bring the examination to an end. As sufficient material had been collected to show that the action which had been taken was justified and necessary in the circumstances, the authorities at Cassel, too, were satisfied. Fortunately for the accused, Rothschild's enemy, Ambassador Bacher, was not in Frankfort at this time; so that the whole painful business passed off well for the family of Rothschild.

French reports [44] on the matter reveal that the French officials found the Rothschild family to be "exceedingly wise and cunning," and to have managed to secure friends in all quarters. The only positive result of the inquiry was to establish the fact that Amschel Rothschild was staying at Prague and was directing the financial speculations of the Elector of Hesse; and that the firm of Rothschild had made small payments to individual leaders of the insurrection. The only circumstance noted which was regarded as of graver import was that the brothers Rothschild had regularly paid considerable

Carl Frederick Buderus von Carlshausen

Silhouette in the possession of the
Hanau Historical Society

sums to the elector's consort, who was staying at Gotha, and to her business manager Kunkel, who also acted as an agent of the elector in promoting the revolution of Hesse against France.

These facts in themselves furnished sufficient material for dealing ruthlessly with the family—if that had been seriously desired; but the Rothschilds benefited by the inhibitions of the rulers of Frankfort and Cassel, who at heart were pleased to have remained faithful to the elector, although they had maintained practical relations with the new French powers. Everything had resulted happily, and the Rothschilds could breathe freely, but it had been a warning to act with even greater precaution in the future. The most important thing was to get the chests belonging to the elector out of the house at once, for in the course of another search the yard cellar might perhaps be discovered. The chests were therefore sent successively through the mediation of a Jewish friend to a business acquaintance of the Rothschilds at Darmstadt—a certain Abraham Mayer—and they stayed with him until the elector returned to his country.

While these events were taking place at Frankfort, Napoleon's campaign against Austria was proceeding. Swift as lightning, Napoleon's genius was thrusting down the Danube to Vienna. He sustained a reverse at Aspern, but on July 6 he made good this defeat by the decisive victory at Wagram.

The elector at Prague had been anxiously watching the changing vicissitudes of the campaign. He had hoped that his tormentor would be speedily beaten and he now saw him coming ever closer to his place of refuge at Prague. When Napoleon was at the gates of Vienna, the elector was seized with terror. He would have to flee again, and in great concern he took counsel with his advisers, and with Amschel Rothschild, who was staying with him, and who was no less terrified than his electoral master, as to whether they should not take refuge in the fortress of Olmütz. At any rate the more valuable articles were sent on there. Seven chests containing securities, and one containing jewelry were actually sent off.

Then came Wagram; Napoleon advanced to Mähren, and Olmütz was seriously threatened. The boxes had to come back, and the elector set out for Berlin, as the king had already offered to shelter him there. But the king now rather regretted having made this offer; Napoleon was too powerful and might resent the elector's being granted asylum in Berlin. The king therefore wrote on January 29, 1810, to put him off, on the ground of *"ménagements délicats"* obtaining between himself and Napoleon at the time. Meanwhile peace was signed at Schönbrunn, no mention whatever of the elector being made in the treaty. Napoleon returned to Paris, whereupon William decided to remain at Prague.

The unsuccessful campaign of 1809 had resulted in the retirement of Count Stadion, the Austrian Minister for Foreign Affairs, and this brilliant man and bitter opponent of Napoleon withdrew for some years into private life. On October 8, 1809, he was succeeded by Prince Clemens Metternich, who was to play such a decisive rôle in the destinies of Europe during the following half-century.

Metternich had only just entered upon his duties when he received a letter from the Elector of Hesse, requesting the minister to support him, and "to restore to his orphaned subjects their native prince, whose presence they so ardently desired." He had great hopes that Metternich would use his influence with the emperor, and he was bitterly disappointed when he learned that he had not even been mentioned during the peace negotiations.

He wrote a bitter letter of complaint to Stadion:[45] "So many worthless people, relying on French protection, are enabled to sin against me with impunity, and nobody now feels that he has any duties toward me; everybody does as he pleases and is actuated by base and selfish motives. I have thus lost more than two-thirds of a fortune that was never very large. That is hard, but harder than everything else is my present condition."

It was highly typical of the elector to suggest that he was badly off; in spite of his losses he was still actually one of the wealthiest princes of his time; but if there were spoils to be divided, he did not want to be left out in the cold on the ground that he was rich enough already. The money motive was always the principal one with the elector, and in this matter he had a perfect understanding with his crown agent Rothschild. Rothschild always advised the elector to ask concessions at every possible opportunity—as, for instance, that claims on him in respect of the troops should be waived, etc.—and the elector got more and more accustomed to following Rothschild's advice, and scarcely took any important financial step without consulting him.

A sum of £150,000 had been invested as recently as December 18, 1809, in three per cent British Consols from interest received on behalf of the "poor" elector. The business in connection with this transaction naturally entailed voluminous correspondence, for the conveyance of which between Frankfort and Prague Meyer Amschel made himself personally responsible. He traveled in a private post-chaise which contained a secret drawer.

The French were anxious to intercept if possible the correspondence between the elector and his Frankfort agents; once they did actually succeed in seizing a letter destined for England which clearly revealed the fact that the Rothschilds were responsible for the management of the elector's funds in that country.[46]

In the meantime an important change had taken place in general European politics. The new personality directing Austria's foreign affairs had brought about a complete reversal of the policy followed previously. Nothing could be achieved against Napoleon by the use of force, and therefore Metternich tried other means.

Napoleon's marriage with Josephine was childless. His union with an imperial princess would increase his prestige and might produce the heir he so much desired. The hitherto hostile states were thus reconciled by the prospect of a marriage, and in January, 1810, the imperial house of Austria gave Napoleon to understand that if he asked for the hand of Marie Louise, the eighteen-year-old daughter of the emperor, he would not be refused. The contract of marriage was signed as early as the 7th of February.

One of the first to be informed of this complete change in the situation was the Elector of Hesse. He immediately wrote again to Metternich to the following effect: "I am writing to your Excellency trusting to enlist your sympathy for my most cherished desires. The marriage which is to unite the two greatest monarchies causes me to hope that I may regain the Emperor Napoleon's goodwill, if our emperor . . . will but intercede in my favor. One word from him to the plenipotentiary of France will secure my happiness, and will at any rate establish me as ruler of one of the liberated states in Germany, even if I cannot regain my own Penates. . . . Surely that monarch will not be able to resist the intervention of his exalted father-in-law, and of an adored wife on behalf of a prince who has never yet understood how he has incurred his displeasure." [47]

The elector also repeatedly pressed Count Stadion to use his influence with the Austrian ruler in William's behalf. The minister had great difficulty in dissuading him from traveling to Vienna.

Although in these letters the elector gave such a woeful account of his condition, he was faring exceedingly well at Prague. He had bought a palace on the Kleinseite where he held court, and he maintained a household of thirty-six persons. He had also acquired the magnificent castle and grounds of Bubenetsch, which was finely furnished throughout, but with due regard to economy. The firm of Rothschild carried through the business matters connected with these purchases.

The actual state of the elector's affairs was well known at Vienna. The financial affairs of the court and of the public departments were getting steadily worse, and the new friendship with France had done but little to lighten the burdens of debt incurred under the recent peace treaty. In the negotiations between France and Austria the Austrian Treasury official Nikolaus Barbier had been so vehement in his advocacy of Austria's interests that the French plenipotentiary on one occasion actually protested against his being present. This clever financial expert had played a considerable part in all the various loan operations which Austria had had to carry out during these wars.

At that time the imperial state had no business relations with the Rothschild banking firm. There were four more or less official discount houses at Vienna, through which the Austrian government arranged its loans and other monetary business. They were the banking firms, Geymüller and Company, Arnstein and Eskeles and Company, Graf Fries and Company, and Steiner and Company. The Austrian government also dealt with the banking firm of Parish at Hamburg in 1809, in matters relating to remittances and realizations—such were the technical terms used at the time—of English subsidy moneys.

The condition of the Austrian state finances was lamentable. The value of her bank notes had fallen steadily during the wars, and the amount of paper money in circulation had risen to the enormous figure of over a thousand million gulden; it was already necessary to pay five hundred paper gulden for one hundred gulden in coin of the realm, this amount soon rising to twelve hundred gulden. In June, 1810, the difficulties had become so acute that an attempt was made to raise a loan of from two to three million gulden on the contents of the Privy Purse, which were deposited in the Vienna Treasury, this loan to be carried out by the four discount firms mentioned above, on the security of mortgage deeds. The banker Eskeles made a journey to Paris and Holland in order to raise this money.

It was also suggested that the state lottery monopoly should be mortgaged, but the four banking firms had not great resources themselves, and were not particularly successful in their attempts to raise credits. Eskeles was forced to report from Frankfort that he had no hope of success, "either in raising money or in mortgaging the state lottery."

In these depressing circumstances Vienna remembered the wealthy Elector of Hesse whom it had been treating so shabbily, and it was suggested that he might be persuaded through Rothschild to grant a loan to Austria. Barbier was entrusted with this mission, and discussed it personally with the elector, and also informed Rothschild of the matter. The elector replied evasively. He said that he must first discuss it with his advisers; and Buderus had pointed out to his master that so much money was already on loan with private persons that it was not desirable to make further investments.

Rothschild also advised against producing capital sums of the amount required by the Austrian court, although he felt that it was not desirable to give the emperor a rebuff. The elector and Rothschild hit upon the idea of suggesting to the emperor that the elector should transfer to him all his individual outstanding claims, and that it should be the monarch's own business to bring the debtors to book. He suggested that the emperor might have more influence and power to effect this, and that he might be able to neutralize any opposition of the French to collecting the debts. The advantage for him would be that he would then have only one single debtor, the Emperor of Austria.

The elector accordingly wrote to Barbier [48] that he would be happier than he could say if his Royal and Imperial Majesty would take over the debts due to him, mentioned in the accompanying schedule. He stated that he was not in a position to grant a loan in any other way than that suggested, as eighteen months earlier he had purchased Austrian government stock of the value of over a million gulden, and funds in England had been sequestrated. If he recovered from his financial difficulties he would be delighted to be of service to his Majesty.

He enclosed a list of thirty-three different clients who owed him sums in varying amounts, ranging from 784,848 reichsthalers down to 6,951 reichsthalers. Apart from several princely houses, the names of privy councilors and counselors of embassies figured in these lists, as well as ministers such as Hardenberg, who owed the elector 140,000 thalers. The total value of all the claims amounted to the sum of 5,832,532 reichsthalers.

This proposal, however, came to nothing. The scheme put forward by Rothschild, and approved by the elector, had been too subtle and complicated, and on the instructions of Emperor Francis a reply was sent to the elector [49] declining the offer, on the ground that the collection of the money would be a process too difficult and uncertain, and not consonant with the dignity of the Austrian state. It was also pointed out that the moneys had been attached by the French government, and that to accept a transfer of these obligations would therefore compromise Austria.

Although the proposal was rejected, it had the important result that for the first time a high Austrian Treasury official negotiated with a member of the Rothschild family.

In the meantime important political changes had taken place at Frankfort. Dalberg's Confederation of the

Rhine had exchanged Hanau and Fulda for Regensburg, and the title of Grand Duke of Frankfort was conferred on the overlord. Dalberg's promotion furnished an opportunity to Meyer Amschel, who was in his favor, of proving his gratitude to Buderus for his good offices in the past, by services other than financial.

Buderus had been continually molested by the French police, and Rothschild decided to put an end to this by persuading Dalberg to recognize the electoral official as a deputy of the estates of the Grand Duchy of Frankfort on the occasion of the handing over of Hanau, and also to appoint him director of the finance committee of the diet. He hoped that when Buderus held this official position he would be left in peace.

Dalberg acceded to Rothschild's request. He steered his course very cleverly between the former powers who were now in exile and the new masters at Frankfort. It was very necessary that he should do so, for he could not uproot himself from the city of his birth. All his possessions were there, and the city was the principal commercial and financial center of the Continent. The Austrian ambassador Baron von Hügel reported enthusiastically regarding the increasing prosperity of Frankfort, which had conserved its wealth through all the difficulties of the war period, and had actually grown richer. "Luxury," he wrote,[50] "has increased incredibly. Cash is turned over much more rapidly. Hospitals, libraries, museums, etc. are provided on the most generous scale; trade and industry flourish, and everyone is full of enterprise."

Hügel emphasized the fact that the city already gave the impression of being one of the pleasantest and most important towns of Germany. "The grand duke," he continued, "takes an active interest in everything. Since I have been here, I have not seen a beggar or been asked for alms. The roses in the gardens are never touched, and in spite of all difficulties the industry of the tradespeople and bankers is exemplary. In fact their difficulties seem to act as an incentive to further efforts. During the last twenty years there has been no bankruptcy of any note. The volume of goods passing through the city is inconceivably great. Plutocratic standards obtain at Frankfort, and persons are judged by the magnificence of their establishments or by the appearances that they manage to keep up."

Hügel pointed out that Frankfort was a focus for trade between northern and southern Germany, and the gateway to France and Austria; and that no less than eight hundred of its citizens had admitted to possessing unencumbered cash to the sum of 50,000 gulden or more, while some hundreds enjoyed annual incomes of this amount and upwards.

Although this description may have been painted rather rosily, it was, in essentials, in accordance with the facts. There were many people at Frankfort who had grown rich, and the rapidity of the rise of the House of Rothschild to wealth and influence had been particularly marked. In view of the progress of his business, Meyer Amschel now decided to define more clearly its internal constitution; and more particularly to regulate his sons' share with greater accuracy than had been done within the framework of the existing concern.

On September 27, 1810, a new deed of partnership was accordingly drawn up between the father and his sons.[51] The main principle of this contract was that Meyer Amschel gave all his sons a substantial share in the business in order to stimulate their industry. They became, not merely indirectly, but directly interested in its continued prosperity. To mark the change the name of the firm was altered to "Meyer Amschel Rothschild and Sons," and Rothschild conveyed this information to all his business friends in a printed letter, in which he emphasized the fact that he was now associating his three sons with him in the direction of the business, which had been established for forty years.

The contract assessed the capital value of the business at a total of 800,000 gulden, 370,000 gulden being allotted to the father, 185,000 gulden each to the sons Amschel and Solomon, and 30,000 each to Carl and James, who had not yet come of age. These shares were allotted to them as their absolute property, and it is noteworthy that Jacob (James) Rothschild, who was barely eighteen years old, was allotted shares to the capital value of 30,000 gulden, as duly earned through the "conscientious carrying out of the business entrusted to him by the old concern."

For the purpose of dividing profit or loss, the business was divided into fifty shares; a multiple of five, having the convenience of facilitating the future division of the business equally between the five brothers, while the smaller fractions made it possible in the meantime to allot shares with due regard to the varying ages and capacities of the five sons. When the time came to divide up the inheritance, each son could acquire an equal fifth share.

On perusing the document, one is struck by the fact that Nathan, who was living in England, is not mentioned in the partnership deed and seems to have been left entirely to his own resources, although he was in close business association with the parent concern, and on the best terms with his family. Under the contract, twenty-four of the fifty shares were for the next ten years to belong to the father, twelve each to Amschel and Solomon, and one each to Carl and James. In point of fact, however, Meyer Amschel was holding the twelve-fiftieths destined for Nathan; but for the sake of public opinion, on account of the French domination, the connection with Nathan, who was living in England, had to be kept secret. We may assume that there was a secret subsidiary agreement with Nathan, accurately defining his relation to the company.

Each partner of adult age was authorized to sign on behalf of the firm. The deed recited that "with the help of the Almighty, Meyer Amschel Rothschild has, through the industry which he has shown from his youth upwards, through his commercial capacity (i. e., business instinct) and through a tireless activity continued to an advanced age, alone laid the foundations of the present flourishing state of the business, and thereby provided for the worldly happiness of his children." It was therefore laid down that the decision in all transactions should remain with him, as being the head of the business. Moreover, he expressly retained for himself alone the right to withdraw money from the capital of the business as he might think fit, whereas the other partners could take out only their annual profits and what was necessary for their households.

It was also laid down that no daughters or children-in-law should have any right to see the company's books. Finally there were provisions against "vexatious litigation," and any partner who set the law in motion was made liable to a penalty for doing so. Before he could appear before the judge he was required to deposit this amount. This article was cleverly designed to lessen the possibilities of disputes between the five brothers; and although they might perhaps have rendered it invalid at law, they fully appreciated its wisdom, and all five solemnly agreed to abide by it.

The deed of partnership gives some insight into the varied nature of the business of the House of Rothschild, and the vicissitudes to which it was liable. As "bad and unrealizable" mortgages, debentures, and outstanding debts of all kinds are mentioned, it is clear that in its numerous undertakings the House of Rothschild sometimes suffered losses and made mistakes. These certainly always brought indirect advantages, as Meyer Amschel continually emphasized to his sons that mistakes have an educational value, and one must never lose courage.

Meyer Amschel was careful to nurse the old connections which the elector had facilitated for him through his relations in high quarters, and to exploit them for the benefit of his house. Whereas previously he had acted as the middleman between the electoral lender and Denmark, he offered as early as December, 1810,[52] a loan of 400,000 thalers to Count Schimmelmann, the Danish finance minister, which loan was to be advanced, not by the elector, but by Meyer Amschel Rothschild and his sons. It was another step towards his gradual financial emancipation from the elector, although, having now arrived at the point of doing business on his own account, he continued to apply in his own interests the business principles so well proved by William of Hesse.

Rothschild carefully watched the general political situation. Though by reason of his personality and origin, and his ignorance of language, he could not possess those qualities which are normally required in a diplomat, he had a sagacious understanding of human nature, entirely free of any preconceived ideas or prejudices. This was of particular advantage in a world which, at the time, was politically topsy-turvy. One really had to be a consummate diplomatist in order to carry on one's business without causing offense, either to the French or to the powers which they were oppressing.

As long as Napoleon's star was in the ascendant, the Rothschilds acted as if they were well disposed to France and her ruler; they lent money both to the French and to the native authorities, delivered flour to friend and foe alike, and hoped to be left entirely unmolested by Napoleon. They felt, as we know today, more secure than they really were. They were running great risks, for instance, in their commerce, or rather illicit trade, in merchandise with England.

It was not till some time after the proclamation of the

continental blockade that Napoleon realized that it inflicted hardship not only upon England but upon France, as France thereby lost her best customer, and the cost of living in that country rose much higher. He accordingly issued various decrees modifying the strict provisions of the continental blockade, so as to permit of a kind of official smuggling under departmental supervision, and also to allow the import of colonial goods on the payment of a very heavy duty approximating fifty per cent of their value. In spite of these alleviations, smuggling was carried on on a large scale, and its direction was naturally concentrated in the commercial city of Frankfort. Napoleon had sent his own spies there, and on receiving their reports he decided to take more active measures against Frankfort.

Buderus had just decided to give to the young crown agent, Carl Rothschild, who was about to attempt to bring to Prague the property which the elector had left in Schleswig, the final account for the year 1807, which the elector required. The official stated [53] that he was not inclined to venture on the journey himself, because he was too closely watched, and feared a further arrest, and the possible confiscation of all his property.

His letter also contained news that would be welcome to his avaricious master. "After long arguments, and as the result of great efforts," he stated, "I have persuaded the crown agent, Rothschild, in effecting the third investment of £150,000 sterling, to charge one-quarter per cent less commission, so that he will deliver the stock for 73¾, involving a saving of £4,521. . . . The younger son of Crown Agent Rothschild will bring over the document relating to the first purchase of stock, as soon as means can be found for sending it safely."

But this could not be carried out so easily; Napoleon's anger because Frankfort did not respect his blockade regulations against England led to more stringent regulations, and Buderus was forced to change his plans completely. "The crown agent, Kallmann Rothschild," he wrote on November 2, 1810,[54] "should proceed to Prague at once, as several French regiments with artillery have come into the town, as well as a host of customs officials. All the gates have been occupied, and nobody is allowed to pass out without being closely inspected; all warehouses have been sealed, and an extensive search for English and colonial goods has been instituted, severe penalties being inflicted when such goods have been discovered.

"The extent of the general confusion and distress which this has caused beggars descriptions. I myself have taken every conceivable precaution, and I feel justified in stating my absolute conviction that the sons of Crown Agent Rothschild deserve the highest praise for the tireless industry and zeal which they have shown in their devotion to your Electoral Highness. Fresh proclamations have been issued, promising a reward of fifteen per cent for information regarding the investment of your Electoral Highness's funds, and the number of spies and traitors under every guise is so great that it is impossible now to trust anyone. From this mild account of conditions here you may graciously be pleased to infer that it would be as impracticable for me to leave as it was formerly to transport the effects in custody at Gottorp. I shall arrange for Crown Agent Kallmann Rothschild to start as soon as it is possible to get a package out of Frankfort."

On instructions from Paris, a general domiciliary search for concealed English-manufactured goods had been ordered at Frankfort. The city which had just been described in such glowing colors by Hügel was now in a panic. Naturally the business House of Rothschild was also affected by this measure. A list was drawn up of two hundred and thirty-four tradesmen who had to pay the heavy duties prescribed for the colonial wares which were discovered.

Meyer Amschel Rothschild was the sixty-eighth name

in this list,[55] and was made liable for a payment of 19,348 francs, which was certainly not a very large amount compared with the sums payable by other tradesmen. Hebenstreit, for instance, paid nearly a million francs, and Bethmann 363,000 francs. Altogether the French collected a total of nine and a quarter millions on the colonial stores discovered at Frankfort. Half the amount payable by Rothschild was for indigo. In view of Meyer Amschel's relations with the grand ducal government and his cleverness at concealment, we may assume that his actual stores of colonial goods were much greater, and that through his connections he substantially reduced the amount which he ought to have paid. Nevertheless this sudden incursion, personally ordered by Napoleon, had distinctly alarmed him.

Meanwhile the elector at Prague had received Buderus's letters, and sent the following reply to his trusty official:[56] "It is a special satisfaction to me that you have induced the firm of Rothschild, in view of the prospect of the further investment of £150,000, to reduce their commission by one-quarter per cent.

"In view of further representations made by the crown agent Rothschild, and having regard to the favorable price, I have decided to increase this investment by a further £100,000 . . . but on the understanding that I shall pay this amount in instalments, and that I am not to be worried about it in any way. At the same time you are to see that the document regarding the first investment reaches me as soon as possible, and that I receive the others shortly afterwards. I note with pleasure that the House of Rothschild has shown its traditional devotion to me even in the present catastrophe at Frankfort. You will kindly convey to them my satisfaction and gratitude."

Meanwhile the Emperor of France had just experienced one of the happiest hours of his life. On March 20, 1811, Marie Louise had presented him with the son and heir he so much desired. The baptism of the French heir, who had been created King of Rome while still in his cradle, was an occasion of unexampled splendor and magnificence. From all their domains, princely personages swarmed to the festivities, to take advantage of the opportunity of expressing their allegiance to the mighty monarch.

The Grand Duke Dalberg, in Frankfort, also desired to go to Paris to do obeisance, but there was a formidable obstacle in the way of his doing so. The journey was very expensive, and Dalberg could not visit Paris except with a retinue such as befitted his rank. But he had no retinue, and in the first instance he turned for assistance to the association of Frankfort merchants, requesting them to lend him eighty thousand gulden for the journey to Paris.

The merchants, who disliked the Napoleonic régime, and could not agree as to the proportions in which the money should be subscribed, declined the request. Dalberg had not applied to Rothschild in the first instance, because he thought the amount was too heavy for a single individual to advance. Meyer Amschel learned of the grand duke's wish, and voluntarily offered to advance him the sum at five per cent. Dalberg could now proceed to Paris.

While Rothschild had always enjoyed Dalberg's favor, this clever action gained for him the full confidence of the grand duke, as is indeed specifically stated in a later French police report regarding the Rothschild family:[57] "Through meeting him in this matter he was so successful in gaining the grand duke's confidence, and secured himself so thoroughly in his good graces, that henceforth the grand duke scarcely ever refused him any request."

He asked for instance for a passport for young James, who was then nineteen years old, and who was sent through Antwerp to Paris, straight into the lion's mouth. His presence was necessary there in connection with certain illicit business that Nathan was carrying out from England, which will be described in more detail later. For the present it will suffice to state that James actually arrived in Paris on the 24th of March, 1811, took up his quarters at 5 rue Napoleon without being hindered, and duly reported himself to the police.

At this time the Rothschild family were kept very much on the move. Apart from their own business, all the members of the family who were capable of traveling were constantly on the road, in order to transact personally the important business of the elector at various places. This is most clearly revealed in the correspondence between Buderus and the elector.

"Young Rothschild," he wrote from Hanau to his master on April 7, 1811,[58] "is actually on his way to London to fetch the certificates of title regarding your investment of capital. He can take the packet of letters with him. His father will gladly make an effort to get the things away from Gottorp . . . and is already making inquiries on this matter. On my advice Crown Agent Rothschild has called in the capital payment due at Copenhagen, and has received 159,600 gulden. Will your Electoral Highness graciously permit me to convey to Crown Agent Rothschild your Highness's satisfaction regarding his manifold activities on your behalf? I am informed by Crown Agent Rothschild that the Prague police have discovered the secret drawers in his carriage. I have therefore thought it advisable not to send my account for last month with the other documents, on this occasion, as it cannot be concealed under the clothes as letters can."

The elector rewarded such news with expressions of genuine satisfaction, and agreed that Rothschild should be acquainted with his satisfaction with him. He was, however, still concerned about the money which he had invested in English stock, in respect to which he had not yet received any document of title. "I feel a real longing, which I think is justified," he replied to Buderus,[59] "to see the documents regarding the investments. . . . I had not been informed that the police here had discovered the secret hiding-place in the carriage. In any case there is no reason to expect anything untoward from that quarter."

Buderus was unceasing in his efforts to exalt the Rothschild family in the opinion of the elector, and to represent all other business houses as unreliable or less accommodating. This was shown in the case of a transaction of earlier origin. The elector had transferred to Meyer Amschel Rothschild and two other Jewish bankers from Cassel an amount of a million Dutch gulden due to him in Holland. In accomplishing this various technical difficulties arose which delayed the payment of the sum in Holland, while the transferees of the debt had already paid out the greater part of the sum involved. Before making further payments, they naturally asked the elector for a guarantee.

In righteous indignation Buderus reported this to his master:[60] "The worst of this business is that it was not entrusted to one single business firm. . . . The agents Stuben Hesse Goldschmidt and the heirs of Michel Simon are most ill-disposed toward your Electoral Highness. Levy, Simon's son-in-law, who manages the business, has gone to such extremes that, as I know for certain, he caused the recent arrest of myself and Rothschild, and furnished the police commissary with the questions on which we were cross-examined with extreme severity."

Buderus now proposed that the Cassel Jews should be made to retire from the business, and that the matter should be entrusted to Meyer Amschel Rothschild alone. The elector concurred in this proposal, and replied as follows:[61]

"I have read with great interest the reports regarding the Dutch loan of a million gulden. . . . You are quite right in holding that it is essential to keep the Cassel

Jews out of this business (although I have always regarded Goldschmidt as an honorable man). . . . I fear that these Jews will not trust the Frankfort agent (Rothschild) and will imagine that there are heavy profits at issue, and demand high compensation for retiring."

In the end the elector left the whole matter to Buderus, and he accordingly put it all in Rothschild's hands.

In general, however, the elector was again in an exceedingly bad mood, first, because Rothschild had still not succeeded in bringing his property from Holstein to Prague, and secondly, because he had received a report from Buderus regarding an electoral loan which had been made to a family called Plettenberg through the intermediary of Prince Wittgenstein, the recovery of which seemed highly doubtful. He was also annoyed by a suggestion made by Buderus that he should again take part in Frankfort loans, of which he had had such an unfortunate experience. It was in a highly nervous condition that he awaited the documents regarding his investment in English stocks, which had not yet come to hand. This mood found expression in an exceedingly angry letter, in which the elector notified the cessation of payments to Rothschild in respect to the English stocks, thereby causing a positive panic in the Rothschild-Buderus firm.

In the course of this letter he said:[62] "After all, my trunks and chests in Holstein contain something more than clothes; there are Hessian debentures, and accounts of various kinds, and a chest containing silver. I will arrange to have them brought to me here direct, for I am weary of giving instructions in this matter to the House of Rothschild year after year.

"I shall dispatch the draft letter to Prince von Wittgenstein, regarding the Plettenberg loan affair, but do not expect that it will have much result. The whole business is a network of intrigue, and I am absolutely determined to sacrifice everything rather than involve myself further with that prince. He has behaved in a shockingly irresponsible way toward me.

"I am not inclined to take part in the Frankfort subscription loan. I am sick of all loans, and I really prefer to have my money lying idle."

Nothing had yet arrived from London, a fact which particularly exasperated the elector. "I am exceedingly worried about this matter," he wrote, "and am most eagerly waiting to hear what you have to say. In the meantime you are to cease making any further payments with respect to these stocks, neither are you to invest in them any further English interest payments. I am still waiting in vain for the documents regarding the capital which I have invested; and in spite of all the confidence which I have in Rothschild, I cannot tolerate this delay any longer. Neither has the registration of the older stocks been effected yet. Lorentz is constantly and emphatically reminding you of this matter. You must see that he is kept fully informed of all my financial affairs in England, and especially of the investments effected through Rothschild, in order that he may keep an eye on them as it is his duty to do, as my chargé d'affaires. You are to see to this without delay."

The elector's fears had been increased by letters from Lorentz, his plenipotentiary in London, who was offended because he had not been taken into the confidence of Buderus and Rothschild in the business which they were transacting for the elector in England. He had suggested to his master that England might conclude an unfavorable peace, which would cause a heavy fall in British stocks, and therefore advised the sale of the securities which had only just been purchased.

Buderus replied to his master in a very injured tone,[63] stating that in accordance with instructions he had stopped payments to Rothschild with respect to the new purchases of stock. He enclosed Rothschild's explanation, which set out the enormous difficulties in the way

Burning of British Goods, November, 1810, at Frankfort-on-the-Main
From a painting in the Frankfort Historical Museum

of undertaking journeys to and from England and safely conveying documents and letters in a time of war and blockade.

Buderus strongly indorsed the remarks of his Frankfort partner.[64] "In my opinion," he wrote, "his judgment is sound and his request is justified. . . . I have not yet informed War Councilor Lorentz of the investments made by Crown Agent Rothschild. It is not desirable that such information should be too widely known." He added that if the elector's instructions in this matter were not countermanded he would forthwith carry them out. . . . "The bank of Rüppell and Harnier," he continued, "is, not to put too fine a point upon it, filled with absolute rage against your Electoral Highness. Although they owe their fortune entirely to your Highness, they behave like madmen, instead of keeping quiet as they ought, and doing their duty by their customers, whom they serve for profit."

In a second letter Buderus wrote: "Rothschild is unjustly accused of having, from motives of secret advantage, delayed the Dutch business, which is probably to the great detriment of your Highness's interest; for it is Rothschild alone who has collected such sums as have reached your Electoral Highness, while the other bankers have made no effort whatever in the matter." [65]

Meanwhile one of the younger Rothschild brothers (probably Carl) arrived at Prague with a detailed report from Buderus, in which that official strongly urged his master not to jeopardize the business of the English investments, which was proceeding so well. Young Rothschild employed all his powers of eloquence to persuade the elector to revoke his veto regarding further payments. He thought that he had gained his object, and wrote to Buderus from Prague, stating that the elector had graciously agreed to continue to invest in British stocks the interest received in England. Buderus thereupon immediately resumed his payments to Rothschild on the elector's account, until he received an instruction from his master, dated December 9, 1811, which did not confirm Rothschild's premature conclusion. Thereupon Buderus made a further effort to impress upon his master that it was in his highest interest finally to cancel the veto on further payments, since otherwise the Rothschild banking firm would be faced with a severe crisis.

"It is my duty," he wrote,[66] "to bear witness to the fact that the Rothschild bankers have not failed to make every possible effort to obtain the certificates of the investments, and your Electoral Highness can have no conception how difficult it is to send important documents between here and London. If your Highness will consider the dangers that would arise if such a document were to fall into the wrong hands you will surely realize that all precautions which human ingenuity can devise must be taken in order to reduce to a minimum the chances of such an occurrence.

"The withholding of further payments to the Rothschild bankers has not increased their efforts to obtain the documents, as these efforts could not be increased. Directly after his return from Prague, the young crown agent Rothschild traveled to the seacoast in order to seek an opportunity for bringing over these documents. He did not feel secure in a Dutch village where he was staying, and went across to Dunkirk, where he has to furnish daily to the police department a satisfactory reason for his living there. According to his last letter, he expects the documents to arrive at any moment and he will then hasten here without any loss of time.

"The power of attorney sent to the bankers Van Notten, under date October 28, 1810, authorizing the transfer of the old stock (under another pseudonym) has been recovered. After leaving Amsterdam, the ship was driven back to the coast, and my letter was delivered in a Dutch village, where a reliable acquaintance of the banker Rothschild has kept it until now. The young crown agent Rothschild has now taken advantage of a favorable opportunity to forward it, and has received an assurance that it has safely reached the other side of the Channel."

Finally, young Rothschild, who had traveled to London, succeeded in smuggling over to the Continent a certificate for £189,500 sterling, and this was immediately forwarded to the elector. William now again consented to the interest on his capital being used for effecting further investments, after noting with satisfaction that the House of Rothschild, which had been highly nervous about retaining this business, had reduced its terms, and declared that it was now willing to deliver the stock for 70 per cent commission. The elector expressed his pleasure in conveying this information to Buderus, and concluded his letter by saying: [67] "I do not fail to realize the difficulties involved in communicating with London, and am therefore exceedingly happy to be in possession of the certificates for £189,500 sterling."

The elector also expressed the wish that one of the brothers Rothschild should reside permanently at Prague, but this Buderus had to refuse. The operations of the family were already so extensive that, with the best will in the world, it was impossible to accede to this request. Buderus wrote to his master:

"Flattering though the suggestion is that one of the Rothschild sons should be allowed to reside permanently in the neighborhood of your Electoral Highness, it is no less impossible than flattering. Their father is old and sick. His eldest son, Amschel Meyer, and his second son, Solomon, who is also delicate, are indispensable to him in his extensive operations. The third son, Carl, is almost continually engaged in traveling in the service of your Electoral Highness, while the fourth son, Nathan, is very usefully established in London, and the youngest,

James, spends his time between London and Paris. They have declared to me that they will spare no effort to carry out your Highness's commands."

The continental blockade was naturally the chief cause of the great difficulties in the way of communications with England. This question had indeed become the crucial problem in general European politics. At Erfurt the opinion had obtained for a time in 1808 that Napoleon and Alexander of Russia would be able to share the dominion of Europe between them. The Emperor of France had particularly in view that he might finally be enabled to subdue England with the assistance of Russia.

For this purpose it was essential that Russia should unconditionally adopt the continental blockade; but the tsar never contemplated sacrificing all his trade with England for the sake of Napoleon. On the contrary, he facilitated the import of goods by sea, and goods of English origin could now easily find their way to other continental states via Russia. Thus the effectiveness of Napoleon's measures was endangered, and as early as the summer of 1811 it was obvious to the whole of Europe that a complete breach between the two most powerful continental states was inevitable, and that war was now only a question of time.

The Napoleonic police consequently applied a much more rigid censorship to all correspondence and secret agreements in territories subject to French rule. Anything addressed to the ruling family of Hesse was subjected to a particularly close scrutiny. A letter dated Frankfort, November 1, 1811,[68] which carelessly mentioned Meyer Amschel's name in two places, and was addressed to the elector's brother, Landgrave Karl, fell into the hands of the French. In one passage the unknown writer acknowledged the receipt of a letter from the landgrave, through the good offices of Meyer Amschel, while another passage read as follows:[69]

"I deliberately read to Rothschild, in his sons' presence, the passage in which your Highness speaks of them so kindly and graciously. They were all delighted."

It was clear from the context that the letter referred to the Tugendbund of which the landgrave was a member, and it was a question of payments which Rothschild had to make on the landgrave's behalf. This letter was immediately forwarded from Hamburg, where it had been intercepted, to General Savary, the commissioner of police at Paris, who instructed Baron Bacher, the French ambassador at Frankfort, to furnish any light he could as to the implication of the letter and the parts played by the persons mentioned in it.

Baron Bacher suggested [70] that they should not proceed against the family Rothschild by domiciliary search and arrest as in 1809, but should act with greater cunning. The House of Rothschild and the other agents of the elector should be lulled into a complete sense of security; their letters should be skilfully opened, copied, and then forwarded. In this way Bacher hoped in a very short time to familiarize himself with their network of intrigue in all its complicated ramifications.

The chief commissioner of police also asked for a report from his commissioner at Mainz, and the letter informed him [71] that the House of Rothschild had formerly been exceedingly active in the trade of colonial goods and English manufactures. But since they had been subjected to a domiciliary search and had had their English goods sequestrated, they had occupied themselves principally with banking business, and commerce in goods confined to the Continent. The Mainz commissioner added that the head of the House was not friendly toward France, although he pretended that he was sincerely attached to that country.

Bacher's advice was taken. The brothers Rothschild were most carefully watched by agents of the French Imperial State Police, both in Frankfort and in France, where they were amongst those who carried on illicit trade with England subject to departmental authorizations; at the same time they were on the best of terms with Dalberg's Frankfort police, although this force was also subject to Napoleon. Dalberg's police commissioner, von Itzstein, who although a Jew, was director of the police of the grand duchy, was a particular patron of Meyer Amschel and of all the Frankfort Jews.

Meyer Amschel Rothschild had long cherished the idea of exploiting Dalberg's friendly feelings for the Jews in the interests of the fellow members of his faith who had formerly been so oppressed, and incidentally of his own family. It is true that a new "status" proclaimed by Dalberg had somewhat improved their condition, but it involved no essential change. For example, the number of Jewish families tolerated remained at five hundred. "Five hundred, only five," indignantly wrote a certain Israel Jakobsohn. "Why not more, and why not less?" [72]

Dalberg, seeing that he could exploit this situation and do a good business deal, allowed Meyer Amschel and his partner Gumprecht to persuade him to commute the annual amount of 22,000 gulden payable by the Jews, into a lump sum, and to grant them the rights of citizenship in Frankfort, thereby making them the political equals of the Christians. At the same time, the Jews were granted their own governing body, known as the "Governing Body of the Israelite Religious Community." Police Director von Itzstein was nominated president, while the other members of the committee were chosen from amongst the most prominent Jews in the town.

In the course of his efforts Meyer Amschel let Dalberg infer that the Jews were prepared to make financial sacrifices, and in the end Dalberg demanded that they should commute the annual payment of 22,000 gulden by a single payment of twenty times that amount. This was a substantial amount of money, but one that the Frankfort Jews could produce, especially as Meyer Amschel alone advanced 100,000 gulden, or almost a quarter of the total sum. He also managed to arrange that only 150,000 of the 440,000 gulden should immediately be paid in cash, and that for the balance twenty-four bearer debentures would be accepted. Jewish circles awaited with considerable suspense, the conclusion of these arrangements, which were so important for their future. If the proposal went through, Meyer Amschel wanted to be the first to bring the good news to the fellow members of his faith.

As he was constantly being begged for information by members of the Jewish community, he requested a recorder of the province, who was friendly to him, to let him have the earliest possible information: "I should be most pleased," he wrote to him in his peculiar German,[73] "if I could be the first messenger of the good news, as soon as it has been signed by his Royal Highness, our most excellent Lord and great Duke, in our favor and that I can inform my nation of their great joy, will you graciously inform me of it through the post, I confess I abuse your goodness and grace, but I do not doubt that your Highness and your honored family have to await great heavenly rewards and will receive much happiness and blessing . . . because in truth our whole Jewry, if they have the happiness to obtain equal rights, will gladly pay with great pleasure all dues that the citizens have to pay."

After some time the matter was put through, and aroused as much enthusiasm amongst the Jews as indignation in the senate and amongst the patrician families, who were hostile to them. It was at once suggested everywhere that Dalberg had received money personally, in addition to the sum publicly mentioned. In this connection pointed remarks were made about the fact that Meyer Amschel and his sons had been appointed official bankers to the grand duchy and that Meyer Amschel had been made a member of the Electoral College of Frankfort. A member of the Austrian Secret Police actually claimed that he knew the amount of the sum, namely 33,000 karolins, which Dalberg had received for his good offices.[74]

The Jewish community certainly had every reason to be grateful to the aged and infirm Meyer Amschel, who had never completely recovered since his operation, and yet still had the energy to apply all his influence and money to secure this improvement in their status. The debentures, to the value of 290,000 gulden, were immediately brought into circulation. One of them, of the value of fifty thousand, was acquired by Dalberg's finance minister, Count Christian von Benzel-Sternau; eight debentures of ten thousand gulden each were taken over by Herr von Bethmann, while the greater part of the amount paid by the Jews in cash went direct to Paris as a payment on account of the electoral domains in Fulda and Hanau, which had been seized by the French, and which Dalberg had repurchased on taking over these two principalities.

The grand duke immediately sold the domains again to private persons for earnest money of three and one-half million francs, payable by instalments, a transaction which, when concluded, would yield 190,000 francs more than France had received for the domains.

When the bargain was concluded Dalberg declared, with somewhat premature joy, "A transaction concluded in so masterly a manner deserves a reward," and rewarded the ministers who had been principally employed in the transaction, and their wives, with presents of 40,000 francs each. In the letter regarding this matter [75] he stated:

"Since I am determined to gain nothing by this business except the welfare of the state, there are still 70,000 francs available out of the 190,000 realized. Of this amount I give 10,000 francs to Privy Councilor von Itzstein as a reward for services rendered in converting into cash the debts of the Jews to the state. I give 10,000 francs to the House of Rothschild for their excellent cooperation. I shall leave the remaining 50,000 francs with the House of Rothschild, as a part payment of what I owe them." [76]

The senate of the city of Frankfort, and the exiles who had formerly been in power, observed these events with concern and ill-will, and were firmly determined, if matters should take a different turn, to do everything possible to undo what had been done. Meyer Amschel's conduct had made him by no means popular with the former authorities of the city; but for the time being they had to look on in impotence, and allow him and his protector Dalberg to have their way.

It was with the greatest suspense that they watched the course of general European politics. The points at issue between Napoleon and Russia had already almost resulted in war. Napoleon collected the *Grande Armée,* the greatest host that Europe had ever seen, in order to subdue the last independent monarch on the Continent. At Dresden he gathered his dependent princes about him at a great court ceremony, and his imperial father-in-law Francis of Austria was also present on that occasion.

The elector in Prague had again begged Francis to avail himself of the favorable opportunity for pleading his cause with the Emperor of France. Emperor Francis was used to such appeals, and paid no further attention to the letter. While the great drama of the Russian campaign was being enacted, the elector remained at Prague, and awaited the outcome of events in a state of extreme anxiety.

Napoleon's army was advancing steadily toward the heart of the Russian Empire, although it was certainly suffering enormous losses. Out of an army of four hundred thousand men, scarcely one hundred thousand entered Moscow. But all that Europe saw was the victorious advance. Owing to the prevailing conditions it was weeks, even months, before further news reached Frankfort. The merchants of that time could not adjust their affairs to events as speedily as scientific discoveries have now enabled them to do.

Meyer Amschel Rothschild's attitude was entirely determined by his sense of the overwhelming power of the Corsican, who was now at Moscow, when the reopening of his old wound quite unexpectedly brought him back to his sick-bed. He did not live to see Napoleon's complete failure in Russia, to be followed a year later by his defeat in Germany, which was followed by the return to his Hessian domains of Rothschild's lord and master the elector.

On September 16, 1812, a high Jewish Feast Day, the so-called "long day" which is set apart for the pardoning of the penitent sinner, Meyer Amschel had been fasting, in accordance with his strict religious principles, and spent many hours standing in the synagogue, sunk in prayer. The same evening he felt severe pains in the region of his wound. He was immediately put to bed, but his condition grew worse. He had violent attacks of fever, and he felt that death was approaching. Thereupon he determined, while he still had the strength in him, to order his affairs, and to make a new will adapted to the most recent developments, to take the place of the earlier will which he had made.

In doing so he was giving effect to an agreement which he had made with all his children, and in accordance with which he sold to his five sons all his shares in the business, his securities and other possessions, as well as his large stocks of wine, for the sum of 190,000 gulden, which of course was far below their real value. His sons were henceforth to be the exclusive owners of the business, and it was clear, although not definitely stated, that after their father's death any inequality in their shares ceased, and each of the five sons henceforth possessed ten-fiftieths, that is, a fifth share, in the business.

The will completely excluded the daughters and their husbands and heirs from the business, and even from all knowledge of it. Meyer Amschel applied the purchase price of 190,000 gulden as follows: he granted his wife Gutle a life interest in 70,000 gulden; the remainder he divided amongst his five daughters. This arrangement served a double object. First, it made it unnecessary on his death to declare to the officials the enormous value, for those times, of the business that was divided between the five sons, and to put the capital bequeathed at the modest figure of 190,000 gulden. Secondly, the business was secured absolutely to the five sons, safe from the possibility of any interference from the sisters and their relations.

The will concluded [77] by enjoining unity, love and friendship upon the children, and any undutiful child that showed an intention of rebelling was threatened with the penalty of inheriting no more than the legal minimum, which was only to be reckoned on the basis of the 190,000 gulden, from which would have to be deducted anything that the child in question had received during his life.

When Meyer Amschel drew up his last will there cannot have been more than two of his five sons, namely Amschel and Carl, at Frankfort, for Solomon was living in Paris, and James, who was maintaining communication between Solomon and Nathan in England, was living at Gravelines on the Channel coast in the Department Pas-de-Calais. These facts, proved as they are by French police records, and the records of visés issued, are fatal to the well-known legend, according to which Meyer Amschel gathered his five sons about his deathbed and divided Europe amongst them. Moreover, his illness had come on quite suddenly and developed so rapidly that the idea of recalling the sons who were abroad could never have been considered.

When Meyer Amschel had thus done everything that lay in his power to secure the future prosperity of his House—which, it is true, he considered in terms only of financial gain—and by clear and simple provision to maintain unity and peace amongst his numerous family, he could look death calmly in the face. Two days after he had completed his will, on the evening of September 19, 1812, his old complaint took a marked turn for the worse. The alpha and omega of medical practice of the time was to let blood, a procedure which simply served to weaken old people who were very ill, instead of giving them relief. At a quarter past eight on the evening of the same day, Meyer Amschel Rothschild, the tireless, cunning, simple, and religious Jew, and founder of the banking firm M. A. Rothschild and Sons, was no longer to be counted amongst the living.

In his last hours he was fully aware that he was leaving a fine inheritance to his sons, but he certainly could not have guessed that he had laid the foundation of a world power which during the first half of the nineteenth century was to exercise an unparalleled influence throughout Europe, and was to maintain this influence almost unimpaired throughout the changing conditions of the second half of the century.

CHAPTER III

The Great Napoleonic Crisis and Its Exploitation by the House of Rothschild

SINCE the French Revolution, the Continent of Europe had been continuously suffering from the turmoil of war, while large territories were subjected to the horrors of the actual battles between the opposing armies. On the other hand, sea-girt England, although she exerted a powerful political influence upon the continental groups, was able to devote her principal attention, practically undisturbed, to the development of her commerce and the prosperity of her citizens.

Through his financial reforms which had assisted the capitalistic development of the state, the younger Pitt had brought order into Britain's internal affairs and thereby made it possible for England, out of her growing wealth, to advance very considerable sums of money to her allies, who were waging war on the Continent with the wealth and the blood of their citizens. Towards the close of the eighteenth century England was indisputably the most important commercial power in Europe, and the House of Rothschild had made an exceedingly clever move in arranging that one of its sons, and the most talented one at that, should take up his residence in that kingdom.

Nathan had first settled in Manchester, the center for the manufacture of all kinds of cloth, as he had long had business connections with that city. In view of the numerous armies that had to be clothed, the cloth trade offered opportunities of making exceptional profits. The sum of money he brought with him—£20,000, which constituted a very respectable capital sum in those days—gave the stranger an assured position from the start, although he could not speak a word of English. Nathan, therefore, came to Manchester, not as a small tradesman, but as a fairly important representative of an established commercial firm on the Continent, with money at his command.

He entered upon his commercial activities with all the enthusiasm of youth, at the same time showing a business acumen remarkable in one so young. He first carefully studied his environment, and his neighbor's methods of making money, and ascertained that profits were made on the purchase of the raw materials necessary for the manufacture of cloth and on the issue of these materials for dyeing purposes, as well as on the sale of the finished article, each of these activities in England being the province of a separate merchant.

Nathan determined to secured for himself the profit at each stage in the process.[1] He bought the raw materials on his own account, had them dyed, and then gave them out to undergo the further processes of manufacture, and finally himself handed them over to the trade. Nathan did not confine himself exclusively to cloth. He bought everywhere, and anything that he thought was good and cheap. Thus he bought all kinds of fancy goods, as well as colonial produce such as indigo, wine, sugar, and coffee. He was not troubled about finding a market, as the parent firm at home required all these things.

The capital which he brought with him was soon doubled and trebled, while his father and brothers derived the greatest benefit from Nathan's presence in England. He enjoyed the life in that country, which struck him as extraordinarily free and unfettered, compared with the oppressive conditions in Frankfort.

As his business grew, Nathan naturally began to establish contact with the capital, which is the heart of Great Britain, and in which all the financial interests of an extensive empire are concentrated. Determined to settle in England for good, he left Manchester in 1804 for London, where he would be in closer touch with those political developments which were producing such profound effect upon commercial life. He realized at once that the fact that he was a foreigner was a great handicap in business, and therefore, as early as the summer of the year 1806, he applied for naturalization as a British subject. His wish was readily granted, as the applicant had resided for six years in the country, and even if he had not yet attained a very prominent position in the business world, he was already honored and respected.

Favored by the keen demand for goods on the Continent, Nathan carried on his business in London with great success, until the year 1806. His intimate experience of English life and character, and his sympathy with the spirit of resistance to Napoleon's plans of world domination which inspired the whole country, soon caused him to adhere completely to English modes of thought. But he avoided publicly identifying himself with any political cause which might have damaged his family at Frankfort, and all his actions were guided first and foremost by business considerations.

Nathan was now twenty-nine years old, and was contemplating marriage. He had made the acquaintance of the daughter of a rich Jewish family. Her father, who had emigrated from Amsterdam, had several small business dealings with Nathan, but their relations had not been sufficiently intimate to enable him to form an accurate estimate regarding the suitor's financial position and general business qualities. The fact that Nathan was living abroad made investigations of this nature more difficult. Nathan, however, with skill and directness, managed to set his future father-in-law's doubts at rest, while the information which the latter obtained from Frankfort confirmed the fact that the Rothschild family were prosperous and respected. Nathan gained his object, and through his marriage was enabled to increase his own fortune by the amount of his wife's substantial dowry; his position was also strengthened by the influence of a father-in-law who was a wealthy and respected merchant in the City of London.

Moreover, his wife's sister Judith Cohen shortly afterwards married the rich and well-known Moses Montefiore, who was thus brought into close association with Nathan, and whose energy, foresight, and sound business sense in regard to all the vicissitudes of the continental wars, which so intimately affected financial operations, Nathan had constant occasion to admire.

Nathan had as yet nothing to do with the elector's investments in England, although his father at Frankfort was endeavoring to get him this business, and had repeatedly urged him to cultivate relations with the elector's plenipotentiary in London. The intimations of the elector's wishes, hitherto received by Count Lorentz, had not been favorable to such an arrangement, but this in no way discouraged Meyer Amschel at Frankfort, or Nathan in London, from continuing their efforts. As has already been stated, the elector soon changed his opinion, and we are now entering upon the period of the investment of large sums in English stocks, as recommended by Nathan. In view of his intimate relations with Meyer Amschel, the elector could not continue to object to the employment of his son Nathan in transacting the business in London.

Another factor in Nathan's favor was the difficulty of getting possession of the documents certifying the purchases of stock, this being not so difficult for Nathan to arrange, in view of his numerous Jewish and non-Jewish connections. Thus Nathan came to be interested in the enormous financial operations of the elector, and as considerable periods of time could be made to intervene between the purchase and the payment of the securities, he sometimes had temporary control of very substantial

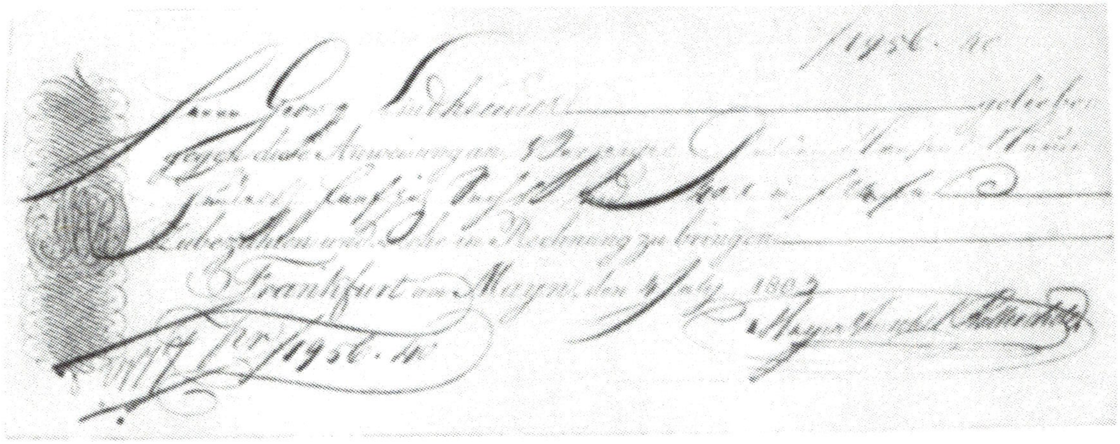

One of the Much Coveted Drafts of Meyer Amschel Rothschild

In the possession of the Frankfort Library

sums of money, which he could employ in safe, short-term transactions, such as, for instance, the purchase of bullion, which was constantly rising in value at that time. It was not known in England how Nathan came to have such sums of money temporarily at his disposal, for the purchases of English stocks on the elector's account were officially made in the name of Rothschild, and apparently for the benefit of that firm, as the elector's funds in England had already been sequestered once.

The credit of the House of Rothschild and of Nathan certainly gained greatly from these enormous purchases, and he came to be entrusted with transactions which, even if he could not immediately meet his obligations in cash, he did not like to lose, as they offered good prospects for the future. Nathan was particularly skilful at exploiting the abnormal conditions of the period, conditions such as always give those with a gift for speculation an opportunity of enriching themselves, while those who stand by passively are reduced to poverty.

Through his continental blockade, Napoleon had revolutionized the whole commercial outlook of England; then, recognizing that his measures had a boomerang effect, he modified them, and actually negotiated with the smugglers, whom the English government encouraged with prizes for breaking through the Napoleonic blockade. The decree of June 15, 1810, practically officially regularized this illicit trade. Certain goods that were required in France, and then gold and silver, were allowed to be brought to France in limited quantities, French products being sent to England in exchange. In order to prevent the smuggling of undesirable articles, there was a special railed-off enclosure at Gravelines for the officially recognized smuggling, the captains of smuggling vessels being required to remain exclusively within this enclosure, and to load and unload their goods under police control.

Nathan took advantage of this officially sanctioned

commerce between England and hostile France, to do business on an extensive scale, both on his own account and on account of the parent firm at Frankfort. But it soon became apparent that it was essential to have an absolutely reliable man at Paris too, to deal with this business. Nathan had written to Frankfort to this effect, and old Meyer Amschel had decided to profit by his good relations with Dalberg's French régime at Frankfort to obtain a Paris passport visé from the French officials for one of his sons, to whom alone he was prepared to entrust so important a position, and also to obtain a letter of recommendation for him to one of the higher French Treasury officials.

A particularly favorable opportunity for this occurred when Dalberg set out for Paris in March, 1811, with the money advanced by Rothschild. It is certainly no mere coincidence that, according to the French police records,[2] James, who was then nineteen years old, started to Paris via Antwerp, and took up his residence in a private house there. It is particularly worthy of note that Count Mollien, Napoleon's finance minister at the time, had been informed of young Rothschild's arrival, and knew of his intention to receive and forward large sums of ready money that were expected from England.

"A Frankforter," the minister wrote to Napoleon on March 26, 1811, "who is now staying in Paris with a Frankfort passport, and goes by the name of Rothschild, is principally occupied in bringing British ready money from the English coast to Dunkirk, and has in this way brought over 100,000 guineas in one month. He is in touch with bankers of the highest standing at Paris, such as the firms of Mallet, of Charles Davillier, and Hottinguer, who give him bills on London in exchange for the cash. He states that he has just received letters from London dated the 20th of this month, according to which the English intend, in order to check the export of gold and silver coins, to raise the value of the crown from five to five and a half shillings, and the value of the guinea from twenty-one to thirty shillings. . . . Such operations would be on a par with the practices of the Austrians or the Russians. I sincerely hope that the Frankforter Rothschild is well informed of these matters, and that ministers in London will be sufficiently foolish to act in this way." [3]

This letter reveals much; it shows that while James Rothschild may have been in Paris before the 24th of March, 1811, without the permission of the police, as soon as he officially arrived, that is, as soon as he reported to the Paris police, he must have had an interview with the minister or with one of the officials of the treasury, this being no doubt due to Dalberg's introduction. Although in sending the guineas to Frankfort Nathan was generally acting in accordance with quite definite plans that suited the British government, James, in order to gain the support of the French departments for these operations, pretended to the ministry at Paris that the English authorities viewed the export of cash with extreme displeasure, and did everything possible to prevent it. He succeeded only too well in hoodwinking Mollien, and through him, Napoleon.

"The French government," says Marion,[4] "viewed with satisfaction the arrival of English guineas at the Channel ports, because they regarded this both as a proof and as a cause of the progressive decay of England." It is true that in his memoirs Mollien afterward tried to suggest that he did not share this view, and that Napoleon derived it from others, but the letter quoted above clearly shows that the finance minister also believed Rothschild.

Nathan wanted just at this time to send exceptionally large sums of ready money to France, having the secret intention that these should ultimately be destined for Wellington's armies, who were fighting the French in Spain. That general had suffered great financial embarrassment since the beginning of the English campaign in

Portugal and Spain. It was not only that the blockade made it difficult to transport large sums by sea, but the devastating storms in the Bay of Biscay were a serious menace to the cumbrous sailing ships of those times. Such consignments were therefore liable to grave risks, and the insurance charges were exceedingly heavy.

As early as 1809 Wellington had had occasion to write to his government in the following terms: "We are terribly in need of funds. . . . The army pay is two months in arrears. I feel that the Ministry in England is utterly indifferent to our operations here.[5] . . . It would be much better for the Governments," he added some time later,[6] "entirely to give up our operations in Portugal and Spain if the country cannot afford to continue them."

This state of affairs continued for two years, and Wellington had to have recourse to highly dubious bankers and money-lenders in Malta, Sicily, and Spain, from whom he had to borrow money at the most usurious rates, giving them bills of exchange which had to be cashed by the British Treasury at great loss. The measures taken by the treasury for satisfying the requirements of Wellington's army were always quite inadequate; finally the British commander wrote indignantly to London [7] that if matters continued thus, his army would have to leave the Peninsula, which would relieve France of important military commitments on the Continent, and expose England to the danger of having a hostile force landed on the island itself. Then his exalted monarch and his subjects would experience in their own country something of the horrors of war, from which they had hitherto had the good fortune to be spared.

A year later things were not much better, and on being reproached for having too casually drawn bills on the English government, Wellington replied with some heat, writing that he was sorry to have to state that sick and wounded British officers at Salamanca had been forced to sell their clothes in order to keep body and soul together.[8]

Such were the conditions under which the British army was fighting in Spain, when an energetic movement in its support was started in London, which at first was directed by Nathan Rothschild on his own account. He had acquired very cheaply a large proportion of the bills issued by Wellington, and proceeded to cash them at the British Treasury. The cash which he thus received—generally in the form of guineas—he sent across the Channel to France, where it was received by one of his brothers, generally by James, but in 1812 sometimes by Carl or Solomon, and then paid in to various Paris banking firms. The brothers obtained from the Paris bankers bills on Spanish, Sicilian, or Maltese bankers, and they contrived, through their business connections, to get these papers to Wellington, who duly received the cash from the bankers. Thus the cash sent from London actually only had to make the short journey from London to Paris, and thence through the intricate network of business firms, who were mostly Jewish, it finally reached the English commander in Spain, through the heart of the enemy's country.

As time passed, however, the supply of cash and precious metal began to be scarce, even in England. Nathan, who had concentrated his attention principally upon business in specie and bills of exchange since the blockade had made ordinary commerce so difficult, closely watched [4] for favorable opportunities of acquiring any consignments of specie that might be available. When the East India Company once offered a considerable amount of bullion for sale, Nathan Rothschild was one of the first customers in the field; and he was able, through having recently received large sums of money for investment from the elector, and through mobilizing his whole credit, which stood very high, to acquire the whole of this stock of gold for himself.[9]

At that time, John Charles Herries was commissary-in-chief, an office that had been created in order to supply both the British army at home and the troops fighting on the Continent with the necessary funds. He was not able alone to meet the demands made upon him. A sailing ship carrying money had again been held up somewhere for weeks, and another consignment which had arrived safely at Lisbon encountered extraordinary difficulties in its further transportation. The British government, and especially Herries, were in the greatest distress.

They then heard of Nathan Rothschild's purchase of gold from the East India Company, and the almost unknown man who had acquired it was sent for by the treasury. Nathan sold the gold to the government at a heavy profit, and, at the same time requested that he should be commissioned to convey the money through France to Wellington in Spain, as he had already been doing to a limited extent at his own expense, asking that he should now do it on a large scale on account of the British government.

Very substantial sums of money indeed were involved, which were sent across the Channel from England to France, as is shown by a letter from James in Paris to Nathan in London, dated April 6, 1812, which was intercepted by the Paris police. Nathan had at that time sent 27,300 English guineas and 2,002 Portuguese gold ounces in six separate instalments through six different firms, to James at Gravelines. James acknowledged the receipt of these amounts, and of bills on the firms of Hottinguer, Davillier, Morel and Faber, to the amount of £65,798. He added that he was glad that it had been possible to send him this money without affecting the rate of exchange, and urged his brother to let him have any commercial news at the earliest possible moment. Both brothers naturally watched the rate of exchange very closely, ceased buying bills when it rose, and acquired them when it fell.[10]

All these transactions were carried through in agreement with the chief French department, and Finance

Minister Mollien. He was flattering himself that England was in great difficulties, that the rate of exchange was against her, and was constantly getting worse through the drainage of gold, while the Bank of France was consolidating its position, and France's currency stood highest in the world. Meanwhile gold pieces were trickling through in complete security, under the eyes and indeed under the protection of the French government, across France itself, into the pockets of France's arch-enemy, Wellington.

But though Mollien was deceived, the activities of the Jewish emigrants from Frankfort were being watched with great suspicion in other quarters. Letters from a local merchant to one of the Rothschilds at Dunkirk, which were intercepted by the French police, revealed the nature of their activities. A police official sent a detailed report on the matter [11] to Marshal Davoust, who was then military governor of Hamburg. After carefully examining the letters he fully appreciated the nature of the Rothschild transactions in France. As the marshal considered the matter to be exceedingly grave, he decided to report on it direct to Emperor Napoleon.

He pointed out incidentally [12] that "the arguments in favor of withdrawing money from England, under which the plotters concealed their maneuvers, lose their force when one considers that the English do everything possible to facilitate its export."

The emperor took note of the report, but did not pay any further attention to it. He no doubt said to himself that Davoust was a splendid soldier, but that this did not imply an understanding of financial matters, in which Mollien's opinion must be more reliable. The chief commissioner of police, however, continued to concern himself with the Rothschild family, of whose relations with Hesse he had long known, and he determined to get to the bottom of their activities (*couler à fond*). He forwarded Davoust's report to Police Prefect Desmarets, instructing him to furnish accurate dates regarding the family, and at the same time wrote in similar terms to Gravelines.

This was in February, 1812, when Carl and James were both in Paris. Desmarets had them watched, and asked the French commissioner of police at Mainz to report regarding the political sympathies of the House of Rothschild, its commercial relations abroad, and its speculative transactions, as well as the extent, if any, to which it was involved in contraband trade.

The police commissioner at Mainz sent a detailed report in reply, in which he emphasized the confidential relations between the Rothschild House at Frankfort and Dalberg, stating that these were so intimate that Dalberg refused practically no favor that a Rothschild asked of him. He added that Dalberg's entourage had certainly given the Rothschild family previous warning of the domiciliary search which was conducted in 1809, and concluded with the words: [13] "As regards Rothschild's political leanings, they are far from being all that they should be. He does not like us French at all, although he pretends to be devoted to the French government."

At the same time the report from Gravelines came in, which confirmed the constant presence, amounting practically to the *"établissement"* of a Rothschild at Dunkirk, and referred to his brother and partner in London.[14] The prefect of police, Count Réal, pointed out that the mere fact that Rothschild was a foreigner was sufficient reason for not allowing him to stay on the coast.

"How could this man be anything but suspect?" he continued indignantly. "What could have been in his Majesty's mind when he permitted the smugglers to trade? Surely it must have been with the intention that this trade should benefit French industry, an object which will not be achieved if London firms can maintain correspondents, not to mention branch offices, in Paris. What are we to think of this Rothschild's sojourn on our coast? A man who has established his brother in London, with whom he actually has common interests?" Réal therefore recommended that Rothschild should immediately be asked to leave the coast.

The Paris prefect of police reported the result of all these inquiries to the chief commissioner, and at the same time proposed that the Rothschild who was living in Paris should be arrested. But the protection of the French finance minister prevented this. Indeed, how could the government suddenly allow persons to be arrested whom it needed for carrying out its own business operations, and from whom the French Treasury accepted reports and advice, while it also entrusted them with commissions? The brothers Rothschild had cleverly made their position absolutely secure before they ventured to Paris into the lions' den, and in spite of all the suspicions of the military and the police, they remained entirely unmolested.

Nevertheless, the position was certainly not without its dangers. Sentiment in high quarters might suddenly change, in which case a Napoleon would have made short work of the brothers Rothschild. A further incident occurred to alarm the French police, and it caused General Savary to institute a further investigation.

A letter which was being forwarded to James Rothschild by a business firm at a special charge independently of the post-bag, which was controlled by the Boulogne police, was intercepted in the course of its journey. The inference was drawn that the brothers Rothschild frequently attempted to evade the censorship, but the writer of the letter, and the responsible police commissioner of the department asserted that the letter had merely been sent by special messenger after the regular post, as it was urgent. The matter was not further pursued, but the police commissioner for Pas-de-Calais was severely reprimanded, his chief giving him to understand that the luxury of his household and his general extravagance were highly suspicious circumstances.

The business of the two brothers Rothschild *à cheval* the warring powers of England and France was so important that it was absolutely essential for the brothers to be continuously on the spot, and even after the death of their father on September 19, 1812, only one of the two brothers who were in France at the time, namely Solomon, returned to Frankfort, whilst James remained in France and was constantly oscillating between Paris and the coast.

James had won the esteem of the Paris business world, through the enormous transactions which he always carried through punctually and accurately. It was at once noted whether he was buying bills or not, and the exchange was immediately affected when there was a rumor that he was going to buy. He set great store by his personal reputation; when a business man once slandered him to one of Nathan's employees, accusing him of an action unworthy of a man of integrity, he never mentioned the matter to the person concerned, since, as he wrote to Nathan, he considered it far beneath his dignity to discuss such a matter.[15]

Great events were now brewing on the Continent; Napoleon had not been able to keep up the myth for long regarding his victorious march to Moscow. The historic burning of that city robbed him of his only resources. Winter was already approaching when Napoleon was forced to decide upon retreat, which meant that the remnants of his army would have to traverse hundreds of miles through ice and snow, pursued by the enemy across country most of which had been laid desolate.

The crossing of the Beresina completed the disintegration of the Grande Armée, and on December 3, two days before Napoleon left it in order to return as quickly as possible to Paris, the famous twenty-ninth bulletin was issued, which, while generally admitting the destruction of the army, laconically reported that the emperor's health had never been better. The whole world received this news with great emotion, and new hopes sprang up in the European states which were under French dominion. But it was not possible to estimate what the future consequences of the catastrophe would be

The reports from Russia made a particularly profound impression at Frankfort. The unexpected news was so disconcerting that at first there was a tendency to regard it all as highly exaggerated—the newspapers had been allowed to report only what the French censorship passed. But soon stray survivors arrived, who told of the inconceivable hardships suffered by the army.

Frankfort was particularly interested in the complete collapse of Napoleon's schemes on the practical side. It is true, contents of the secret report of the paymaster general of the Grande Armée were still unknown. He had set out for the campaign with fifty-five cartloads of cash, drawn by four horses apiece, and seventy-eight clerks. He had been able to rescue only one cartload, containing two millions in gold, which he hoped to get safely to Königsberg, but he was not even prepared to guarantee that.

"My staff," he reported,[16] "no longer exists; they have all perished from cold and hunger. Some of them whose hands and feet have been frozen have been left at Vilna. All the account books have been taken by the enemy. Nobody thinks of anything except saving his own skin, and it is quite impossible to stem the panic. . . ."

Amschel Rothschild, the eldest son, and now head of the Frankfort firm, was just engaged in building a new banking house in the Bornheimerstrasse at Frankfort. He was enormously excited by the news of Napoleon's collapse; in view of the firm's extensive operations, which, ranging from Spain to Denmark and from Prague to London, already embraced the half of Europe, such sudden changes affecting the distribution of power on the Continent of Europe were bound to have most far-reaching consequences. It is true that his firm had friends in both camps, but it was important that, if either of the political structures collapsed, or showed serious signs of instability, the center of gravity of the firm's business should be rapidly shifted to the victorious side.

However, things had not yet reached this point. Through his enormous energy, Napoleon succeeded in rapidly improvising a new army, with which he meant to turn the tide of events. Frankfort continued to be occupied by the French, and Rothschild had to go very warily.

It is true that everywhere in Germany people smelled freedom in the air. In the public streets of Hesse the cry was heard, "Long live the elector, long live Russia!" Napoleon's so-called allies in the Russian campaign fell away, one after the other. Prussia allied herself with Russia and declared war on France, and Napoleon felt exceedingly uncertain even about the attitude of Austria. In April Napoleon was again campaigning in Saxony, and in the operations of the year 1813 he won one or two brilliant victories, but could not drive his enemies completely out of the field.

The bond between these became closer as time went on. England again offered Prussia and Russia her all-powerful financial support. In the Treaty of Reichenbach of June 14, 1813, she offered Prussia £666,666 as a subsidy, if that kingdom would put eighty thousand men in the field. Russia received twice the amount for twice the amount of men. On August 10, after Metternich's world-famous interview with Napoleon, Austria's attitude was also decided. The minister, who had completely changed his policy, left the Emperor of France, whom he had once made the son-in-law of his emperor, in the lurch, and Austria joined the coalition against Napoleon.

The Elector of Hesse also watched the course of events with satisfaction from his exile at Prague. He again requested the Emperor of Austria to reinstate him as speedily as possible in his dominions. He felt that the end of his sufferings and persecutions was at hand.[17] He who had so often begged the emperor and Marie Louise to intercede with Napoleon on his behalf, now spoke of himself as the German prince who had remained true to the cause, and as the protagonist of the German nation (*Verfechter des teutschen Reichs*) ; he certainly did not forget to remind the emperor of the undertaking that he was to be "guaranteed against any loss." He was, however, glad to contribute temporarily to the common war-chest and to send troops to reinforce the allies. Buderus was instructed, in spite of the general shortage of money, to obtain the sums necessary for this purpose. He applied to the House of Rothschild, and received one hundred thousand thalers, which enabled the elector to make several payments to the allies.

The unity of front which had thus been established led to some success in the further course of the campaign. In spite of her constant financial embarrassments, Austria played an important military part in the war. England also came to her assistance, and under the Treaty Alliance of Teplitz of October 3, 1813, she contracted to pay after October of that year, a million pounds in monthly instalments, in return for which Austria undertook to place 150,000 men in the field.

The day of Leipzig, October 18, 1813, was the final turning-point in Napoleon's career. The great general was forced to yield to the powerful coalition. At one blow the whole of Germany was liberated up to the Rhine, the Confederation of the Rhine fell to pieces, the King of Westphalia fled, and Dalberg voluntarily resigned his grand ducal dignity at Frankfort. The exiled princes now returned to their states, and on November 11, the Elector of Hesse also left Prague and reached Cassel soon afterwards, where the populace received him with acclamations.

These events were propitious to the business policy of the House of Rothschild. The prince to whose riches they owed their prosperity, and with whom they stood on such a unique footing, thanks to the assistance of Buderus, had now been reinstated. He immediately set about making good his financial losses, and reestablishing his position amongst the princes of Germany. This naturally reacted favorably upon his court banker.

In other respects the position at Frankfort left much to be desired; the fall of Dalberg did not mean merely the loss of a personal patron; the Jews lost the man who had sold them rights which had placed them on an equality with other citizens. The final payment was not yet due, and there was the risk that the senate, which consisted of members of the old patrician families, would on getting into power again revoke all the concessions that had been so dearly bought. The old municipal constitution was reestablished, but without regularizing the legal position of the Jews; and it was a bad sign that the redemption of the debentures which were falling due under the contract for the purchase of their freedom was refused.[18]

There was only one way of dealing with the situation: the House of Rothschild would have to prove itself so useful through its financial services, to the most important powers of the victorious coalition, that the victors would call the citizens of Frankfort to order if they should really proceed to act with hostility against the Jews.

While the first principle of the House of Rothschild was to amass wealth, the liberation of the race from oppressive restrictions contributed indirectly to this end, since it would facilitate intercourse with the rest of the world, and thereby increase the possibility of financial gain, which in turn would serve to increase its power. At this critical time the most important services were rendered to the Frankfort firm, not by its new chief, but by his incomparably more talented brother Nathan, in England, whose flair for finance amounted to positive genius. He now enjoyed the elector's full confidence. When in 1812 the Prince Regent of England seemed to be inclined to repay £100,000, Nathan was instructed to receive this amount, and to invest it in consols. This transaction brought him into immediate touch with the private finances of the royal family.

As Great Britain was the financier of the powers which were fighting on the Continent, and was also maintaining armies of her own abroad, enormous demands were made on the British Treasury in 1813. The officials were not equal to the task of raising the money or of sending it to the Continent. It had already been necessary for a naturalized foreigner to demonstrate that there were other ways of raising and sending money than for Englishmen abroad to draw bills on England. That method had a very bad effect on the English rate of exchange, which at the end of 1813 had already fallen by one-third.

Herries, who was charged with the sole responsibility for sending money to the Continent, again called in Nathan Rothschild to his assistance. While his principal problem was to supply the enormous sums that England had to provide under the subsidy contracts that she had just concluded, it was even more urgent and more important for the final overthrow of Napoleon to afford every possible support to Wellington, who was still pressing for money, but who was now free to advance into French territory, as Napoleon had transferred his best troops and generals to Germany.

Herries invited Nathan, whose name was still almost always wrongly spelled by the British Treasury, to a conference regarding the measures to be taken. The English official was completely convinced by the clarity and logic of the scheme for sending money which Nathan submitted, and requested him to draw up a memorandum for the chancellor of the exchequer, explaining the methods to be adopted for rendering prompt financial assistance to the Duke of Wellington. The technical problem was now somewhat different, since Wellington attached most importance to being supplied with French currency.

In the interests of England, as well as of his own pocket, Nathan had hitherto worked almost consistently against Napoleon; but he had done it as inconspicuously as possible for fear of compromising his brothers on the Continent. Even now that Napoleon was retreating, and was soon to be fighting within the former frontiers of France itself, he still kept well in the background, although he adopted the anti-Napoleonic cause with all the more enthusiasm, since the Russian disaster and the defeat at Leipzig seemed to imply the end of Napoleon's power. Lord Liverpool, first lord of the treasury and prime minister, and Vansittart, chancellor of the exchequer, approved the scheme submitted by Herries, and in a secret letter entrusted its execution to Nathan's experience and discretion.

Nathan Rothschild thereupon proceeded personally to Holland and collected, in close cooperation with his brothers, the French metal currency with which the Continent was flooded, but which, owing to the blockade, was naturally unobtainable in England.[19] James also acquired French cash on the spot in Paris, and managed to smuggle it across to his brothers in Holland. The sums thus collected were then shipped from the Dutch coast to Wellington's headquarters, this transaction becoming easier as his troops advanced from the west coast of France. In this way, a constant stream of gold and silver in current French coin flowed to the British army, which was thus enabled to pay in French money, whilst the allies, advancing from the east, were deprived of any such cash resources.

In the interests of the brothers Rothschild the secret was exceedingly well kept; Herries had every reason to be satisfied with his, and his country's relations with the foreign Jew, and did not grudge him the enormous profits which he was making. In later years Nathan himself stated that this was the best business he had ever done.[20]

Meanwhile the victorious allies had advanced beyond Frankfort, and had established their general headquarters in that city. The Emperor Alexander of Russia, the King of Prussia, and the Emperor Francis met in the ancient city where the Holy Roman Emperors were crowned. Metternich came with them, rejoicing in the triumph of his policy. The outward signs of the great change in the political situation were therefore particularly apparent at Frankfort, the home of the Rothschilds.

It is not surprising that the family regulated their future conduct accordingly. As yet they had had no relations with Austrian statesmen, but the brothers Rothschild now proceeded to sound members of the imperial entourage with a view to getting an opening. Accompanying Metternich was a previous acquaintance of theirs, Barbier, vice-president of the Austrian Treasury, who was responsible for the financial arrangements of the Austrian army. It was with him that the unsuccessful negotiations regarding the electoral loan had been carried on. Amschel accordingly called on him, and attempted although at first with little success to secure his interest and that of his powerful master Count von Metternich.

The name of Metternich was now on everybody's lips. The success of his policy had enormously strengthened the minister's position. It was a fair assumption that in the future he would exercise a very decisive influence in all matters affecting Austria, even in financial matters, although they did not come strictly within his province. In spite of his other outstanding qualities, Metternich had not a sound economic sense, either in public matters or in his private affairs. He spent money rather thoughtlessly and extravagantly on his private account, and his natural inclination was to make finance secondary to foreign policy, rather than the reverse.[21]

The Emperor Francis had repeatedly come to the rescue of his minister with personal loans, and had waived their repayment later.[22] Metternich had also frequently had recourse to various bankers, including such Frankfort bankers as Bethmann and the brothers Mühlen. As far as can be ascertained, he had had neither official nor personal relations with the Rothschild family before the year 1813.

Metternich was conscious of his own uncertainty in financial matters, and therefore relied largely on the advice of his indispensable secretary and counselor, the brilliant publicist Frederick von Gentz. This man had got to know the count intimately during the years 1802-1803, while he was still in the Prussian civil service and Metternich, who recognized his distinguished literary talent, was ambassador at Dresden; and it was Metternich who induced him to transfer to the Austrian civil service.

Gentz was even worse than Metternich at managing his private affairs, and unlike the count, was completely unscrupulous in getting money from anybody he could, from his own or from foreign states, from persons who desired orders or titles, and wherever opportunity offered. In spite of this, and of the fact that he often managed to earn considerable sums of money with his pen, he was in a constant state of financial embarrassment owing to his extravagant manner of life, and was repeatedly on the verge of complete ruin. This, however, did not prevent him from being always on the most intimate terms with all the great men of his day, with poets and statesmen, with princes and the higher nobility, as well as with Jewish bankers and merchants.

Humboldt knew him well, and Goethe was interested in him too. Humboldt wrote to Goethe on one occasion:[23] "You have perhaps heard that a few weeks ago

James Baron von Rothschild
From a painting in the Frankfort Historical Museum

poor Gentz went completely bankrupt. It is weakness, and not extravagance that has brought him to this pass." Later events were to give the lie to this statement of Humboldt's; it would scarcely have been possible for anyone to dissipate money more thoughtlessly and extravagantly than Gentz.

In spite of these personal characteristics, Gentz had a bent for political economy, and had taken a very good course in that subject in England, where he stayed for some time. While studying in that country he had made the personal acquaintance of Herries, who translated several of his writings into English, and maintained a correspondence with him. He also told him of the firm of Rothschild. Gentz did not stay with Metternich at general headquarters, but he corresponded with him constantly on financial matters.

The Austrian state was again urgently in need of funds for continuing hostilities, as it had been decided to carry the war into the enemy's country across the Rhine. The immediate problem was to convert into cash the remaining instalments of the subsidies from England. This had been done hitherto by the four Viennese banking firms, but the government was not very satisfied with their services, and Gentz, for personal reasons apparently, was not on good terms with them. He therefore wrote to Metternich to say that as far as he was aware, the four Viennese firms had no exclusive right to conduct the financial affairs of the state, and recommended the Frankfort banker von Herz. But he too proved to be very disappointing; he succeeded in making several hundred thousand for himself, but got rid of the bills at absurdly low rates, thereby also damaging English credit. The problem as to who should carry through these transactions still remained to be solved.

A letter from Count Ugarte to Metternich indicated how much they were exercised as to the best means of getting the English money over.[24] Ugarte observed that in the past the English government had generally sent the subsidies in cash, and in gold and silver bars, while only a small portion of them had been realized through "mercantile" channels. Now, however, that the precious metals were scarce in England too, this was difficult to arrange.

"We have to reckon," he wrote, "that on the average at least a third of the subsidies will be lost on the rate of exchange, and this is another reason for trying to get the amount of the subsidies increased to as high a figure as possible, since, if for example six millions are sent over, we shall only be able to realize four millions at the outside." This remark of one of the highest Austrian government officials clearly reveals how governments were taken advantage of in such transactions, and what huge profits were derived in the course of remitting these sums from England to the Continent.

Now there were several cogent reasons for the employment of Frankfort firms. They naturally did what they could to bring influence to bear in this direction, on Metternich and his advisers, and Ambassador Baron von Hügel pleaded the cause of the Frankfort bankers. He had already on a previous occasion written to Count Stadion to say that of all the cities in Germany, Frankfort ought to be specially considered in connection with the financial measures of the imperial court. He said that there was no commercial center in Europe that would collaborate as readily as Frankfort in efforts to improve Austria's credit.

To crown all, Metternich simultaneously received a dispatch from the ambassador in London, Baron von Wessenberg, stating that the four Vienna firms had hopelessly mismanaged the realization of the English bills of exchange.[25] They had made the mistake of instructing no less than four firms on the same day and in the same market, to obtain bills on Paris and Amsterdam, so that their joint action naturally forced up the rate of exchange.

The imperial treasury had thereby incurred a loss of thousands of pounds, which would have been avoided if the business had been carried through by a single firm which would not have feared the competition of its rivals.

In accordance with a memorandum of Metternich's, the Emperor Francis issued a letter[26] in which he strongly enjoined the persons concerned to expedite the realization of the English subsidies as far as this could be done without incurring substantial loss. He also commanded that careful investigations were to be made as to the most advantageous method of procedure, adding that since he understood from a trustworthy source that the four firms had not handled the matter in a practical way, and the business could be carried through much more profitably from Frankfort, no further contracts should be made with those firms unless it could be shown that that was the best and most certain method of achieving the desired object.

Ugarte had requested the four banking firms to send in a written reply to the statement contained in Wessenberg's report, since he himself was inclined to support them, as they charged a commission of only one-quarter per cent; and he instructed Barbier at Frankfort to report as to whether the bills could really have been cashed at a much higher figure in that city. At this point Metternich intervened, also urging that Frankfort should be considered. Thereupon Ugarte summoned a secret commission at Vienna, and this commission naturally pronounced in favor of the four well-established local banking firms, whose credit stood high and who could be controlled more effectively, as they were on the spot.[27]

Meanwhile imperial headquarters had been shifted to Freiburg in Switzerland, where Gentz joined Metternich. In view of the conflict of opinion the emperor Francis dealt with the matter by instructing Ugarte to do nothing for the present.[28] But as in the early months of 1814 the allied armies advanced into France from all directions and the statesmen of the allied powers were busily engaged alternately in fighting and negotiating with Napoleon, it was all that they could do to raise the money necessary for the further conduct of the war.

The firm of Rothschild at Frankfort made every effort to get into touch with the Austrian government which was so sadly in need of funds, and they knew through Nathan that it received large sums from England. Nathan did all he could to achieve this object, and had already secured the support of Herries. At the beginning of 1814 Amschel Rothschild at Frankfort succeeded in obtaining the order to issue the pay of the imperial officers who were passing through or stationed in Frankfort, the accounts to be settled by the Austrian paymasters. That was at any rate a start.

Meantime the shortage of money at army headquarters in Freiburg had become acute. The army needed as much as two million gulden a month, so that further English subsidies, which the English government had agreed to under the Treaty of Chaumont, were exceedingly welcome. Austria was to receive £1,666,666⅔ or a monthly payment of £138,888⅔. In point of fact there was never occasion to pay out this sum, for the allies soon gained a decisive victory over Napoleon, and entered Paris on March 31; whereupon, after Napoleon's abdication, the first Peace of Paris was signed.

The elector immediately sent his sincerest congratulations to the emperor as the liberator of Europe, as usual accompanying this expression of feeling with a request that he should be compensated for his losses.[29] The elector had been a profitable example to the Rothschild family. He was always importuning the authorities to protect his interests, but he did so in rather an aggressive manner, whereas the Rothschild brothers, though no less persevering, always contrived so to frame their requests that they seemed to be concerned only for the interests of the state or the person with whom the decision lay.

Austria had already received the English payments due to her for the first three months of the year. The instalments for April and May were still due, as well as two payments for the return of the army, a total of £555,-555⅓, the remittance of which amount had to be arranged. The firm of Rothschild put in for this business, and in order to support it, Herries had proposed to Vienna that Austria should arrange for the money to be sent through Frankfort. In agreement with Nathan Rothschild, the Englishman, who regarded Frankfort as the most important financial center in Germany, had appointed his own plenipotentiary in that city, a certain Chevalier von Limburger, who was to conduct any negotiations regarding subsidies. He was a German Jew, and the proprietor of an important tobacco factory in Leipzig, but he enjoyed the confidence of the English commissary-general Herries.

Meanwhile the Rothschild brothers had been ceaselessly urging Barbier, who was still staying at Frankfort, to avail himself of the services of their firm for the financial affairs of the Austrian imperial government. They now decided, with the assistance of Herries and Limburger; on launching a final attack. On July 28, 1814,[30] two of the Rothschilds called on Barbier on behalf of the firm in general, and informed him that they had received instructions from the Chevalier von Limburger, the plenipotentiary of the English commissary-general, to ask whether Herries's proposals regarding the settlement of the balance due to Austria of the English subsidies for 1814 had been accepted at Vienna or not. At the same time the brothers Rothschild handed him a letter in which they offered their services in that connection. The letter was:[31]

Your Excellency:

In accordance with the permission graciously granted to us, we have the honor to offer your Highness our most obedient service and most humbly beg your Excellency to honor us with your high confidence, and to commission us to realize your claims on London. As our brother is himself established in London, we can easily make use of bills on that city, and enjoy many advantages which enable us always to obtain the best price. Your Excellency has had occasion to observe that we have acquired large sums from London and Vienna, with the intention of ourselves profiting by such exceptional circumstances. If your Excellency will lend a favorable ear to our petition we shall undertake most faithfully to serve your interests and to prove the high value that we attach to your Excellency's gracious goodwill, and, in return for our efforts and our services we shall be absolutely satisfied with the customary trade commission. . . . Comforting ourselves that you will favorably accede to our request, we beg to remain with all due respect,

Your Excellency's most obedient servants,

MEYER AMSCHEL ROTHSCHILD AND SONS.

Not long afterwards they wrote again, more succinctly: "We beg most submissively to inform your Excellency that today we are paying at the rate of 132 to the pound (on July 28 it would only have been 127) and that we are appropriating £200,000 for this purpose, and beg your confirmation of our action." [32]

Barbier forwarded the two communications to Ugarte at Vienna, and felt it his duty to add that in his opinion the offer should not be accepted, as Viennese firms and Austrian subjects were entitled to be considered. He suggested, however, that the proposals of Herries and Limburger should be considered, even if the Rothschilds' were not.[33] Barbier did not know at the time that the motive behind their proposals, although hitherto they had only recommended Frankfort in general and had not specifically mentioned the firm of Rothschild, was to secure that the whole business should be taken over by the House of Rothschild.

He was soon to be enlightened on this point; Carl Rothschild left him no peace. On August 5 he had another interview with Barbier, and gave it as his opinion that the English rate of exchange was then very favorable. He stated that he had received a communication from Limburger on the previous day and, in accordance therewith, he desired to make a definite and advantageous offer in writing regarding the realization of the further subsidies due to Austria.

Barbier reported this offer to Vienna, adding that he had taken no steps to conclude the arrangement, and ended by saying: "The House of Rothschild now does more business in English paper than all other firms put together, and this may be largely due to the fact that one member of the firm is established in London and another in Paris, and that the firm has to carry through several substantial remittances of money on account of the English government itself." [34]

The fundamental idea at the back of Herries's mind, a plan that Nathan had inspired, was that in view of the English government's unfortunate experience of the methods of middlemen, it should itself control the realization of the subsidies, and thereby prevent the frustration of its efforts for improving the English rate of exchange. Whilst Nathan supported Herries in these efforts, he profited by the occasion to get his firm established with the continental powers, and to induce Herries to entrust him with the remittance of the English subsidies to the three greatest powers, mindful that the connections thereby resulting would enable the firm in the course of time to secure other important business with the financial administrations of those powers. In this way he hoped gradually to secure for his firm a privileged position as state bankers to the four principal powers that were engaged in defeating Napoleon.

A letter from the firm of Rothschild to Barbier, dated Frankfort, August 8, 1814,[35] while making constant refences to Herries and Limburger, already entered into details concerning the remittance of the remaining £500,000, this serving as an introduction to the following proposal, which concluded the letter: "If your Excellency should be prepared to regard this unofficial proposal as acceptable, we would not fail to inform Herr von Limburger of your views, after which we may be in a position most dutifully to submit a formal offer."

Whereas Barbier and the treasury official Schwinner, who was on his staff, had hitherto dealt only with such firms as Bethmann, Metzler, Wertheimber, etc., the firm of Rothschild had now entered the field with the determination to drive all rivals out of it. The offer was duly sent in and forwarded to Vienna by Barbier. At the same time he observed to Rothschild that it was too vague to be accepted, and that this was not an ordinary banking transaction subject to the usual business risks, but was based on the proposal of the English commissary-general, and was therefore of an official nature.

Rothschild replied that Limburger was shortly coming to Paris, and that he had therefore not been able to frame his proposals more definitely. The Austrian Treasury would not have to pay any commission in respect to such transactions, although in all similar business which his firm had had to carry through for the English government, it had received a commission of two per cent. All he wanted was an opportunity to demonstrate his zeal on behalf of the imperial court.

Rothschild proceeded to enter into details as to the method by which he proposed to carry through the transaction, as he was hereby able incidentally to relate that the firm of Rothschild had already carried through similar business on an enormous scale for Russia and Prussia. At that time England had to pay ten million thalers to Russia and five million to Prussia. She agreed that this payment should not be immediately effected by bills of exchange, but should be made in monthly instalments of a million thalers.

It was further indicated that if the two states required the money at an earlier date, bankers could temporarily advance the amount. Knowing of this term in the contract, Nathan had told his brothers at Frankfort immediately to advance money to Prussia and Russia. These advances were actually made, so that at his interview with Barbier, Rothschild was able proudly to inform him that his firm had advanced to the Russian court four million gulden in cash and that his elder brother Solomon had gone to Berlin to carry through this important business.

A few days later Rothschild further informed Barbier,[36] with the object of impressing him, that his firm had received payments of the value of 750,000 francs in English crowns, and that this amount could also be applied to a settlement of the subsidies.

In the meantime, Count Ugarte's reply to Barbier's communications of July 28 and August 1, in which Barbier had first informed him of Rothschild's offers, was received. "As your Excellency . . . quite rightly observes," wrote the count, "it will be more profitable and safe for Austria in realizing the English subsidies to use native firms that enjoy the protection of her government, than to have recourse to foreign firms, over which her government has no control, and in which one cannot have the confidence . . . necessary for such extensive operations, as one would have no control over their activities, and they would not be able to offer security for the very considerable sums entrusted to them." Ugarte also expressed the view that in any case it would appear more advantageous to discount the English bills at Vienna, as the pound in that city was dealt in at nine gulden, three kreutzers, whereas, according to the latest report, it was only worth nine gulden at Frankfort. "There can therefore be no question," he continued, "of accepting the firm of Rothschild's offer to take over twenty thousand pounds sterling at the price they have suggested, of 8.48 gulden."[37]

The Rothschild proposal was therefore declined for the time being. Ugarte had failed to be convinced, and even Barbier had not been won over by the Brothers Rothschild. However, they did not lie down under this refusal. As they knew that the English government was working through Commissary-General Herries, on whom Nathan was bringing all his influence to bear, to get these financial transactions entrusted to them, they never thought of relaxing their efforts in that direction.

Limburger had just arrived at Frankfort with new instructions from England, and Amschel thereupon wrote personally to Barbier:

> Most honored sir, gracious vice-president!
>
> We have the honor most dutifully to inform your Excellency, in accordance with instructions, that the Chevalier von Limburg has arrived here with the purpose of negotiating with the three ministers or comishairs (*sic*) of the high powers, regarding the outstanding subsidy, we repeat our request for your high commands, and are with great respect and devotion
>
> Your Excellency's most obedient servants
>
> MEYER AMSCHEL ROTHSCHILD & SONS.
>
> Frankfort, August 22, 1814.[38]

The uneducated style of this letter, written by a member of the second generation of the family, since it had risen into prominence, contrasted strongly with other communications from the firm, which were only signed by one of the chiefs. Such communications indeed, in contrast with the practice of most bankers of that time, were always models of style and calligraphy, and therefore very easily read and understood—a fact which made a good impression on the government departments, who appreciated them as being above the usual standard. When, however, a Rothschild unexpectedly took the pen into his own hands, his style and spelling immediately revealed the low standard of education obtaining in their father's house. This did not, however, prove to be the slightest obstacle to the development of their commercial gifts. It merely provoked understanding smiles from the diplomats and highly placed persons with whom they had to deal.

As Austria was not inclined to accept the Rothschild offers, greater pressure had to be brought to bear by England, and it was decided accordingly to send Limburger to Vienna.[39] The statement that Carl Rothschild had made to Barbier, regarding his firm's financial dealings with Prussia and Russia, was in accordance with the facts. Herries had gone to Paris to carry through the subsidy negotiations with the representatives of the powers personally, and to convert them to Nathan's system under which the subsidy payments would not be effected by drawing bills on London at considerable loss to both parties, but through payments quietly carried through by the brothers Rothschild on the Continent.

In Paris, James Rothschild, who was most familiar in that city, had placed himself at the disposal of the commissary-general, and he was in turn introduced by Herries to the representatives of the victorious powers who were staying there. As a negotiator was required for the discussions at Berlin, Solomon was instructed to travel from Frankfort to the Prussian capital, and carry on the detailed negotiations there. In this way the five brothers played cleverly into each other's hands, and just as their father had contemplated, gave one another complementary support in all undertakings.

France had undertaken, under a convention dated May 28, 1814, to pay the allied powers twenty-five million francs as a lump sum, representing contributions that had not been levied and stores that had been left behind. Austria's share of this money was eight and two-thirds million francs. France deposited as securities for this amount, papers known as *bons royaux,* and the firm of Rothschild immediately applied for the business of cashing these in Paris at a commission of one-half per cent.

Rothschild again called on Barbier, and attempted to secure this business for his firm, as far as Austria was concerned, too. He was careful to mention that he had already been entrusted with a similar transaction by Russia, and that 250,000 new Dutch Rand ducats which were destined for Russia had already been deposited with his firm.

He brought a written application in support of his suggestion, and submitted to Barbier letters from the most important business firms in Paris,[40] from which it appeared that monetary conditions were so easy that the bonds could be negotiated at a very desirable rate at that time.

"If you should be graciously pleased," the letter ran, "to take advantage of these favorable circumstances, and to entrust us with the discounting of the *bons royaux* belonging to the royal and imperial government, you shall have no cause to complain of the industry and care with which our brother who is living in Paris will carry through this business. We would always duly pay over to your Excellency exactly what we received for the securities, subject to the customary commission of one-half per cent, with which we should be fully satisfied."

Without replying to the brothers Rothschild, Barbier submitted this letter, with some relevant observations of his own, to Ugarte, adding that certain other firms, including Bethmann, had also applied for the business.[41]

The Rothschilds were endeavoring at the same time to secure a third piece of business which was just then offered. An agreement had been arrived at between the Prussian finance minister and the Austrian Governor-General of Belgium, under which a sum of 9,500,000 francs was to be paid by the Belgian Treasury to the three eastern powers in equal proportions, on account of the expenses of occupation. Knowing of this arrangement, one of the brothers dropped the remark casually, in the presence of Barbier, that the firm of Rothschild had recently sent eighty thousand gold napoleons to Brussels, and would shortly have to transmit to that city further large sums of money on England's account.[42]

Barbier recollected the fact that Austria was to receive this payment in Belgium, and in view of what he had just heard, he thought it would be well for the firm of Rothschild to deal with this matter and asked whether they would undertake the business. Rothschild immediately pledged himself to pay out any amount which he received in Brussels in francs, in thalers or good bills of exchange at Frankfort, after deducting one-half per cent commission.

Barbier was entirely dependent on Vienna in such matters; he had first to report to Count Ugarte, and wait for his decision. At that time, quite an interval had to elapse before a reply could be received to a letter, and government departments were also exceedingly slow in dealing with correspondence. The brothers Rothschild submitted a detailed plan to Barbier, regarding the remittance of the money from Brussels on July 29, concluding with the words:[43] "We shall request your Excellency one-half per cent commission for our expenses and trouble, beyond which you will not have to bear any further expense whatever. If, on the arrival of the money here, we can secure more favorable terms for your Excellency, we shall certainly not fail to furnish you with such proofs of our disinterestedness."

The use of the word "disinterested" is not entirely to be sneered at. Often, especially when as in this instance they desired to gain a new customer, the firm of Rothschild was wont to emphasize that it was particularly concerned with the interests of the other party to the transaction, and business was often undertaken at a quite modest profit, sometimes even at a loss, with a view to securing much more important business at a future date, whereby any such loss would be made good. It was exactly the same principle that old Rothschild had applied in his dealings with the Elector of Hesse, when at the beginning of their connection he sold him coins and antiques far under their real value. This principle had paid, for by 1814 the Rothschilds were doing business that ran into millions.

Barbier faithfully transmitted to Vienna all the offers that were made to him, and received Ugarte's reply a month later.[44] This was not favorable to the foreign Jews, and showed a preference for relying on native bankers. He could not, however, entirely ignore Barbier's suggestion regarding the transfer of the money from Brussels. He therefore wrote to say that he considered Rothschild's offer to be generally acceptable, but limited the amount which they were to handle to about one-half of the total; and in order to avoid all risk he instructed Barbier to arrange with the firm of Rothschild that the receipt for payment at the treasury in Brussels should not be handed to them until the sum had been paid in cash or in good Augsburg bills, or appropriate security had been furnished.

Barbier hastened to arrange an interview with the firm of Rothschild, and with the firm of Gontard, who were collaborating with them, but he could not persuade them to agree to carry through the business on such terms. In spite of their desire to enter into relations with Austria, they wanted at least to have the advantage of being able to dispose of such a large sum for a short space of time, during which they could have employed it very profitably within the scope of their numerous activities. They were also somewhat offended at such a demonstration of lack of faith.

"The heads of these firms observed to me on this point,"

wrote Barbier to Ugarte, "that these conditions were not at all customary in such transactions, and might indeed be prejudicial to their credit; that certainly no other firm would accept such conditions, and that in a business in which they were charging only an exceedingly modest commission, they could not make advances in cash . . . especially at a time when they had so many other opportunities of employing their funds much more profitably. Rothschild further remarked that much greater sums were entrusted to him by the English government, and that other governments also did not fail to accord him similar confidence, while several millions of gulden that belonged to the Elector of Hesse-Cassel and were invested in government loans in London, Vienna, etc. were simply inscribed in his name."

Barbier admitted the general justice of the Rothschilds' contention, but said he could not take bills that had not been accepted or indorsed by a substantial firm as in that case he would have no security except the property of the drawer, "although," as he wrote, "the firm of Rothschild, as well as that of Gontard, are known to have very solid resources, and, together with several other firms in the 'second class' as regards their resources . . . enjoy a very good reputation and a no less extensive credit."

Bethmann, with whom Barbier next negotiated, stated that he would be doing the business at a loss, and that he must ask for a higher commission. On Barbier pointing out that Rothschild had only asked for one-half per cent, and that Bethmann must therefore realize that it would be difficult to get a higher commission approved, Bethmann replied that Rothschild could carry through the business much more easily than he could, because he had to make considerable payments to the English troops in the Netherlands, on account of the English government.

Limburger also, to whom Barbier applied, refused to handle the business, since his authority extended only to the payment to the three allied courts of the English subsidy still outstanding. At the same time he remarked that in accordance with the instructions which he had received, he was leaving the subsidy business to the direction and personal supervision of the firm of Rothschild, since these transactions required the cooperation of an active banker with very good connections; and that that firm had actually to make considerable payments for the English troops and would therefore be able more easily than any other to deal with the remittances in question.

In spite of this new offensive in favor of the House of Rothschild, the business was entrusted to Bethmann, on the ground that the property of that house was "well known to be so great as to require no other security than a duly binding contract or a debenture." This was a triumph of Bethmann over Rothschild, and it was due to the fact that the importance and financial greatness of the firm of Rothschild, which at that time was still of very recent date, was not appreciated at Vienna, and even Barbier had more faith in the old Christian firm of Bethmann than in the upstart Jewish firm.

Nathan was annoyed at this failure, but was all the more obstinately determined to gain his object. However, before this could happen, Ugarte would have to make way for a new man at Vienna, Count Stadion, and Barbier would have to be won over, which was not accomplished until 1815, in Paris. For the moment, the assiduous attempts of the firm of Rothschild to obtain big business with Austria had failed, and it had to content itself with the modest duties of handling the Austrian war-commissariat account at Frankfort, which indeed served to maintain its connection with the financial departments of the Austrian government.

From the foregoing description of the nature of the business transactions of the Rothschild family, it is evident that they were mainly concerned with overcoming the tremendous difficulties to which international monetary dealings were subject, owing to the political conditions of those days and the backward state of communications.

Baron von Hügel's elaborate report [45] as to the way in which a sum of 8,353 gulden and 74 kreutzers could most safely and cheaply be sent from Frankfort to Vienna, makes strange reading today. At first he wanted to entrust the amount to a non-commissioned officer who was leaving for the imperial city with a consignment of official documents; but on reflection he thought it was too dangerous to entrust such a large sum to a soldier, as one could never tell what chance accidents might befall him on the way, and endanger the property confided to him.

After such pondering Hügel finally had recourse to the Rothschilds, and asked them whether they could not issue a bill on Vienna for the amount. The firm replied that they were prepared to issue such a document, and to make it a bill payable at sight, but that they would have to charge a commission of one per cent, a sum of 83.30 gulden, which sum was certainly less than the cost of sending the remittance by post-chaise. Such special circumstances yielded opportunities of profit which the Rothschild family most skilfully exploited by establishing a kind of clearing-house between the three brothers in London, Paris, and Frankfort; and this system was soon extended to Vienna.

Nathan was the father of this idea. Although the third son, he was more and more tending to become the directing brain of the firm. His association with Herries, who relied upon him to an increasing extent, although concealed from the public became increasingly intimate and more profitable both politically and financially. The services rendered by Nathan, not only covered an extensive field, but were also most varied in their nature. After the fall of Napoleon, to which Nathan's financial measures in support of the Allies and of Wellington had contributed not a little, his business expanded in a quite unprecedented manner. Thereupon he immediately availed himself of every opportunity of rendering services to the Bourbons, who had returned to France with the support of the Allies, thus smoothing the path for his brother James in Paris.

The exiled Bourbon heir, who was later King Louis XVIII, had been living at Hartwell in Buckinghamshire since 1807. When the Allies invaded France in 1814, he appealed to his divine right to the throne, and decided to go to Paris immediately after the fall of Napoleon. However, he lacked the money necessary to undertake the journey and make his appearance in France with the magnificence proper to a king. The king applied to the English Treasury, requesting it to advance the necessary capital. As French currency and bills on Paris were required, the application was sent to Herries to deal with, and he called in Nathan.

Nathan was delighted to have such an early opportunity of proving himself useful to Louis XVIII, and with the assistance of his brother James in Paris he acquired bills payable in that city, to the value of 200,000 English pounds.[46] He placed them speedily at the disposal of the new king, and thus made it possible for him to land at Calais on April 26, 1814, and to enter Paris on May 3.

Although to Herries's considerable satisfaction, Nathan carefully preserved the close veil of secrecy covering his activities, and let Herries get most of the credit, whilst he contented himself with the commercial profit and the fact that the transactions served to introduce him to other governments, on this occasion Nathan was careful to see that the newly established monarch learned of his share in the transaction. For this seemed to him to be of great importance for the future position of the firm of Rothschild in France.

The development of this branch business was to be entrusted to James, who had already made himself at home in Paris, and who was widely traveled, although he was only twenty-two years old at the time. His appearance, it is true, was not exactly prepossessing. He looked very Jewish; he had red hair and deep-set eyes, and a good complexion, but he had a wide mouth, a prominent hooked nose, and pursed-up lips. During his earlier years in Paris, he showed an almost servile politeness to everyone. He had obviously acquired the habit at Frankfort, where the status of the Jews was very low, but as he grew more successful and his position improved he gradually lost it. Moreover, James was an exceedingly acute, honorable, and clever banker, whose talents can be rated only a little below those of his brother Nathan. Above all, he had a fair share of the other's abundant energy.

In the life of feverish activity which developed in Paris after the conquest of that city, when officers, diplomats, bankers, and business men flocked to it from all sides, James was absolutely in his element. He was seen everywhere, in government offices as well as on the Bourse and in diplomatic circles,[47] and made great efforts to establish himself in society. He actively supported Herries and his brother Nathan in their efforts to cash the English subsidies without depressing the rate of exchange, and Nathan was able to show in a report to the English Treasury that hundreds of thousands were saved by the new method.[48]

Under the Paris Treaty of May 10, 1814, the French government had undertaken to meet certain obligations incurred by responsible officials, either in France itself or in the conquered territories. To collect these amounts the creditors found it necessary to employ middlemen. James was appointed as the agent of numerous banks and organizations that had claims of this nature, and he was also engaged in the interests of the Elector of Hesse and other minor German princes.

His personal mode of life was exceedingly modest. He lived above a small courtyard, although his business dealings had not only won him the respect of commercial circles but had also brought him substantial profit. He had already decided ultimately to settle in Paris, just as Nathan had taken up permanent residence in England. He was, however, not in such a hurry as his brother to get naturalized, partly because he wanted to watch the course of developments in France after the stormy time of the revolution and the Napoleonic period; and since France could not at that time place any obstacles in the way of a subject of the victorious powers, he wanted to register his own firm in Paris. If occasion should arise the powers were always ready to exert diplomatic pressure in favor of their subjects. James did in fact register his business without getting naturalized, his name appearing in the Paris trade almanac for 1814 as resident in the rue de Pelletier.

Whilst the House of Rothschild was getting well established in Western Europe through the activities of the two brothers, in its native town it had to fight for recognition, owing to the aversion of the citizens to the Jews. The growing wealth of the Rothschild family at the expense of Christian firms was viewed with displeasure at Frankfort. Buderus had completely succeeded in eliminating their rivals. The firm of Van Notten at Amsterdam had put up a fight longest, but that firm, also, failed to survive Buderus's systematic propaganda with the elector.

In a letter dated May 13, 1814, Buderus had written to the electoral plenipotentiary Lorentz, at London, expressing his dislike of that firm in the following words:[49] "The worthy bankers Van Notten must be small-minded people. On one occasion, when I was very hard-pressed because I was waiting for assistance from England, I drew £35,000 on them. They showed the most extraordinary anxiety about the repayment of this sum. I hope they are now easy in their minds. The Rothschild bankers at Frankfort, on the other hand, have advanced over half a million, and have rendered services of every kind in a cheerful spirit." Buderus did not fail to express similar views to the elector, so that the rivals of the brothers Rothschild had the ground completely cut from under their feet as far as the Hessian prince was concerned.

The Frankfort Jews had nothing to fear from Austria and Prussia. When Grand Duke Dalberg left Frankfort, the firm of Rothschild was a creditor of his for considerable sums, including the following items: 22,900 gulden for supplying flour to France; 71,181 gulden advanced in connection with the transactions affecting the Fulda property; and 50,000 gulden advanced to Dalberg on account of the Jewish tax commutation payment, which was not yet due.[50] Baron von Hügel, who after the occupation of Frankfort took part in its civil administration, charged all these claims to the city budget, on Amschel's application, to the great indignation of the senate. The city finances were in a state of confusion, but the claims of the House of Rothschild seem to have been satisfied.

The inhabitants of Frankfort particularly grudged the Jews the equal political rights, which they had obtained, it was held, by methods of indirect bribery. The threatened attitude of their native town caused the brothers Rothschild to be seriously concerned about the future of the parent company on which their power was founded. They decided to make every effort to prevent the Jews of Frankfort from losing any of those rights which they had bought during Dalberg's régime.

The new constitution of Frankfort, and therefore the decision regarding the future status of the Jews, was one of the questions to be settled by the Vienna Congress, which was to meet on October 1, 1814. The choice of Vienna was not very acceptable to the Rothschilds, for Austria was the state which had hitherto so obstinately refused to enter into close business relations with them, and her statesmen, such as Ugarte, still did not really trust the upstart Jewish firm at Frankfort. Moreover, the Rothschilds well knew the strict police control to which foreign Jews were subjected at Vienna, and how greatly all Jews were restricted in their freedom to do business in Austria. As they were determined, however, to secure the desired business connections with the Austrian state, they were not tempted to make the realization of their plan more difficult through possible conflicts with the police authorities at Vienna.

Such considerations caused the House of Rothschild to refrain from sending a member of the family there. The Frankfort Israelites sent old Börnes, Jacob Baruch, and J. J. Gumprecht, as their representatives. They were closely watched by the Viennese police; indeed their expulsion was ordered and sanctioned by the emperor himself; but Metternich intervened, and prevented this from being carried out. Metternich's intervention was probably due to the fact that he had known Baruch when he was ambassador at Frankfort. There is no proof that Rothschild had any particular influence with the minister at that time.

The Jewish representatives at Vienna adopted the method of giving presents; thus they offered Humboldt three magnificent emerald rings, or four thousand ducats —presents which he refused, whereas Gentz gladly allowed himself to be bribed. The brothers Rothschild had of course contributed to these funds; but they still kept quite in the background.

The general discussions of the proud assemblage of princes and diplomats at Vienna took their course, and sometimes went through critical phases. At one time, indeed, it seemed as though two main groups of powers would form, the differences between which threatened war. This seemed to Napoleon, who was fully informed at Elba of all developments, to be a suitable moment for putting into execution his plans of returning and regaining the throne.

On March 1, he landed on French soil with a handful of faithful adherents. Three weeks later the magic of his name had reinstated him in the palace of the Tuileries in Paris. Louis XVIII and his court had fled from the capital. Napoleon hoped, not only that the Congress of Vienna would collapse, but that some of the powers represented there would adopt his cause. Actually nothing of the kind occurred. While negotiations at Vienna had hitherto hung fire, it was now clear to everybody that delay was dangerous and that quick action was essential. The powers unanimously turned against the disturber of the peace, and determined on concerted action.

The other matters were settled hastily; and half-measures were sanctioned, such as the constitution of the German Confederation. This formed thirty-nine communities into a confederation of states, each one of which was to remain independent, while having a common governing body, with Austria presiding over the Federal Diet, whose seat was to be Frankfort-on-the-Main. It was in Metternich's interest to keep Germany disunited. Controversial matters such as the Jewish problem were to be discussed later by the Federal Diet, while in the meantime existing arrangements were to remain unaltered in the individual states.

Metternich informed the plenipotentiaries of the Israelite communities in Germany of this decision,[51] assuring them that the Federal Diet would respect the welfare of the Israelites and that he himself would urge that full rights of citizenship be conferred on the Jews. This was good news, and the delegates hastened to send a copy of Metternich's statement to the House of Rothschild, anxiously waiting tidings at Frankfort.

However, the time had not yet come to raise this question. It was far more important to overthrow Napoleon, who was again collecting his military resources in France. On March 25, 1815, the four principal powers had renewed their alliance. Each of them undertook to provide one hundred and fifty thousand men, except England, which undertook to send subsidies instead of the full amount of troops.

Napoleon was to be finally destroyed by a joint effort. It was therefore again necessary to arrange to transfer the subsidy payments from England to the various continental powers, and substantial sums would have to be paid to Prussia and Austria. Prussia particularly was again in great financial embarrassment, and unless this were immediately relieved, her future military action would suffer. Herries and Nathan now redoubled their feverish activities. Toward the end of April, Nathan sent in one instalment the sum of £200,000 to the Prussian government. It was conveyed by Solomon, who traveled to Berlin for this purpose. When this amount proved inadequate, Solomon without previously consulting Nathan, granted a further advance of £150,000 on the security of the English subsidy, at a rate which was certainly very profitable to himself.

Herries retrospectively sanctioned this operation. Not only did he make no objection, but he also allowed England to assume the considerable loss on exchange which Solomon's high rate of profit had meant for the Prussian government.[52] His profit was not Solomon's only gain on this transaction; in return for his ready willingness to advance such a heavy sum on his own responsibility, the Prussian government conferred on him the title of commercial adviser, a distinction that raised him above the majority of his rivals.

Meanwhile in Austria a change had taken place in the direction of the government's finances. Count Ugarte had retired, his place being taken by Count Stadion, the gifted and eminent statesman who was such a bitter opponent of Napoleon. Having hitherto been engaged exclusively in diplomatic matters, he had not as yet made himself familiar with finance. He therefore entered upon his new office with some misgivings. Grillparzer,

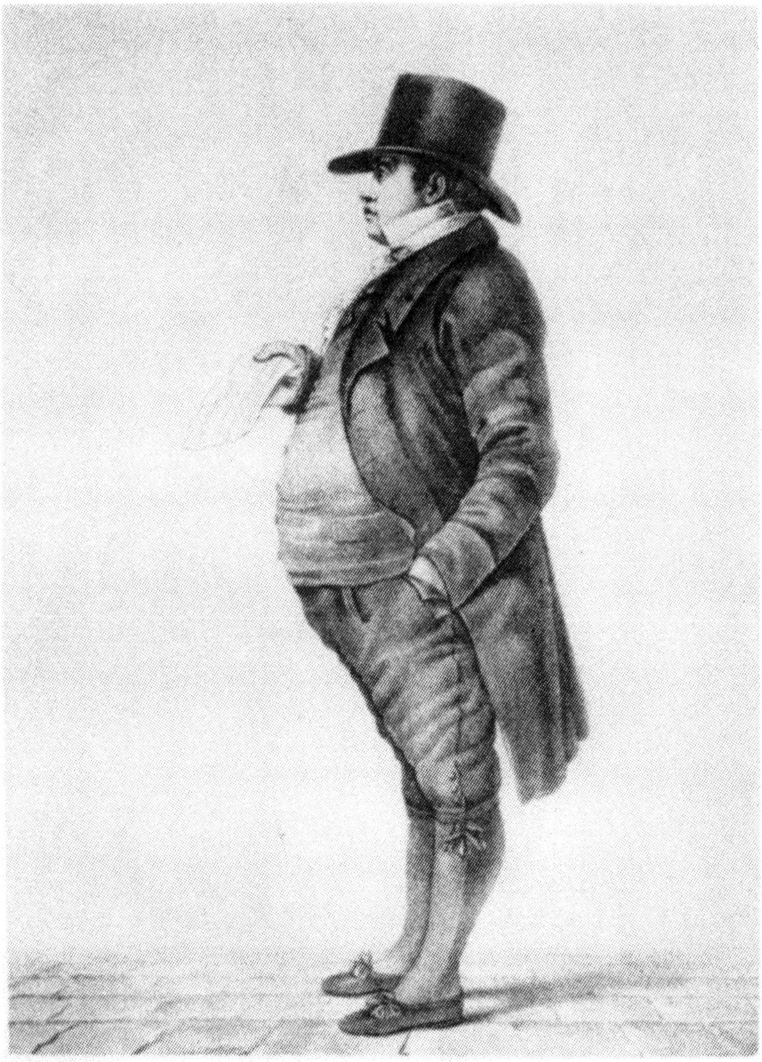

Nathan Rothschild

From a painting in the possession of the
Vienna National Library

who thought so highly of Stadion that he described him as having more character [53] than any other person he had ever met, noted in his diary [54] that Stadion had himself admitted to possessing very little knowledge of finance.[55] In spite of his greatness in other directions, a finance minister such as this would naturally seem an easy mark for clever bankers and financiers who were out to get business. In view of the change of atmosphere at Vienna and the added prospect of new English subsidies, the brothers Rothschild immediately made themselves felt again, both indirectly through Herries and Limburger, and by direct applications to the Austrian government.

However, Stadion as yet knew little about them, and as Nathan's heavy transactions were still purposely kept in the background, he had no information about these either, so that his whole knowledge regarding the origin and business of the House of Rothschild was exceedingly vague. He suddenly noticed that Meyer Amschel and Sons described themselves as "I. and R. Crown Agents" in a letter, and signed themselves as such. Stadion inquired at the Foreign Office about this from Metternich—who had been advanced to the rank of prince after the battle of Leipzig—stating that he could not understand their signing in this way, since the treasury had no knowledge as to when and in what connection the Rothschilds had acquired this title from the Austrian court. In view of the inferences that might be drawn from its use, he felt it his duty to ask Metternich for further information on the matter.[56]

The following reply to this note was received: "With reference to your inquiry . . . regarding the title of imperial-royal crown agents assumed by the Frankfort business firm of Rothschild, the secretary of state has the honor to inform you that there is no record in his department of that title having been granted to the said firm, and that he has no information whatever on the matter." [57]

The fact was that the Rothschilds had not signed as

imperial-royal, as Stadion thought, but as imperial crown agents, as they were entitled to do in accordance with the decree of January 29, 1800, issued by Emperor Francis in his then capacity of Roman-German Emperor.[58] In any case the incident showed the extent to which the Rothschild family were distrusted in Austria.

In Frankfort, also, they met with every kind of opposition. In order to hinder them in the development of their constantly increasing business, an attempt was made to force the two brothers who were living at Frankfort into the army, in view of the special efforts being made to raise men to resist the return of Napoleon. They turned anxiously to Nathan for help, and he determined to use this opportunity of intervention for addressing a homily to Austria, as he realized that very definite pressure would have to be brought to bear from England, if Austria were at last to be roped in as a customer. The House of Rothschild had already established a virtual monopoly in carrying out the subsidy arrangements of the Island Kingdom.

Nathan went to Herries and acquainted him with the situation; and Herries induced the Foreign Office to make representations to Herr von Neumann, Austrian counselor of embassy in London, in accordance with which Neumann commended the House of Rothschild to Baron von Hügel, the Austrian plenipotentiary at Frankfort. His letter ran as follows:[59]

Sir:

The English Government has requested me most particularly to commend to your Excellency's consideration the House of Rothschild at Frankfort, which carries out the transfer of our subsidies. This firm is represented by several brothers, one of whom is established here, and is employed by the British government in connection with all their principal financial operations on the Continent. By reason of the confidence which he enjoys, and the extensive nature of his operations, both he and his brothers have incurred the envy of the Frankfort bankers to such an extent that an attempt has been made to torment [*tourmenter*] them by forcing them to do military service. As the English government appears to be most anxious that this firm should not be annoyed in any way, and as this appears to be a matter that directly concerns our service, I felt that I ought not to fail to transmit this request. I therefore ask your Excellency to grant that firm every help and protection that lies in your power.

Baron von Hügel immediately forwarded this letter to Vienna, where it was submitted to Metternich and Stadion, and it did not fail of its effect. No further opposition was offered to the Rothschild brothers' undertaking the transfer of the subsidies; and in general the interstate financial transactions were all carried through more easily, since Stadion allowed his officials abroad much greater scope than had Ugarte. The new finance minister was inclined to leave more to their personal initiative and judgment, as he realized that they being on the spot were in a better position to know what conditions were, and as the cumbrous methods of communication made it impracticable to correspond on matters requiring an immediate decision.

At this time Herries himself visited Frankfort, where his commissioner, Limburger, was negotiating with the treasury commissioner Schwinner in regard to the amounts to be paid to Austria, which Stadion would have liked to receive in coin or bullion. Herries emphatically demanded that in this matter the House of Rothschild should be granted as free a hand as possible.

Napoleon's return had suddenly upset their plans and made new measures necessary, and the commissary-general and Nathan were kept exceedingly busy. In the campaign against the bold adventurer the most important thing was to raise cash and especially French currency. As they could not obtain French coins anywhere, Herries on Nathan's advice had gold louis minted, in order to supply the armies.

In the middle of June, Napoleon resumed the campaign. France was supporting him only half-heartedly, for after all these wars everyone was longing for peace, and was willing even to put up with foreign invasion. Now, however, the French were faced again with a demand for new sacrifices and blood and treasure, and with a struggle against superior forces. For a short time the fortune of war seemed again to smile upon Napoleon, but as early as June 18, 1815, the Emperor of France met his fate at Waterloo. He was completely and decisively beaten—abdication, captivity, and banishment to St. Helena were the result.

On the resumption of hostilities in France, Herries and Nathan had returned to London, and were anxiously awaiting news of the result of the conflict. Nathan and his brothers had always made a particular point of letting one another have news as speedily as possible, either directly or through their business friends, of any important event that might influence their business, or be a determining factor in new undertakings. Nathan had promised prizes for the most speedy supply of news to boats sailing between England and the Continent. He also instructed his agents throughout the world to give him the earliest possible report regarding the outcome of the expected conflict. Such measures were of particular importance at that time, because none of the modern methods of conveying news had been invented—the stage post, that is a series of messengers, being the usual way of obtaining it quickly.

Nathan's arrangements worked perfectly for the battle of Waterloo. One of his agents, whose name was Rothworth, waited at Ostend for news of the result. He succeeded in obtaining the first newspaper account of the successful issue of the battle, and with a copy of the

Dutch Gazette fresh from the printers, he caught a boat just sailing for London. He entered the British capital very early in the morning of June 20, and immediately reported to Nathan, who conveyed the news of victory to Herries, and through him to the British government.

The government were at first skeptical, as they had not received any direct information, and Wellington's envoy Major Henry Percy did not arrive with the field-marshal's report until the 21st of June.[60] The members of the British government were tremendously impressed by Nathan's advance knowledge of such an important event; and when this became generally known, the public, who were just beginning to learn of the extent to which Nathan was employed by the English Treasury, began to invent all manner of legends regarding the method by which Nathan had acquired this knowledge and the manner in which he had exploited it.

Some said that he had a private service of carrier-pigeons; others that he had been personally present at the battle of Waterloo and had ridden to the coast at top speed. In order to make the story more romantic, he was said to have found heavy storms raging when he reached the Channel and to have crossed at the risk of his life. Nathan was also alleged to have exploited the news on the stock exchange, thus at one stroke creating the enormous fortunes of the Rothschilds.

Nathan naturally applied the early information that he had obtained to his own profit in his business dealings; but the substantial part of the fortune of the Rothschilds had been amassed through the profits realized in the financial transactions which have already been described; the successful issue of the battle of Waterloo merely served to increase it, and to open up wider fields for profitable business in the future. This was all the more so as England had been victorious and Nathan had transferred the center of gravity of the Rothschild business to her side.

In spite of the fortunate issue of the campaign, which had lasted barely six days, England continued to pay the subsidies to the continental powers. The House of Rothschild was, for instance, instructed by the English Treasury—that is, by Herries and Nathan—to pay Austria £277,777 on demand, for the months of August and September, this amount not to be subject to any discount, so that Austria should receive it in full.[61] The commission due to the brothers Rothschild was paid by England herself. The payments were continued up to and including December.

Stadion had expressed the wish that as much *coin* as possible be sent. This made the transfer more difficult and produced a fall in the exchange; it was due to the continuing distrust, which even Schwinner, Austria's representative at Frankfort, was not able to dissipate. The English alone emphatically countered this attitude, and the resulting correspondence clearly shows how highly the wealth and position of the young firm of Rothschild were already rated in England, or at any rate in the authoritative circles of Commissary-General Herries, as compared to their standing in Austria.

"The . . . exchange value [of the pound]," wrote Schwinner to the Austrian embassy in London in November, 1815, "was constantly rising during the early part of November; after the 9th it weakened because Rothschild, having reason to believe that Austria would insist on receiving her considerable payments in cash, refrained from purchasing bills offered by foreigners. This circumstance would appear to justify the view of the English commissioner Baron von Limburger, in which Commissary-General Herr von Herries, who was here a few months ago, concurred, that the more the House of Rothschild were granted a free hand . . . the more certainly would the exchange value of English bills be maintained.

"In this connection the firm of Rothschild have offered bills with respect to the November and December instalments . . . similar to those that have already been accepted and fully cashed in previous payments to the extent of several millions. Nevertheless, in spite of the fact that the generally recognized standing of the firm of Rothschild should be sufficient guarantee for these instruments, I felt that I must adhere to those rules which must always be strictly observed, lest unexpected difficulties should be met in cashing bills of exchange. I considered that this condition was met when Baron von Limburger gave a written undertaking on behalf of the English government that that government would in any case indemnify the imperial and royal treasury if any loss whatever were suffered in realizing the bills accepted by Rothschild." [62]

Schwinner had on a previous occasion expressed his misgivings to Limburger regarding his responsibility for any loss "resulting from the lack of solidity of the firm of Rothschild." Limburger had on that occasion replied to him in the following terms:

"I have the honor to acknowledge the receipt of your valued communication of even date. I cannot possibly give the slightest credence to the rumors which you have communicated to me, and which I regard as malicious slanders deserving of severe punishment. In order, however, completely to set your mind at rest I have to repeat to you on behalf of my government the verbal statement made to you by the commissary-in-chief, Mr. Herries, that even if the accepted bills are not met, the Imperial and Royal Austrian government shall in no wise suffer loss, but that they will be indemnified if there should unexpectedly be any loss in cashing the said bills. I have to point out first that in the case of the considerable amounts which you have already received in such bills, no such occasion has occurred and secondly, that the House of Rothschild is itself too rich and too powerful not immediately to make good any such loss without requiring the intervention of my government." [63]

Schwinner transmitted the whole of this correspondence to Vienna, where it was brought to the attention of Metternich and Stadion. As they were both hearing such completely satisfactory accounts of the firm of Rothschild from all quarters, and more particularly were learning of the enormous credit which that firm enjoyed, confidence was completely established at Vienna. From now onwards the firm of Rothschild was most extensively employed by Austria, even in business which had nothing whatever to do with the English subsidy.

Thus Nathan had succeeded, while remaining behind the scenes himself, in establishing his brothers on the Continent in the confidence of the Austrian Treasury. This was to be the starting-point of an even more intimate association with governing circles in the imperial state, which was to develop within the next few years.

While the position of the Rothschild family abroad became more and more important and their wealth attained prodigious dimensions by reason of the great interstate financial transactions which were entrusted to them, they had to fight in their native town of Frankfort to secure the equal political rights of the Jews which had been granted during the period of French dominion. In spite of the decisions of the Congress of Vienna and in spite of Metternich and Hardenberg, this equality was threatened by a hostile senate. Now, however, emboldened by the position which they had won with the great powers, the brothers Rothschild felt in a position to make more definite efforts on behalf of their fellows.

The newly created Federal Diet which met at Frankfort had an important voice in this matter, and the Rothschilds determined to gain the responsible representatives of the powers for their cause. From the first, they had a true friend in the representative of the Elector of

Hesse, who had already reestablished everything in his own territory, including the soldiers' pigtails, just as it was before, and who was again at loggerheads with his estates regarding financial matters and the question of the separation of the state treasury from the prince's privy purse.

On October 17, 1816, he had nominated, as his envoy to the German Federal Diet, the administrator of his financial affairs, the old supporter of the Rothschild family, Buderus von Carlshausen—who in the meantime had advanced to the dignity of privy councilor and president of the Chamber. Von Carlshausen had recently been in Paris, on business in connection with his master's claims for compensation, and had specially commended the elector's interests to James. He was now to serve as a kind of liaison officer between the elector and the House of Rothschild, as indeed he had always been. Only positions were now somewhat changed; hitherto it had been the Rothschilds who had asked favors; now it was the elector and Buderus who tried to maintain a close connection. The brothers Rothschild certainly did not forget what they owed them, and endeavored as far as possible to meet all their wishes. But the elector's business had fallen very much into the background since the family had got accustomed to transacting business running into millions with the states of Europe.

In any case, the first important relationship of the Rothschild family had worked out to the benefit of all concerned. The elector had had his scattered resources most ably shepherded during the confusions of the Napoleonic war; Buderus had been made an exceedingly wealthy man; and the extensive operations of the Rothschilds themselves had been made possible through the moneys originally entrusted to them by the elector. They naturally urged Carlshausen to make strong representations in favor of Jewish interests at the Federal Diet.

Solomon and Carl Rothschild next turned to the Prussian chancellor Prince Hardenberg and transmitted to him a copy of the letter that Metternich had sent to the Jewish representatives at the Vienna Congress, adding the following covering letter: [64]

> In humble confidence we beg to submit to your Highness the enclosed document which is of such fateful import for the destinies of the Israelite community.
>
> After all that your Highness has done for our community in recent years we cannot but hope that your Highness will not withdraw your powerful support at this decisive moment. That, and that alone, can secure a tolerable existence to the Frankfort Jews. Everything depends upon the Commission nominated by the Federal Diet proceeding according to just and reasonable principles in dealing with this matter; and any influence exerted by your Highness in that direction cannot but have the most satisfactory result. We therefore beg to submit our most humble and relevent request that you will most graciously convey to the royal Prussian Ambassador at Frankfort, as speedily as possible, those general instructions which are indicated in the enclosed letter. This is the only means of salvation left to us.

This letter was necessary because there were definite signs that the senate was not likely to pay much attention to the decisions of the Congress of Vienna. This fact had financial consequences; for some of the debentures issued by the Jewish community in connection with their liberation had not yet been met. The Jews did not wish to pay the money until it was certain that the rights which they were thus purchasing would be secured to them. The firm Meyer Amschel Rothschild and Sons wrote in similar terms to Hardenberg and Metternich, saying that they had been informed that all the duly acquired rights of each class of the inhabitants at Frankfort would be maintained, and that there was therefore no further obstacle to the debentures being redeemed.

"As none of the principal magistrates at Frankfort," the letter continued, "have as yet taken any action in this matter, and the holders of these debentures are pressing more and more for their payment, we humbly request you to take the necessary steps, so that these obligations may be paid without further delay.

"We venture to hope that our most humble request will be graciously granted, since the necessary money has long been available, and it will be paid as soon as the necessary action in this matter has been taken." [65]

Before this money was paid, the Rothschilds wanted to receive an assurance from the city of Frankfort that it would not attempt to dispute the agreement with Dalberg of December 28, 1811, regarding the equal rights of the Jews. Both the persons appealed to agreed; and Hardenberg wrote to Metternich that he considered the request to be right and just, that the city of Frankfort could not legally raise any objection, and that it would be advisable for the two courts jointly and emphatically to enjoin Frankfort to recognize the agreement as binding and to fulfil it.[66]

Count Buol-Schauenstein, Austria's plenipotentiary, and therefore president of the Federal Diet, was, in contrast to his superior Metternich, no friend of the Jews, and had reported his views to Metternich at Vienna. He held that Grand Duke Dalberg had sold the rights of citizenship to a crowd of Jewish families for a song.

"Trade," wrote the ambassador from Frankfort, "is still the only means of livelihood which the Jews adopt. This nation, which never amalgamates with any other, but always hangs together to pursue its own ends, will soon overshadow Christian firms; and with their terribly rapid increase of population they will soon spread over the whole city, so that a Jewish trading city will gradually arise beside our venerable cathedral." [67]

Buol's attitude was bound eventually to result in a conflict of opinion with Metternich, but for the time being no decision was made in the Jewish question, and the question of the status at Frankfort remained in the balance.

Paris offered opportunities of important new business, and all the members of the Rothschild family were kept fully occupied exploiting them as far as possible.

The victorious powers inflicted a heavy war indemnity on France, appointing four commissioners of the principal powers to settle the precise terms and receive the money. They met at Paris under the presidency of the Austrian, Baron von Barbier. The amount of the indemnity was fixed at seven hundred million francs, to be paid within five years in fifteen instalments of 46,666,-666 francs, commencing on December 1, 1815.

At once the difficulty arose of arranging for these payments to be transmitted to the powers. James, perceiving the great possibilities of profit that the situation offered, advised his brothers and urged them to do everything possible to get the order for remitting this French tribute.

The brothers had to meet heavy competition. Austria still employed her four banking firms, which were represented in Paris; while Baring and other big firms in England endeavored, in connection with the Paris banking firm of Ouvrard, to get the business. All the firms were eager to exploit the opportunity to the utmost, and all the financial and banking world was considering the methods by which the great indemnity could be settled.

Barbier received a proposal from the Baring-Ouvrard Company which was unacceptable because, as Barbier reported,[68] "the bankers insist on enormous advantages being assured to them, without guaranteeing our principal objects, namely, complete security and advances before instalments fall due." Austria intended, among other things, to divert large sums to Colmar for various purposes, mainly of a military nature. The four Viennese firms had very poor connections in Germany, and it was not practicable to make use of them.

The question therefore was whether the Messageries —the overland postal services—could be entrusted with this task, or whether recourse should be had to bankers as an intermediary. Barbier felt anxious about the first method, the roads being exceedingly unsafe so soon after the confusion of the war. This was indicated by the fact that the postal company refused to accept liability for *"les vols à main armée,"* after a mail-bag had been rifled on another journey.

Barbier reported as follows to Stadion:[69] "I am informed that the Frankfort bankers Rothschild and Gontard have undertaken entirely at their own risk to transfer certain sums of money required for the Wurttemberg regiments that are remaining in France, and that they have been granted a commission of one and a half per cent for their services. This amounts to exactly double the transport costs demanded by the Messageries. I have also heard that they have demanded one and a quarter per cent for sending money to the Russian regiments. I suggested to them that they should remit our money at their own risk for a commission of one per cent, to cover all expenses; but they definitely stated that the expense and the danger were too great for this commission to cover them. I had therefore no alternative, after lengthy negotiations with them, except either to grant the commission they asked or to adopt the cheaper but somewhat unsafe method of sending the money by the Messageries."

The Messageries were certainly cheaper, but an accident to a single remittance might make this manner of transport exceedingly expensive. Barbier therefore closed with the firms of Rothschild and Gontard, and on January 6, 1816, they dispatched the final letter regarding the transfer of the first amount of 2,200,000 francs to Colmar.

"Allow us," they wrote,[70] "to add the assurance that

we shall apply our united efforts to carrying out this to your complete satisfaction. . . . We could not offer a lower commission because we cannot yet accurately estimate the expenses involved. We shall, however, make it our duty to reduce this commission in the case of future remittances if circumstances permit. We venture to trust that your Excellency will be disposed to let us know when future payments have to be made, in order that we may be able to quote you the cheapest terms."

Accepting responsibility for all risks of carriage, the two firms undertook the transfer of these moneys from Paris to Colmar for a commission of one and a quarter per cent on the payments made. This was not so serious for them as it might appear, since they did not really transfer any money at all, but through their extensive connections acquired the equivalent sum at the place of payment itself. Thus without incurring any risk, they were able to book the high commission as pure profit.

After this system had been in force for some time, the general commanding at Colmar, Baron Frimont, who regarded the commission as excessive, intervened, and attempted to get the money over by military couriers. However, after trying to do this for two months, he admitted himself beaten, and himself requested [71] that these remittances and the issue of officers' pay should again be carried out by the firms of Rothschild and Gontard, "as has already been found to be the most reliable method in connection with military payments at Frankfort."

They did not confine themselves to this business. Soon payments running into millions [72] were carried through by Rothschild and Gontard on account of the French indemnity to Vienna, the most important part of which was entrusted to Eskeles and Geymüller. Nevertheless, the Austrian government continued to give considerable orders to the four Austrian firms; and in their competition with them, Rothschild and Gontard had to make exceptional efforts to be allotted even a small proportion of the

French indemnity to Hamburg. Competition was exceedingly keen.

At last the brothers Rothschild succeeded in winning over Barbier, Austria's financial representative in Paris, whose attitude toward them had hitherto been neutral. As time went on he became an ardent supporter of the Rothschild family and of the Frankfort bankers who were working in conjunction with them. This is revealed by the correspondence which passed between him and Count Stadion, who dealt with the matter in a thoroughly businesslike and impartial manner.

Stadion recognized the conscientious services rendered by the Rothschilds in remitting the subsidies; and Nathan saw that the minister was fully informed from England of the part which they had played. With Napoleon a captive at St. Helena, the period of subsidy payments was completely at an end, so it was no longer necessary to keep this business a strict secret. Nor did Nathan consider it desirable to do so, since their credit and reputation would gain if it were widely known that those enormous sums had been handled by the House of Rothschild.

We must bear in mind that during the period between October, 1811, and October, 1816, no less than £42,500,000 [73] had passed through Herries's hands. Almost half of this had been forwarded to the various continental recipients through the intermediary of Nathan and his brothers. In Herries's memoirs, published by his son, are extracts from a memorandum [74] prepared for competent authorities, which speaks of Rothschild in the highest terms. Of course in praising Rothschild, Herries was indirectly taking credit for himself, since he after all was responsible, and would have had to bear the blame for any mistakes.

Herries wrote that it was possibly solely due to the banking firm of Mr. Rothschild and his brothers that he had been enabled to carry through the exchange operations so successfully. He said that the greatest gratitude was owing to these gentlemen, who had devoted themselves entirely to the public service, and that the reward which they would receive would have been fairly and honorably won.

Herries certainly emphasized [75] the fact that he had always kept Nathan strictly under his control, had never allowed him to take any steps without his express consent, and had had him almost constantly with him in his room; but he also stated in a private letter to the chancellor of the exchequer that he owed it to Mr. Rothschild not to miss this opportunity of bearing witness to the skill and energy with which he had carried out this service, quite unobtrusively and in such a manner that the rate of exchange had not been unfavorably affected. Even if we regard Herries's testimony as biased, there can be no doubt that Nathan rendered magnificent financial services, from which, it is true, he personally reaped substantial profits.

The Austrian finance minister Count Stadion was just about to undertake the task of putting his country's finances thoroughly in order, reducing the amount of paper money in circulation, and as far as possible reducing Austria's public debt. He required a large amount of ready money for these purposes. This he had the prospect of obtaining through the Austrian share of the French indemnity, but as the payments were distributed in instalments over a period of years, and as he required money urgently, he decided that he would try to obtain an advance on the amount due.

He therefore wrote from Milan [76] to Barbier in Paris: "If your Excellency should receive any offers of an advance on the security of the contributions due in the next few years, I am of opinion that they should be considered, for they would assure us the advantage of obtaining a certain sum for the treasury at an early date."

Barbier replied to his minister as follows:

As such an offer could be expected to be made only by a very substantial banking company, I contrived to introduce the subject in the course of conversation with the firm of Rothschild. But it awakened no response. Yet a short time ago young Rothschild stated to me that it might now perhaps be possible to arrange the settlement of the Austrian share of the indemnity for the four last years at one stroke, saying that if I had the necessary authority to undertake such an operation it might be possible to enter into negotiations. I asked him to put his suggestion in writing; but he replied that he was unable to do so until a commissioner had been definitely instructed by Austria to enter into such negotiations.

This is as far as matters have gone at present; and I am led to infer that the proposal is at present merely a tentative suggestion on the part of Rothschild, who would try to find partners for the scheme if our court would express an opinion in favor of it. . . . Rothschild spoke of the enormous discount of forty per cent.

Barbier emphasized the fact that the entrepreneurs were speculating on an enormous profit and that Rothschild was paving the way thereto by mentioning this heavy discount. Barbier estimated the loss involved through such advance payments at "only" about twenty percent. He stated that it would require special considerations to make it desirable to incur a loss exceeding twenty percent.

It is true that the demands put forward by the Rothschilds were extremely high, and the benefit to be derived from such a transaction was positively enormous. But the very offer, implying as it did that the brothers Rothschild and their business friends were in a position immediately to supply cash to the tune of countless millions of francs, shows how strong the financial position of the Rothschilds had now become. There was nobody else in the field in financial transactions on this scale, and the

Rothschilds meant to turn their privileged position to account.

Austria's urgent need of money, and the hope of getting better terms for the advances from the brothers Rothschild inspired Stadion to a clever move. He would put the family, who, handicapped by their origin, were making every effort to improve their social position, under a special obligation. After the conclusion of the subsidy transactions, the Rothschilds had repeatedly appealed to Baron von Handel and to Schwinner at Frankfort to recommend to the emperor recognition of their services; and Schwinner had forwarded this request to Count Stadion, the minister of finance. Stadion gladly availed himself of the opportunity thus offered.

Of the subsidies amounting to approximately £1,800,000 (15,000,000 gulden) [77] which were made available in the year 1815, the four Viennese discount houses first discounted an amount of about 2,750,000 gulden, for which the Austrian government paid a commission of one percent. The money, however, was not forthcoming as speedily as had been hoped, and the Austrian government was compelled to ask the four banking firms for advances on the payments. On these they had to pay interest at the rate of six percent. They were therefore exceedingly pleased when the English government consented to make the moneys payable in large amounts and even to pay several months' instalments in advance through the firm of Rothschild. Thus Austria no longer had to pay any commission, and thereby saved one percent in that respect, as well as saving six percent on any advances.

In the finance minister's report to Emperor Francis the following passage occurred: [78]

> Count Stadion flatters himself that his Majesty will approve of the manner in which this business was carried through. In this connection he feels it to be his duty to recommend that the services of the Frankfort banking firm Meyer Amschel Rothschild

and Sons should be recognized, since the efforts of that firm contributed in a special degree to securing the prompt payment of the English subsidy moneys, and in the present circumstances it may be necessary to have further recourse to the good offices of that firm. . . . The firm has very large resources and enjoys an even larger credit. It can carry through transactions that appear vast to a private person on the Continent, because the British government employs it in the most extensive operations and therefore supports it with the necessary funds.

An examination of the subsidy transactions reveals the fact that the House of Rothschild alone paid out 12,203,822.43 florins with respect to £1,442,000. The report of the former high commissioner, who was in charge of the subsidy payments at Frankfort at the time, shows that Rothschild always paid most punctually, and that on various occasions, such as in changing foreign coin and bills, he showed the greatest desire to help without taking any undue advantage.

After the subsidy transactions had been carried through, the head of the firm expressed a wish that the services which he rendered might be publicly recognized by your Majesty. High Commissioner Schwinner was asked for his opinion as to the form which such recognition should take. He discussed the matter with the director of the Grätz police, Göhausen, who was then at Frankfort. . . . Göhausen suggested that the head of the house should be granted the honorary title of imperial and royal councilor, a like title having been granted for similar reasons to the brothers Kaula, in Hanau and Stuttgart, and to other Israelites. The grant of a title of nobility, on the other hand, would excite the envy of Christian banking firms and would create a particular sensation at the present time, as the rights of citizenship of the Jewish community at Frankfort are the subject of negotiations.

High Commissioner Schwinner does not recommend that the title of I. and R. councilor be granted, as it is customary to confer this distinction upon eminent public servants. He favors the granting of an imperial title of nobility, believing the apprehensions of the director of police to be unfounded. Since then Rothschild has repeatedly asked for some recognition as an encouragement both to himself and to others.

Count Stadion begs to state by way of recapitulation: The services rendered by Rothschild are not of a kind that may be suitably rewarded by conferring an order; but the civilian medal would hardly come up to his expectations. In view of his own wealth, a reward in money or money's worth would be even less appropriate. And such in any case would have to bear some relation to the high dignity of the donor and would therefore have to be very considerable. In the opinion of Count Stadion orders are more suitable as a reward for officials, but as Rothschild has already many officials under his direction, an order is not likely to impress him. Count Stadion therefore requests that as a public mark of your Majesty's satisfaction with the services rendered by the Frankfort firm Meyer Amschel Rothschild and Sons, your Majesty will graciously confer on the two brothers of this firm resident here, the German hereditary title of nobility, free of all dues, and will authorize him, Count Stadion, to convey to the firm in a special letter your Majesty's satisfaction.

This report was sent to Privy Councilor Barton von Lederer. He was the right-hand man of Count Zichy, the secretary of state and lord of the privy seal, and had accompanied the emperor when he fled from Napoleon in 1809. On that occasion he had won his confidence and affection. When the reorganization of Austria was undertaken after the Congress of Vienna, Count Zichy was placed at the head of the central office for dealing with all matters affecting the reorganization; and it became his duty to consider the suggestions that were made from various quarters and to express his opinion upon them.

Although Stadion was so enthusiastic about the services rendered by the Rothschilds, Lederer remained comparatively unmoved. He regarded them simply as a calculating family of money-makers who were only concerned with their own interests, and he accordingly sent in a detailed report in which he argued against granting them a title of nobility. At the beginning of his statement Lederer gave a short synopsis [79] of the movements of the pound sterling before and after the battle of Waterloo, based upon the payments actually made by the Rothschilds.

In the year 1814, it was as follows: the pound sterling was worth on the average	8 fl	11⅛	x
In 1815, before the battle of Waterloo	7 "	42⅗	"
In 1815 after the battle of Waterloo	8 "	50¾	"
Taking the whole year 1815	8 "	23½	"
Taking the two years 1814 and 1815	8 "	21¾	"

Lederer's memorandum continues:

I now pass to the question of rewarding the two brothers Rothschild, raised by the minister of finance in his report. In this connection two questions have to be considered: 1. In this business, have they conferred a benefit on the Austrian Treasury, and wherein does this benefit lie? 2. How can this benefit be suitably recognized?

As to the first, it was not until June, 1815, that the firm of Rothschild was employed as the business agent of the English government, in connection with the realization of the subsidies. It looked after the payments for that government, for which service it no doubt received a liberal commission, its duty being to maintain the rate of exchange between England and the Continent in favor of England and to improve it. The firm of Rothschild never had any right to ask Austria for a commission on the payments which it was effecting on behalf of the English government. In acting wisely in this matter, it deserved the compliments of the English government, whose intentions it was carrying out. The rate of exchange at which funds were transmitted before and after the battle of Waterloo indicates how far its success was due to fortunate circumstances and how far to its efforts. In effecting the payments accurately and punctually, the firm of Rothschild was but doing its duty. Even the fact brought forward by Schwinner, that they made the payments to the governor-general at Frankfort and to his military departments—payments for which the Austrian Treasury was responsible—out of the subsidy moneys, without charging any special commission for these transactions, cannot in my opinion be counted very much to its credit. It was paid a commission on the whole amount by England, and it cannot have been any more trouble to the firm to divide the payments among the various departments than to pay the whole amount into the central treasury at Frankfort. In any case I cannot conceive of a business firm doing business except in its own interest. The business man undertakes transactions in order to make a profit, and he should not pretend to having conferred an obligation where he has not done so.

Count Stadion thinks it desirable to secure the good-will of a firm of such extensive credit with a view to the future. I must confess that I cannot see how this is to be obtained by conferring any distinction whatever on the House of Rothschild. They will carry through transactions for the Austrian financial administration again in the future. If they see the chance of making a profit, they will ask us for business; but if they do not, they will decline to do business for us, even if the chiefs of the firm have been honored by your Majesty.

The balance-sheet is the first and most powerful

factor in determining the business man's attitude. However, since the firm of Rothschild has carried through such considerable financial transactions for the Austrian Treasury, whereby the payment of commission was saved, I consider that it would be proper and consonant with your Majesty's dignity to give both brothers Rothschild a proof of your favor.

In this connection I cannot agree with the suggestion that a hereditary title should be conferred. Such titles should be the reward of service only. In this case there is the special consideration that the brothers Rothschild are Israelites. It is true that there have been cases in which your Majesty has decided to raise Israelites to the ranks of Austrian nobility, e.g., Baron Arnsteiner and Ritter von Eskeles.

On the other hand the claims of the Frankfort Jews to full rights of citizenship are now the subject of discussion, and although I would not venture to express an opinion as to whether honors should be conferred upon Jewish business men when the result of the negotiations in the diet is pending, I suggest that if your Majesty is inclined to act upon Count Stadion's proposal, the views of the minister for foreign affairs should first be ascertained. Personally I consider that the most suitable thing would be that your Majesty should make a gift to each of the two brothers Rothschild of a gold snuff-box bearing your Majesty's monogram in diamonds. Count Stadion might be consulted as to the monetary value of such a gift.

Count Zichy, to whom this memorandum was submitted for his observations, sent it on to the emperor with the comment that he considered Baron von Lederer's argument to be sound but that he could not immediately agree that the proposal should be rejected. He suggested that since Prince Metternich was best informed as to the conditions of the Israelites in Frankfort. and in view of the fact that the firm of Rothschild had really rendered services to the imperial treasury, Prince Metternich should be asked to express an opinion.[80]

Emperor Francis accordingly officially requested Metternich to express his opinion regarding Stadion's proposal, asking whether the existing circumstances of the Jews at Frankfort did not make it politically undesirable to distinguish a Jewish business firm in that way.[81]

The matter was therefore to be decided by Metternich, the man who, as has been stated, was well-disposed to the Frankfort Jews, and who had concurred in Stadion's making the proposal. Metternich reported verbally to Emperor Francis in favor of ennobling the Rothschild family.

Mindful of the important financial and political considerations on which Stadion's proposal was based, and which were further emphasized by Metternich, the emperor agreed, although he felt that the minor nobility would view the ennoblement of foreign Jews with very mixed feelings. The patent conferring the title of nobility on Amschel and Solomon, in recognition of their services in realizing the English subsidies, was issued from Schönbrunn on September 25, 1816.[82]

Meanwhile, it had been pointed out to Stadion that the two other brothers, Carl and James, whose services were also required for the operations that were being planned, might feel slighted, and a few days later Stadion recommended that these two brothers should also be ennobled. Emperor Francis issued an order in council to this effect, dated October 21, 1816.[83]

No sooner had the document been signed than Ugarte had the fact recorded in the official Vienna papers. Stadion expressly thanked the chancellor for doing so, a fact indicating the importance which he attached to the whole matter. At the same time he informed Ugarte that he had asked both the brothers Rothschild to submit a de-

Original Sketch for Coat of Arms Submitted by the Rothschild Family in 1817

Coat of Arms Adopted by the Rothschild Family in 1817

sign for a coat-of-arms, and to state whether they wished to adopt a prefix of nobility.[84]

Stadion had informed Ugarte of the reasons for conferring a title of nobility, as set out in his report to the emperor, and added: "I do not consider, however, that the patent should enter into any details as to the services rendered, but that there should be merely a general statement to the effect that since the two brothers Meyer Amschel [*sic*] Rothschild and Solomon Meyer Rothschild have carried through a loan most meticulously and punctually—the English subsidy transactions during the year 1815—and have also shown an exceptional readiness to render services outside their actual duties, his Majesty has been most graciously moved, etc., etc."

In accordance with Stadion's request, the brothers Rothschild submitted a design for a coat-of-arms. This was enclosed with a letter written by Solomon Rothschild's own hand,[85] explaining the design, and reading as follows: "First quarter, or, an eagle sable surcharged in dexter by a field gules (having reference to the Imperial and Royal Austrian Coat-of-Arms); second quarter, gules, a leopard passant proper (a reference to the English Royal Coat-of-Arms); third quarter, a lion rampant (with reference to the Hessian Electoral Coat); fourth quarter, azure, an arm bearing five arrows (a symbol of the unity of the five brothers).

"In the center of the coat a shield gules. Right-hand supporter, a greyhound, a symbol of loyalty; left supporter, a stork, a symbol of piety and content. The crest is a coronet surmounted by the Lion of Hesse."

In submitting the design the Rothschilds asked that a separate patent of nobility should be prepared for each of the four brothers, as they lived in different countries. The design was duly sent to the Heralds' College (there was such an institution in Austria at the time) with a request for their observations. The college replied that they saw no objections to preparing four patents, but that it was "necessary to proceed with the greatest caution, particularly in the case of members of the Jewish nation for various reasons, and more especially because they are not familiar with the prerogatives of nobility." They added that although the usual fees were being remitted, they considered that the Rothschilds should pay 150 gulden for the special grant and that they could hardly resent this charge in view of the great distinction that was being conferred upon them.

"As for the coat-of-arms," the report continued,[86] "they ask for a coronet, a center shield, supporters, the Leopard of England, and the Lion of Hesse. According to the rules of heraldry, the gentry are entitled only to a helmet; their suggestion is entirely inadmissible since otherwise there would be nothing to distinguish the higher ranks, as coronets, supporters and center shields are proper only to the nobility. Moreover, no government will grant the emblems of other governments, as nobility is conferred for services to one's prince and one's country, but not for services to other countries. The lion is a symbol of courage only, which does not apply to the petitioners."

A design such as the Heralds' College considered suitable was attached to the report. The seven-pointed coronet, to which the petitioners were not entitled, and which was no doubt intended to express their wish for the title of Baron, had disappeared, together with the heraldic animals supporting the shield, and the lions of Hesse and England. Only the half-eagle and the arm with the arrows remained; but the hand was grasping, not five but four arrows, this being in accordance with the curious fact that Nathan, the brother who behind the scenes had had most to do with the English subsidies, was not yet recognized in any way.

The recommendations of the Heralds' College were accepted in every detail, and the design submitted by them duly became for some years the coat-of-arms of the Rothschild family, as laid down in the patent dated March 25, 1817. Although the ennoblement only carried a modest "von," the new rank was of no little importance. We must remember that at that period the higher nobility were dominant in almost all the states of Europe. They occupied all the highest positions in the state and were in a most favored position financially as compared with other citizens. For a Jewish family who had to fight hard for their position in their native city, the Rothschilds' imperial patent was a particularly rare distinction, and involved an important step forward in their fight for social recognition. As soon as the nobility had recovered somewhat from their annoyance, it became much easier for the brothers Rothschild to make their way socially.

The event was naturally very helpful to the relations of the House of Rothschild with Austrian statesmen. They did not take over the business of paying the whole of the huge French indemnity in advance instalments, but partial payments were made through them. They also transferred the moneys to Colmar as well as larger amounts sent to Mainz for the purpose of building fortresses.

Austria was owed three hundred thousand Dutch ducats by Russia for advances made to Russian troops during the Napoleonic wars and accordingly drew bills on the Frankfort firm of Rothschild, which were due in December, 1817, and January, 1818. In reply to Barbier's inquiry, James Rothschild wrote a considerate letter [87] saying that he could not accept the bills because the order from the Russian finance minister had not yet been received.

"If, however," he wrote, "it is your Excellency's wish that these bills be accepted by me . . . I am gladly prepared to do so if your Excellency will be so kind as to give me an assurance that the bills in question are in order and that I will receive the report of the Imperial Russian Ministry of Finance."

The brothers Rothschild further offered,[88] in conjunction with Gontard, to provide three hundred thousand ducats, at five percent interest and one percent commission, a few months before the due date. "We flatter ourselves," they stated, "that your Excellency will appreciate the reasonableness of our proposals, and we venture to assure your Excellency that our principal desire has been to give further proof to the I. and R. Court of our constant zeal in their interests. Moreover, we are prepared to modify our proposals if an alteration in the rate of exchange in your favor should make this possible at the time when your Excellency has occasion to accept them."

Barbier supported the Rothschild proposal, attacking the four Vienna firms and observing that in his opinion the Rothschilds worked better and more cheaply.[89] But plans had now been changed at Vienna, where the bills were wanted to be paid only when they fell due, and inquiries had been made of the four Vienna firms as well as of Rothschild and Gontard regarding the simple transmission of the ducats to Vienna.[90]

The brothers Rothschild named their conditions and went on to say: [91] "If the treasury should later desire to receive in advance the above-mentioned amount of three hundred thousand ducats, we shall always be ready . . . to provide it. If, however, we should make such an advance your Excellency will find it not unreasonable to grant us a commission of one percent in addition to the interest rate of five percent per annum. We flatter ourselves that your Excellency will regard our various proposals as just, and venture to believe that we have made every possible effort in our power to furnish further proofs of how greatly we desire to continue to be honored with the treasury's confidence."

The letters show how cleverly the Rothschilds contrived to clothe their proposals in polite phrases and how they were always concerned to present their case as if their one desire was to make themselves useful, while the other party would derive all the profit and advantage.

While endeavoring to secure the custom of Austria, the brothers did not neglect the other states. Similar advances on account of the French contribution appear to have been suggested to Prussia and Russia, and in February, 1817, a loan of several millions was made to Prussia in the name of Rothschild. The Elector of Hesse, it is true, had a large share in this.[92] The brothers Rothschild still carried out really big transactions in conjunction with their patron or with other firms, but the time was soon to come when the five brothers would act alone, and one great firm after another would fall before them.

They were now again concerned to secure their position in Frankfort. The Jewish community had sent a request for assistance to Baron von Humboldt, the Prussian minister who was at that time acting on the diet; and Rothschild had appealed to the young German legal luminary and statesman Sylvester Jordan to use his influence with Count Buol at Frankfort, who had known Jordan since his earliest youth.

"The banker Rothschild," [93] Jordan accordingly wrote to Buol, "one of the richest bankers in Europe, who has nothing to worry about except that he is a Jew, has most emphatically implored me to commend to your Excellency the interests of the Jews in general and of his House in particular. Hardenberg has already sent instructions in this matter to Humboldt. The senate of Frankfort is determined to confine them to the Jewish quarter, which is naturally distasteful to a banker who is worth millions."

In the middle of December, 1816, a printed memorandum with no less than thirteen enclosures, regarding the

Jewish rights of citizenship, was sent to the diet, amongst the signatories being Amschel and Jonas Rothschild, as well as Jacob Baruch and old Bernes.

Meanwhile the brothers Rothschild were working assiduously abroad to extend their influence within the countries where they were living. In Austria their persistence had met with the greatest measure of success, and accordingly they redoubled their efforts in that country to secure new honors and titles. It did not take them long to realize that friendly social relations were of the greatest use to them in their business in each country; but it was just in this matter that they often met with great difficulties in London and Paris.

It was exceedingly hard for poorly educated German emigrant Jews to get into the higher social circles, even though they were rich. James had so far been most successful; at the excellent dinners which he gave he was already entertaining diplomats such as the Austrian ambassador Baron Vincent, and once even a prince of the blood royal, Paul von Wurttemberg. But he also met with numerous rebuffs.

Nathan and James hit upon the idea of asking Austria to grant them the dignity and office of honorary consul. On receiving such a nomination they would more or less belong to the diplomatic corps, whereupon many doors hitherto closed must necessarily be open to them as persons of official standing. Moreover, the title of consul of a great European power such as Austria was at that time, would be bound to raise their prestige and their credit in the business world. They wrote to Amschel at Frankfort asking him to obtain the title for them in Vienna; and he immediately wrote to Metternich: [94]

MOST EXCELLENT PRINCE, MOST GRACIOUS PRINCE AND LORD!

We have had the good fortune on various occasions to experience the proofs of your Highness's

> most gracious good-will, and we are therefore emboldened most respectfully to make the following proposal. Our brothers, the chiefs of the branches in Paris and London respectively, Jacob M. von Rothschild and Nathan M. Rothschild, honored through the distinction recently received by our family and their gracious elevation into the ranks of the nobility, are inspired by the most zealous desire to be able to devote their energies to the service of the I. and R. Austrian Government. They would feel they had found a means of satisfying these natural desires if one of them were nominated I. and R. Austrian Consul, a position which is at present vacant both in Paris and in London.
>
> This position depends upon the nomination of your Princely Highness, and we therefore most submissively venture to request that your Highness may be pleased to accede to our humble wish. The I. and R. Government can find no more loyal, zealous, and indefatigable servants than our brothers; and we flatter ourselves that the connections which we have established with the governments of France and England would make it easy for us, both in a general way and in individual cases, to be useful to the I. and R. trade with those countries. We should be happy to be placed in a position to do so in this honorable manner, and to receive this further distinction.

Amschel wrote to Stadion at the same time [95] stating that it was not the desire for further honors that caused him to ask that his brothers should be nominated as consuls, but his sincere desire to prove himself of ever-increasing usefulness to the I. and R. Austrian Government. He was certain that the relations which both brothers had established with the governments of the countries where they were living would aid them in being of use to the I. and R. Austrian subjects, especially in commercial matters, and that the granting of their submissive request would enable his whole House to apply all their energies in the most varied ways to the service of Austria's commerce.

Carl Rothschild also appealed to Count Zichy,[96] whom he knew through business dealings, informing him that the Austrian ambassador in London, Prince Esterházy, had written to Metternich in support of Nathan's nomination and requested the same favor of him. Zichy forwarded Rothschild's letter to Metternich, with the remark [97] that although the matter did not come within his province he ventured to observe that this firm already appeared to have rendered important services to the Austrian treasury, and would through its riches and influence, especially in England, be able also in the future to give pecuniary aid to Austria.

It was to be a long time before these requests were granted. The Austrian state machine worked slowly, and several objections and difficulties cropped up, which could be overcome only by years of work. It was only through their close association with Metternich and Gentz, whom the brothers Rothschild cultivated in the ensuing period of congresses, that they were enabled to smooth the way, so that three years later there was no further obstacle to the desired nomination. Before they could achieve their object, however, they had a long row to hoe.

But the brothers Rothschild worked assiduously toward any goal which they had set themselves to achieve, notwithstanding all the difficulties that arose and the years during which their patience was tried. In the end they got what they wanted. Their unremitting efforts and their persistence in urging their cause, undismayed by any rebuffs, secured for them the unique career that had been destined for their family.

CHAPTER IV

The Brothers Rothschild During the Period of Congresses, 1818-1822

THE great fortune of the Rothschilds had been made; it was now a question not only of preserving it but of developing it and of employing it as remuneratively as possible. The convulsions through which all the states of Europe had passed, and the enormous military efforts made during the preceding quarter of a century, had produced general confusion in their finances, which could be straightened out only by hard work in peace conditions.

Every state had been spending money lavishly for a long time, and the resulting shortage of money was very acute. The poverty-struck states had to acquire the cash necessary for their recovery from those who had succeeded in profiting by war conditions to accumulate riches as contractors or through financial operations. Foremost among these was the House of Rothschild, and it gladly lent money to princes and states, as the repayment of such loans through their subjects was secured. Thus it advanced moneys to numerous small princely families, especially to those of the neighborhood, while its relations with the Elector of Hesse remained outwardly unchanged.

Although he was the third son, Nathan incontestably took the leadership among the five brothers. His long and fortunate connection with the English government had taught him both the advantage of concentrating on really big financial operations, and the comparative safety of carrying through such operations with powerful states. For the concern of these for their public credit and their prestige made them regard it as essential to carry out their obligations punctually. Nathan was not in the least inclined to rest upon his laurels, or to limit himself to the preservation and enjoyment of the family's great fortune. His aim was to increase the power of his House; and he held the view that in order to win a victory, ducats, like soldiers, had to be concentrated in mass suddenly and unexpectedly upon a wisely selected point.[1] This was the dominant note in the policy of his House during the following period.

In order to apply this policy it was necessary, now that his firm enjoyed the high regard of the business community, that he should secure his position in society as well. The Austrian patent of nobility had given him a good start in this direction; but his native city and the senate of Frankfort continued to adopt an unfriendly attitude toward the Jews, including the Rothschild family. Amschel at Frankfort, who had been placed in charge of the campaign against the senate, used every opportunity for exerting external pressure upon the authorities of the city, especially through Prussia and Austria. At the beginning of the year 1818 a favorable opportunity occurred for again enlisting the support of the Prussian Chancellor Prince Hardenberg, who was well disposed toward the Jews.

The state finances of Prussia were, like those of Austria, in great confusion. The deficit was large, and it seemed not improbable that the pay of civil servants and of the army would have to be suspended. The treasury lived from hand to mouth, and the king himself was being dunned by small tradesmen. In these circumstances, Barandon, the London representative of the Prussian Mercantile Marine, had recommended that a loan should be raised in England, and that for this purpose recourse should be had to Nathan Rothschild. Hardenberg readily agreed, and asked Amschel at Frankfort, whom he knew personally, to use his influence in favor of securing this loan. Amschel consented, and used this opportunity of again appealing to the chancellor on behalf of the members of his faith at Frankfort.

"At the present time," he wrote,[2] "when his Excellency the Minister and Envoy to the Diet, Count von Buol, is with your Excellency, I beg to renew my most humble representations regarding the fate of the members of my faith here, who are awaiting in great suspense the decision of the diet. We place our greatest hopes in the honored Prussian government, and cherish the most sincere wish that the principles recognized by it will be applied, convinced that your Highness knows too well how to appreciate the cultural progress made by our community during the last forty years to allow the way to their further development and improvement to be barred, or them to be limited in this respect."

Hardenberg was quite willing to accede to this request, since in doing so he would be acting in accordance with his own personal convictions. He had, however, a difficult task with his king, who was not well disposed to the Jews. The monarch told him the measures he could apply if action were taken by the magistracy of Frankfort, but at the same time expressed the desire that the wishes of the magistracy should be met as far as possible. "In any case," the resolution concluded, "I do not wish Prussia to support the Jews in the diet."[3]

On this Hardenberg angrily commented: "First *ad acta*. We have at any rate the decisions of the Congress of Vienna to go upon."[4]

However, the king came off his high horse, for Hardenberg had made him realize that the Prussian state would need the brothers Rothschild for a loan, and that it would not be good policy for Prussia to alienate them by an attitude unfriendly to the Jews in the Diet of Frankfort. The majority of the diet were in any case in sympathy with the desires of the senate at Frankfort, and the rights which the Jews had acquired in 1811 seemed therefore to be in peril. Only the powerful influence of Metternich and Hardenberg had so far restrained it from taking a definite decision hostile to the Jews.

Amschel regarded the head of the House of Bethmann, which was being more and more overshadowed by the Rothschilds, as a natural enemy of the Jews; but Bethmann refused to admit that this was so. "If Herr James," he wrote at the time to David Parish, "will but visit me at Frankfort, he will soon realize that I am not influenced by any nonsense about Christians and that I have no prejudice against a reputable Jew. I have often attempted in vain to disabuse Amschel of the stupid illusion that I am opposed to the demands of the Jewish community at Frankfort in so far as they are reasonable. The fact that I am suspected by my fellow Christians of taking the Jewish side should convince him, if nothing else will, that he has no ground for his attitude." [5]

Amschel Meyer certainly was greatly interested in keeping on good terms with Prussia and Austria. Prussia's acute financial distress seemed to provide a further excellent opportunity of earning a large amount of money, and he did all he could, in close collaboration with his brother Nathan in London, to induce Prussia to come to the Rothschilds for refuge.

That kingdom had very good reason to look around for money, for in 1817 the state was carrying a burden of twenty millions of floating debt, interest being charged on part of this amount at the extravagant rate of twenty percent per annum, the payments being met by further borrowings each year.[6] Apart from this, the annual budget showed a deficit of several million thalers. Prince Hardenberg, by the king's command, accordingly instructed the Director of the Prussian Treasury to negotiate a loan. The director, Christian von Rother, was a highly competent official and Hardenberg's right-hand man in financial matters, and he had come into special prominence in raising money during the wars of liberation.

"It is essential," wrote the prince to Rother,[7] "that we should obtain money for various purposes. *The maintenance of the state urgently calls for it.* I am eagerly waiting to hear from you. Act with decision and courage."

Rother first tried Berlin firms, but they attempted to exploit the difficulties of the situation, and, as he reported to the king, the conditions which they proposed were "exorbitant and humiliating." In Holland he had no success either; but he fared better at Frankfort. As Prussian commissioner of finance he had already come into contact with the House of Rothschild in Paris, and he now succeeded in getting on exceedingly good terms with Amschel Meyer.

Amschel referred him to his brother Nathan in London, as the most likely person to make the loan a success. Hitherto, Barandon had conducted the negotiations in England, but he was not liked by the House of Rothschild. Rother, on the other hand, the brothers had known in Paris, and they regarded him as a more pleasant person to deal with. Indeed they preferred him in every way, and were exceedingly gratified when he came to London and Barandon was left out in the cold.

They were now dealing only with two friends of their House, Rother and the Prussian ambassador in London, William von Humboldt, the brother of the great explorer Alexander. He himself was not only a diplomat, but also a distinguished scholar and philosopher. Humboldt understood little of money matters, and he left his private estate to be managed by Rothschild, whereas Rother was regarded as a financial genius in his own country. Humboldt was certainly a complete believer in Nathan Rothschild's indisputably superior talent for finance. He reported in this sense to Berlin, using words which are especially remarkable coming from such a man.

"If the loan is to succeed here," his report ran, "this can be managed in my opinion only through Rothschild.

. . . Rothschild is now easily the most enterprising business man in this country. . . . He is a man upon whom one can rely, and with whom the government here does considerable business. He is also, as far as I know, just, exceedingly honest, and intelligent. But I must add that if business is given to him to carry out, it will be necessary to fall in with his ideas. For he has acquired the independent habit of mind developed by riches and a fairly long sojourn in this country, and he is now engaged in such a constant number of financial transactions that it will not greatly affect him if one of them fails to come his way. He wants to take over the whole loan himself; on this point he is likely to be exceedingly firm, and he has asked in advance that the Prussian consul here, against whom he is prejudiced, shall not be allowed to interfere in the matter in any way." [8]

Humboldt's report is all the more valuable as an expression of opinion, since he proved his independence in concluding it by advising against the acceptance of the loan, this being of course quite contrary to Nathan's wishes. Rother, on the other hand, speedily came to terms with Nathan regarding a loan of five million pounds. This he considered advantageous for Prussia, as other important states were able to obtain money by loan only in small amounts.[9] In spite of the ups and downs of the negotiations, exceedingly cordial relations seem to have been maintained throughout between Rother and Rothschild. At any rate this is indicated by their correspondence at this time. Rother wrote to Solomon Rothschild,[10] who was also in London at the time, that he had been glad to make the closer acquaintance of his brother Nathan, whose character and intelligence he felt compelled the greatest admiration.

Solomon's reply was full of friendliness and candor. His letter was, he indicated, an expression of his sincerest feelings, and Nathan and Solomon assured Rother, when he left, that he could travel with a light heart.

He had achieved "a splendid piece of business, and they were his devoted, loyal, and eternal friends." [10]

This way of getting into the good graces of the Prussian negotiator did not fail of its effect. Rother was delighted that he had carried the business through and that on the day on which the agreement was concluded Nathan sent a ship to Hamburg with a million thalers as a payment on account.

Rother had, if possible, been even more strongly impressed than William von Humboldt by Nathan's influence. "The Rothschild in this country," he reported to Berlin,[10] "is a most estimable person and has an incredible influence upon all financial affairs here in London. It is widely stated, and is indeed almost a fact that he entirely regulates the rate of exchange in the city. His power as a banker is enormous."

The loan, which was issued at an average price of 72 per cent, turned out to be "a splendid piece of business" for Rothschild, as it never fell below the price of issue, and in 1824 actually reached par. The House of Rothschild therefore had every occasion to be pleased with this, the first big state loan which they handled, and they were encouraged to develop this line of business on a large scale. This loan was the first of several.

The brothers had formed valuable friendships through these negotiations, and William von Humboldt introduced them to his famous brother Alexander. It was not long before he was seen dining at Rothschild's house in London. Nathan was more frequently the guest of William von Humboldt, whose wide education and extensive knowledge certainly provided a contrast to the Frankforter who had risen so rapidly. Humboldt expressed himself candidly about him in a letter to his wife.

"Yesterday," the letter runs, "Rothschild dined with me. He is quite crude and uneducated, but he has a great deal of intelligence and a positive genius for money. He scored off Major Martins beautifully once or twice.

Martins was dining with me, too, and kept on praising everything French. He was being fatuously sentimental about the horrors of the war and the large numbers who had been killed. 'Well,' said Rothschild, 'if they had not all died, major, you would presumably still be a subaltern.' You ought to have seen Martins's face."

The Rothschilds were anxious to maintain their friendly relations with the Humboldt brothers. Solomon also did his best to be agreeable to them whenever possible. Meeting Caroline von Humboldt at Carlsbad on one occasion, he overwhelmed her with attentions. She wrote to her husband: "I have had several callers, and among others Herr von Rothschild, the brother of the one who is looking after your affairs at Frankfort. He made some exceedingly comic remarks to me. He thanked me, in the course of his conversation, for receiving him, and said, 'Your Excellency ought to come to Frankfort again. We could do with a lady like you there.' It sounded extraordinarily funny. He also asked me whether he could be of use to me in the matter of money and said that his purse was at my disposal." [11]

The Prussian loan, which the brothers Humboldt arranged with the Rothschilds, furnished another excellent illustration of the way in which the three brothers worked together.

While Solomon and Nathan were dealing with that business in London, Amschel Meyer was meeting an awkward situation at Frankfort. In the case of propositions which the firm did not like, they could excuse themselves by pointing out the difficulty of obtaining the agreement of *all* the brothers—that is, of five persons who usually were widely separated from one another—this agreement being necessary for any substantial transaction.

These tactics were adopted in a matter involving the Crown Prince of Hesse, who was constantly at loggerheads with his father. The elector was now seventy-five years old, and failing. In contrast to his parsimonious father, the crown prince had made himself popular by a manner of life from which many persons profited. This involved very heavy expenditure, and the heir's need of money was all the greater since the appanage allotted to him by his father was—according to his ideas at any rate—ludicrously inadequate. The consequence was that the prince found his way to the firm which owed its rise and prosperity to his father. He applied to Rothschild for a loan.

Naturally, this was done quite in secret, without the knowledge or consent of the elector. At the beginning of 1818 the prince requested a loan of 200,000 reichsthalers, which the House of Rothschild granted; but before six months had expired he asked for a further advance of 300,000 reichsthalers. On this occasion he remarked that the House of Rothschild had the fullest information regarding the elector's affairs, and could therefore easily provide for the subsequent repayment of the loan.

Carl Rothschild happened to be in Cassel at the time. The prince immediately summoned him, and informed him that he had again applied to his firm for money, making the same remark to him as he had made to the firm. Carl Rothschild left the audience chamber in reflective mood. He thought it exceedingly strange that the prince should already have incurred further debts, and he was somewhat annoyed at the remark which he had made in asking for the loan. There was a risk that the old elector might come to hear of his son's borrowings, and they would arouse his indignation not only with his son but also with the firm of Rothschild. Carl Rothschild met a chamberlain in the anteroom, and made some remark which may have sounded ill-tempered about the request for a further loan.

After returning to Frankfort Carl took counsel with Amschel, who was there alone; the result was embodied in the following letter:[12]

MOST EXCELLENT PRINCE!

We have the honor to acknowledge your Highness's most gracious letter of 28th ultimo. We must confess that having but recently handed to your Highness the considerable loan of 200,000 reichsthalers, we did not expect to be asked for a still greater amount. Your Highness will be graciously aware that we can act only in agreement with our absent brothers, and we shall therefore not fail to communicate to them your Highness's letter, asking them for their views. In the meantime we would most submissively beg for a gracious explanation of the following passage in your Highness's letter, in which your Highness is pleased to state: "You have the best possible knowledge of the elector's business here, and it is therefore particularly easy for you to reimburse yourselves through discounting bills."

Our knowledge of the elector's affairs extends only to such business as we are entrusted to carry out. It is impossible for us to retain a single farthing and to apply it in the interest of your Highness, for we furnish the fullest accounts of the smallest transaction and send them to Cassel.

This letter was to fulfil a double object: it would stave off the prince for the time being, and it would also be a protection against any reproaches from the elector if the matter leaked out.

The letter displeased the prince exceedingly; he perceived the rebuke and would have liked to reply indignantly. But he restrained his feelings as he still hoped to get money from the Rothschilds. However, he felt that in these circumstances it was difficult for him to carry on the negotiations personally. He accordingly selected Buderus as a go-between, requesting him to keep the matter strictly secret from the elector.

"Having learned of the chance arrival of Baron Carl von Rothschild," the prince wrote to Buderus,[13] anticipating the future title of the family, "I felt that I should inform him of the application I had made to his firm, and did so most politely. He, however, replied in a most unfriendly way, and permitted himself to make remarks behind my back which are not consonant with my honor." The young prince stated that nevertheless he still had confidence in the firm, and begged Buderus to use his influence to help him out of the awkward situation. He suggested that the Rothschilds' letter must be based upon a misapprehension. "I for my part," he continued, "could of course never have thought of such a thing, my intention being to indicate to him that he would be fully secured as he would have me more or less in his hands."

Buderus hastened to carry out the wishes of the heir to the throne, his future master. He went to Frankfort and remonstrated with Carl Rothschild for making the remark to which the elector's heir had taken exception. Carl Rothschild protested that he had made no remark regarding the further loan to anyone excepting Holzförster, the gentleman in waiting, who was kept fully informed of the financial affairs of the heir. Buderus reported to the young prince: [14] "I have succeeded in persuading *Finanzrat* Carl, who was the only one of the brothers at Frankfort, temporarily to advance a few thousand friedrichdors. *Finanzrat* Solomon of London has gone to a spa, and *Finanzrat* Amschel is also traveling. It will require a month to obtain the replies of the absent brothers."

However, the heir to the throne was persistent. He immediately informed Buderus that he was not going to be fobbed off with a few thousand friedrichdors, and added a remark which savored strongly of a threat.

"I know," [15] he wrote, "that these gentlemen will be entirely guided by what you say, and my gratitude in future to Privy Councilor von Carlshausen will be commensurate with his readiness to do me a service now." The letter went on to make proposals as to how the 300,000 reichsthalers might in spite of everything be obtained from Rothschild.

The faithful Buderus felt very bitter about this ungracious reply. He could not force the banking firm to hand out money at the point of the bayonet. "I most humbly assure your Highness," [16] he replied, "that the will to carry out your desires is not lacking, and that I would spare myself no labor or sacrifice to that end, for I find my greatest satisfaction in the success of my endeavors. Nevertheless, with the best will in the world I am unable to dispose of another person's property, or to dictate to him how he should deal with it."

Buderus reported that he had immediately sent a further pressing request to the firm of Rothschild, and had received the following communication from Carl: [17] "I am anxious to accede to his Highness's request, and assure you that if it depended on me alone there would be no obstacle to its being immediately granted. However, in the present instance consultation with all my brothers, who are now away, is particularly necessary. Our funds have been to an extent tied up in the recent negotiations for considerable loans, and I am unable to my infinite regret . . . immediately to come to a decision. Nevertheless, your Excellency may be assured that we shall make every possible effort to satisfy his Highness's requirements."

Meanwhile Solomon had returned to Frankfort, and it was decided after all to advance the prince the money he wanted on very special security. By a deed dated October 15, 1818, he mortgaged not only "all his real and personal property to the exclusion of nothing whatsoever," but also any property of which he might become possessed in the future in any way whatever.[17]

Three months had scarcely elapsed when the prince was again in need of money. He himself felt that Carlshausen would think it strange that he should already want another 100,000 gulden; and he first tried to see whether he could "acquire" the money from his father's friend, a lady whose politeness led him to expect that she would not refuse his request.[18] The Countess von Hessenstein evaded the question of a loan in her reply.

The young prince would have gladly paid the firm of Rothschild ten percent interest if only he could have got the money. Von Carlshausen was instructed by the Rothschilds to inform him that the firm never accepted interest at ten percent as this would be a usurious rate. Thereupon the prince wrote as follows to his father's loyal servant:

"I am well aware that the House of Rothschild can loan no capital sums in cash at five percent without loss, and at the same time that the prestige of the firm is too great to allow them to take a higher rate of interest—a fact which is entirely to their credit, although in these times no objection could be made to the higher rate. I am therefore confident that your Excellency will, with your usual kindness, use your good offices with the House of Rothschild to persuade them to grant me a further loan of four hundred thousand thalers." [19]

This request moved the firm of Rothschild to indignation. "Your letter," they wrote to Carlshausen, "arrived at the same time with the letter embodying the resolve of our brother at Berlin, in accordance with which it is plainly impossible for us to provide a sum exceeding the five hundred thousand reichsthalers in cash already advanced, especially in view of the fact that we have had to make the most exhaustive efforts to provide that sum." [20]

The use of the word "resolve" in this letter calls for special comment, this word usually being reserved for the decisions of sovereign rulers; also, it was apparently not so "plainly" impossible to advance the money, for on April 1, 1819, this third loan was also granted and the prince received the money he wanted.

Scarcely two years later the elector died; his son succeeded to the government and to his father's great possessions, and the Rothschilds had their money repaid in full with all interest due.

A far-reaching political development now diverted the firm's attention from such minor loan transactions, concentrating it exclusively upon the higher politics of Europe. The victorious powers had decided to meet in a congress at Aix-la-Chapelle, there to establish new relations with the France of the Restoration, as well as to discuss the question whether the armies of occupation should be withdrawn, and alleviation granted for the indemnities to be paid. England and the eastern powers were still suspicious of France; and the interest aroused by this congress was so great that the monarchs of the Holy Alliance attended it in person, while England was represented by the two foremost men of the day, Lord Castlereagh and Wellington.

Metternich meant to use this opportunity to secure the support of the tsar and the King of Prussia for his schemes by playing on their fears of revolution and general upheaval. Besides the numerous statesmen, the most prominent bankers and merchants of Europe flocked to Aix-la-Chapelle, scenting prey. Most of them traveled through Frankfort and availed themselves of the opportunity of getting into touch with the financial wire-pullers in the commercial center of Germany. Metternich too had come to Frankfort on September 3, 1818, accompanied by Gentz.

Gentz was his secretary and adviser in money matters; but he was interested not only in his country's but also in his own personal advantage. With rare candor he notes in his diary that in 1815 he received a purse with three hundred ducats and one with eight hundred ducats from Russia, and that Prussia had given him—an Austrian civil servant—eight hundred ducats and two hundred gold napoleons as a gratuity.[21] He was also quite open about the fact that the Jewish banker Lämel

Frederick von Gentz
From a portrait by I. Lieder in the Vienna National Library

had given him money and that Parish had given him a share of the Austrian loan of May, 1818. Gentz called such transactions "pleasant financial dealings."[22] His way of referring to them is so candid that one gets the impression that the circumstances of those times prevented his being in the least conscious of anything improper in such gifts.

Prince Metternich came into contact with all the local magnates at Frankfort, including Bethmann. He seems not yet to have met Rothschild personally at this time, but this defect was more than made good by his right-hand man Frederick von Gentz. The brothers Rothschild were well aware of the great influence that Gentz exerted upon Metternich in matters concerning the state finances, and through him upon the minister of finance, Count Stadion. They knew also that Gentz was bribable, whereas they naturally did not venture to approach Metternich in such a way.

Amschel Meyer and Carl Rothschild therefore called on Gentz immediately after his arrival. This visit resulted in verbal agreements of a financial nature; and they also requested him to use his influence with the prince toward securing his support in the question of the Frankfort Jews; for at that time the senate[23] was attempting to dispute the competence of the diet to deal with the Jewish problem, arguing that it was a purely local matter. The pressure brought to bear by the Rothschilds upon Gentz, and through him upon Metternich, resulted in the senate's objection being disallowed, and a commission of the diet being appointed to mediate between the two parties.

This decision, taken on September 10, 1818, moved the brothers to call on Gentz again on September 12, and to "engage his interest" by a further detailed exposition of the whole matter. Gentz suggested that Hardenberg should have his attention called to the subject again as he would meet Metternich at Aix-la-Chapelle and would be able to discuss it with him. The brothers needed no pressing to do this, and wrote to Hardenberg in the following terms:

"Your Highness's gracious sentiments toward us, as well as your well-known tolerance in matters of religious opinion, gives us reason to hope that you will graciously grant this letter your favorable consideration. The question at issue is the final decision in the matter of our position as citizens. This is a most important question for us now, since the welfare of those who confess our faith depends upon it, and is constantly occupying our thoughts. We are exceedingly anxious not to let pass the opportunity of the meeting between your Highness and his Highness the Prince von Metternich to ask that he should come to a final favorable decision regarding our destiny, and we await his decision in confidence. In venturing to appeal as strongly as possible to your Highness we hope that it may be vouchsafed to us to look with confidence to the future." [24]

During the sixteen days which Gentz spent at Frankfort the brothers Rothschild very frequently came to see him; he was invited to dine with the Rothschilds at five o'clock on September 22, Frau Herz and General Volzoven being among those present at the dinner. Amschel made no slight effort to have distinguished people at his table; but, as Johann Smidt, Mayor of Bremen, stated,[25] it was not in accordance with contemporary customs and manners to admit a Jew to so-called good society. No Christian banker or merchant of Frankfort had yet invited a Jew, not even one of the Rothschild brothers, to dine, and the delegates to the diet did not do so either. However, several people were beginning to depart from this tradition, and accepted invitations from the Rothschilds, either from an absence of prejudice, or from motives of personal interest.

Gentz arrived at Aix-la-Chapelle September 25, a few days after Metternich. A brilliant society had met in that city for the congress. Besides monarchs and statesmen, it included financial magnates such as Baring and Hope, who were negotiating the French loans in connection with the payment of the war indemnity. The firm of Rothschild had sent two brothers to Aix-la-Chapelle, Solomon and Carl. The latter was accompanied by his bride, the beautiful and intelligent Adelheid Herz, whom he had married on September 16, so that his business journey to the congress coincided with his honeymoon. In the case of the House of Rothschild even the most important personal considerations had to yield to important business, and to such a unique opportunity for forming extensive new connections.

Through Gentz, Metternich was brought into actual touch with the two brothers at Aix-la-Chapelle. Gentz fell completely under their influence, and his diary constantly records their visits. On October 27 Solomon handed him eight hundred ducats, which he stated he had won by speculating for him in British funds.[26]

On November 2, Gentz again records [27] "pleasant financial dealings" with Solomon, and on November 12 the brothers, together with Gentz and Parish, lunched with Metternich. In spite of his heavy work in keeping the minutes of the congress, Gentz spent the whole of the next day working on a memorandum stating the case for the Jews of Frankfort, no doubt in return for financial considerations. He called upon Carl's young wife, who was highly flattered to be waited upon by the secretary and confidant of the man who was playing the leading rôle in the illustrious assembly. At the Rothschilds' request, Gentz supported Dr. Buchholz, whom the Jews had sent to Aix-la-Chapelle to secure a favorable decision. Even if this proved fruitless, the European Areopagus was at any rate led to view the question in dispute from a friendly angle.

The congress broke up on November 14, 1818. Its conclusion brought profit to the House of Rothschild, although the principal parts among the bankers had been played, not by them, but by Baring and Hope. The Rothschilds, however, took over bills from that firm. They had successfully put forward the demands of small princes and above all through Gentz they had obtained a profound insight into the activities of the men who were the determining factors in European politics. Moreover, they had formed invaluable connections for the future of their House; and more especially they had made the closer acquaintance of Metternich, the most powerful man in Europe at the time. The brothers therefore left Aix-la-Chapelle in a state of high satisfaction.

Gentz was no less satisfied. He had been widely complimented for his work during the congress and had collected two orders, as well as six thousand ducats. He also attached great value to having "taken part in the most instructive conversation with the most powerful men in the commercial world, while the intimate secrets of the greatest financial dealings that have ever been transacted between men were negotiated in his little room." [28]

It is true that Gentz liked to see himself in a romantic light, and was wont to exaggerate anything with which he had to do; but the negotiations at Aix-la-Chapelle as to the manner in which France should pay the 270 million francs of war indemnity still outstanding did in fact constitute a formidable financial transaction. Metternich returned home with his sovereign, but Gentz returned at the end of November via Frankfort, where he spent about a week.

His diary shows that the first week in December, 1818, was spent in almost daily visits to or from the Rothschilds, and in long conversations and discussions with the members of the banking family. Hour after hour Gentz worked in favor of the Jews of Frankfort. To this period must be attributed the conclusion of the agreement that was so profitable to both, providing the Rothschilds with an important source of political information and a connection with Metternich, while enabling Gentz to carry on his extravagant manner of life, and to indulge in his expensive middle-aged amour with Fanny Elssler. The relationship continued until his death.

From Frankfort Gentz proceeded home via Munich, where he received a letter from his friend Adam Müller.

The public had learned something of the part played by the brothers Rothschild during the past critical years, and Gentz had told Müller more. Müller, as a result, suggested that his friend describe in a short sketch the rise of the House of Rothschild.[29]

Gentz replied as follows: "I was delighted with your idea of a monograph on the Rothschilds. It is one of the brightest and most happy notions that I have heard for some time. The word is all the more appropriate since the Rothschilds really do constitute a special *species plantarum* with its own characteristics. They are vulgar, ignorant Jews, outwardly presentable. In their craft they act entirely in accordance with the principles of naturalism, having no suspicion of a higher order of things; but they are gifted with a remarkable instinct which causes them always to choose the right, and of two rights, the better. Their enormous wealth (they are the richest people in Europe) is entirely the result of this instinct which the public are wont to call luck.

"Now that I have seen everything at close quarters, Baring's most profound reasoning inspires me with less confidence than the sound judgment of one of the more intelligent Rothschilds—for among the five brothers there is one whose intelligence is wanting and another whose intelligence is weak. If Baring and Hope ever fail, I can state with confidence that it will be because they have thought themselves cleverer than Rothschild and have not followed his advice. I am writing to you *con amore* about these people and their business, because they were my recreation at Aix-la-Chapelle and at the same time I learned a great deal from them."

These remarks of Gentz's are valuable because they occur in a confidential private letter to a friend. We shall see later how differently Gentz was to speak about the same Rothschilds in a work destined for publication for which he received a princely fee from the family.

While the International Congress temporarily brought the three brothers, Amschel, Solomon, and Carl into the foreground, James in Paris and Nathan in London had not been inactive. Nathan in particular had succeeded in carrying on his activities in dealing with large loans, and had issued twelve million pounds of English State Loan. This business does not itself appear to have brought much profit to the firm of Rothschild, but it secured its prestige in the eyes of the British Treasury, and demonstrated to the whole world that in the face of native competition it had maintained its position as the banker of England—a nation which now, after Napoleon's overthrow, was rejoicing in its undisputed political power and wealth.

James in Paris was in constant close association with Barbier, the chairman of the Austrian Liquidation Committee in that city. He continued his efforts in rivalry with other firms, to secure the handling of the war indemnity, and so extended his business.

While the House was thus prospering throughout the world, its existence was suddenly most seriously threatened in the home town of Frankfort. The family had just lost one of its best friends there—the man to whom must properly be ascribed the important part of having first held the ladder on which the House of Rothschild had climbed to such heights. On August 3, 1819, while sitting at his desk in Hanau, Buderus had a stroke.

A short glance at the papers which he left shows that he had spent his whole life in meticulous devotion to the exacting work of accountancy. The son of a poor schoolmaster, he had risen to the rank of privy councilor and head of the treasury. He had acquired a fine estate and was possessed of about one and a half million gulden.[30]

All this was, however, a trifling reward, when one considers the services he rendered to the elector during the Napoleonic period, and the enormous portions of the elector's possessions he rescued.

His devotion to duty had not made him popular, for he was reproached with having acted with too great harshness in the elector's interests. Von Carlshausen seems to have realized this at the end of his days, and there is a suggestion of self-justification in the concluding sentence of his will, which reads as follows:

"I have done what was in my power to provide for my dear children. I have considered no sacrifice and no effort to be too great where the furtherance of their happiness has been concerned, and my whole life has been a consistent endeavor to place their welfare on a firm foundation. God has blessed my efforts . . . and you, my dear children, hearken to and follow a father's last counsel: guard carefully the property which I, with God's help, have industriously acquired. It is burdened neither by the tears of the oppressed nor by the curses of the defrauded. Endeavor to increase and secure it through economy, order, industry, wisdom, clemency, and piety. Shun greed and usurious avarice that blights all virtue. Have naught to do with unjust acquisitions. Always remember that contentment is the crown of riches."[31]

The House of Rothschild owed an infinite debt of gratitude to the dead man. It is true that under the contract he had had his share in the business, and to this fact indeed he owed the greater part of his wealth. But this was of small account in comparison with the services which he had rendered in excluding all rival firms from the rich elector's business, and with the possibilities which he had created of applying the elector's money to consolidate the credit of the banking firm and to secure its great business.

It was in its native town that the rise of the House had aroused the greatest envy and hatred. A Frankfort police report of that time gives a fairly good picture of popular feeling in the old imperial city:

"The occasion of a day of penitence," [32] the report runs, "being held to commemorate a big fire that occurred at Frankfort a hundred years ago, through which four hundred houses were destroyed, clearly brings out the feelings of the Christian inhabitants against the Jews. According to the story, much property is supposed to have been stolen by them. In general, any opportunity for showing envy and ill-will is welcomed, all sense of justice being forgotten, although many rich Jews are a source of substantial income to Christians. Any right-thinking person will condemn the fact, for instance, that a caricature ridiculing his ennoblement [33] was recently pinned to the door of the Jewish banker Rothschild at Frankfort.

"Rothschild, although he indulges somewhat in display, provides many people with an opportunity of earning money thereby, and is exceedingly benevolent to the poor whether they be Christians or Jews. The capacity of this Jewish commercial and banking firm is shown by the fact that it has taken over a loan for England, of which we have just been informed. It is noteworthy that the firm of Rothschild secured the business in competition against others. A few days ago the firm on receiving a special message from Vienna bought fifteen thousand Métalliques; the price of Austrian securities immediately rose, and the stockbrokers got extraordinarily busy."

The revelation of the firm's power had the most exaggerated results. In such a highly emotional period as Germany was passing through, a rapid development of this kind was bound to have a particularly exasperating effect upon contemporaries and rivals. All thinking people in Germany were greatly stirred by the desire for freedom and national unity. On March 23, 1819, a fanatic's dagger cost Kotzebue his life because of his attacks on the national party. The emotion, artificially held in check by Metternich, everywhere vented itself upon the Jews.

A farce called *"Unser Verkehr"* ("Our Neighbors") was played throughout Germany, which, to the uproarious applause of the spectators, ridiculed the manners and customs of the Jews.[34] The author was unknown, and everybody said that the House of Rothschild had offered a reward for his discovery.

In August, 1819, the Conferences of Ministers, over which Metternich presided, met at Carlsbad to decide upon the notorious measures against any movement of liberation; the resulting excitement found an outlet in a violent outbreak of popular passion against the Jews. Würzburg was the first town in which acts of violence were perpetrated. The populace gathered together in groups which marched past the Jews' houses, smashing windows and breaking down doors. They began to loot. "Hepp! Hepp! Down with the Jews!"[35] resounded through the streets. Similar scenes occurred in Bamberg and other towns.

The Jews of Frankfort were all the more dismayed by these occurrences, as there had been menacing signs of a similar movement developing in that city. Amschel Meyer Rothschild and his two brothers, who on account of their wealth were likely to be the principal object of any attack, began to feel that their lives were seriously threatened, and to consider the question of flight.

One of the brothers seems to have spoken of their intentions to an Austrian official, for, writing on August 6, a secretary of legation at Frankfort reports as follows:[36] "I have the honor tentatively to inform you that I have learned from a reliable source that the Jewish banking firm of Rothschild here intends to leave Frankfort for good; they are going to apply, through the imperial minister of finance Count von Stadion for permission to settle in Vienna. Their intention is still a close secret here.

When they give effect to it, it will cause an enormous sensation both among the municipal authorities and in the whole business community, and the splendor of Frankfort will be considerably dimmed. It will probably serve to heighten the bitter feeling against the Jews, and the departure of the Rothschilds will be a fatal blow to them."

Frankfort soon caught the contagion of the anti-Jewish disturbances in the other cities of Germany. They were all the more likely to culminate in deeds of violence in that city since the populace knew that in its hatred of the Jews it enjoyed the sympathy of the highest authorities in the town. The occasion for the outbreak was a trifling one. On the evening of August 10, 1819, some youths walked through the Jewish quarter provocatively shouting "Hepp, Hepp!" Several Jews who happened to be standing at their doors joined to drive the youths out of their street, and beat one of the brawlers who had fallen into their hands. Thereupon the rumor spread through Frankfort like lightning that a Christian had been killed by the Jews.

Crowds collected instantaneously and moved shouting through the Jewish quarter, breaking up windows and shops with stones. The house of the Rothschilds was also attacked, and all their window-panes lay scattered about the streets. The family had had to take refuge in the back room, where they listened trembling to the threatening shouts of the mob.

On the morning of the 11th, the words "Hepp, hepp," the slogan for driving out the loathed Jew, were inscribed in large letters at all the street corners. Thereupon several wealthy Israelites left the inhospitable town of Frankfort, and the brothers Rothschild nearly followed their example. As the disturbances increased the senate began to be alarmed that the Jew-baiting might develop into a general rising. The available troops were called up to hold the excited populace in check. Moreover, the delegates to the diet, feeling particularly concerned about the attacks on the House of Rothschild, which had important financial connections with most of the governments represented at the diet, demanded that counter-measures should be taken. A general resolution of the diet was proposed, requiring the senate to take strong measures to protect the security and property of the Jews.

Count Buol would certainly have been acting in accordance with the wishes of Prince Metternich in pressing energetically, at any rate on behalf of Austria, for such measures to be taken by the senate. Buol, however, who was hostile to the Jews, hesitated and waited for instructions. Not so the Prussian representative, Counselor of Embassy Himly. On the very morning of August 11 he gave a "most worshipful council of the free city of Frankfort to understand[37] that he had the fullest confidence that the council would take the most appropriate measures for punishing the attack made upon the house of the royal Prussian commercial advisers, Meyer Amschel von Rothschild and Sons, and would assure their persons and property adequate protection against similar risks in the future." Himly added, "The undersigned kindly requests the earliest possible information regarding the measures which an honorable council have taken in this matter."

The mayors Metzler and von Usemer replied that the disturbances in the Jewish quarter had immediately subsided, and that the senate had taken the strongest measures to prevent their recurrence. The senate added to this statement that the protection of the laws extended to all the inhabitants, and therefore also to the merchants Rothschild, and that the events of the previous night would be reviewed most strictly, and the ringleaders punished.[38] This read well, but bore little relation to reality, for although actual attacks upon the houses of the Jews ceased, the hatred of their inhabitants had come into the open, and this kept the Jews in a state of anxiety.

James in Paris had heard with great alarm of what had occurred at Frankfort, and had urged his brother to leave his home. "You will have read in the public press," he wrote to David Parish at Carlsbad, "how on the night of the 10th of this month mobs collected in the streets of Frankfort and poured forth threats and imprecations upon the Jewish community. Prompt measures on the part of a praiseworthy senate have scattered the ring-leaders and, according to the last reports I have received, have restored order.

"You can readily imagine that such occurrences are as unpleasant as they are unexpected nowadays. What can be the result of such disturbances? Surely they can have the effect only of causing all the rich people of our nation to leave Germany and transfer their property to France and England. I myself have advised my brother at Frankfort to shut down his house and to come here. If we make a start I am convinced that all well-to-do people will follow our example, and I question whether the sovereigns of Germany will be pleased with a development that will make it necessary for them to apply to France or England when they are in need of funds.

"Who buys state bonds in Germany, and who has endeavored to raise the rate of exchange if it be not our nation? Has not our example engendered a certain confidence in state loans, so that Christian firms have also taken heart and invested part of their money in all kinds of securities? The Jewish community in Germany is not allowed to learn the various crafts, so that there is nothing left for them to do but to become dealers in money and stocks.

"A man generally has the greatest confidence in the securities of the country in which he lives; if the peace of the rich in Germany be disturbed, they will find themselves forced to emigrate for their safety; and they will certainly not take any interest in the funds of a country where their life has been obviously endangered. The object of the agitators at Frankfort seems to have been provisionally to collect all the Israelites into a single street; if they had succeeded in doing this, might it not have led to a general massacre? In that case would the public have had any scruples about plundering their houses?

"I need not point out to you how undesirable such an occurrence would be, especially at a time when our house might be holding large sums for the account of the Austrian or Prussian court. It seems to me to be really necessary that Austria or Prussia should devise measures to be applied by the senate at Frankfort for energetically dealing with occurrences such as those of the 10th of this month, and thus making each man secure in his possessions.

"I am sure you will be so good as to speak to his Highness Prince Metternich about this matter, and your friendship for me makes me feel confident that you will appeal to him strongly on behalf of our nation. I am informed that Herr von Bethmann was particularly conspicuous among those who endeavored to restore order." [39]

The advice which James gave from abroad did not take into account the important interests that would have to be sacrificed if the firm that was so deeply rooted in its native city, where it was the center of an intricate network of business connections, were to change its headquarters. The brothers who were resident at Frankfort did certainly consider the question of leaving the town, but when order had been restored they gave up the idea for the time. Amschel Meyer, as head of the firm, was tied to Frankfort. But in Solomon and Carl, who were freer to move about, the events at Frankfort had produced a certain uneasiness, which made them inclined to welcome any future opportunity for settling elsewhere.

Baron von Handel attentively noted the results of the Jewish disturbances. Some rich Jewish firms such as

Ellissen and Speyer did actually transfer their headquarters to the Hessian town of Offenbach close by; and a persistent rumor was maintained that the Rothschilds would follow them.

"The great and rich House of Rothschild," Handel reported to Metternich, "is supposed to be not entirely averse to the idea of leaving here; and if they should do so, they would probably take up permanent residence in Paris or London, where they already have branches. The question suggests itself whether it would not be in our interests to offer them the prospect of a good reception in the I. and R. states, and to induce the House to emigrate to Vienna." [40]

This report was communicated to the committee of the treasury dealing with commercial affairs at Vienna.[41] The next day another letter from Handel arrived, stating that the inclination of the Rothschild banking firm to leave Frankfort was becoming more and more marked. The treasury committee for commercial affairs transmitted these to the ministry of finance and the interior for their information and observation, adding [42] that Amschel von Rothschild spent a hundred and fifty thousand gulden on his household alone and that he gave twenty thousand gulden a year to the poor. The committee were of opinion that the firm of Rothschild was at liberty to apply to be received in the I. and R. states. Count Stadion thereupon wrote the following to the minister of the interior, Count Saurau:

"The president of the treasury committee has informed me in the enclosed letter of his intention to invite the Frankfort firm of Rothschild to settle in Vienna, and also of the means whereby, subject to my agreement, he proposes to prepare the way to this end. The settlement of the House of Rothschild within the Austrian dominions would without doubt be of great advantage, and the proposal is therefore deserving of every support, although Hofrat von Handel's letter does not suggest that the

House have expressed any desire to emigrate to the Austrian dominions. It merely raises the question whether an effort should be made to induce them to do so." [43]

As the reception of the Jewish families was a matter that concerned the minister of the interior, Stadion referred the suggestion to him, with the request that he approve it. Count Saurau sent his reply direct to the president of the treasury committee, conveying his decision to Stadion in the form of a copy of that letter, which read as follows: [44]

> I venture first to call your Excellency's attention to the fact . . . that it is still quite uncertain whether the firm of Rothschild intends to leave Frankfort. Still less may we infer (from the reports) any clearly expressed preference for settling in Vienna. It would seem indeed exceedingly doubtful whether the House of Rothschild would choose for permanent residence a place where its principal would, in view of his religious persuasion, be subject to more restrictions than in any other state. Your Excellency must be aware that foreign Israelites may reside here only on obtaining the special "toleration" permit, which cannot be issued until they have duly received the provisional authorization for wholesale trading.
>
> The department is not competent to make an exception to the I. and R. regulations regarding this matter, and its action would be limited . . . to approving the request of the House of Rothschild for permission to reside, if submitted. In view of the complicated conditions, which are not likely to attract the House of Rothschild, it would seem especially desirable to avoid any step that suggested an invitation, and to leave it to them to apply, since special exceptions can be made only with the personal approval of the emperor. Meanwhile your Excellency may rest assured that we are far too well aware of the advantages that would in many respects accrue to the imperial state of Austria through

> the settlement of such an eminent firm within its borders, not to advise his Majesty most emphatically to give his consent as soon as a formal or definite application in this matter is received.

Handel was accordingly instructed that if the House of Rothschild made inquiries at the legation he was to indicate that they should submit an application. In any case, the report of the department revealed that it desired the House of Rothschild to emigrate to Vienna.

This was all the more remarkable as the position of the Jews in Austria was far from being an enviable one. They had not the right of owning land in any part of the imperial dominions; law and custom excluded them from administration and the courts, from the practice of the law and from the teaching profession, from all higher posts in the army, and from any political functions and offices. They were restricted in the matter of marriages; they had to pay poll tax and report themselves to the Jewish office, and foreign Jews were allowed to remain in the country only for a short period.

Such were the circumstances in which the highest officials in the state of Austria were trying to induce a foreign Jewish family to settle in the country. But that family was enormously rich; its financial influence was immense; and money overcame all other considerations. Soon a Rothschild House was to be established in Vienna too.

Frankfort was becoming exceedingly uncomfortable for the Rothschild family. The brothers were constantly receiving anonymous threats. One letter[45] informed them of the day on which Amschel was to be murdered by a secret society formed for the purpose of driving the Jews out of Frankfort. In spite of all this the firm continued to carry on its business undisturbed, the Austrian side of it particularly developing with the help of Metternich and Stadion.

Solomon Meyer Rothschild
From a portrait by I. Lieder in the Vienna National Library

Austrian affairs were chiefly left to Solomon. In mid-July of that year the firm of Rothschild had undertaken jointly with Gontard to arrange for the transfer from Naples of large sums of money which that kingdom had owed Austria since the intervention of 1815. Also sums to the value of about three million francs, payable in satisfaction of Austria's claims upon France, were transmitted to Vienna, the firm of Rothschild receiving one percent of the payments effected.[46] Finally, the brothers had heard from a confidential source in Milan that there was an amount of money in the state treasury there[47] which the government wished to transfer to Vienna. They immediately offered to carry this out.

It involved a transmission of two million lira in gold coins, and Solomon, who was again staying at Vienna, quickly got into personal touch with the treasury in order to discuss the best means of sending this sum from Milan to Vienna through exchange operations. The firm of Rothschild stated that they would undertake the transfer of any sum whatever at the cheapest rate possible, and that they could arrange the business to the greatest advantage of the imperial interests.[48] For this service they and the firm of Gontard received one-half percent commission and one-eighth percent brokerage, so that for the simple transmission of the money from Milan to Vienna they received 12,933 lira in gold.

Their extensive transactions necessitated a voluminous correspondence, the rapid transmission of which was a difficult problem under the primitive conditions of those times. It was not only that posts were slow and far between; there were special dangers attached to the postal service because the contents of correspondence was not treated as inviolable. A large part of Germany was still served by the Thurn and Taxis post bureaus which were divided into lodges and non-lodges,[49] according as their officials were or were not the confidential agents of the Viennese Cipher Service.

If a letter came to a lodge office, it was carefully opened before being sent on, read through, and any important passages were copied. As these "intercepts," as they were called, were always laid before the authorities, such action, often abused, was greatly feared. Even Count Stadion did not hesitate [50] personally to invent "intercepts" in order to ruin persons who were a nuisance to him. Sometimes the couriers themselves intercepted letters in transit.

"Such inspection," Bethmann wrote on the occasion of a visit to Vienna,[51] "is inevitable, and Rothschild and Parish are as little able to avoid it as Herr von Geymüller, although the latter enjoys the full confidence of Prince Metternich. Solomon Rothschild yesterday told me that his brother had recently again received three letters from him in one day."

The brothers Rothschild naturally thoroughly understood the position. As they had a great deal to say to one another that they did not wish anyone else to hear and also attached great importance to the speedy receipt of news in advance of normal methods, they decided to have their own system of couriers. They would be reimbursed for the heavy expense of this arrangement at one stroke if their firm thereby received early news of any political event that might affect the exchange.

An example of this occurred when the Duke of Berry was murdered. The duke was the nephew of the King of France, and as Louis XVIII had no children, the hopes of the Bourbons were centered upon him. As he was leaving the opera on February 13, 1820, he was assassinated by a political fanatic who thought to save France by exterminating the Bourbons. According to Handel's statement [52] the Rothschilds heard of this long before anyone else; they made appropriate arrangements for themselves, and then made the event known. This resulted in an immediate fall in all state securities, and produced "general consternation."

The courier system was at first inaugurated between the three brothers in London, Frankfort, and Paris. When the business with Austria accumulated, and Solomon's visits there grew more and more lengthy, the couriers extended their route to include Vienna.

The Austrian representatives in London, Frankfort, and Paris, being in constant communication with the House of Rothschild, soon realized that reports could be more speedily sent in this manner and, as remarks on numerous documents showed, frequently entrusted the Rothschild couriers with the most important and secret letters, without considering whether the Rothschilds might turn the tables and themselves "intercept" the state communications. This certainly cannot be proved, but it is highly probable, for on one occasion, when the brothers entrusted a letter to an ambassador, the letter was immediately "perused." Proof of this is furnished by the following two letters: on November 28, 1819,[53] Handel reported as follows to Metternich: "The banker Carl von Rothschild, who left for Vienna today, asked us to put several letters to various German ministers meeting at Vienna, which he had been asked to take with him, in a packet and seal it with the embassy seal, so that he could bring them over the frontier without risk. I made no difficulty about acceding to the request of Herr von Rothschild—who like other Jews is exceedingly timid but is a person of sound character—because this favor made it possible to see the contents of the letters. Rothschild duly sent them to me and although I had not time to peruse them all, I was able to scan the more important."

The other letter was from [54] Le Monnier, the secretary of legation at Frankfort, to the director of the secret service department at Vienna. It ran as follows: "Herr Rothschild [no doubt Amschel Meyer], whom I often meet at Count Buol's as well as at Baron von Handel's, has asked me to allow him to send his letters to his brother in my bag. I did not raise any objection as I did not think it advisable to refuse; but I venture to suggest that you should inform the secret service department of this fact so that they may look out for these letters and intercept all those under my address."

It is not at all unlikely that the brothers Rothschild, who must be credited with a reasonable amount of intelligence, sometimes deliberately had letters sent through the embassies in order to put them in possession of facts which had been invented or adapted for definite purposes.

The financial position of all the states which had been engaged in prolonged military operations much needed to be set in order, now that peace and tranquillity had returned. In Austria, Stadion was dealing with this problem in collaboration with Metternich. Metternich was personally concerned to see that Stadion was profitably occupied in the financial matters, to which he had been sidetracked when the chancellor succeeded to the Foreign Office. His rival would then feel that he had plenty to do, and the financial strengthening of the monarchy would assist the policy of the chancellor. There were thus two men controlling the destinies of Austria who were well disposed to the Jews in general and to the House of Rothschild in particular.

In 1816, in addition to the interest-bearing state debt, there was an almost equal amount of paper money in circulation which was worth a quarter less than its face value. Stadion's efforts were directed toward preventing any further fall in value, through the issue of loans and other measures such as the founding of a national bank. The Métalliques loan, so called because the interest on the bonds was payable in precious metal, constituted a beginning. Stadion was in agreement with Metternich that the House of Rothschild should always be treated with consideration politically, with a view to inducing it also to participate in a loan. Since these were Metternich's plans, it is not strange that he should have been much irritated by the anti-Jewish attitude of the city of Frankfort.

Frankfort was described as a center of unrest [55] in the reports from the delegates at this period. This was quite enough reason for Metternich, who scented revolution and upheaval everywhere, to feel displeased with that city. He accordingly intervened to prevent the diet from leaving the settlement of the Jewish problem to the municipal departments. Metternich and Stadion also decided to accede to the request made a year and a day previously that Nathan should be appointed consul in London. On March 3, 1820, the emperor gave his formal sanction in this matter.[56]

The ambassador in London, Prince von Esterházy, was instructed [57] to inform Nathan of his new sphere of activity, and to encourage him "through friendly advice and any other suitable means to carry out his duties in the manner which the state expected." Official instructions were simultaneously sent to Nathan in London [58] informing him not merely that he should duly carry out the duties imposed upon him by the I. and R. embassy, but that he should, without waiting to be asked, regularly convey to them any information he received regarding events that might directly or indirectly affect the government's policy.

On Metternich's instructions Handel, the minister at Frankfort, had in November, 1819,[59] entered into negotiations with Rothschild for the big loan that Austria wanted to place with the firm.

Since that time the distinctions and favors already described had with deliberate intent been accorded to the House of Rothschild. Nathan now had a position in the consular corps of the British capital, a fact which was exceedingly valuable to him both socially and in business. He was able to give Amschel powerful support in his struggle for the rights of the Frankfort Jews.

The ground had thus been well prepared for a favorable reception of the Austrian loan. The national bank required about 55,000,000 gulden in order to withdraw the paper money from circulation. On April 4 the emperor had authorized the minister of finance to issue the loan, which in accordance with Stadion's suggestion was to be done in two parts. On April 7 the first 20,000,000 gulden were, in accordance with Solomon's suggestion, issued to the firms of Rothschild and Parish in the form of a lottery loan, a method which was still unusual at that time, and which never failed of its effect upon the general public.

Nothing was said at the time of the negotiations that were already in progress for the issue of a further 35,000-gulden loan; and everyone subscribed to this loan in the confident belief that it would be the only lottery loan for the time being. The conditions were very oppressive to the Austrian state, although the redemption of the loan extended over quite a long period; under the agreement, the state had to repay in all 38,000,000 in return for the 20,000,000 then advanced. This naturally produced an adverse opinion in the general public, which was ignorant as to the general financial position and Stadion's intentions, and had only these figures to go upon.

A contemporary police report states [60] that the announcement of the Rothschild lottery loan had had a very bad effect upon public sentiment. The government's credit when it had scarcely begun to recover was appreciably lowered.

"As far as the Rothschild loan is concerned," the report continued, "I feel a genuine difficulty in deciding where to commence with my description of the exceedingly unfavorable impression . . . made by this financial operation, not only upon the Viennese public, but also upon the inhabitants of all the provinces. It would not be in accordance with the modesty due from one in my position to record the harsh expressions used by the opponents of this measure in describing it as a monument of frivolity, caprice, and self-interest—indeed as being an immoral transaction. There have probably not been such numerous critics and opponents of any previous financial operation.

"I heard a guest at an At Home exclaim, 'This loan is one of the most wicked things that have been done at the expense of our pockets for twenty years, and that is saying a great deal!' One thing generally felt about this loan is that the manner in which it was made public inevitably made it unpopular from the start. To notify the inhabitants of a state that 20,000,000 were being borrowed from a foreign Jew, for which 38,000,000—very nearly double the amount—would have to be repaid, is regarded as treating one's subjects as beneath contempt. . . . It is felt that the announcement of the loan in the Wiener Zeitung amounted to the finance minister's saying: '*I am well aware* that your expenditure being greater than your income you have not enough money to pay your taxes. Now in order that in future you may be still less able to pay them I shall still further limit the amount of money in circulation and therefore your income. In return for this benefit you will have to pay 38 millions to the Jew Rothschild.'"

The writer of this report emphasized the fact that there appeared to be no conceivable excuse for excluding the public from participating directly in such an advantageous financial speculation as the lottery loan, and for putting it in the hands of a foreign Jew. Citizens were being compelled to purchase the lottery bonds from foreign Jews at a premium of from 10% to 18%.

"I am assured by bankers here," the report continued, "that the profit which the contractors have made out of this loan is enormous. To the four millions granted them by way of commission must be added what they will realize through the sale of the bonds, which they do not issue at under 100 gulden. The Rothschild who is living here himself admits that this profit will increase from year to year, and that he hopes the bonds will rise to 200 by the second drawing, and to 400 by the tenth drawing! And this is not at all unlikely, since Rothschild is holding back the sale of the bonds, thereby increasing his chances of a tremendous gain.

"The whole transaction is felt to be a shameful Jewish swindle arranged between the Rothschilds and the crown agent Joel. The latter is supposed to have persuaded the minister of finance, or rather his department, to agree to it, and in return Joel or Joelson is alleged to have received 1,000 bonds, Count Stadion 2,000, and Burgermeister, the secretary of the treasury, 500. I personally regard all these statements as slanders without any foundation. The feeling about the loan was so bitter at first that a proposal was made among all ranks of society to form leagues, the members of which should pledge themselves not to take bonds exceeding the value of 100 gulden from the Rothschilds."

There were other critics who did not deny that Stadion's intentions were honest, but gave him to understand that they believed the minister of finance had been hopelessly done.

The figures contained in this police report somewhat exaggerated the facts, but expressed the feeling of the public that enormous profits had been made out of this business. In spite of the declared boycott there was an extraordinarily brisk demand for the Rothschild lottery bonds. The offices were literally besieged with applicants, and the bonds soon rose to 110, 120, 150, and even higher.

The Augsburg Allgemeine Zeitung had published articles by Gentz and other agents of the Rothschilds, which under the title "Financial Letters" recommended the "exceptionally favorable lottery." Enticed by these developments, Stadion decided in accordance with the authorization which he had received, to issue the further

35,000,000 gulden four months after the first loan. Rothschild and Parish paid out 35,000,000 gulden of convention currency in cash in twelve monthly instalments, in return for acknowledgments of indebtedness. The terms were such that the state would have to repay 76,821,515 gulden as capital and interest in return for the 35,000,000 gulden which it had received. In addition the state paid a commission of 4%, amounting to 1,400,000 gulden.

These conditions which were approved by Emperor Francis made the loan one of the most lucrative transactions of the time. For the firm not merely exploited the public's gambling instincts to sell the bonds at a good price, it also influenced the rate of exchange through its connections with the principal bourses. It was obvious that the Rothschilds would have to reckon with the fall in the price of the twenty-million issue as soon as it became known that a further loan of thirty-five millions was to be made so soon afterwards. But before this was made public they had placed the original issue at a price well above par, so that when the second loan was issued the earlier bonds were almost all in other people's hands.

There was naturally at once a storm of indignation against the enterprising bankers; but the first issue soon recovered, and the bonds of both issues were eagerly sought. The public indignation subsided; the Austrian State had its millions in cash; and the Rothschilds remained in undisturbed possession of their profits.

The negotiations necessitated by these important and extensive transactions had made essential the continuous presence in Vienna of a member of the Rothschild House. The discussions were carried on almost exclusively by Solomon Rothschild, although he was acting in concert with his brothers. This enormous business, however, required constant personal attention in its further stages also; and it was therefore necessary for Solomon to try to obtain some permanent *pied à terre* at Vienna. The laws of the country did not allow a foreign Jew to buy a house of his own, and perhaps such was not his original intention. The firm did not yet contemplate establishing a branch similar to those in London and Paris, although this was done eventually as the result of its intimate association with the finance and policy of Austria.

Solomon Rothschild had taken up his quarters in one of the leading hostelries of Vienna, known as the Hotel of the Roman Emperor, No. 1 Renngasse. It had some of the most distinguished visitors at that time, including the King of Wurttemberg in the year 1820. This was the only hotel with a large concert room,[61] and its acoustic properties were excellent. Beethoven often gave recitals there, and occasionally he stayed, it is supposed, at the Roman Emperor.

Solomon lived at the hotel until he was given the freedom of the city of Vienna. Eventually, it is true, he was the only guest in the hotel, for he occupied all the rooms. In the end he bought the building, as well as the house next it, No. 3 Renngasse. This is still in the possession of the family, while an insurance company acquired what was once the Roman Emperor Hotel.

Meanwhile Metternich's confidence in the firm of Rothschild had increased. The family perceived this, and when they saw any signs of big business they would let him know through Gentz that they would like to carry it out. James had learned in Paris that the allies had decided in 1815 to put aside twenty million francs of the Paris war indemnity for the erection of a fourth confederate fortress on the Rhine.[62]

James in Paris and Solomon in Vienna immediately offered to send this money to Frankfort so that the diet might have it available in current coin at their headquarters. Metternich was unduly attracted by the firm's offer to transmit the funds without charging commission or anything for expenses, and overlooked the profit to be derived on the rate of exchange. He therefore decided

Johann Philipp Count von Stadion
From a portrait by Perger
in the Vienna National Library

jointly with the Prussian secretary of state that this business should be carried through by the firm of Rothschild.

The two brothers, by a concerted arrangement, each made an offer that, if the money were left in their hands, the one in Paris would pay 3½% and the one in Vienna would pay 3% until the building work on the fortress actually commenced. That might be a long time yet, as indeed events proved. Barbier observed in this connection (in a letter to Buol) [63] that in carrying out Metternich's instructions he had arranged that the diet should retain the right to demand security for the twenty millions from the House of Rothschild if this sum were deposited with them.

"The House of Rothschild," he wrote, "is undoubtedly one of the richest and best-established firms in Europe, but we thought it wiser to take this precaution as over twenty million francs are involved, which may be on deposit with them for quite a long period if the construction of the new fortress should be still further delayed."

Thus while the government itself paid 5% for ready money it left this large sum on deposit with the firm of Rothschild at 3½% interest for an indefinite time. The banking firm got the advantage of this unexpectedly cheap money just when important political events in the South of Europe threatened to disturb the peaceful atmosphere that had been prevailing since the Congress of Vienna.

The Liberals in Spain had forced the promise of a constitution from King Ferdinand VII, who had been reinstated there. Civil war continued in that country, while the victory which the Liberals had won infected the excitable population in other lands similarly oppressed.

Revolution broke out in the kingdom of Naples, where the nationalistic aims of the secret league of the Carbonari had affected wide circles of the population. On his restoration by the Austrians in 1815 King Ferdinand I, an upholder of the principle of absolute autocracy, gladly accepted Metternich's condition that he should make no concessions to the Liberals, and should govern in accordance with the Metternich system. Now, however, that he was threatened by popular rising, he yielded all along the line and made the ringleader, General Pepe, commander-in-chief, and pledged himself to a constitution on the Spanish model.

A similar movement was making progress in the island of Sicily, where the king's ministers had to make way for new men who were popular with the Carbonari. One of these ministers was the brilliant Luigi Cavaliere de Medici, who managed to maintain order in the finances in spite of the extravagances of the ruling family, and the privileges of the nobility and priesthood.

Metternich, who was watching over Europe like a guardian angel, resented any signs of resistance to his "principle of legitimacy." He had been deeply disturbed by the news from Italy, which was within Austria's sphere of interest. If the revolutionary spirit should spread from Naples to the North and infect the territories that were under Austrian dominion, there was no saying what the results might be. He saw that his political system, his influence, which already extended through the whole of Europe, and the very existence of all the old legitimist monarchies were endangered. He felt that every effort must be made to meet this peril, and summoned another conference of monarchs to consider the point. The conference met at Troppau in October, 1820, to discuss the principles to be applied if revolutionaries tried to impose changes in the form of government anywhere in Europe.

The congress was moved to Laibach, and Metternich arranged that the King of Naples should be asked to attend. Scarcely had the king crossed the frontiers of his revolutionary country before he forgot all the concessions he had granted to the people, and assured the envoy of the eastern powers that they had been wrung from him by force, and that he loathed constitution and Carbonarism. The congress decided in January, 1821, in spite of the objections made by England and France, to restore order in Ferdinand's kingdom by occupying Naples. Metternich had succeeded in a masterly manner in gaining over the tsar to his point of view.

"It is a matter of indifference," he stated to that monarch,[64] "whether the word be Bonaparte or the sovereignty of the people; they are equally dangerous and must therefore both be resisted. The Neapolitan revolt, and everything connected with it, must be completely stamped out, or else the powers themselves will be destroyed."

Metternich concentrated absolutely on his one great political object, the overthrow of revolution. The troops and money necessary for this purpose had to be forthcoming, and it was up to generals and financiers to see to the ways and means.

The news of Metternich's plans, involving as they did heavy additional expenditure, came as a severe shock to Stadion, who had done so much to put Austria's finances on a sound basis. He saw the edifice which he had spent years to erect shaken to its foundations. The revolutions had also affected the bourses, and state securities were falling in price. Metternich, however, succeeded in being so convincing through his influence with the press, and the passionate communications sent by him from Laibach, that even those who had reason to be alarmed about their property became adherents of Metternich's plans of armed intervention in Naples. The chancellor had inquired of Stadion as to how the money could be found, and whether Naples would subscribe to a loan. Stadion sent the following confidential letter in reply:[65]

"Even our financiers, led by Rothschild and Parish, are anxious to see our troops across the Po at the earliest possible moment, and marching on Naples. I have written to Count von Mercy regarding the Neapolitan loan.

I suppose you have spoken only to Rothschild about it? I have never mentioned it to Parish, because I do not know how far Rothschild wants him to come into such a business (*parceque je ne sais en combien Rothschild voudrais de lui dans une pareille affaire*). In any case it is essential to lay our plans carefully so that the money does not merely come in at one door to go out of the other."

As Stadion considered the matter more closely, he began to feel distinctly uneasy. In normal circumstances the deficit for the year 1821 would have amounted to eight million gulden; but very heavy additional sums of money were now required for the expeditionary force to Italy, and the greater part of this cash would have to be found immediately. As Stadion came to consider the heavy demands made upon the treasury by Metternich's policy, he felt a growing sense of bitterness. Metternich, the chancellor whose financial ideas did not extend much beyond a general realization that a state no less than a private individual must have money, carried out his policy without any consideration of the cost. Stadion was expected to produce the necessary funds as if by magic, and he really was at a loss how to do it.

The chancellor advised Stadion to see the Rothschilds, and urged him to discuss with the brothers the means for raising the amount necessary for the campaign. The emigrant Jews from Frankfort had suddenly become the sheet-anchor for Austria's two leading statesmen, one of whom exercised an influence upon the destinies of Europe extending far beyond the boundaries of the imperial dominions.

While at Laibach, Metternich had asked Count Nesselrode, the Russian minister for foreign affairs, who was just about to leave for Vienna, to urge Stadion to ask Solomon Rothschild to come himself to Laibach and express his personal opinion there regarding the issue of loans to Russia and Austria. The chancellor also wrote a letter to Solomon Rothschild on January 29, 1821, making this suggestion, but Solomon was not prepared to leave Vienna at a time when the political situation was such that prices on the bourse were fluctuating violently from day to day. He therefore wrote the following letter to Count Nesselrode:[66]

> YOUR EXCELLENCY:
>
> With reference to the business matter under consideration, I venture most respectfully to observe that a discussion on this matter at Laibach, and my presence there, might give rise to numerous and probably highly inaccurate newspaper reports. Persons with base motives would unearth the fact that a loan to the most gracious of monarchs was being discussed; rumor would be piled upon rumor, and this would not be at all agreeable in the highest quarters. For this reason I submissively venture to suggest to your Excellency—and Finance Minister Count von Stadion agrees with my proposal—that the business be negotiated here with our finance minister. My continued presence here would dissipate all rumors, while everything would be carried on under the strictest seal of secrecy, and the business could be transacted in peace and quietness.

Solomon Rothschild sent a similar communication to Count Stadion at the same time, and the count immediately wrote[67] to Metternich to say that in his opinion Solomon's contention that neither he nor any other banker should go to the congress at Laibach was absolutely sound.

"In addition to the arguments which he has brought forward," he wrote, "I submit that the following points have to be taken into consideration. The loan in question (which ought to cover the costs of the expedition), can be only a Neapolitan loan, guaranteed for the greater security of the powers. It can be prepared under these conditions, but its formal conclusion must take place in Naples, after our troops have entered the city and occupied it. . . . Until that moment the public must know nothing whatever about it; for the loan would go very badly if we were only like the person in the fable offering the bear's skin, and it could be issued only on very unfavorable terms. It would immediately suggest that we were in lack of money, which fortunately is not yet the case; but the mere belief that we were would seriously damage not only our credit but our political position generally.

"Rothschild is here able to control his business and his correspondence from the center, and day by day, in collaboration with our finance department and his business friends, to decide upon the steps or transactions that seem to him appropriate to prevailing conditions. He cannot carry on his work effectively anywhere but here, while it is only here that we can examine the means that he adopts to carry out the wishes and intentions of the governments. These means must be brought into harmony with our general system of credit, since the loan is destined ultimately to find its way into the Austrian Treasury. . . .

"I feel myself compelled to observe that whatever view one takes of the situation Austria alone will have to bear the burdens of the military operations until Naples is occupied. When we get there it appears to me that the three following matters will have to be dealt with: first, our troops will have to be entirely maintained by that country; secondly, we shall have to obtain compensation for the costs otherwise incurred through their stay in the kingdom of Naples; and thirdly, we shall have to obtain an indemnity that will partially make good our advances.

"Rothschild believes that if the sum exceeds—the loan ought not to be too heavy—one million pounds, or about twenty-four million francs, *cela se pourrait faire pour ainsi dire une bonne fortune à Londres.* I have not yet gone far enough into the matter to be able to judge how far his hopes are well founded."

At the same time Solomon wrote the following letter to Metternich:

> Your Highness was graciously pleased to send me your command of the 29th ultimo. Although it gives me great pleasure to show my zeal in fulfilling your Highness's wishes at all times, and happy though I always am to wait upon you, I feel it my duty to avoid doing anything which would attract attention. . . . A journey to Laibach at this time would arouse such attention, and would give rise to all kinds of conjectures. . . .
>
> Ever devoted to your Highness's commands I beg to remain in deepest respect
>
> Your Highness's Most Obedient Servant,
>
> S. M. von Rothschild.[68]

Stadion's letter had revealed the whole plan that was to be carried out: Naples was to pay everything, and Rothschild was to arrange loans at the expense of that country, the proceeds of which were to be applied for paying for Austria's unwanted intervention.

Meanwhile things had begun to move. The Austrian, General Frimont, crossed the Po on February 5, 1821, with 43,000 men, and began to march on Naples. Solomon Rothschild perceived with satisfaction that Austria's statesmen were dependent on him for finance, and saw the prospect of realizing substantial profits. He accordingly hastened to place sums at their disposal, with a view to securing the possible business at Naples entirely for himself.

Stadion wrote to Metternich:[69] "Rothschild and Parish"—who had apparently, against Rothschild's wishes, been informed of this affair by Gentz—"are provisionally offering to make me advances and to transfer sums direct to Naples apart from the loan. Rothschild is already concluding agreements in Paris and London for this purpose, or at any rate he says he is."

A week later Stadion wrote saying: [70] "For some days Rothschild has been effecting transfers of money to one or several banking firms (in Naples), and by the time we get there about three million francs will be available. These can be immediately placed at the disposal of our government. I only wish that I could always be informed of the requirements in good time so that I could make the necessary arrangements. Until the day before yesterday nobody asked for a single gulden of cash for the whole march of our troops from the Po to the Neapolitan frontier; and then a courier arrived demanding an urgent credit of 250,000 gulden at Florence. It seems to me that this should have been foreseen and provided for a long time ago. Fortunately, Rothschild has money and credit everywhere, and he was therefore able immediately to provide me with the advance I wanted, as well as an additional advance of 100,000 gulden. . . ."

Stadion was already relying largely upon the House of Rothschild, which rendered that statesman the most welcome services in his embarrassment, although certainly not without cherishing the hope that they would be duly rewarded. The finance minister had sent Metternich a detailed scheme regarding the contemplated Neapolitan loan.

"I am awaiting," he wrote to the chancellor, "your reply to my last memorandum regarding the Neapolitan loan, so that I may carry the matter further with my friend Solomon Rothschild. It is absolutely impossible for him to travel to Naples, and he is asking one of his brothers to come over from Frankfort and go on to Naples. This brother is expected by the end of the month. He has also written to Paris to say that a confidential servant of his firm—by name Salicey—who is thoroughly familiar with Naples, should proceed there without delay." [71]

Finally Stadion complained that he no less than the

public had been kept completely in the dark for ten days regarding the progress of events and the present position of the troops.

Solomon had realized that it was absolutely essential that a member of his firm should go to Naples. It was not exactly pleasant to go there as there was a revolution in progress, and the Austrian troops would have some hard fighting; nevertheless Solomon summoned Carl, the only one of the five brothers who so far had no independent sphere of his own.

Carl had, since his youngest days, been accustomed to making long journeys on his father's business. Now at the age of thirty-three a promising field for his activities was offered him, although it was in a country that he had only once casually visited, and the language of which he did not know. This, however, did not affect the matter, for it seemed to be a merely provisional arrangement, and Carl little guessed that Naples would come to be his permanent place of abode. On March 1, Carl Rothschild arrived at Vienna from Frankfort and immediately called on Stadion.

"Un petit frère Rothschild," Stadion reported to Metternich,[72] "has just arrived here on his way to Naples. I am engaged in working out with the two brothers the most important conditions regarding the loan which they will issue. I hope to send young Rothschild to Laibach next Wednesday, or at the latest next Thursday. You will there be able, my dear prince, to inform him whither he should then proceed. I hope that it will be to Naples, and that you will have occasion to send him as speedily as possible."

On March 6, Carl did in fact go to Laibach. Stadion was hoping that in the course of its advance the army would acquire a few millions for the Austrian Treasury, which was sadly in need of them. "I have to point out," he wrote, "that the declaration of war by Naples without a shot having been fired is sufficient ground for us to declare our right to indemnity from the date when our troops crossed the Po." [73]

Meanwhile the Austrian army was approaching the Abruzzi, which was the easiest territory between Austria and Naples for the enemy to defend. Its march was somewhat delayed through the insufficiency of provisions and of money. Count Ficquelmont, who was accompanying the army on his way to take up his duties as ambassador at Naples, wrote: "We are all suffering acutely from the disastrous shortage of money." Application was made at Rome to Torlonia and other banking firms, but in vain. A stirring appeal was made by Metternich with a view to remedying these evils. On receiving a report from Vienna, Metternich had published a statement regarding the whole expedition, in order to pacify the Viennese public, who did not understand what business Austria had in Naples. Count Sedlnitzky welcomed this step, wishing the chancellor luck in carrying on his policy on the grand scale, and reported: [74]

"Through an arrangement made in the nick of time by the thoroughly worthy House of Rothschild and other firms, regarding Wertheimer's failure, the market here has been saved from being flooded with Métalliques bonds, and a gradual rise in their value as well as in that of other state securities has been effected. This has had an excellent effect upon public opinion in the middle classes and in the business world."

The minister of police considered the critics and malcontents to be especially numerous among so-called men of learning, and even in several higher circles and in the army. "Nevertheless," he wrote, "we may count ourselves fortunate, if we compare public sentiment here with that in other countries."

Stadion, however, who was constantly receiving applications for money, was not equally satisfied. He viewed the future with dismay, and was utterly at a loss to see how he could provide the money for everything that was being done. He suddenly heard that a general had stated during the court ball that the emperor had recently commanded the pay of the Neapolitan Expeditionary Force to be increased, and a new recruiting law to be carried into effect which would add almost 100,000 men to the strength of the army.

"I was absolutely overwhelmed with surprise," he wrote in alarm to Metternich,[75] "by this news, and by the manner in which I learned it. If this is true, it will involve a permanent additional expenditure on our armies of more than ten millions. I have not got this money and I see no prospect of getting it. Things cannot go on like this. I feel that I have already reached the utmost limit of what is possible. . . .

"It is very easy to send out handbills, but in order to translate them into reality the emperor must find a man who can feed fifteen thousand men with five loaves. I cannot refrain from protesting against the way things are being done. His Majesty does not allow himself to spend even two hundred florins on his gardens; he does not sanction a pension to save a poor family from hunger without sometimes consulting me several times in the matter. And now we are to have an additional expenditure of ten million which it is difficult to justify. . . . So far from consulting me in fixing this sum, which is far beyond anything we can possibly raise, it was not even thought worth while to inform me of the decision.

"In such circumstances my position, which I have always regarded as the great misfortune of my life, has become quite impossible. For years I have been refused the means . . . of putting things straight, but at the same time I am regarded as an inexhaustible source of money. I am required to fill the glass at any moment it is put before me. Such a method of proceeding certainly puts an end to my responsibility in the matter. Even if, after all the other sacrifices I have made, I cast aside the last shreds of any respect that I may enjoy in the world, this will not bring additional revenue to the monarchy or save it from financial disaster.

"I write to you today, my dear prince, in the bitterness of my heart. It is difficult to remain calm under such conditions. Besides, I feel it to be my duty to state the unvarnished truth, when, as in the present instance, the truth is of such importance. Farewell, my dear prince, make such use of this letter as you think fit."

In some such mood as this, Stadion wrote two memoranda regarding the general financial position of the country, and sent them to Metternich. "The problem is," he submitted, [76] "how to save at least some part of our existence. I cannot possibly conceal from you any longer that I am weighed down and oppressed by a load of misfortune. I have reached the point when I fear that any day I may find that I am quite impotent and helpless to do any more work. I will carry on with the strength that remains to me, until I drop. But do not expect any great services from a man who is weakened as I am."

The finance minister's panic left Metternich unmoved. Clear before him lay the path that he had recognized as the right one, and had ruthlessly followed. He was determined not to deviate from it until he reached his goal.

"We have embarked upon a great undertaking, one that contains the possibilities of greater results than any of our times," he wrote to General Count von Bubna. [77] "It is great, for upon its success or failure the whole future depends; not merely the future of the Austrian monarchy but that of the whole of Europe. . . . It was impossible for us to take any other action, for it is a matter of life or death. . . .

"Everything now depends upon success. I hope that one or two hard blows will decide the issue. If not, the result will be the same as if we had ventured nothing; the revolution will engulf, first Italy, and then the world.

I will spare no effort until I am killed myself. . . . Meanwhile, farewell. I shall not see you this year, but I shall certainly see you next year unless the world has been destroyed."

While Metternich was using proud words such as these, he was being besieged with the most urgent requests from the army to furnish money for its innumerable needs.

In the meantime Carl Rothschild had arrived at Laibach and had called on Gentz, who immediately informed his princely master of young Rothschild's arrival. Metternich asked Carl, through Gentz, whether he would be prepared to travel in his service, and whether he was able, without any loss of time, to make payments to the army. The chancellor also desired to know how moneys could be speedily and safely conveyed to Rome.

Carl replied as follows: "I have the honor to reply to your Princely Highness's gracious inquiry of today that I am prepared to undertake the journey at once to any place where your Princely Highness may bid me go, and to do everything in my power to see that the payments which you have graciously commissioned me to make to the army are carried out with the greatest possible speed and precision. If your Princely Highness will most graciously inform me what sums, and at whose disposition you wish them placed in Rome, I will then . . . send a special messenger to instruct Signor B. Paccard, a member of a firm who is in Milan, to transfer any sums required to Rome without delay, and if necessary to travel there himself. . . . I have only to add, with all humble respect, that we will, on this occasion as always, use our endeavors to satisfy the wishes of his Majesty, which indeed is always our sole aim." [78]

Carl Meyer von Rothschild, who thus came into prominence, was personally the least gifted of the five brothers. He had little talent for adapting himself to his environment, had an awkward manner, and was over-strict in his observance of the religious practices of an orthodox Jew. His principal asset was a pretty and intelligent wife, who won everybody's affection and thereby made people forget many of her husband's errors. In spite of the distance which separated them, Carl remained, at any rate in really important transactions, under the control of his brothers James and Solomon.

Meanwhile the Austrian army had advanced almost without a battle. The encounter at Rieti was just a small skirmish and was described by Ambassador Count Ficquelmont as the most ridiculous thing he had ever seen. "Our advance is uninspiring," he reported,[79] "as we are completely unopposed, but our political victory is all the greater."

Everything therefore seemed to be proceeding satisfactorily, when a very bad piece of news was received. After his return King Victor Emmanuel had inaugurated a severely reactionary régime in Piedmont. For example he made the possession of a certain amount of property a necessary qualification for being allowed to learn to read and write; he had the botanical gardens at Turin destroyed, and wanted to destroy the marvelous bridge over the Po, simply because they were the works of Napoleon. He naturally opposed all nationalistic movements among young people. The risings in Spain and Naples were accordingly joyfully welcomed in Piedmont.

When the Austrian troops started for the South, a rising broke out in Alessandria too, the object of which was to secure a constitution, and the abdication of the autocratic king. The news of these events caused dismay at Laibach. The assembled diplomats were like a swarm of bees that has been disturbed. Gentz reported:[80] "This unexpected news is a very hard blow to me and to all of us. I remained with the prince until half-past four in a kind of stupor, and then I tried to eat something.

Meyer Carl Baron von Rothschild
From a portrait in the Frankfort Historical Museum

Rothschild came to me in a state of great emotion; I had enough sang-froid to be able to calm him."

Carl Rothschild was just about to start for Italy in accordance with Metternich's wishes, and these events caused him the most serious alarm. The impression made at Vienna was no less profound. Stadion completely lost his nerve. "The situation is terrifying," he wrote to Metternich.[81] "Never, not even in the darkest hours of the revolutionary wars, has an event produced such an effect on the Vienna bourse as the latest news from Italy. . . . If the enemy were at the gates there could not be more unreasoning panic. The whole of the population of Vienna is rushing to the bourse to get rid of our public securities. . . . Our credit (which has only just been established) is on the eve of vanishing completely. I shall be forced to suspend the conversion of paper money into cash or banknotes on demand. To do so would be exceedingly painful to me, for it would mean destroying in one day the labors of the five preceding years. . . .

"This is the first step to our destruction. It is impossible that a loan should be considered either at home or abroad at a time when our securities are becoming worthless. . . . Judging from the way things are going we shall have to give up all hope of getting any financial assistance from Naples. . . . There is so much popular unrest of a very marked character that each day may bring a fresh catastrophe and make further desperate measures necessary."

During this period Stadion repeatedly called in Solomon to examine the situation with him and ask his advice. If, however, he hoped for comfort from him, he was doomed to some disappointment. Solomon too had suffered from the sudden fall in the value of securities, and could not himself help being somewhat affected by the general panic. It was not until he received reassuring news from his three brothers in the West of Europe, that he was able to take a less gloomy view of the situation.

The panic reached its height on March 22. On that day Stadion wrote again to Metternich, describing the complications in Naples and Piedmont as amounting to the destruction of Austria.[82] He wrote: "If all the misfortunes that appear imminent today come upon us at once, I must confess I see no hope of salvation. Nevertheless we must try to put an end to the Naples adventure as speedily as possible, and thus at least save the army's honor. All troops should be withdrawn to within our frontiers and kept in readiness to meet attacks from abroad and from the revolutionary spirit at home."

Metternich said nothing, but proceeded to set troops in motion for quelling the revolt. It was Stadion's business and not his to raise the necessary money. The former had already spent money which was earmarked for the year 1822, and his pronounced sense of responsibility caused him to take a darker view of recent events than was strictly justified. Metternich, however, infected his imperial master, who was staying with him at Laibach, with his own spirit of resolute calm, and the emperor wrote a reassuring letter to the King of Naples. The king had just left Laibach, having borrowed the money for the journey to Florence from the Emperor Francis, as he had no funds himself. While assuring the king that his interests were identical with his own, the emperor did not forget about the repayment of the journey money, and issued instructions that the cash should immediately be provided out of the Rothschild loan which was being planned in Naples.[83]

On March 24 the expeditionary force had entered Naples without encountering serious resistance. The news of this event put an end to the rising in Piedmont; Lombardy remained quiet; and the general information received at Laibach gave reason to hope that the whole movement would die down. In a short time Metternich was able to feel that he had reestablished his system in both countries. It was now possible completely to reassure Carl, and to persuade him that the journey to Florence, where the King of Naples was still staying with his retinue, was absolutely safe. Before he started on the further journey to the capital at the foot of Vesuvius, the Austrian troops there would have reestablished complete order and security.

It was on March 23 that Gentz had made these reassuring observations to Carl Rothschild, using the opportunity to ask for a small personal loan. Carl, who was not so quick at appreciating Gentz's influence as his brothers had been, made difficulties, with the result that, to use his own words, "an unpleasant discussion" ensued.

When he got back home Rothschild learned that Metternich wished him to leave for Florence on the following day. He felt some misgivings regarding the disobliging attitude he had adopted toward the right-hand man of the all-powerful chancellor; and he thought that his brother Solomon would be annoyed with him if he had parted from Gentz in ill-will. He accordingly called on Gentz late that evening in order, as the latter put it, "to make good his error."

Metternich had given Carl Rothschild a letter of introduction to the Austrian general, Baron Vincent, who was staying at Florence with the King of Naples. The general had long known of the Austrian government's financial intentions regarding a loan to be issued in Naples. He knew that the Allies had agreed with the king at Laibach that the costs of the expedition should be borne by the kingdom of Naples from the moment when the army crossed the Po, and that the cost of maintaining the army in Naples should also be borne by that kingdom. Metternich had sent Vincent the following instructions on the matter as early as March 1, 1821:

"The point regarding the loan is of great importance for our finances. We wish to facilitate the work of the

Neapolitan government so that they will be able to provide for the first needs of our army and fulfil some of their obligations to us. Count Stadion has already entered into negotiations on this matter with the House of Rothschild. . . . It is desirable in our financial interests that this house should be given the preference, and the king also is prepared to proceed on these lines. The firm has the necessary means at its disposal, and I therefore believe that it will be possible speedily to come to terms with it. . . .

"It would be redundant to point out to your Excellency that the fact that Count Stadion was compelled to make enormous advances to the Neapolitan Expeditionary Force has made him exceedingly anxious to insure that these moneys shall be gradually repaid. He is the more concerned about this since, if the monarchy were to incur such a heavy loss, the resulting financial embarrassment might produce results which nobody can foresee." [84]

Shortly before Carl Rothschild's departure Metternich followed up these instructions with a letter [85] stating that Rothschild was coming only in order to negotiate for the Neapolitan loan. Although this firm had not yet put forward definite terms, Metternich wrote, it was desirable that the Neapolitan government should hand over to the House of Rothschild bonds coming within the scheme of their general system of credit at a fixed price, and leave it to the firm to reimburse itself by issuing these bonds at its own risk at a price which would yield it a profit.

Should the House of Rothschild demand a guarantee from Austria for the due carrying out of the obligations of the Neapolitan government, Vincent was authorized to accept such a condition if it was necessary. He was urged, however, to ask Rothschild to put his proposals into writing, and to press for a speedy conclusion of the agreement. This was urgent in the interests of Austria's finances. In general he should show courtesy to Carl Rothschild and introduce him to the Neapolitan minister, Prince Ruffo, so that Rothschild could deal direct with him. Metternich concluded by saying:

"We must naturally take no direct part in these business negotiations, but we are very much interested in their success. The loan is destined to cover a part of the costs of the expedition, as well as to meet the expenses of maintaining and paying our army. You are invited, therefore, if Herr von Rothschild's first proposals are accepted by the Neapolitan minister, to facilitate the conclusion of their business through your good offices."

Carl Rothschild arrived in Florence on March 31. On Vincent's introduction he had a short interview with Prince Ruffo,[86] but he was coolly received and was not given any explanation as to the minister's intentions. He had to wait for news from James, who had been requested by Solomon to express his views regarding the Neapolitan business. Vincent advised Rothschild to go to Naples and inform himself as to the prospect on the spot, for Ruffo had been absent so long that he was completely uninformed as to the financial situation. The Ambassador took the opportunity of borrowing 1,000 ducats[87] on the government's account, the advance for his official expenses having long been exhausted. Rothschild gladly lent the desired amount.

Although the agreements were kept secret, and nobody knew that that firm had been granted absolute priority, the news of a loan to be issued by Naples became known in other banking circles. A Milanese, by name Barbaia, approached Vincent, and in agreement with certain French firms offered[88] to advance thirty millions to the Neapolitan government at an issue price of 60%. "My one fear is," Vincent replied, "that this may conflict with our arrangements with the House of Rothschild and confuse them." Barbaia was not a negligible rival. He was already known to the King of Naples, and was received by him in Florence on this occasion too. Vincent as speedily as possible gave Carl Rothschild precise information regarding the offer.[89] "You will," he remarked, "be in a better position than anyone else to say what value should be attached to this offer."

This problem itself naturally did not engage Carl's very close attention, but it was valuable to him to be informed of his rivals' plans as speedily and accurately as possible, in order to be able to take appropriate counter-measures.

On April 6 he proceeded to Naples. Vincent gave him a letter to Ambassador Count Ficquelmont, informing the count of the offer being made by Barbaia, and of Austria's anxiety that the loan should be intrusted to the firm of Rothschild. The king himself did not yet dare to return to Naples. In accordance with Metternich's instructions the general commanding at Naples meanwhile restrained the newly installed government from considering loans proposed by various Italian banking firms before Rothschild should have arrived. When he arrived on April 12, Count Ficquelmont immediately introduced him to the government, who informed him that they wished to take up a loan of twelve million ducats—about twenty million gulden.

Under pressure from the Austrian general the government had ignored Barbaia's offers, although the Milanese had brought a letter from the King of Naples recommending him. The king had instinctively felt that the House of Rothschild would act in Austria's interests rather than his own; but he was king only by the grace of Austria, and that country could call the tune.

The House of Rothschild stated that they were prepared to grant a loan of ten million ducats.[90] They added that they would at first make only six millions available, the balance to be paid when they had placed the six million. The bonds were to be issued at 54; 3% commission was to be paid; and an undertaking was to be given that during the continuance of the agreement no new loan should be issued. Moreover, in any future loans the firm was to be given the preference before any other. For sinking-fund purposes and for greater security they demanded that the state domains should be pledged.

These were hard conditions. Public securities then stood at 60%, so that the issue price was very low, and all the more favorable to the Rothschilds, as they intended to issue the state bonds (which had hitherto been dealt with only on the Naples bourse) and, through their London and Paris houses, to put them on the market in those cities. The Neapolitan finance minister, Marchese d'Andrea, considered the proposals to be far less advantageous than those of certain Neapolitan firms, and therefore entirely unacceptable. The minister was of opinion that instead of helping the state the conditions would be a serious blow to its credit, since it was impossible to place any confidence in a government that sold its securities at such a low rate. He held that there was no reason for selling bonds at 54 when the ruling price was 60. The government was not so pressed for money as those appeared to believe who put such proposals forward.[91] Meanwhile, news had been received that the revolution at Naples had collapsed.

Ficquelmont summoned Carl Rothschild and told him that Austria was desirous that the House of Rothschild should handle the loan. The ambassador requested him not to make it too difficult for Austria to bring the necessary pressure to bear upon the Neapolitan government, but to moderate his terms somewhat.

Rothschild replied that his first proposals were not his last word in the matter; he had been asked to make an offer, and he had done so by way of opening negotiations. The good news received from Piedmont made it possible for him now to offer better conditions. The ambassador also asked Rothschild to avoid, if possible, saying anything about a guarantee by the powers. Carl promised to do what he could, and Ficquelmont assured him of his full and very powerful support with the Neapolitan government. That government owed its very existence to the Austrians, and it was obvious that it would have to conclude the agreement with those whom the Austrians wished.

The ambassador at Naples had completely understood what was in the minds of the leading men at Vienna. "If the House of Rothschild carries through a loan of any kind," he wrote to Metternich, [92] "that fact will provide us with the necessary security. As we have not yet made any direct or positive demand for reimbursement of our expenses, I did not feel that it was possible to include in the terms of the loan any explicit condition regarding direct payments to Austria [by the House of Rothschild]. Herr Rothschild, who always keeps our interests in view in the negotiations, has therefore inserted the words in his draft terms, 'payable to those who shall be authorized to receive the money.' This condition will become applicable when our direct negotiations have settled the amount to be paid to us."

The ambassador was anxious that the Neapolitan finances should be spared as much as possible so that there should not be any doubt as to Naples' ability to pay the expenses of Austria's expeditionary force. "If the current expenses for the maintenance of our army," Ficquelmont wrote to Metternich, "can be met out of the ordinary revenue of the state, the whole amount of the loan could be paid into our treasury, except perhaps the first two or three instalments, which the government will require . . . in order to put the taxing system in order."

Shortly afterwards the loan was issued, 16,000,000 ducats being taken up at 60 ducats for the 100 ducat bond. Rothschild allowed other Italian banking firms to take some small part in it in order to keep active opposition down. The government pledged itself not to issue any further loan before 1824, and if it required to issue further loans, to give the House of Rothschild the preference.

Carl joyfully reported the conclusion of the business to Metternich.[93] He emphasized that in accordance with Metternich's wishes he had made no mention of a guarantee by the powers, writing: "Moreover, I hope that, if peace only lasts for a little while, the loan will soon be fully subscribed, and it will not be necessary to ask for guarantees for the balance, as in that case all state securities will rise in value, and the Neapolitan securities will follow suit . . ."

The plan had succeeded, and Austria had thereby put the House of Rothschild in the saddle at Naples. This was not done from motives of disinterested friendship, and the brothers Rothschild paid for the privilege—with Neapolitan money. Meanwhile the forces of reaction were playing havoc at Naples. People were arrested in thousands, the death penalty and long terms of imprisonment were meted out to the Carbonari and the revolutionary officers. A strict censorship was also instituted. These conditions continued after the return of the king, and as all these things were being done under the protection of Austrian bayonets, the foreïgn troops did not gain any sympathy in the country. All classes, excepting the conservative upper class, regarded them as undesirable guests; and resentment against the Austrians was heightened by the fact that theÿ were using a clever foreigner to force the country itself to pay for their occupation.

About this time death came to the man in whose service the Rothschild family had grown great. On February 27, 1821, the Elector of Hesse had a heart attack. With the words,[94] "I shall lose this battle," he expired. His death had nothing like the importance to the Rothschild family that it would have had about ten years earlier, when their transactions with the elector constituted almost their only, and certainly their most important, business.

The new elector spent a great deal of money, but he had not the commercial ability of his father, and the relationship with the Rothschilds was limited to casual transactions of minor importance. Amschel at Frankfort carried on the business of making loans on an extensive scale to princes and other important personages whom he desired to cultivate. James and Nathan put the Neapolitan securities on the market in London and Paris, making the interest due in London payable in British currency, a fact which induced many people to invest their money in these securities, carrying as they did a high rate of interest. The result was that soon after their issue they rose considerably in price.

Nathan was clever at securing people's support, and at getting publicity for himself. A young clerk from the commercial department of the treasury at Vienna, by name Anton Laurin, had been sent to study in England for some months during the summer of 1820, and was naturally referred to the Austrian consul in London, Nathan Rothschild. Nathan showed a great deal of kindness to Laurin, as he naturally assumed that he would send a report home. He acted as his mentor, and invited him frequently to dinner and supper.

He was so successful in securing the young man's affection that Laurin gave the most ecstatic not to say extravagant and almost tedious accounts of him when he returned home. He sent in such an enthusiastic report to his chief that the latter decided to convey the essential points in it to the emperor, with the request that Nathan should be specially commended.

After recounting how Nathan had helped Laurin, the president of the commercial department of the treasury proceeded to state in his memorandum to the sovereign: "Laurin at the same time reports as to the disinterested work done by this consul, and as to his efforts to be of effective assistance to Austria's credit, industry, and commerce. He states that Rothschild waives all consular fees, actively assists Austrian subjects . . . has secured a quotation for Austrian state securities on the London stock exchange, helps Austrian sailors generously . . . from his private resources. Nathan is prepared with his own ships to establish a direct service between London and Trieste; he has sent a collection of seeds of rare foreign plants for your Majesty's gardens, as well as several articles of interest in industry and the arts for the Polytechnic Institute without asking for any payment; he is still collecting models and various objects of this kind with a view to bequeathing them to that institute.

"It is not for me to express an opinion as to the value of the services rendered to the credit of the Austrian state by Consul Rothschild; in this connection I can but humbly lay before your Majesty the London stock-exchange report for the 6th ultimo, which he has sent me. In this your Majesty may be graciously pleased to observe that Austrian state debentures are specially mentioned, together with their price, under the designation Austrian Loan. The other efforts referred to above by Consul Rothschild for facilitating and extending Austrian trade, the industrious and disinterested manner in which he carries out the duties of the consulate, so graciously intrusted to him by your Majesty, his generous help to unemployed Austrian sailors, and his efforts to enrich your Majesty's gardens and the Polytechnic Institute deserve proper recognition.

"Through establishing a direct monetary exchange on London, Rothschild has indisputably greatly facilitated commercial and financial transactions. If he succeeds, as he undoubtedly will, in view of the disinterested patriotism of his aims and methods, in establishing direct communication between London and Trieste, the beneficial results to our commerce will be even more marked. Through carrying out this one conception he will earn the well-deserved gratitude of a considerable portion of the Austrian trading community and consuming public. . . .

"I hope that your Majesty may graciously realize from

a perusal of these few lines what an important and beneficial influence upon the trade and industry of the monarchy the nomination of this man as Austrian consul is having. . . . Our former consuls in this country, which is so uniquely adapted to trade and industry, did . . . absolutely nothing for the monarchy, confining their activities to collecting substantial fees from our subjects. . . . The newly appointed consul, Rothschild, has in a very short time done more than all his predecessors put together. I therefore feel it to be my duty to bring his meritorious activities to your Majesty's knowledge, and at the same time most dutifully to beg that your Majesty's satisfaction may accordingly be conveyed to him." [95]

In his memorandum to the emperor of March 6, 1821,[96] Count Stadion confirmed the statements of Ritter von Stahl, adding that the Rothschilds also deserved praise for the greater facility with which, under the existing critical conditions, the financial requirements of the army in Italy could be met.

These two documents were also sent to Count Zichy for his observations, who passed them to Privy Councilor Baron von Lederer, who gave his opinion in the same skeptical vein he had used when the ennoblement of the family was under consideration.

"The alleged special services of Nathan Meyer Rothschild," he wrote, [97] "are connected partly with his activities as Austrian consul in London, and partly with his relation to the finance departments. If it is due to Rothschild that Austrian government securities are quoted in London stock-exchange reports, and if the transfer of money to Italy has been facilitated through the good offices of the House of Rothschild it must be remembered that the interests of the brothers Rothschild are identical with those of the finance departments.

"The brothers Rothschild are at the head of the business which concluded the last two loans with the Austrian financial administration, so that they are clearly interested in obtaining a market for Austrian securities abroad, and particularly in London. When banking firms undertake to remit money they are rewarded by a commission set aside for the purpose, and are able to profit by differences in the rate of exchange. I would therefore attach more importance to Nathan Meyer Rothschild's disinterested manner of carrying out his duties as Austrian consul, and would venture immediately to concur in the proposal that he should be acquainted of his Majesty's satisfaction, if I did not feel that the occasion for doing so is somewhat unsuitable.

"A clerk of the commercial department of the treasury, by name Laurin, obtains leave to travel to England. He is given a letter of introduction to Nathan Meyer Rothschild, who receives him in a friendly manner, and supports him in his endeavors to extend his knowledge in the fields of industry and commerce. He returns full of praise of the way he has been received, and takes the opportunity of commenting in high terms on Nathan Meyer Rothschild's disinterested and zealous conduct as consul.

"I am far from wishing to cast any doubt upon the facts that he brings forward, but as he made the journey purely as a private person, and not on any official mission, it was not his business to put these facts forward through official channels, and to take the responsibility for their accuracy. In my humble opinion the statement he volunteered should merely have led to an inquiry on the matter being made through the Austrian Embassy; and it seems to me that this omission can still be rectified."

The emperor, who was not yet fully aware how deeply leading statesmen had committed themselves to the House of Rothschild, did indeed command that further information should be asked for regarding Laurin's statements that Rothschild carried out his duties in such a disinterested manner. Ritter von Stahl, however, stuck to his guns, and was particularly emphatic in pressing the interests of the House of Rothschild. As he knew that James in Paris desired the dignity of an Austrian consul-general, for the same reasons as his brother in London, he suggested, on March 30, that James should be appointed.

The highest quarters did not give any immediate decision in this matter, but the Neapolitan revolution occurred shortly afterwards, involving the close cooperation between Metternich and the House of Rothschild. It was no longer thought either desirable or possible to refuse the brothers anything, as it depended upon their attitude whether or not Austria should recover the money spent on the expeditionary force. Solomon gave his brother James at Paris to understand that he should renew his application to be appointed consul-general, for now was the critical moment, as the Austrian government was more or less in a cleft stick. As it was under an obligation to the House and closely associated with it, it could not turn the request down.

James asked Solomon, as he stood so well in Vienna, to put forward the request himself. Solomon drafted a petition to the emperor, and handed it to Stadion, who, in consideration of the indispensability of Solomon and his family, conveyed it to the emperor with the following memorandum: [98]

"I venture to support this petition, which your Majesty was previously not pleased to entertain, for the following reasons, which relate particularly to present circumstances, and to conditions obtaining during the last few years. Your Majesty is fully aware of the highly important services which the House of Rothschild or, more accurately, the various Rothschild firms established in the principal capitals of Europe have rendered in the complicated difficulties of the present time.

"To the energy and resources of the Rothschilds, to their tireless efforts to apply large sums of money at points where they were immediately required to stem the tide of events, I owe the fact that I have been able continuously, in all places, and at the right moment, to provide what was necessary for military operations, without interfering with our internal services or the measures to restore our credit. In the precarious state of Austria's finances resulting from recent events, it was only thus that popular feeling and the government's credit could be maintained at the point where they now stand. Through the Rothschilds' clever management, the cost of the extensive monetary movements during the military operations was low compared with any other method of remitting money.

"Through the great services which the Rothschild firms have rendered to us during a most eventful period, their existence has become most intimately bound up with that of the Austrian monarchy. They have incurred the envy and hatred, and to a certain extent the persecution of the whole Liberal party in Europe; and although the extent of their wealth, their firmly established reputation throughout Europe, and their constant rectitude in business matters have so far protected them from the consequences of malicious intrigues, it is really essential that their services should be recognized by our court and that they should enjoy the explicit protection of your Majesty in the principal markets of the world, in order that they may have the necessary strength to resist all these machinations and to continue as useful to the monarchy in the future as they have been in the past.

"This is particularly the case in Paris as being the headquarters of all Liberal activities in Europe, and the city in whose bourse the loans of all states are handled, with no inconsiderable effect upon their value.

"The president of the commercial department of the treasury has laid before your Majesty proofs of what has been done to promote our trade by the Rothschild who has been appointed consul-general in London. Even more successful have been his efforts to develop a market for the sale of our securities in England and to establish arrangements for directly discounting bills of exchange between Great Britain and the Austrian markets.

"Paris is as indifferent as London to religious distinctions, and the appointment of one of the brothers Rothschild as Austrian consul-general in Paris should be of real service to the commercial and financial interests of the monarchy. Moreover, Rothschild waives the right to any emoluments connected with such an appointment, which he desires only for the distinction attaching to the office as being likely to afford him some protection against the hatred and persecution of the Liberal party in that city."

There was much truth in Stadion's report. The Rothschilds had in fact made themselves unpopular with the more Liberal section of the public abroad, through the contracts which they had made everywhere with the re-established reactionary governments. Stadion was not aware that in spite of their particularly conservative sentiment, especially in Austria, they cultivated relations with the other parties as well, lent money here and there, and thus secured themselves against a political reaction such as was always possible.

The envy of other firms was increasing to a prodigious extent as the power of their house grew. In Paris their position was particularly delicate. For the Bourbon kingdom, with the weak Louis XVIII and the Ultras, who were all the more powerful, was far from popular, and the strictly royalist minister, Villèle, who was at the head of the government, was hated by a large part of the population. The brothers Rothschild, however, had necessarily become intimately connected with the new régime and, moreover, as the bankers of the Holy Alliance, they were sending French gold abroad in large amounts.

James Rothschild was often the target of veiled attacks, and once he felt actually constrained to call upon the prefect of police to lodge a complaint regarding the large number of threatening anonymous letters which he was receiving.[99] Through being appointed consul-general he hoped not merely to raise his social prestige, but also to achieve greater security under international law. It is true it was not realized at the court either of Paris or of Vienna that James Rothschild was in close association with the liberal-minded Duke Louis Philippe of Orléans (afterwards King of France). James frequently advised him in money matters, and was very often a guest in his house.

Emperor Francis referred James Rothschild's application to be appointed consul-general to the commercial department of the treasury, with the instruction that they should let him have their observations upon it. Ritter von Stahl did not need to be asked twice to do this. He immediately transmitted the application to Stadion with the following observations:[100]

"England and France are by far the most cultivated states in Europe; in them agriculture, industry, and commerce flourish in the greatest harmony, and it is therefore most important for us to have in their capitals commercial agents who are experienced men, and enjoy an extensive credit. . . . As far as commercial and industrial matters are concerned, I cannot suggest a more suitable person for his Majesty than the head of the Paris House, James von Rothschild.

"I made his personal acquaintance during his last stay here; he is a young man of parts, who is intimately acquainted with several members of the Polytechnical Institute in Paris, and of the Conservatoire des Arts et Métiers, as well as with many of the most cultured French manufacturers and business men. Moreover, he expressed to me his readiness, as his brother in London had done, to cooperate in every possible way in promoting our industry and commerce. For this purpose he immediately ordered some interesting machines, which he is giving to our Polytechnic Institute, assuring me that he did not wish in any way to lag behind his brother in London in proof of his devotion to the House of Austria.

"Finally, the consideration that James Rothschild is a Jew seems, in my humble opinion, to constitute no greater difficulty than in the case of his brother in London. It is true that in the decision regarding the appointment of the London Rothschild as consul, which decision is attached to the application, your Majesty expressly laid down that it would have to continue to be the rule that no Israelite should be appointed consul. Yet if the exception made by your Majesty in favor of the London Rothschild has proved in the highest degree beneficial, it is likely to be no less so in the case of the Paris Rothschild.

"In Paris, too, the consuls . . . have no specially representative character . . . and as, under the French constitution, the Israelites enjoy the same rights of citizenship as all other French subjects in France, I am of opinion that your Majesty may graciously permit an exception to the rule to be made in the case of James von Rothschild such as you have graciously permitted to be made in regard to the London Rothschild.

"While the commercial and industrial reasons for acceding to James von Rothschild's request are weighty, the financial considerations are still more important. This point it is not necessary for me to labor; your Excellency is fully aware that since the recent crucial events in Italy the combined Rothschild houses have rendered far greater services than they had rendered even at the time when his Majesty, with your Excellency's approval, was graciously pleased to appoint the London Rothschild to the office of consul. It is certainly a factor of no small importance in the success of such vital operations to have the support of all these wealthy firms."

In conclusion, Ritter von Stahl strongly urged that Metternich should be asked to express an opinion as to whether there was any objection to the proposal from a political point of view, so that a further report to his Majesty might be made as speedily as possible.

Metternich duly wrote to Herr von Stahl: [101] "As all considerations of a commercial, industrial, and financial nature make it desirable to grant this application, I have to add only that from a political point of view there is no reason why Solomon von Rothschild's wish should not be granted."

On August 11, 1821, James von Rothschild was duly appointed consul-general in Paris. Thus another of the five brothers had climbed a rung in the ladder of social position.

Immediate payment for his Majesty's favor was required. Since the Austrian army had entered Naples, the Neapolitan government had met all its expenses, including pay; but ten days after so whole-heartedly supporting the petition, Metternich instructed Count Ficquelmont in Naples to get from that government the money that had been expended from the moment when the army crossed the Po. The finance minister had already pressed impatiently to be indemnified for these expenses.[102] The advances already made were estimated at 4,650,000 gulden, and the money was to be repaid in Vienna in six monthly instalments, commencing on August 1, 1821.[103] Metternich sent a private letter to the count, together with these instructions.[104]

"The ministry of finance," wrote the chancellor, "attaches very great importance to the punctual and reliable repayment of the moneys which you are hereby instructed to demand from the Neapolitan government, and it will not tolerate any further excuses for delay. With this end in view, it has concluded an agreement with the House of Rothschild under which . . . Herr Rothschild in Naples has been authorized to make an arrangement with the government in order to facilitate these payments. . . . I have the honor to request you to get into communication with Herr Rothschild on this matter, and to support such proposals as he may consider it desirable to submit to the Neapolitan government. The object of these proposals will be to make it easier for the government to effect a payment that might cause it some embarrassment without the assistance of this banking firm, and at the same time to facilitate the punctual receipt of a considerable sum of money by our treasury, in the payment of which no further delay can be suffered, as it constitutes a part of our annual budget."

Although he did not succeed in arranging for the Neapolitan government to repay the whole of this amount, Count Ficquelmont managed to obtain compensation to the extent of 4,000,000 gulden, 500,000 to be payable on August 31, 700,000 in each of the following three months, and 1,400,000 in January, 1822.[105] The first amount was paid to Carl Rothschild and transmitted by him through his brother Solomon to the Austrian government. It had been possible to make this payment out of existing funds, but further payments were to be met out of the loan of the House of Rothschild.[106] Thus part of the money subscribed for the loan never reached the Neapolitan Treasury at all, but was made over to Austria direct by the House of Rothschild, although Naples bore the whole burden of the loan.

The government of that kingdom at this time made the request of Carl Rothschild that in consideration of certain additional advantages he would, if possible, make his loan payments to them earlier than was provided for under the agreement. Rothschild agreed, on condition that he was allowed to deduct the first two instalments of 700,000 gulden, and transmit them direct to Austria. Carl reported the conclusion of this agreement to Count Ficquelmont, stating:

"I am accordingly glad to be in a position . . . to give your Excellency the assurance that the first two payments are secured, and that I shall be making payments to your Excellency, instead of my brother making them in Vienna.

Amschel Meyer von Rothschild
From a portrait by William Hobday
in the Frankfort Historical Museum

Your Excellency will no doubt realize that this was the principal reason which led me to fall in with the suggestion—at some sacrifice to myself. For I was thus able to satisfy your Excellency's wish that the payments in question should be secured to the I. and R. Treasury, and at the same time furnish further proof that I am always prepared to make every effort in the interest of his Majesty's service. As for the balance of 1,400,000 gulden (out of the total of 4,000,000 gulden) due in January, I shall try to deal with this sum in a new loan which the royal government of Naples intends to issue shortly. . . ."

Carl Rothschild had thus endeavored to meet the convenience of all parties. He made it easier for the Austrians to recover their expenses, and he paid the instalment on the loan to the Neapolitans before the agreed dates. He himself did not do badly, for in June, 1821, the bonds he had underwritten at 60, already stood at 76½! The court of Naples had been in such urgent need of the advance payments on account of the loan that when Carl agreed to make them, he received a special letter from the finance minister.[107]

"His Majesty," the letter ran, "has instructed me to communicate to you in his royal name, his full and gracious satisfaction with the consideration you have shown in the matters affecting the treasury."

The king's debts to the emperor were also settled through the House of Rothschild by making a deduction from the loan. The balance, so far as it was not used in the maintenance of the Austrian army, was not spent either carefully or usefully. In spite of all the loans, therefore, the country continued to be oppressed by financial stringency; and the Neapolitan ministers were constantly complaining of the annual charges (amounting to nine million ducats) for maintaining the Austrian army, which made any reasoned finance impossible.

But Austria insisted upon its pound of flesh, and Stadion's attitude was positively petty when Carl Rothschild transmitted the moneys to Austria in bills due in three months. The finance minister demanded immediate payment in cash, as Naples was required to pay the money free of all charges in Vienna. Carl took the stand that without his intervention and willingness, the Neapolitan government would have been absolutely unable to carry out the obligation it had incurred to the Austrian court to pay four million gulden, so that he had felt himself justified in adopting this method of remitting the money.[108] Henceforward, however, he paid in cash, and simply debited the expense of remitting the money and the loss on exchange to the Neapolitan treasury.

In such circumstances the first loan was naturally soon exhausted, and the Neapolitan finance minister found it necessary to apply to Carl Rothschild for a second loan. After lengthy negotiations a loan of the nominal amount of 16,800,000 ducats was arranged at the end of November, 1821, which in view of a wider market and the resulting improvement in price was underwritten at 67.3 in spite of the fact that the state's indebtedness had increased.

When the amount of 1,400,000 gulden fell due on the last day of January, 1822, the finance minister himself asked Rothschild to make the payment out of the loan,[109] as Naples was not able to find the money; for the support of the Austrian troops was a constant heavy burden on the treasury. Stadion's financial program with regard to Naples was carried through quite ruthlessly; and Metternich was able to point out to the finance minister that thanks to the Rothschild intervention, which he had advised, the undertaking that Stadion had so much dreaded had been completely financed by Naples.

Metternich fully appreciated the services rendered by the House of Rothschild, and was prepared at Solomon's urgent request to devote greater energy henceforward to securing the emanicipation of the Jews. Slowly but surely, the rich Jewish bankers, who had been brought into touch by the Rothschilds with the delegates to the diet at Frankfort, improved their social position. Severely though they had been shunned before, the change became apparent during the first months of 1820. The Rothschilds and other representatives of the commercial world gave big dinners, and the bearers of the most noble names, as well as persons in every kind of high office, were seen at their tables. In this way they often acquired items of news that they could turn to account in business.

"Since arriving here," the Bremen burgomaster Smidt wrote from Frankfort,[110] "I have found to my great astonishment that people like the Bethmanns, Gontards, Brentanos eat and drink with prominent Jews, invite them to their houses and are invited back. When I expressed my surprise I was told that no financial transaction of any importance could be carried through without the cooperation of these people, they had to be treated as friends and it was not desirable to fall out with them. Having regard to these facts the Rothschilds have been invited by some of the ambassadors."

During this period Amschel Meyer Rothschild's wife was invited to a ball at the Prussian Legation in Frankfort. Smidt specifically recorded his opinion regarding the Rothschild family in a report of a conversation with the delegate to the diet, Count Buol.[111]

"This house," he observed, "has through its enormous financial transactions and its banking and credit connections, actually achieved the position of a real power. It has to such an extent acquired control of the general money-market that it is in a position either to hinder or to promote, as it feels inclined, the movements and operations of potentates, and even of the greatest European powers. Austria needs the Rothschilds' help for her present demonstration against Naples; and Prussia would long ago have had to discard her constitution if the House of Rothschild had not made it possible for her to put off the evil day. Several medium and small states have also had recourse to its financial power in their difficulties. This puts it in a strong position to ask for favors, especially for a favor of such an apparently trivial nature as the protection of a few dozen Jews in a small state."

At the end of May, 1820, Metternich sent a dispatch to the reluctant Buol instructing him to support most of the Jews' wishes in the diet. Buol, however, was inclined to follow out his own predilections, so that there was no immediate change in the situation; indeed the senate showed a tendency to revert to increased harshness in dealing with the Jews. Thereupon Metternich firmly admonished Buol to put an end to this state of affairs, with the result that the diet sent a kind of ultimatum to the senate.

The chancellor went even further; he traveled to Frankfort himself, and decided publicly to honor the Rothschilds there by accepting an invitation to dine with them. He had let Amschel Meyer know this through Solomon at Vienna, who had just come into prominence again through an action which had won sympathetic recognition in high quarters. The I. and R. Court Theatre at the Kärntner Tor was again without a lessee, and the only applicant, Dominik Barbaia, was unable to find the deposit of fifty thousand gulden in cash required under the terms of the lease. The House of Rothschild stated that they were prepared to guarantee and pay this amount to the I. and R. Treasury, whereby, as the document of guarantee stated, "the further continuance of an entertainment worthy of the dignity of the imperial court and the capital city" was assured until the year 1824.[112]

On his arrival at Frankfort, Metternich received the following letter from Amschel Meyer Rothschild: [113]

> MOST EXCELLENT PRINCE! MOST GRACIOUS PRINCE AND LORD!
>
> I hope your Highness will not regard it ungraciously or consider it as a presumption if I make so

> bold as to ask your Highness to do me the gracious favor of taking soup with me this noon.
>
> Such a favor would mark an epoch in my life; but I would not have ventured this bold request if my brother in Vienna had not assured me that your Highness did not entirely refuse his entreaty to grant me this gracious favor.
>
> The Austrian gentlemen here have assured me that they will also be present in such a case. If your Highness wishes to come at another time, please command me, for any man feels himself happy to be in your Highness's company.

Metternich accepted the invitation and, accompanied by his intimate friend Countess Lieven, came to lunch with Amschel Meyer, an event which did not fail of its effect upon the diet and upon society in Frankfort. The two burgomasters of Frankfort, although invited, did not come. The senate, however, was prepared to make all the concessions asked for, except to agree to the designation, "Israelite citizens." Metternich had seriously to emphasize his "definite wishes" to the obstinate Buol, instructing him to act "in strict accordance with them." But the senate remained obdura. , Buol practiced passive resistance, and the Jewish problem remained unresolved.

While making these social and diplomatic efforts on behalf of the Jews in general and of the Rothschilds in particular, Metternich instructed Gentz to see that the House of Rothschild did not suffer in the press. Because of the close association of that House with Austria, which was ruthlessly repressing all liberal movements in Germany, the more radical sections of the German public, and their papers, were venturing to pass some rather hostile judgments upon the House of Rothschild, in spite of the prevailing censorship. Gentz had repeatedly to listen to Metternich's reproach that he had not got the newspapers sufficiently in hand. For whenever an article unfavorable to the Rothschilds appeared in a German paper,

Solomon pressed Metternich to use his influence to prevent such occurrences in the future. Even the Frankfort letters to the Allgemeine Zeitung, published by the firm of Cotta, contained such attacks. Gentz felt that it was his duty to intervene.

"Sir," he wrote on October 18, 1821, to Cotta, "you will have heard from other sources that there is again grave dissatisfaction here regarding the manner in which the Allgemeine Zeitung is edited. . . . It seems to me all the more necessary that if you are really anxious that the A.Z. should continue to circulate in the Austrian states without restriction, you should at least mitigate such offending passages as convey the impression of hostility to Austria. . . .

"I refer to such articles as those of Frankfort origin, which have been appearing with some frequency lately, and which comment upon the financial operations here and the rate of exchange in a manner unfavorable to Austria and her credit. It is true that the general sense of these articles reveals the fact that they are directed, not against our state securities, but against the House of Rothschild. Under prevailing conditions, however, it is obvious that the moves attributed to the House of Rothschild always react upon our state credit, and are generally more damaging to it than to the Rothschilds, who in such cases are well able to help themselves."

On December 4, 1821, Gentz wrote again, saying, "The constant attacks upon the House of Rothschild invariably, and sometimes in the most outrageous manner, reflect upon the Austrian government by necessary implication, since everybody knows they are transacting important financial matters with that House, which is not only unimpeachable, but honorable and thoroughly respectable. The persistent rumors regarding new loans are invented simply and solely in order to undermine the confidence which our public securities have won and which they deserve." [114]

The Allgemeine Zeitung was thereafter banned throughout the whole dominions of the Austrian monarchy. Cotta, who although no friend of the Jews was a sound business man, was exceedingly displeased at this and requested Stegemann, the editor-in-chief, to be more careful, as Gentz—and they both knew well that meant Metternich—had complained bitterly about the paper.

Stegemann replied:[115] "In view of the letter from Herr von Gentz which you have been kind enough to communicate to me, I gladly give my formal promise not to accept . . . anything in future relating to the value of Austrian public securities, or *anything whatever* relating to the House of Rothschild (at least as affecting its relations with Austria). This means of course that I shall have to adopt a new, very cautious, and colorless attitude to affairs. . . . In point of fact, I know nothing of any *attacks* against the House of Rothschild, unless the remark that Madame Rothschild has received her first invitation from the Prussian minister constitutes an attack."

In a word, Cotta and Stegemann submitted, and for the time being the brothers Rothschild did not have to bother much about the very widely read Allgemeine Zeitung. The zeal Gentz had shown in this matter was not attributable entirely to Metternich's instructions. Since his return from Laibach to Vienna he had grown more and more intimate with Solomon Rothschild. He often had occasion to confer with him on behalf of his chief regarding the Neapolitan loan, and on one occasion Metternich made a very friendly remark to Gentz, regarding the attitude of the House of Rothschild in this matter.[116]

It happened that on the following day Gentz met Rothschild at a dinner given by the banker Eskeles at Hietzing; and he hastened to inform him of the "remarkably flattering remarks made by the prince." This produced, as Gentz himself records in his diary, results most favorable to himself.

"This morning," he notes,[117] on June 24, 1821, "Rothschild paid me a very long visit; he told me the same remarkable story about his money and family affairs as I had recently heard from the prince. At the same time he gave me the account of my share in certain recent financial operations, from which it appeared that, entirely contrary to my expectations, nearly five thousand gulden were due to me."

Gentz's diary for the next few months is full of notes of meetings with Rothschild, and constantly mentions his "very agreeable communications," [118] and "important financial arrangements." [119]

At the end of the year Rothschild specially demonstrated his gratitude for all the information he had received, and for the influence that had been brought to bear upon Prince Metternich and the press. "Rothschild breakfasted with me," Gentz notes in his diary on December 22, 1821, "and gave me a proof of real friendship for which I cannot feel too grateful to this excellent man at a time when all my income from the principalities has come to an end,[120] and nothing is done by those in authority to compensate me somewhat for this loss." [121] Finally, Gentz played his part in bleeding the Neapolitan treasury, and Rothschild assisted him in this matter too.

On New Year's Day Rothschild waited at Gentz's house until he came back from Metternich in order to tell him that a courier was leaving for Naples next day, and that Gentz might send an urgent reminder regarding the gratuity promised him by the court of Naples. He, Solomon, would see that the matter was put through by his brother Carl and General Koller, the intendant general of the Austrian troops. Gentz and Rothschild had become positively inseparable; the friendship certainly cost Solomon a great deal of money, but the cost was negligible in view of the advantages which it brought him.

The restoration of the Neapolitan kingdom by the Austrians placed heavy burdens upon the people. Count

Ficquelmont estimated that Naples had to pay 23 to 24 million gulden, or 12 to 13 million ducats, for the annual upkeep of the Austrian army; [122] he himself was terrified at the magnitude of the amount. "If the burdens that we impose," he reported to Vienna, "are so oppressive that they are more than the country can stand, all parties will unite in desiring our departure. Instead of being a protecting power we shall become oppressors. The end of it will be that we shall not be able to remain as long as our interests and those of the kingdom of Naples require."

The ambassador also stated emphatically, as he had often done before, that the finance minister was entirely incapable, and that there was only one man who could restore order, namely, Luigi de'Medici, the former finance minister, who had been overthrown by the revolution. All the other foreign representatives were also of this opinion, but the king feared Medici as a man whose intellectual gifts would not accord well with his own autocratic temper. Ficquelmont discussed this matter with Carl Rothschild, and Rothschild also thought that it was only by appointing this descendant of the eminent Tuscan noble family—a man of outstanding honor, energy, and administrative talent—that the material recovery of the country could be assured.

Although Medici had enemies among the royal family, such as the Duke of Calabria—to whom he had refused to give money for the duke to squander in an irresponsible manner—successful pressure was brought to bear by the Austrian government with the result that he was reappointed finance minister at Naples in the spring of 1822. The new minister did succeed with great difficulty in getting the country out of its serious embarrassments.

It is true that not even he was able to deal with the demands of Austria, but he proved himself a pertinacious accountant, and managed to knock down considerably the maintenance expenses of the Austrian army, the returns for which had always been scaled up very generously.

He contrived to make the second Rothschild loan last longer than his incompetent predecessors had done in the case of the first loan, but in December, 1822, he was compelled to have recourse to a third loan, the extent of which was 22 million ducats nominal. Later on he raised a fourth loan of 2½ million pounds sterling at the rate of 89⅘, in order to acquire the necessary funds for paying the Austrian army for a further period, and for covering the deficit in the budget.

Through arranging for the loan to be issued in sterling instead of in ducats Nathan expected especially to interest English investors,[123] and in this he was successful. By February 26, 1824, the loan was already quoted at 96.75. The public debt of Naples, which before the revolution had stood at 28 million ducats, had risen by the year 1824 to no less than 104 million ducats nominal, yet the bonds appreciated so considerably in value that some Neapolitan public securities stood at 108 in April, 1824. It might have been expected that as the amount of the debt increased these quotations would fall, since, the income having remained comparatively stationary, the security for repayment of the debt diminished as the debt increased in amount.

The ambassador Ficquelmont fully appreciated the position when he wrote: "It was therefore another's credit and not that of Naples that caused the prices to rise, namely, the credit of the House of Rothschild. The value of its public securities is therefore not a reliable basis on which alone to found an estimate regarding a state's welfare. By so doing one might be gravely misled.

"Securities at Naples have risen in value because a wider market for them has been found. London and Paris have become the principal centers through which they are sold. It has not been possible for Naples to contribute in any way to the result, since Naples merely punctually paid the interest on its debt. . . . A small portion of the funds has found its way to Austria, the balance, . . . which was not placed in Naples, has been gradually absorbed by powerful banking firms in London and Paris, which derive their profit from fluctuations in value, and have thus recouped themselves (and a great deal more) for the capital sums which they have advanced." [124]

Thus, briefly stated, the financial policy of the Rothschilds in Naples was summed up. Carl Rothschild had originally gone to Naples with the intention of remaining there only for a short time, as its occupation by Austrian troops was intended to be a temporary measure; but local conditions made it necessary that these troops should remain in the country for a much longer period, unless by withdrawing them Metternich was prepared to risk having the king and his reactionary supporters driven out of Naples.

While the Austrians remained, the presence of Carl was an urgent necessity; and his wife, who had embarked on the journey to Naples as a pleasure trip, made arrangements for a prolonged stay. Carl extended his business, and finally contrived to make himself indispensable to the Neapolitan court in financial matters. He struck roots in that beautiful city of southern Italy, and what had at first seemed likely to be a brief business sojourn was destined to develop into permanent residence. And the House of Rothschild acquired a new center of operations in the world.

In spite of Stadion's efforts through Rothschild and military pressure to get in the money expended in Naples, the Austrian budget had got into a state of sad confusion. The rising in Piedmont had cost a great deal of money, and the military expenses had attained colossal figures. In despair Stadion reported to the emperor and Metternich [125] that the excess of expenditure over revenue was such that there was a permanent annual deficit of at least 20 million gulden, or more than one-sixth of the total budget. He urged the necessity for putting an end to this disastrous state of affairs. If it were to continue for a longer period of years, it would involve the downfall of the monarchy.

Stadion stated that another loan to cover this deficit was urgently required, and suggested recourse again to the House of Rothschild, whose wealth had increased prodigiously of recent years. Moritz von Bethmann, who was staying in Vienna in February, 1822, expressed the following opinion regarding the House of Rothschild: [126]

"I can understand that the Rothschilds prove exceedingly useful instruments to governments, and am far from wishing to cast aspersions on them or from envying them their good fortune. Solomon especially is a man of the most estimable character, and I am exceedingly fond of him. I have heard from a reliable source that Solomon Rothschild has stated that the annual balance sheet of the five brothers showed a net profit of six million gulden in 20-florin measure. This is certainly a case where the English proverb applies: 'Money makes money.'

"Observing their industry and judgment, we may expect their business to continue to flourish; indeed one hopes so, since the overthrow of this Colossus would be terrible. The harmony between the brothers contributes largely to their success. None of them ever thinks of finding fault with another. None of them adversely criticizes any of the others' business dealings, even when the results do not come up to expectations. Solomon has won people's affections here, partly through his general modesty and partly through his readiness to be obliging. Nobody leaves him without feeling comforted."

Stadion's gloomy report regarding the condition of the public finances induced the emperor to give his agreement to a loan being obtained from the House of Rothschild. Rothschild was approached in March, 1822, an amount of 28 to 30 million gulden being mentioned. The treasury official, Baron von Pillersdorff, wrote a considered report on the offer sent in by the firm.[127] Rothschild proposed that 30 million gulden should be issued at 70%, so that the loan certificates to be issued would represent a nominal capital sum of 42,957,000 gulden. As interest was allowed to be deducted, even before the money was paid, a capital amount of 42,875,000 florins would have to be issued in respect of cash received, amounting to 28,785,717 florins.

"If we compare the real underwriting figure (allowing for the deduction of interest) of 67%," Pillersdorff's report continued, "with the ruling price which averages 75%, we find there is a difference of eight points, or 10⅔% in favor of the underwriters, which would mean a profit to them of 3,428,000 gulden. It further appears from the above statement of the case, that the interest payable on the suggested loan would amount to 7½% per annum.

"The view to be taken of these conditions," the report concluded, "follows naturally from a consideration of the figures detailed above. In my opinion they are exceedingly onerous and less favorable than any previous proposals, having regard to the fact that the first loan, concluded when Austrian credit was in its infancy, was a daring experiment. They are unacceptable in view of all the reactions that would result. . . .

"Taking all these considerations into account, the proposals put forward do not seem to me such as should be accepted, even as a basis for further negotiation. It would certainly be a severe blow to the country's credit if it became known that, in the circumstances indicated above, a loan had been concluded at the price of 67%, especially when one bears in mind that the treasury would have to meet the reproach of having confined itself to a single offer."

The House of Rothschild was accordingly informed that the treasury was prepared to carry through a financing operation with them and Parish, if this could be arranged on favorable terms, but that the proposals made could not be regarded as such. Moreover, the treasury wished to take up only a small amount. The Rothschilds, who wanted to get the business at all costs, replied in the following terms: [128]

"We hasten hereby to inform your Excellency that we have just heard from our houses in London and Paris, that several firms in those cities have informed them of their desire to invest capital in Austrian funds, and thereby to participate in a loan arranged for his Majesty's service. In view of our friendly relations with those firms, we should be exceedingly glad to meet their wishes as far as we can. So we venture to inform your Excellency, in connection with the offer (we have now made) for underwriting twelve million gulden of five per cent loan, that we are prepared in any event to offer one and a half per cent more for the amount decided upon than is offered by any other firm."

The Rothschilds sent in a second letter on the same day, in which, together with Parish, they endeavored to get the large loan. They tried again to induce the finance minister immediately to issue the loan on a larger scale, as they stated,[129] "principally in order that the credulous and uninstructed public should have no occasion to believe that a similar operation would be repeated at an early date." The letter concluded: "In the full conviction, that none, not even the smallest circumstance of any significance escapes the profound insight and business acumen of your Excellency, we are confining ourselves briefly to indicating the above consideration and are content to leave the appreciation of it entirely to your Excellency's wisdom and judgment."

When the Austrian Treasury did not accept this offer, Solomon Rothschild felt personally aggrieved. He took his troubles to Gentz, who had just received a gratuity of three thousand ducats from the court of Naples, through Carl Rothschild's interventions. Gentz reports [130] how

Baronial Coat of Arms Finally Granted to the Rothschild Family in 1822

Solomon described, with many tears, how inconsiderately he had been treated in more than one quarter, in connection with his new loan proposals.

This failure was soon compensated for by other important transactions. Nathan had just concluded a loan of three and one-half million pounds with Prussia, and the repercussions of this transaction were felt as far as Frankfort and Vienna. Concurrently there were a large number of small loans arranged in Germany and Austria, with the higher nobility, who were short of money in both countries.

The loan, amounting to nine hundred thousand gulden, which Prince Metternich himself obtained from the House of Rothschild on September 23, is of particular interest. It was a perfectly straightforward business; the loan bore five per cent interest, and was to be repaid by 1834; in fact the prince repaid it in full in 1827. There was nothing in the least suggestive of bribery about the transaction—Metternich was no Gentz—but it was bound to make the chancellor, who thus became Solomon's debtor, feel not entirely free in his dealings with him. At all events it had the result that Metternich was more inclined to be sympathetic to the personal wishes and requests of Solomon Rothschild and his brother.

The chancellor had known for some time that the brothers Rothschild were not content with the simple "von" that they had acquired in the year 1817, and that they had their eye on the title of baron. Upon Gentz one day sounding Metternich as to whether a request in that direction was likely to meet with success, the chancellor gave him to understand that he would raise no objection. The brothers accordingly put forward this request, mentioning their services to Austria. And it was granted; by an imperial decree, dated September 29, 1822, all the brothers and their legitimate descendants of either sex were raised to the rank of baron.

Thus most of the objections raised by the College of

Heralds, the court officials, and Baron von Lederer, were automatically discounted. The Rothschilds obtained the seven-pointed coronet which, as a rather broad hint, they had drawn on the coat-of-arms submitted in 1817. The lion on the coat was also granted, and instead of the four arrows which the hand had grasped since they had been admitted into the ranks of the minor nobility, there were now five, symbolizing the five brothers. They were also granted supporters, a lion and a unicorn, and three splendid helmets adorned the coronet. The motto, "Concordia, integritas, industria," was intended to express the harmony between the brothers, as well as their honesty and tireless industry.

In view of the enormous value attaching to any title of nobility in those times, the promotion to the rank of baron signified for the Jewish House, which only twenty years ago had been almost entirely unknown outside its native town, an almost immeasurable increase of prestige. The private life of the brothers also changed from this time. They occupied luxurious dwellings in Frankfort, Paris, and London. Only the aged Gudula stuck faithfully to the family house in the Jewish quarter until her death in 1849 at the age of ninety-six.

Their efforts firmly to establish their social position also met with success, especially as the stories of the family's wealth had invested its members with a kind of legendary halo. They consciously encouraged this belief in their wealth and their power, for they fully realized that it increased the credit of their House. Astonishing though the achievements of the five brothers had been since their father's death, they showed no sign yet of flagging in their efforts. They were driven by the constant urge to accumulate ever-growing riches, and to increase their power and prestige.

CHAPTER V

The Rothschild Business Throughout the World

THROUGH his vigorous intervention, Metternich had restored peace after his fashion in the Apennine Peninsula. The chancellor, however, was constantly apprehensive for the future of his system and the principle of legitimacy, and dreaded the spread of liberal and democratic ideas. When the fires had been quenched at one spot they burst out at another on the broad continent of Europe. Attention was now directed to the Greek rising, and to the civil war in Spain, which had been continuing since 1820.

In this country, which had wrung a constitution from the king, the opposing forces of the Right and Left were still in conflict. During the summer of 1820 the radical members of the Cortes treated the king practically as a prisoner, and on June 22 of that year Ferdinand VII wrote to the King of France requesting him to send forces to his assistance, and also endeavored to induce the other great powers to assist him against his own subjects.

The idea of intervention did not appeal particularly either to the King of France or to his chief minister Count de Villèle, although one party, that to which Chateaubriand belonged, was very much in favor of it. The matter had come to be one that concerned the whole of Europe, and Metternich had grown accustomed to intervene decisively in any important European crisis. He had found that the most effective way of doing so was through the congresses of sovereigns, such as had repeatedly been held of recent years. These congresses gave him the opportunity of using his persuasive powers to the full.

On October 20, 1822, another such congress met, this time at Verona. Metternich and Gentz accompanied the emperor to Verona as they had to Laibach, and profiting by their previous experience they took Solomon Rothschild with them. For it was obvious that if it were decided at Verona to apply measures of compulsion to Spain, the resources for this would have to be forthcoming immediately. As the House of Rothschild had proved so useful in the case of Naples, it was desired to make use of it if necessary on this occasion too. In the case of the congress at Laibach, Solomon had felt misgivings about leaving Vienna; but he made no difficulties now.

When Solomon arrived at Verona he learned from several representatives of the powers there of a rumor abroad that the House of Rothschild had offered a loan to the government which had come into power through the revolution, and which was threatening its own king, or that the Rothschilds had at any rate entered into negotiations with this government. Such conferences may actually have taken place; but it was of the utmost importance to the Rothschilds that Metternich should be reassured. He must not be left in any doubt as to the fact that their House was lending its support only to the legitimists and the conservative régime. Solomon therefore two days after his arrival at Verona hastened to write a letter to the chancellor refuting these rumors:[1]

"Most gracious Chancellor," the letter ran. "On my arrival at Verona I was amazed to learn that men of standing here believe that our House has contracted or intends to contract a loan with the Spanish government. Your Highness is far too familiar with the sentiments of myself and my brothers to give such a baseless rumor more than a moment's consideration. It is so wholly inconsistent with our general reputation that I do not think it necessary for me to go into explanations regarding the matter. I will confine myself to stating that your Highness may rest assured that we have never concluded any loan with the Spanish government, that we shall not conclude any such loan, and that we have refused such offers as have been made to us in this matter as decisively as we have, in your Highness's knowledge, refused similar offers in the past."

Solomon had spoken the truth. He had had nothing whatever to do with any arrangements with Spain; his brothers certainly, especially Nathan who lived in liberal England, often did things which they did not immediately communicate to the other brothers, and which these learned of only after the *fait accompli;* but on this occasion there had actually been no agreement concluded with Spain. After handing his letter to Metternich, Solomon called on Gentz. Alexander von Humboldt had just left him. Humboldt was attached to the King of Prussia's suite, and he had been discussing problems of high philosophy with the "Pen of Europe." In order to assure himself of Gentz's support during the congress, Rothschild held out to him the prospect of further profitable transactions, and Gentz noted with satisfaction in his diary that Rothschild had discussed with him "matters which although not so high were far more pleasant." [2]

During the whole period of the congress Solomon and Gentz had been inseparable, and both had derived the greatest advantage from their association. Gentz introduced Solomon to the representatives of Russia, and the delegates of the tsar's dominions soon concluded a loan of £6,000,000. Apart from the business profit realized on this transaction, Solomon contrived to increase his personal prestige.

"Rothschild and his Paris brother had the Order of Vladimir conferred on them yesterday," Gentz wrote [3] to Pilat, the editor of the Oesterreichischer Beobachter, which was the most widely read Viennese newspaper at that time. He would be very much pleased if this fact could be mentioned in the papers in an appropriate manner in the near future. "I do not feel that this can conveniently be done in the Beobachter; its proper place would be in an article on Verona, and as you have not published such an article yet, there would be something comic in this being the first item of news from here.

"We must, however, do everything possible to satisfy such a good and loyal person as Rothschild. You might give this matter your thought. In any case please see that it is mentioned as soon as possible in the Allgemeine Zeitung. Have the following statement printed in that paper: 'In recognition of the distinguished services rendered to the Russian Empire by the House of Rothschild in various important financial and credit operations the emperor has conferred the Order of Vladimir upon the barons Solomon and James von Rothschild.' Do not say St. Vladimir and do not refer to the class, which neither I nor the Rothschilds know."

Sometime later Gentz had occasion to send a reminder to his friend and wrote: "You have not replied to me regarding the Order of Vladimir conferred upon the Rothschilds. The baron is asking me every day whether you have forgotten about it. He is particularly anxious that the news should be featured in the Beobachter, and I do not see why this should not be done. At all events the news should be mentioned by you in the Allgemeine Zeitung before somebody else prints it in a misleading and possibly a malicious manner."

In the end the distinction was duly announced in both papers, and the news that the mighty empire of the tsars was also having financial dealings with the House of Rothschild appreciably assisted in raising its credit with the general public.

Meanwhile Solomon had inaugurated a private service of couriers between Verona and Paris and Vienna, and the Rothschilds proceeded to exploit the news about the congress, which they thus received in those capitals before anyone else.

At first it was not by any means certain whether armed intervention in Spain would be decided upon. Even Metternich was not entirely in favor of it, and as war with Spain was therefore not expected[4] French securities kept rising in value. Suddenly, on the arrival of a courier from Verona, James Rothschild sold French bonds to the nominal value of five million francs. The following day it became known that the banker Ouvrard, who was also staying at Verona, had concluded a loan with the Regency Government, which had been set up by the supporters of absolute monarchy in Spain for the duration of Ferdinand's captivity.

It was certainly natural to draw the inference that the congress was taking the side of the king, and a sharp fall in French bonds resulted. The capital of France reechoed with reproaches against ministers who had constantly averred that they were determined to avoid war with Spain. The slump became more and more acute, until, a few days later, the British ambassador got news from Vienna. It then became generally known that no decision had yet been taken, and Wellington was continuing, on behalf of England, to oppose the proposal for intervention. The securities now began to go up, and the good news was confirmed by Rothschild.

On November 18, Villèle wrote to his representative at Verona to say: "The Rothschilds' courier is causing our securities to rise again. He is spreading the news that there will be no intervention. I do not believe in these deceptive booms, which entail fresh variations in the rate of exchange and heavy losses to many persons,[5] especially when there may be a risk of war later."

The House of Rothschild was thus using the general political situation for the purpose of doing profitable business because it was able to get news early. James had been alarmed by the contradictory reports that had followed so rapidly upon one another. Solomon had confidentially informed him that important decisions were obviously pending at Verona, and that the French government would play the leading part in them. Solomon suggested that it would be exceedingly useful if James would come to Verona personally.

James quickly decided to make the journey, and on November 22 Solomon introduced his brother James to Gentz at Verona. On the following day the two brothers dined with Prince Metternich. A few days later, on November 26, Solomon planned to take advantage of his brother James's presence in Verona, and go himself to Vienna. Gentz had just given him a secret report on the congress, and several letters which he wanted taken to Vienna. But a post from Rome informed him that their brother Carl was shortly to arrive from Naples. Solomon postponed his journey for two days. The three Rothschilds had thus an opportunity thoroughly to discuss Neapolitan and Spanish affairs, and the probable result of the congress. After this Solomon and James returned home.

At the beginning of the congress, Solomon had been sending so much news from Verona to Vienna that the bulky Rothschild postal-packets attracted the notice of the postmaster at Schärding. He felt called upon to draw the authorities' attention to this exceptionally voluminous correspondence. This naturally did not particularly excite them, since numerous communications were entrusted to the Rothschild couriers by Metternich and Gentz themselves.

The decisions of the congress did finally lead to armed intervention by France in Spain. The congress passed off with great brilliance and duly impressed the world at large. The ancient arena at Verona was the scene of a magnificent banquet, which was attended by all the members.

Rossini, who was then at the height of his creative powers, charmed the members of the congress with melodies from his operas. Solomon, who had known Rossini in Vienna, introduced him to James at Verona, and this proved to be the starting-point of a friendship which was to develop into intimacy in Paris, especially during the last ten years of their lives.

Solomon dealt with Prince Metternich's personal expenditures at Verona—amounting to 16,370 lira—as indeed the House of Rothschild had furnished[6] all the cash spent in Verona, drawing it partly from France and partly from the various money-markets of the Lombard-Venetian kingdom.

The relations between Austria and that House were constantly growing closer, and her leading statesmen were scarcely able to refuse any request put forward by one of its members.

On September 30 the commercial department of the treasury received an application from Nathan, asking to be appointed Austrian consul-general in London. He pointed out not only that he had punctiliously performed the duties enumerated in his official instructions, especially in the matter of rendering assistance to Austrian seamen—doing so without asking for any compensation—but that he was the sole consular representative of a foreign power in London who had not the rank of consul-general.[7] He promised not to relax his watch on Austrian commercial interests in the future, and also most conscientiously to carry out any instructions which he should receive. The commercial department of the treasury strongly supported this application, and Metternich sent it forward to the emperor with the following memorandum:

"The said Rothschild has for a considerable period occupied the office of Austrian consul in London, to the general satisfaction of his chiefs, and in a disinterested spirit has carried out his duties often involving personal sacrifices, from which he never shrank where the prestige and the interests of your Majesty's service were involved. Your Majesty is moreover graciously acquainted with the services rendered by his House to the imperial state. The incongruity of his present rank in relation to the commercial agents of other foreign powers in London, who generally are styled consul-general, cannot fail to injure his official prestige."

Metternich also pointed out that James in Paris already had the title of consul-general, and Emperor Francis accordingly granted the application. So Nathan now held the same position in London as his brother in Paris. That city was the center now of Rothschild enterprise. The question of intervention in Spain was still the dominating issue, and as in this matter England was sharply opposed to the conservative groups in Russia, Austria, and France, it was inevitable that there should be a corresponding conflict of opinion within the House of Rothschild.

Metternich, with his legitimist policy, had Solomon completely in tow; Amschel was not so prominent, but owing to the Jewish problem at Frankfort, he had to follow the direction indicated by his protector Metternich, while James in Paris was so closely bound up with the leader of the ministry, Count de Villèle, and anticipated such advantages from this connection that he too was compelled to fall in with the conservative group, who were all-powerful on the Continent. Carl at Naples was also a dependent upon Austria, so that Nathan in liberal England was in an awkward position with regard to his four brothers on the Continent.

As a naturalized Englishman, and as banker of the richest state in the world, he personally would have wished to fall in with its political opinions as completely as possible. Indeed, it was necessary that he should do so, as otherwise he would speedily have lost his connection with the British government, and any possibility of doing big business in the future.

After the conclusion of the indemnity transactions in Paris, James had succeeded in getting on good terms with the Bourbon court, and especially with the leading minister Count de Villèle. He had often been able to oblige influential persons in matters of finance, a fact which assisted him in his efforts to consolidate his position. Soon after his appointment as consul-general James had taken the magnificent Palais Fouché formerly occupied by Napoleon's commissioner of police, and the magnificent style in which he lived served to enhance his prestige. He was still a bachelor, a fact that somewhat limited his social activities, but also made it easier for him to make his way into exclusive circles, some of which still showed great reluctance to admit the Jewish parvenu, and only did so when personal interests made it appear desirable. Conditions, however, gradually improved in this respect as his wealth increased. James also benefited by the fact that the great Paris bankers of that period such as Laffitte and Casimir Périer were either liberal, or indeed almost revolutionary, in their views, while others such as Delessert, Mallet, and Hottinguer were too nervous to undertake risky ventures on a large scale.

In 1823 James offered to place funds at the disposal of Villèle, and informed him that he was prepared to come to his assistance in alleviating the financial embarrassments of the treasury. James's first important transaction with the French Treasury consisted in undertaking the sale of 6% Royal Bonds. When at the end of January, 1823, the campaign against Spain was decided upon, James gave Villèle to understand that he was prepared to deal with the big loan to which the chamber had agreed. Villèle bethought himself of the precedent of Austria and Naples, and suggested that Rothschild should in a similar way raise the money necessary for intervention in Spain through negotiating a Spanish loan payable to France.

Fundamentally, however, James was as reluctant as Villèle to embark on hostilities against Spain, for these might seriously interfere with his financial scheme. His attitude is revealed in some intercepted correspondence between him and a Spanish banker called Bertran de Lis, who was endeavoring in association with the Liberals to secure the fall of the Spanish Ministry, in order if possible to prevent the French from intervening. San Miguel's Spanish ministry had, in view of the French menace, obtained authority from the Cortes to change the seat of government and the royal residence. The king would gladly have dismissed the government, but the menaces of an excited populace caused him to refrain from doing so. If the fall of the ministry could be brought about in some other way, France might perhaps be induced to regard this as indicating an improvement in the position and abstain from taking action.

Such was the state of affairs when a letter arrived from Rothschild's confidential correspondent at Madrid. "We are at this moment," wrote Bertran de Lis to the House of Rothschild in Paris,[8] "struggling to overthrow the ministry and to replace it with persons better qualified to guide the ship of state. I am convinced that we shall succeed in our endeavor, and I am therefore anxious that you should bring these facts to the attention of your government, so that they may cease taking any hostile action. I am asking you to do this in the confident expectation that a solution may be found consistent with the honor of both nations, which will assist in maintaining peace throughout Europe. I hope that you will support me in this endeavor as much as possible; but if you see that nothing can be done, and that a breach is imminent, I hope that you will send me a special messenger at my expense, so that I may regulate my actions accordingly in settling my financial affairs."

The same correspondent subsequently attempted in various ways to communicate items of important political and business news to James; but these appear to have been intercepted as they never reached their destination. The first letter to get through seems to have been one dated March 29, 1823, in which Bertran de Lis wrote:[9]

"It is our desire to avoid war, and in order to carry through the business that we have in hand, I feel I should let you know the line of action which in my view your government should adopt to this end. For one thing I feel they should cease any hostile operations until new ministers have been appointed. . . . In this way we might perhaps reach an agreement satisfactory to both nations, and one that might also bring us advantages of a general nature, and also such as we may turn to account in our business."

The writer of this letter proceeded to deal with the current situation in Spain in some detail, and concluded with the warning: "It is important also to use every precaution in carrying on this correspondence; for it would be exceedingly painful to me to be compromised in this matter in which I am convinced that the public interest is identical with my personal interest."

In spite of the precautions that were presumably taken, the correspondence fell into the hands of royalists, and was duly brought to the attention of Metternich at Vienna. He was highly indignant that one of the Rothschilds, who always pretended to be so conservative, and denied that they had anything to do with Liberals, should suddenly be discovered in dealings of this character. Gentz was instructed to speak to Solomon about it. Solomon was at great pains to invent an explanation, and Gentz noted in his diary:

"I have just had a little discussion with Rothschild about the incredible story of his brother in Paris, who is suddenly appearing in the rôle of intermediary between the French ministers and a revolutionary banker at Madrid." [10]

Meanwhile the French had seriously embarked upon intervention in Spain. On April 7, 1823, the Duke of Angoulême, nephew of the king, crossed the Spanish frontier. He encountered no opposition, and pressed on far into the country toward the capital Madrid. It was

Villèle's task to provide the moneys required by the French army, and now that the die had been cast James Rothschild hastened to offer his services to the minister. His first action was to hand the minister a letter of credit in favor of the Duke of Angoulême addressed to a bank in Madrid that was closely connected with the firm of Rothschild.

Villèle forwarded this document to the duke. "This is," he wrote in a covering letter,[11] "in the nature of a courtesy, but I was afraid of offending Rothschild, who has been and still is exceedingly useful to us in our financial difficulties, if I did not accept it. As soon as the army has entered Madrid Rothschild will send an official of the firm, or perhaps one of his brothers, to that city. I would request your Royal Highness to grant this banking firm your very special protection, as its intervention may be exceedingly useful to us in the future, both in the matter of rendering financial assistance to the army, and also in the matter of the Spanish loan, if such a loan can be usefully launched."

Angoulême did not share Villèle's view that the letter of credit was to be regarded as a mere courtesy. "I consider," he replied, "that it would be exceedingly useful to avail ourselves of the facilities that Rothschild enjoys for providing ready money at Madrid." He held that this was a speedier and more economic method than sending money from France. He fully agreed that Rothschild should be treated with consideration, as recommended by Villèle, who it was clear had learned much from the Austrians in Naples.

James was thus placed firmly in the saddle, and was enabled to carry out his measures under the protection of the two most powerful men in France at that time. It is true that Villèle revealed a certain attitude of suspicion toward bankers in general, regarding them as voracious beasts of prey out for money.

On May 23 the duke entered Madrid without opposition, and set up a regency, which was to rule with modified absolutism until the king should have been liberated from the Cortes. This government, however, in spite of its dependence on French troops, soon threw all counsels of wisdom and moderation to the wind. In order to fill its empty treasury it attempted to arrange a loan with Ouvrard and an agent of the House of Rothschild, who had come to Madrid with the French army.

Villèle warned Angoulême not to allow the regency to have a free hand in this matter. "For," he wrote,[12] "where the body is, there will the vultures be gathered together to devour it." He referred to the bankers, not excluding Rothschild, who would undoubtedly have offered the regency oppressive loans.

Meanwhile the Cortes had carried the Spanish king off to Cadiz, and Angoulême proceeded to invest that city and to liberate the king. "Cadiz is the key to the whole problem," Villèle wrote to the duke.[13] "By force and negotiation the king must be got out of the hands of the rebels. Your Highness knows that his Majesty has given you *carte blanche* to enable you to succeed in this venture, and that we have plenty of money in reserve which is available for any of your requirements. Moreover, with the letter of credit which I have sent to you, your Highness can draw bills up to any amount on the House of Rothschild in London for making payments to those who may deliver up the king."

In order to meet all this heavy expenditure Villèle had been negotiating for some time for the flotation of a considerable French loan. The minister still found his dependence upon the House of Rothschild irksome, and gave vent to his feelings in a letter to the duke: [14]

"Although I have nothing but praise for the manner in which Herr Rothschild has served us while I was in difficulties, I should like to float a loan which would make me independent of these people."

The cold facts were destined to turn out rather differently, and through this loan of 23 million francs, which was offered for public tender, Villèle was to be bound more closely than ever to the House of Rothschild. In open competition with three other banking firms, James Rothschild, encouraged by his brother Nathan, offered 89.55%, the next highest price offered being 87.75%. The importance attached by the House of Rothschild to the conclusion of this agreement is most clearly evidenced by the fact that Nathan from London, Solomon from Vienna, and Amschel from Frankfort had all hurried to Paris for the negotiations.

Both parties were delighted with the arrangement. Villèle was pleased since he had scarcely hoped that such conditions were possible for France, engaged in a venture like the Spanish intervention, especially in view of the fact that the country was already burdened with a foreign debt of 400 million francs.[15] He reported enthusiastically to the duke on July 11 [16] that the bonds on that date already stood at 91.25, and that the loan had therefore appreciated 2 1/3%.

The four brothers did everything possible to extend the European market for this French loan. Villèle congratulated himself on having got the loan underwritten at such a high figure, and explained his success as follows: "Monsieur Rothschild, whom the King of Portugal asked for a loan of 25 million francs, had the courtesy to ask King Louis XVIII for his permission before consenting. This is an example of the efforts which the financial powers were making to intervene in politics. Moreover, Rothschild of London, Rothschild of Frankfort, and Rothschild of Paris are all here, a fact which contributed not a little in giving me the confidence necessary to fix the minimum price at 89.5%."

Villèle thought that he had carried through quite a clever deal, but this loan, which constantly rose in value, and reached par as early as February 12, 1824, proved to be a new and abundant source of profit to the issuing firm.

Villèle now reverted to his scheme that the duke should present a skilful ultimatum demanding the liberation of the King of Spain and his family. Villèle advised that he should bring money plentifully to bear in this matter,[17] and should have an unlimited supply of credit at his disposal through Monsieur Belin, the Madrid agent of the House of Rothschild, so that he could draw bills up to any amount on the House of Rothschild in London. James agreed that he might accompany the duke if he left Madrid. Belin's signature was sufficient to release amounts which it might otherwise be exceedingly difficult to procure. Without his assistance it would be impossible to use bribery for the liberation of the king. "This man," Villèle wrote to the duke, "is personally known to the majority of those whose support we need, and it will be much more attractive to them to receive the price of their infamy secretly in London than to be paid in gold which they would have to withdraw at their own risk from a city invested on all sides."

Villèle had entirely forgotten his former feelings about the Rothschilds, and he had extensive recourse to the convenient services rendered by the firm at home and in Spain.

"Your Highness," he wrote to the duke,[18] "can use the House of Rothschild's money for all your financial requirements, whether necessitated by the service of the army or by the negotiations. In connection with the latter its agent's banking relations with the principal banking firms of Cadiz may be useful to you." He suppressed any misgivings at having brought Angoulême into such close contact with Rothschild. "Finance and trade," he wrote, "are the friends of peace, but they always wish to secure peace at the expense of honor; nevertheless, having the safeguard of a man of your Highness's temper and sentiment as a counterpart, we need not be anxious about allowing these gentlemen to intervene."

In Spain matters took the course that France had

desired. On June 23, 1823, the duke had reached Cadiz and was prepared to launch his attack. The forts surrounding the city were speedily captured. The necessity actually to take the town by storm did not arise. In accordance with Villèle's advice the duke made free with the Rothschilds' money; bills were drawn on Nathan Rothschild to the amount of nearly two million francs in favor of various members of the courts, and of the persons who held the king captive.

When the military position at Cadiz had become hopeless, and those who had accepted bribes promoted mutinies in the garrisons, the Cortes finally broke up, and released the king. It is true that he was first forced to sign a document containing all kinds of promises for a moderate form of government, in accordance with the constitution; but everybody knew perfectly well that he would not keep them. Thus the King of Spain was not in the end required to feel under an obligation to the powerful support of the House of Rothschild for his release from his own subjects of the liberal party. Neither was the duke forced to feel that he owed it to the banking firm that, after speedily overcoming all difficulties, he was enabled to return to Paris as a conquering hero.

The services which the House had rendered to the French government, however, enhanced its prestige at court and with Villèle to an enormous degree. James began to surround himself with luxury, and to patronize science and the arts; he furnished his house at No. 40, rue de Laffitte magnificently. He received the Cross of the Legion of Honor.

After the intervention, the course of events in Spain was, to Metternich's delight, exactly similar to what had occurred at Naples. An absolute monarchy was reintroduced, the liberals being savagely persecuted. The constitution vanished. The Roman Inquisition functioned again, and the government went far beyond what the

French government had wanted to achieve by intervention.

Ferdinand's new absolute government had money troubles no less than its predecessor; and the king appealed to the monarch of France, pointing out that his work was not yet completed, and that he lacked such a financial foundation as would be provided by a loan. Villèle applied to James Rothschild, who, in conjunction with Nathan and the British bankers Baring and John Irving, offered a loan of 120,000,000 piasters[19] to be subscribed for at 60%. The bankers demanded, however, that the whole of Spain's Colonial revenue should be mortgaged, this being the only revenue that had suffered little through the civil war, and in addition they required that France should give a formal guarantee.

An agreement was not concluded at the time, since Villèle replied to the bankers[20] that his first consideration must be his duty toward France. He could not agree to a guarantee by France without endangering its political and financial interests. He would, however, gladly advise the Spanish government to regularize its administration and to apply moderation in its general policy, in order to create the confidence necessary for such agreements. These were fine words, but they offered no tangible security for calculating business men, and accordingly the bankers withdrew their offer.

Metternich and Gentz had attentively watched the course of events. Rothschild's relations with Gentz had become, if possible, still more intimate, and the sincerity of Gentz's diary is attested by nothing more than by the entries of the 6th and 9th of January, 1823: "Rothschild called on me in Vienna. Everything is going magnificently and money in profusion. . . . January 9. I have been informed by Rothschild that a remittance of a thousand ducats is on its way from Russia."

Rothschild was assiduous in impressing Gentz with

the riches and power of his family. On January 13, 1823, he favored him with over an hour's discourse on the position of his firm and its enormous resources, showing him some "eloquent and exceedingly interesting documents."

The firm had in fact grown so powerful that it now proceeded to conclude most important transactions, in which it had formerly allowed other firms such as Gontard and Parish to participate, entirely on its own. The brothers may have learned that the Austrian finance minister once more had occasion to think of them. England had recently demanded the repayment of some old debts owing by Vienna, and it appeared that Solomon's and Nathan's services would be required again. Metternich and Gentz were therefore anxious to be obliging at this time, especially in matters that did not cost the state anything. They did not have to rack their brains to find an opportunity of showing their good-will, for together with Börne, Solomon had been "hammering at [Gentz] about this wretched question of the Frankfort Jews." [21]

The growing power of the House of Rothschild, which had originated in Frankfort and now had dealings with most of the more important states, caused the Frankfort Jews to stiffen in their attitude. They now demanded as a right what they had formerly begged as a favor. While Solomon and Gentz were pressing Metternich to help the Jews of Frankfort, Solomon's coreligionists there were carrying on a constant campaign against Count Buol, delegate and president of the diet who was so markedly hostile to them. Their efforts finally resulted in Count Buol being recalled, and this constituted an important victory for the House of Rothschild.

Buol's successor, Baron von Münch-Bellinghausen, was instructed to settle the Jewish problem as speedily as possible, since it was Austria's intention to support such demands of the Israelite community as were just. Amschel

Meyer Rothschild was quite unrestrained in his demonstrations of joy. On the day when the new president of the diet arrived, Rothschild gave a big dinner, to which all the delegates were invited.

"I should have preferred," Münch stated in his report to Metternich,[22] "not to have made my first public appearance in this manner, but as the affair had already been arranged I thought that I ought not to be too nice; moreover I made the acquaintance of all the delegates before the session."

Matters now began to move; Münch-Bellinghausen followed out Metternich's ideas in quite a different way from Buol, and in August, 1822, the question was settled in a manner highly satisfactory to the Jews. It is true that many restrictions were still maintained. Thus only fifteen Jewish marriages were allowed in each year;[23] no Jew was allowed to possess more than one house, and Jewish trade too was not free from all restrictions. The Jews, however, were henceforth counted as "Israelite citizens"; the ghetto was done away with, and they had full liberty of movement within the town.

They regarded these concessions as a victory, and Rothschild gave a dinner to celebrate them September 3, to which he invited both burgomasters, as well as the delegates to the diet. The former, however, again stayed away because, as Schwemer said, they did not feel in a mood for celebrations.[24] The debentures issued in 1811 under Dalberg's agreement for the liberation of the Jews were now fully redeemed. This fact also indicated that the Jews were satisfied. Thus the matters in dispute in the Jewish question, which had been pending for eight years, were finally settled by the diet acting in a judicial capacity. The principal credit for this was due to Rothschild. Both the town and the Jews sent deputations to thank Baron von Münch, who did not fail to report this fact to Metternich, as he knew well the importance Metternich attached to this question.

The reasons for supporting the Frankfort Jews were well known in Austria. Count Stadion had been negotiating with Rothschild and Parish, the underwriters of the last Austrian loan, since the spring of 1822 for a loan to cover the estimated deficit of 20 million gulden. They had stated that they were willing to underwrite 20 millions at 67, and then at 68.5%, but Count Stadion, whose recent experience in such matters had made him more cautious and critical, thought that these terms were not sufficiently favorable, or were, as he expressed it, "oppressive." [25] He therefore looked around for other offers, and for the first time in the experience of the Austrian government these were forthcoming.

Stadion wanted to borrow only 12,000,000 gulden at first; he fixed the final date for submitting tenders at April 14, 1822. The Paris banker Fould, representing a group of Paris firms at the head of which was Laffitte, offered to underwrite the 12,000,000 at 69%. Parish and Rothschild made a second offer to take over the loan at 69½, while the Viennese banking firm of Geymüller offered 72¾. A conference of ministers was summoned for April 13, to consider the tenders.

Solomon Rothschild was particularly anxious to secure the loan, if necessary without the cooperation of Parish—with whom he had recently had several differences—as this would provide him with a further opportunity for exploiting the advantages enjoyed by his firm for the sale of securities through their branches in the most important markets in Europe. He learned through Gentz that other firms were not merely in the field but had actually offered better terms than his, and he therefore decided to write to Stadion.

When the finance minister went to attend the conference on April 13, he was handed a letter from the firm of Rothschild just before entering the conference room. This letter bore the signature of that firm alone. The firm stated that they were prepared in any case to offer ½%

more than might be offered by anyone else for the loan which was to be issued.

The conference first decided that 20 million gulden should be issued at once instead of the smaller amount that Stadion desired. It was then considered whether or not any attention should be paid to Rothschild's late offer. The conference was agreed that Rothschild's letter was manifestly irregular. Applicants had been required to submit tenders under seal by April 12. Rothschild had done so jointly with Parish, but their offer had been less favorable than that of Geymüller. The second letter, although dated April 12, had not been given to Stadion until the following day. The minutes of the conference pointed out that "the irregularity of this procedure consists in having failed to observe the final date imposed upon all applicants for submitting their tenders—a fact which Rothschild is obviously trying to conceal by antedating his offer—and also in the lack of precision in the offer itself."

Metternich and Count Zichy expressed the opinion that Rothschild's offer should not be accepted, but that it should not be rejected either, and proposed that the whole matter should be negotiated afresh. With regard to the French banker Laffitte, whom he suspected of liberal sympathies, Prince Metternich stated that he feared the banker might be actuated by other than purely business motives. He added that he felt similar misgivings regarding Geymüller's offer, since it was possible that he was acting in concert with Laffitte.

While Metternich used his influence in favor of the House of Rothschild, Stadion took the opposite line, adhering to his view that Rothschild's retrospective tender should be ignored, and that the offer of the firm of Geymüller should be accepted as the best offer sent in by the time fixed.

Stadion was of the opinion that the financial interests of the state required that competitive tenders having been asked for, it was essential that the conditions laid down should be strictly observed, and that Rothschild's retrospective offer should therefore not be considered. "This is the first time," he emphasized, "that the treasury has had the gratifying experience of finding several competitors tendering for a loan. They will come to us again, and perhaps with even more favorable results in the future if we prove to them that belated offers are not considered. If in the present instance we act otherwise, it may be assumed that henceforth we shall have no possibility of securing *genuine* competition, and we may therefore pay dearly in time to come, for any immediate advantage." Finally, with reference to the objection made to Laffitte on personal grounds, Count Stadion observed that it would be quite impossible in any case to prevent him from being an unrevealed participator in a loan, and that even if Rothschild's offer were accepted this contingency would still have to be reckoned with.

As there was no way of bridging these differences of opinion the conference broke up without result. It was therefore necessary for the emperor to give the final decision, with the result that Metternich's views prevailed. The emperor issued the following decisions in council:[26]

"On the question whether 12 or 20 millions should be issued, the general political situation should be regarded as the determining factor, and Metternich should accordingly be consulted. A new date should be fixed for submitting tenders indicating that belated offers will not be considered."

Another year was to pass before the new big Austrian loan materialized. In April, 1823, the deficit up to the end of the financial year 1824 was estimated at no less than 35,000,000 gulden. It was now decided to issue a loan of 30,000,000. Four firms, including the House of Rothschild, jointly provided this sum in cash, receiving 36,000,000 five per cent debentures payable in coin, at 82 gulden per cent.[27]

Prince Clemens von Metternich
From a portrait by I. Lieder
in the Vienna National Library

While Austria was suffering from these difficulties, her aggressive foreign policy—especially the expedition to Naples, which was viewed very critically in England—had given rise to the belief that the finances of Austria must be in a most flourishing condition if it had so much money to spend on such objects. The Opposition in the British Parliament had for some time been reproaching the ministry for failing to demand payment of debts which had been incurred by Austria even before the revolutionary war.

Before the system of the English subsidies had come into effect, Austria had been granted two loans by England, to the value of £6,220,000 for financing its campaigns, and in the excitement of the Napoleonic wars, this fact had fallen into the background. With the addition of compound interest the debt had, by the time of the Congress of Verona in 1822, risen to an amount exceeding £23,500,000. Austria had already been approached at Aix-la-Chapelle regarding the repayment of the loan, but Metternich had refused to pay, and all the negotiations since had proved fruitless.[28] For Stadion definitely stated that if England insisted upon its demands it would mean the collapse of Austria's finances, which had been so laboriously resuscitated.[29]

When Metternich adopted a policy at Verona which was opposed to that of England, Wellington again reminded the chancellor that his government was pressing for the payment of this debt. He was not asking for the whole gigantic sum mentioned above, but was prepared to waive all interest charges, compound and simple, and would even be satisfied with a capital payment of £4,000,000. This amount, however, Austria must pay in any event. Even this was a very considerable sum, representing about 40,000,000 gulden in convention coinage, and it constituted another dreadful surprise for Stadion.

Metternich realized that it was his policy which had induced this claim to be brought forward again, and he endeavored to reach an agreement in personal conversation with the British commissioner Sir Robert Gordon, who had been dispatched for this purpose. Various solutions were considered and rejected. Finally Metternich offered a lump sum of 30,000,000 gulden five per cent debentures at an issue price which involved the reduction of the total claim to about two million pounds. He then had recourse to Solomon Rothschild, asking him to try to influence the British government through his brother Nathan. Solomon immediately wrote a confidential letter to Nathan on the matter.

"The British minister," he wrote,[30] "has as yet made no reply to this proposal . . . It is probable that England will not at once unconditionally accept the offer of the Austrian government, but will attempt in one way or another to obtain better terms. Whatever the reply may be, however, I do not believe that the Austrian government will vary their original offer . . . If it were to act otherwise, and all at once to put in circulation new public securities amounting to so many millions, the Austrian government would be dealing a severe blow to its credit, which is being raised by a businesslike and intelligent administration to a point commensurate with the country's greatness.

"You are a business man yourself, and will therefore be best able to appreciate these circumstances, so that it would be redundant for me to explain myself further. What I have written has been communicated to me in confidence by his Excellency Prince von Metternich, and it is merely intended to inform you of the general position. *In any case* you may, although only *confidentially* (for you have no official instructions) discuss the matter with the chancellor of the exchequer, and endeavor to convince the English of the fairness of the offer which is being made. As I am aware of your devotion to the government here, I feel confident that you will be grateful to me for giving you an opportunity of proving yourself useful and well disposed to them in such an important matter, and that you will show all the wisdom and caution necessary to assist it in attaining its ends. I hope that you will be able to inform me of the success of your endeavors by the next post . . . "

Nathan thereupon got in touch with the bankers Baring and Reid-Irving, and also with the British government, and succeeded in persuading the government to agree to a payment of £2,500,000, whereas the negotiators, after at first asking for more, finally obtained from the Austrian government 30,000,000 florin 5% cash debentures at an issue price somewhat exceeding 82 2/3 %. Stadion agreed to the offer made by the three firms mentioned above,[31] and on October 31, 1823, Solomon was able to send the following report to Metternich:[32]

MOST GRACIOUS CHANCELLOR!

It is with particular pleasure that I take this opportunity of informing your Highness of the pleasant news, that after considerable effort I have at last succeeded, in collaboration with my colleagues in London, in concluding the transaction with the English government on the basis of the amount of 30 million gulden 5% Métalliques Bonds. I have thus faithfully carried out the promise made to you on my departure, and am most happy to have been able to terminate a matter outstanding for so long, entirely to the satisfaction of the wishes of the imperial government.

I have been expressly requested by my colleague to endeavor to secure that the government of his Majesty the Emperor shall grant a commission of 2–3% to the underwriters in view of the fact that the transaction is such an advantageous one to the treasury. Mindful of the just and loyal principles of the government here, I may feel justified in assuming that if I submitted such a request it would not fail to receive consideration. But the reflection that my services and my zeal in this matter have resulted in such definite advantage to the state, and effected such large savings, is so exceedingly pleasant that I gladly renounce the possibility of deriving any further emoluments. I have made a similar statement recently to his Excellency, Count von Stadion, and therefore flatter myself that I have given occasion for his Majesty to feel satisfied with me, and have earned his gracious consideration.

Your Highness will no doubt deign to appreciate with your customary gracious condescension the efforts that I am making in the interests of the imperial state, and I confidently flatter myself that you will graciously consider a request with which, lest I should seem immodest, I do not venture to trouble your Excellency yet. I am waiting to communicate it to you verbally. I await with extreme impatience the moment when I shall have the happiness of seeing your Highness again and in the best of health, and when I shall be able personally to renew the assurances of my most profound regard. . . .

As a matter of hard fact the whole transaction constituted a bull speculation in Austrian public securities by the three firms concerned. Their expectations were fulfilled directly after the negotiations had been concluded, for as early as January, 1824, the Métalliques showed a marked appreciation in value.

When the conclusion of the whole affair was reported to Emperor Francis, with a suggestion that the Austrian mediator Kubeck should be commended, Count Zichy wished to avail himself of the opportunity for obtaining some imperial recognition for the House of Rothschild. He minuted on the memorandum requesting the emperor's confirmation that, although the firms carrying through the settlement of this loan, which had so materially improved the credit of the Austrian state on the London Stock Exchange, had indisputably had their own interests in view, they, and especially the House of Rothschild, nevertheless deserved recognition for the able way in which they had handled the business. Such a demand for Austrian securities had been produced that the last loan was already quoted at a premium of over 5%, while by making their credit available the firms had succeeded in the difficult matter of satisfying the English government.[33] Zichy accordingly proposed for the emperor's consideration that the following sentence should be added: "And we take cognizance of the efforts made by the London banking firms which have so materially raised Austria's public credit."

Baron von Lederer, however, added that in his view the services rendered in arranging the loan in England consisted merely in an intelligent appreciation of the circumstances; and that on this service the banks had already realized no inconsiderable profit as shown by the prices of the securities published in the English papers.

Emperor Francis drew his pen heavily through Zichy's "frill," and took "cognizance with satisfaction" of the fact that the matter had been settled.[34] The whole transaction proved to be one of the most profitable pieces of business in which the House of Rothschild had ever engaged. The bonds continually increased in value, their average price in 1824 being 93, and in 1825, 94. It is obvious that the brothers Rothschild succeeded in very profitably realizing on the 30 million gulden debentures which they had subscribed at 82 2/3. It is not possible to estimate the actual profit, but according to the statement of Neumann it already amounted to £1,824,600 at the beginning of April.[35] Solomon Rothschild's "pleasant feelings" and the magnanimous gesture with which he refused a commission or "emoluments" are thus readily intelligible.

It is not surprising that, since Vienna offered opportunities of doing such excellent business, Solomon should have grown more and more attached to that city. In spite of the restrictions imposed upon foreign Jews, his relatives also were attracted by the idea of settling there. One of these was a cousin of Solomon Rothschild, called Anton Schnapper, who was about to marry the daughter of William von Wertheimstein, Rothschild's Vienna manager, a Jew who had received the imperial "toleration" as a private wholesale merchant.

Through Solomon's powerful influence Anton Schnapper contrived to obtain an audience from the emperor, and to submit his request for toleration, and permission to carry on business. Although the emperor gave his consent, much time elapsed, as was the case with all applications, before formal sanction could be given, and the impatient young man decided again to make application to the emperor, but in writing.

"Your Majesty," the application ran,[36] "The undersigned desires henceforward to be included among the millions of fortunate subjects who enjoy the merciful and just rule of your Majesty. I was born at Frankfort-on-the-Main, and I am the son of honorable parents, my mother's name having been Rothschild. I have worked for several years as an assistant in the business of this well-known firm, and acquired such knowledge as goes to make a competent and honest business man.

"I now desire to settle in this city as a wholesale merchant, and to unite myself in the bonds of honorable matrimony with the virtuous daughter of the licensed wholesale merchant of this city, William von Wertheimstein. My request for 'toleration' and for authority to act as a wholesale tradesman has already been considered by all the departments concerned, found to be in order, and has been submitted to your Majesty for approval. May your Majesty be pleased most graciously to accede to this humble request, and speedily to grant it, and thus establish a family which in return for this priceless favor will never weary of beseeching the Almighty in their daily prayers to grant prosperity to your Majesty and your Majesty's family."

Schnapper sent this in with the observation that his first application was still lying in his Majesty's office. "You have on several occasions," he wrote to Solomon,[37] "kindly promised me your support in this matter, and in view of the bonds of blood and friendship that unite us, I hope you will have the kindness to concern yourself with it now."

Solomon kept his word, and requested Metternich[38] very kindly to emphasize the importance of this petition quite briefly to Martin, his Majesty's principal private secretary, as his Majesty's signature was still required.

Metternich's position was such that a word from him put the matter through at once.

Stadion continued to employ the House of Rothschild in important financial operations. In February, 1824, the firm undertook to produce old 200 gulden bonds to the value of ten millions for a commission of 2½%,[39] if he were granted new 100 gulden 5% bonds in return for each 200 gulden bond. Solomon indeed wanted to increase the sum to twenty million, subject to the condition that during this period the old debt should not be reduced, and that the strictest secrecy should be observed during the whole scheme. The offer came to Hofrat von Lederer for his opinion, and he at once minuted that he doubted whether the House of Rothschild would find it so easy to carry through the business to the tune of twenty millions.

He was to prove right; for in February, 1825, the House of Rothschild asked to be allowed to reduce the amount to seven (from ten) millions. In the meantime the older bonds had increased considerably in value, and the result was a loss to the firm. The House of Rothschild naturally did not do all its business at a profit; but if it ever failed to do so, or actually suffered a loss, the brothers generally succeeded in their efforts to reduce it to a minimum, and above all, to keep it secret. The firm's transactions, even outside Austria, were constantly increasing in scope, and its undertakings were beginning to extend beyond Europe to other continents.

Brazil had, in 1821, also imposed a Cortes constitution upon its sovereign the King of Portugal, with the result that separation from the mother-country was decreed and the king's son Don Pedro was proclaimed constitutional emperor. This occurred with the support of England, but against the will of the conservative eastern powers, and especially of Metternich.

While the four brothers on the Continent were under Metternich's sway—James alone allowing himself occasional secret ventures with the liberals in Spain—Nathan had to do his best to follow the general political tendencies of liberal England. When, therefore, in 1824 Brazil was unable to fulfil its obligations to another London firm, Nathan intervened to the great satisfaction of British statesmen, taking over Brazil's liabilities, and in 1829 he concluded a loan of £800,000 with the new imperial state. This enabled Brazil to put her finances in order, while Nathan did not suffer financially.

However, such loans, being suggestive of liberal sentiments, would naturally arouse resentment amongst the conservative powers, and they also gave rise to considerable difficulties amongst the five brothers. Fundamentally the brothers were in complete agreement regarding their aims, and they had no intention in any circumstances of adopting any definite political line. Their adaptability made it impossible to do anything of the kind. But those Rothschilds who were living within the sphere of Metternich's power, and especially the Viennese Rothschild, were forced at any rate to pretend that they stood exclusively for the conservative tendencies represented by Metternich's system. It was often exceedingly difficult for them to explain away or put a good complexion upon Nathan's actions, a fact which frequently led to embarrassing situations.

At this time occurred an event of great importance to the House of Rothschild. On May 13 Solomon Rothschild came to see Gentz in a state of great excitement, and told him he had just received news that Count Stadion had suddenly had a stroke at his home. A man of the most scrupulous personal honor, and the most indefatigable industry, he was profoundly ambitious, and so permeated with the spirit of devotion to duty and with a sense of the importance of his work, that he took all the vicissitudes of his difficult office deeply to heart; he therefore used up his reserves of energy more quickly than other men. The excitement and the strain of the events of the last few years had prematurely worn him out. He died two days after the stroke, and was succeeded in office by Count Nádasdy.

This was a serious loss to the Rothschilds, for they owed it to Stadion more than to anyone else that they had come to Vienna. It is true that during the last years of his life he had grown much more skeptical and critical in his attitude toward the brothers; but they were so intimately connected with Austrian finances that a new minister, had he wished it, would have had the greatest difficulty in eliminating them. Even Metternich, who secretly cherished feelings of suspicion and aristocratic pride toward the Jewish parvenus, never thought of such a thing.

Moreover, Gentz and the Rothschilds themselves took care that no serious misunderstanding should arise. As Gentz reports, Rothschild not only repeatedly saw Metternich at his office during this period, he also often had meals with the prince; and Solomon's big dinners with thirty or more guests were attended by ministers and ambassadors and many members of the aristocracy. Through his numerous invitations, Solomon extended his connection, and got ideas for his operations.

The center of gravity of the House of Rothschild's business was at that time in France. The former leader of the royalists and head of the government in that country had not forgotten the financial assistance rendered by the House of Rothschild at the time of the Spanish expedition. As it was his ambition to set France on her feet financially, it occurred to him that he might avail himself of the assistance of the House of Rothschild in this also. At that time France had to pay no less than 197 million francs interest on its public indebtedness. Villèle meant to reduce this intolerable burden by converting the 5% loan, which already stood at par on February 17, 1824, to a loan at a lower rate of interest, namely 3%. In this way he anticipated saving about thirty-four millions annually in interest. Villèle thought out his scheme and then made a detailed proposal to James Rothschild in Paris.[40]

The minister showed that in spite of the expense of the Spanish war, he could make his budget balance without a further loan or additional taxation. "In these circumstances," he wrote, "it appears to me to be possible to take advantage of the conditions that have caused public securities in England and throughout Europe to appreciate in value, for the purpose of carrying through the conversion of our 5% bonds into 4 or 3% bonds."

Villèle asked James to cooperate in this plan, which was not to affect French credit. He meant in this way to convert no less than 150 million bearing 5% interest, and to issue to the underwriters a corresponding amount of 3% bonds at 75. The minister hoped that the 3% bonds would also soon rise in value; and he offered to allow the underwriters to keep the saving in interest during the first year after the conversion of the bonds bearing 150 million in annual interest had been effected.

James immediately informed his brother Nathan in London of the French finance minister's proposal for this gigantic transaction. All the brothers, and especially James, tacitly recognized Nathan as having the best financial brain. His connection with the British government also made him the most influential of all the brothers. The finance minister not only had sent his proposal to James in writing, but also had repeatedly discussed it with him personally, and immediately after such discussions, on the 2nd, 3rd and 4th of March, 1824, James sent a private courier to his brother Nathan in London. On March 6, Nathan, after consulting with the banker Baring, sent James the following reply: [41]

"MY DEAR BROTHER: . . . the brothers Baring, as well as I myself, will be pleased to be of use to the French government in their plans for reducing the interest payments; and as the scheme seems to have been well thought out, there should not be much cause to fear for the result. At the same time, it is absolutely essential that the finance minister should be in complete agreement with us, and that no difficulties should arise in carrying out his intentions.

"It is quite clear that the present price of the bonds is maintained by speculators who have been exceedingly lucky for some time, and will no doubt continue to develop their success by further speculating on a rise. Such persons, however, have not the power to assist the finance minister in a scheme embracing such far-reaching possibilities, unless it be supported by such eminent capitalists as Messrs. Baring and Rothschild. I am sending you the draft of a scheme which I should like to have submitted to the minister, and the success of which would undoubtedly be of enormous importance to the country and to the government."

In this drafted scheme Nathan explained that the finance minister would have first of all to secure the chamber's consent to the operation, the government being allowed a completely free hand to carry through in the most advantageous way possible, as was done in similar cases by the British Parliament. In essentials, Nathan followed Villèle's proposal that he should jointly with Baring underwrite 150 million 3% bonds. He asked only that, in the event of the operation being less successful than was anticipated, the minister should be authorized by the chamber to issue treasury bills up to 100 million francs, so that in such a case Baring and Rothschild would be able to get money by cashing these bills, and would not be forced to sell the bonds.

"If the results work out satisfactorily," wrote Nathan, "the firms of Baring and Rothschild, who will apply all their energy and risk their property in carrying out the French minister's scheme, must expect to receive as their reward the profit which this operation will yield during the first years. The minister must persuade the bank to discount at 3%, and also to lend money on the bonds.

"His Majesty will thus be in a position when the chamber reassembles, to inform his subjects and the whole world of the flourishing condition of French finances, and that, too, directly after a war which has restored the Spanish Bourbons to their throne and to the hearts of their people. . . ."

If the whole operation were to go through successfully, and if 150 million of annual interest charges were really to be cut down from 5% to 3%, the saving effected by the French government would run into many millions, and the House of Rothschild was to receive the benefit of the first annual saving thus made.

Villèle and the two firms soon arrived at an agreement. Nathan had applied his experience in British transactions of a similar nature, and the whole matter had now to be submitted to the public.

When the chamber reassembled, the King of France referred to the contemplated operation for reducing the rate of interest payable on the public debt. The proposal came as a surprise to the public. The bonds were held by many thousands of small people, and the news made a great sensation because innumerable investors felt themselves hit, and most of the bondholders understood only that they would in future receive three francs interest instead of five.

Meanwhile the bonds had been driven up to a still higher figure, reaching 104 and 106. Each man felt himself threatened in the possession of this valuable paper, and a storm artificially raised by Villèle's enemies broke out. This was increased by making enormous play of the government's statement that the former émigrés should be compensated out of these savings. Vincent, the Austrian ambassador in Paris, reported that these operations would furnish the banking powers with fresh fields of gain, and that their avarice would lead them to suggest similar plans to all other governments.

The scheme met with harsh criticism in all quarters, the most devastating being contained in a report from Paris to Metternich, which concluded with the words: "The rentiers are wild with indignation, but Villèle will attempt nevertheless to carry the thing through, for he is a minister *quand même*."[42]

The king was so upset that he did not dare to show himself in the streets of Paris, fearing demonstrations by the small bondholders. Nevertheless, at the expense of his popularity he consistently supported the plans and intentions of his prime minister.

There were exceedingly severe critics of the rôle which the House of Rothschild played on this occasion. Ouvrard attacked them with special severity in his memoirs.[43] As, however, he belonged to the party which was hostile to the Rothschilds, his statements can be accepted only with reservations. There was no immediate prospect of the House of Rothschild making either profit or loss, for the proposals were carried in the lower house by a very small majority, while the members of the upper house, most of whom had strong personal interest as bondholders, rejected the proposal on July 3, at the instigation of Chateaubriand. Thus, the scheme failed.

Gentz does not seem to have been speaking so well of his friend Solomon at this time, or possibly he wanted to impress Metternich with the fact that he could assert his independence of the House of Rothschild. In any case he wrote to the chancellor on June 11, 1824: "I am secretly pleased that Villèle's finance operation has not gone through. It will do no harm if that gentleman's arrogance is somewhat reduced. Besides, the scheme itself was exceedingly unjust and cruel; and France will certainly be impressed by the fact that the hundred thousand families who would have been hard hit by it owe the fortunate event entirely to the *aristocratic* opposition. Also there can be no harm in the coalition of big bankers having suffered a rebuff which will somewhat damp their ardor for getting new business. Everything must have a limit, and the all-powerful firms were beginning to go beyond theirs. They obviously had a fully prepared scheme for carrying through similar reductions in interest in all the principal states. It will now be as much as they can do to get out of the French scheme with a whole skin . . . and if I were Solomon Rothschild I would retire with all my millions after losing such a battle." [44]

If this remark was meant seriously, Gentz was to prove very much mistaken. It was not the habit of the Rothschilds to throw up the sponge at the first reverse. Moreover, one must be cautious in drawing conclusions from a perusal of the letters that passed between the brothers and Austrian politicians, as the letters suggest that they were inspired by unqualified devotion to the state of Austria, which would not have been consistent with their position with regard to other governments.

Carl Rothschild at Naples in particular soon realized that it would not be at all advisable for him to be regarded there merely as the agent of a foreign power. The occupation by the Austrian troops could not last forever, and it was all the more necessary for him to cultivate relations with the local authorities since he was strongly inclined to settle permanently in Naples, and to found a new branch, the fifth, of his House there.

As the king and the members of the royal family at Naples were always in need of money, Carl had several opportunities of obliging them. His constant business dealings with the finance minister, Medici, resulted in their getting on very good terms in spite of the payments to Austria. While on the one hand the Rothschilds assured Austria of their anxiety to see the state paid by Naples, Carl protested to Medici that he would do everything he possibly could to lessen the burden that Naples had to bear. The results soon became apparent; Medici began to examine and criticize the accounts sent in by Austria for the maintenance of the troops. Ficquelmont now lamented [45] the fact that the sums to be paid by Naples had not been fixed once and for all, and demanded in 1822. He suggested that in that case Medici would not have had time to examine Austria's disbursements so closely.

"The real reason," he stated in a report to Vienna, "that he is induced to increase his demands, and to make difficulties, lies in the fact that he obviously knows of the savings that we are effecting; as Rothschild is transmitting them to Vienna, we may practically assume that Medici is bound to know of them, for Rothschild's staff is in too close touch with Medici's for this to be avoided.

"It would have been better to leave this business to the quartermaster's department of the army, as was done in the case of the first occupation of Naples; in that case nobody would have known the amounts that we transmit to Vienna, and we would also have saved the charges which we pay to the House of Rothschild. Our departments send in exaggerated accounts, and I should not like to have the task of defending them. It is exceedingly annoying that the figures made up by the accounts department should be submitted to a foreign government without revision. This is the most certain way of compromising us."

It was a bold admission to state that the expeditionary force was being used to get more money out of Naples than the expenses actually incurred; but Count Ficquelmont must be given considerable credit for the fact that he opposed these exaggerated demands, and pointed out that the annual claim of 13 million ducats, sent in by Quartermaster-General Koller, was gaining for the Austrian the enmity of the whole country.[46]

The king also was forced gradually to realize that he would not much longer be able to dissociate himself from the movement that pressed for the recall of the Austrian troops, for Medici daily reminded him of what terrible burdens the occupation imposed upon the kingdom, and how his sovereignty was limited thereby. But the king feared the outbreak of another revolution; and as he did not trust his own soldiers, he attempted to recruit Swiss regiments. These negotiations came to nothing because of the expense of raising the troops.

The king then proceeded to recruit in Ireland. The brothers Rothschild had very skilfully introduced this idea to him. Great disturbances had broken out in that country as a result of the wretched conditions under which the poor peasantry, oppressed by their landlords, were living. Nathan had come into contact with an Irishman, the Irish London banker Callaghan, who thought that the British government would also be in favor of such recruiting, as it would draw off dissatisfied and poverty-stricken elements of the population. Nathan saw the opportunity of killing three birds with one stone: he would be rendering a service to the English government by diverting a troublesome element; to the King of Naples by providing the neutral troops that he so much wanted; and, in addition, he would do good business for himself.

It was Nathan who, having prepared the ground in

England, advised his brother Carl to make a proposal on these lines to the King of Naples.[47] He enclosed the Irishman's letter, which stated that the difficulties that might previously have been put in the way of such a scheme had disappeared, now a new government had come into power. Callaghan stated emphatically that the overpopulation of Ireland, where it was scarcely possible to keep body and soul together, was at the root of all the trouble, and that it was positively desirable that some of the population should emigrate.

Carl Rothschild handed the letter to the minister Medici, telling him of Nathan's proposal. Medici hastened to inform the king of both these facts, the king's one wish being to have at last some sense of security.

Shortly afterwards King Ferdinand fell ill, and died on January 4, 1825. He was succeeded by Francis I, who was personally no less frivolous and extravagant than his predecessor, and was far from possessing a strong character. Under his rule the state of the kingdom tended to get worse rather than to improve. He too had reason to feel anxious about his personal safety, and in 1825 it was decided to recruit four Swiss regiments for Naples, and the Irish project was discarded. The incident illustrates how the Rothschilds would apply their energies in the most varied spheres, if there were any prospect of rendering a service to those in power, and incidentally filling their own pockets.

Meanwhile James was actively engaged in negotiations in Paris for a new Spanish loan, which the Madrid government wanted to put through at any price. Busy though he was, he contrived to steal time to make a journey to Frankfort in early July, 1824, in order to marry his nineteen-year-old niece Betty, the daughter of Solomon. He was acting in accordance with the wish of his dead father—which had come to be regarded in the family as an unwritten law—that the sons should refrain as far as possible from introducing other families into their circle by marriage, and should in no circumstances marry a Christian.

Even on this journey James took with him private letters and dispatches reporting on the situation in France, from the Austrian ambassador to Prince Metternich, who was staying at his country place, Johannesberg. Forgoing his honeymoon, immediately after the marriage, James had to return to Paris as his brothers Carl and Solomon were there, carrying on discussions with the Spanish negotiators.

The three brothers decided that one of them should go to Nathan in London with a Spanish plenipotentiary, and ask him to try to persuade the House of Baring to participate in the loan. The Rothschilds, however, demanded that the seventy-two millions which Spain owed to France for her intervention should be included in the loan; to this proposal the Spanish government raised objections. As the Rothschilds in any case had little confidence in Spanish conditions, and tried in vain to secure a guarantee from other powers, the negotiations on this occasion also came to nothing.

On September 16, 1824, King Louis XVIII died. His brother, the former leader of the conservatives, succeeded to the throne as Charles X. He was already sixty-seven years old, and firmly convinced of the necessity of still more definite reactionary measures, as well as being full of religious intolerance. Villèle remained in office for the time being, so that as far as the Rothschilds were concerned, there was no immediate change in the political and financial situation in France.

During this period their business expanded in all directions; Nathan founded a big insurance company in England, the Alliance Insurance Company; Amschel was collaborating with Bethmann, Gontard, and Brentano in a scheme for founding a bank at Frankfort, although through the opposition of the senate it came to nothing.

As the Rothschilds' business expanded, their correspondence naturally became more voluminous, and they found it necessary strongly to reinforce the system of couriers with which they had covered Europe. This circumstance entailed a consideration of the question whether their correspondence could be more closely watched.

In this connection the suggestion made by a Milan postmaster is illuminating. "I have often noticed," he reported to Vienna,[48] "that the Rothschild clerks who travel as couriers from Naples to Paris about once or twice a month take with them all the dispatches of the French, English, and Spanish ministers, accredited in Naples, Rome, and Florence. In addition to this not inconsiderable correspondence, they also deal with the communications passing between the courts of Naples and Rome and their legations at Turin, Paris, London, Madrid, Lisbon, etc., as well as all private letters that are of any importance.

"These couriers travel via Piacenza. As we have an Austrian garrison there, under the command of the reliable Colonel Eberl, it might perhaps not be impossible to *induce* one or another of these clerks to hand over their dispatches for our perusal. Such an examination should yield profitable results, especially if we wait for a favorable or important moment. A room at Piacenza under the protection of Austrian soldiers would be all that we should want in order to do everything necessary without attracting attention."

Since diplomatic correspondence was involved, this proposal concerned the chancellor, and was duly brought to Metternich's notice. He felt that it would be awkward to accept the suggestion. The scheme could turn out to be a double-edged weapon, as he himself often made use of the Rothschild couriers, and matters of the greatest secrecy might come to the knowledge of a subordinate postal official. On the other hand, Metternich would have been exceedingly glad to get hold of the private correspondence between the brothers Rothschild and, as the technical term went, to submit it to "manipulation."

The result of these considerations was the issue of the following order: "The couriers of the House of Rothschild passing through Lombardy on their way from Paris to Naples, or from Naples to Paris are, when carrying dispatches bearing the seal of the I. and R. Consulates-General in those cities, to be regarded and treated as official couriers; if, however, they should be found carrying any letters which have nothing to indicate that they are of an official nature, such letters shall be subject to the usual regulations in force." [49]

Hormayr, the former director of the Vienna State Archives, who had been banished because of his association with the Archduke Johann in his venture for founding the so-called "Alpine Kingdom," was a bitter enemy of Metternich and the emperor. He was thoroughly familiar with the manner in which correspondence was tampered with, and used this knowledge for making a violent attack upon Metternich and Solomon Rothschild. He even went so far as to state [50] that Metternich had, in agreement with Solomon, waited at Fischamend, two stages from Vienna, for a post bearing important news from Constantinople, and held it up for two days.

"This was done to gain time in order to have two or three days to rig the market, and to make some hundreds of thousands for the chancellor, Zichy, and the rest of the pack of thieves, with the German fortress caretaker [50a] Rothschild, the King of the Jews and the Jew of Kings, at their head."

As far as Metternich's relations with Rothschild were concerned, these exceedingly offensive allegations were far from the facts; but it certainly was possible, through holding back news received by courier, to gain time for profitable deals on the exchange, and this was no doubt done.

The firm of Rothschild, which had now literally attained world-wide dimensions, was to enter upon a difficult period. The long years of peace which England was enjoying led that country to seek profitable investment for the enormously increased wealth which it had acquired since the successful termination of the Napoleonic wars. There was also an increasing tendency to unsound speculation, and a flood of new flotations. As the Central and South American republics freed themselves of Spanish dominion, they seemed to offer desirable opportunities for doing business in agricultural produce and mines.

At the end of 1824 there was feverish activity in the City. Companies sprang up like mushrooms, and millions of pounds in cash were subscribed. Almost all the principal London firms took part in this movement; [51] but the Barings and Rothschild, who regarded it as unnatural and artificial, held aloof. The year 1825 proved that they were right. The South American mining ventures collapsed, and numerous undertakings apparently on a solid foundation experienced the same fate, in a crisis that was becoming more and more general, and was spreading from London to the whole of Europe. Consols fell appreciably, and foreign public securities threatened to follow their example.

In these difficult circumstances, Wellington remembered the signal services Nathan had once rendered to him under the much more dangerous conditions of war. He consulted him as to how the crisis should be met, and Lord Liverpool's government followed Nathan's advice.

Nathan had intended to go to Paris to meet Metternich, who was staying there in 1825, but in view of the critical economic situation, he could not think of leaving London, and wrote the following letter to Metternich:

"It has been my daily endeavor to travel to Paris, in order to express to you the gratitude I owe for the gracious and fatherly kindness which your Highness has shown to the Rothschild family for so many years. The date of my journey was actually fixed, but an entirely unexpected event unfortunately frustrated my intentions. The British funds, which had reached a very high level, have fallen rapidly, because of incorrect inferences drawn by the English from the meeting of sovereigns. I am accordingly forced to remain here to prevent if possible any further fall, the government being unwilling that I should be absent at this time.

"I hope your Highness will not misinterpret my absence, and will appreciate the obvious urgency of the matter which detains me . . . since, if a further fall in the funds is not speedily checked, the movement will spread abroad, and even affect the I. and R. Austrian funds. Nevertheless I cherish the hope that financial circles here will soon regain their confidence, and am looking forward to making the journey then, and waiting personally upon your Highness. Meanwhile I beg that your Highness will graciously accept my written expressions of thanks in the spirit in which they are offered, as proceeding direct from my heart, for I pray constantly to the Almighty that our beloved sovereign emperor may long be spared, and that your Highness may flourish." [52]

Thanks to Nathan's skill, the developments in England did not result in excessively serious losses to the House of Rothschild, in spite of the crisis through which that country passed, but the firm was severely affected indirectly by the commercial crisis in Paris. In spite of the change in the general situation, the French minister Villèle had adhered to his conversion scheme, and although the Rothschilds were much less enthusiastic about it than they had been a year ago, James was so closely bound up with the French minister that when Villèle took the scheme up again in May, 1825, he could not stand entirely aloof.

He certainly did not conceal his misgivings. While Metternich was in Paris, James openly said to him that it was wrong of Villèle to resume the operation at that time.[53] James was more explicit in the following state-

The Pedler on Horseback
Caricature of the House of Rothschild

ment to the Austrian ambassador, Baron von Vincent: "There are times when such an operation may be opportune. Last year the finance minister was assured of the success of his scheme; he was supported by powerful firms, and a large volume of English money was available for investment in France, but now it is flowing into other channels. The return of the capital sums that find their way to America is only partial, and much slower. Most of the banking operations in Europe are not carried through on a cash basis, but this is not the case in America. The . . . operations of Mr. Huchinson in England are moreover exactly contrary to those of M. de Villèle. When one also considers the constant complaints in the press which bring the measures proposed by the ministry into bad odor, one cannot but fear that it will find itself deprived of the necessary resources." [54]

Villèle, however, was not to be restrained. He succeeded this time in carrying his proposals in the upper chamber as well, and he proceeded to put his long-cherished plans into operation. The Rothschilds could not exclude themselves from the scheme, but they went into it very cautiously. The Paris market was reacting to the fall in prices in England, and as success was largely dependent upon a boom in French securities, the prospects were far from propitious.

James remarked to Vincent on July 7, that it was a long time since he had seen the Paris market so dull. He shared the antagonism of a certain party toward M. de Villèle, and he said it was certainly not his fault that the House of Rothschild was regarded as seriously compromised in having supported the government.[55] This was a dig at Nathan, because James was a little jealous of Nathan's outstanding reputation.

The difficulties of the whole undertaking were increased through the public opposition of the authorities at the Bank of France. This was shown in the fact that they suddenly demanded the repayment of considerable sums advanced by the bank to the treasury. James was, however, not altogether confident that he was right in taking up an attitude opposed to the operation. The matter might succeed in the end, and in that case James would have suffered a humiliating reverse. He accordingly thought it advisable to say [56] to Vincent as early as June 8, that in spite of the bank's hostility to Villèle and to the House of Rothschild, matters could still be arranged, and Villèle's plan would yet succeed.

Somewhat later, after the chambers had accepted the draft bills, James for a time saw everything in glowing colors, and wrote a letter to Metternich expressing his changed views:[57] "You may now be assured that Villèle has won his case. The bonds will be a great success, and he will defeat all his opponents *because he is right.*"

On June 18, Solomon, who was also staying in Paris, made the following statement: "I am now able to say that notwithstanding all the vigorous attacks to which M. de Villèle has been subjected hitherto, and is still being subjected, in my view, his financial scheme will go through; and the count, who enjoys his Majesty's confidence to an exceptional degree, will be strengthened in his position; while the enemies of peace and of the ministry will be deprived for a long time yet of the pleasure of seeing it fall." [58]

Metternich condemned this remarkable change of opinion with the remark: "In Paris Rothschild said to me that Villèle was *wrong.* It is often so with the world's judgment." [59]

James's first view had really been the right one. The general financial situation throughout the world did not in fact admit of such an operation's being carried through at that time. The government succeeded only in converting 30 millions to 3% bonds, and these quickly fell from 75 to 62 and 63.

Four of the Rothschild brothers—Nathan alone was absent—were assembled in Paris in August to take counsel regarding the steps to be taken to limit the loss resulting from the decline in the 3% bonds. They admitted [60] that they had not reckoned with the possibility of such an unexpectedly sudden fall. The four brothers finally went to consult the family oracle Nathan, in London, with a view to taking energetic measures to save the situation. Villèle's conversion scheme, however, could not be improved in any essential now. Even the 5% bonds were quoted some points under par at the end of the year. All they could hope to do was to limit their losses, and in this they succeeded to a certain extent; but the whole affair was an unfortunate piece of business.

In other, more distant fields also, the Rothschilds had not been over-lucky in their investments during that year. After several fruitless attempts at reconquering Haiti, the second largest island of the Antilles, it had to be surrendered by France, on the payment of an indemnity of 150,000,000 francs by the new republican government. This government borrowed the necessary money, the loans being taken up by a French syndicate, including Rothschild and Laffitte. The Republic of Haiti was never able to meet its obligations; and even though the French government eventually indemnified the two firms for their losses, the transaction had to be put down as unprofitable.

Whether the brothers Rothschild were fortunate or unfortunate in their dealings, their names were on everybody's lips; legends gathered around their activities and their wealth, and they were accredited with the most fabulous schemes by the general public. Thus the story gained currency in Austria that Rothschild had one day demanded the immediate repayment in convention coinage, of no less than 40 million gulden which he had lent the state. On being told that it was impossible to repay this sum, Rothschild was alleged to have proposed that he should either be handed over the whole customs revenue throughout the imperial dominion for a certain period, or be granted the monopoly of the purchase of fleece in the Austrian dominions, whereby he would have been able to dictate the price of textiles. Although these rumors were obviously untrue, they indicated the estimation of the power of the House held by the public, whether it was well or ill disposed.

The Rothschilds were becoming the central figures in the jokes and caricatures of comic papers. In 1825 a caricature making fun of their versatility was circulated in Frankfort and South Germany. The drawing showed a Rothschild on horseback, with samples of all his businesses; wine-casks, seeds, buttons, etchings, state securities, umbrellas, pens, magic lanterns, etc., on his way from the north to the south of Europe. The easily interpreted legend ran: "Blueshield, commercial traveler, does business in all branches of trade." [61]

The brothers did in fact engage in every conceivable kind of venture, and they were approached with all sorts of schemes. Persons in high places especially had recourse to them for loans. Among them was Marshal de Marmont, Duke of Ragusa, formerly governor in Illyria under Napoleon I. He had joined the Bourbons after Napoleon's fall, and got on good terms with Metternich. As a reward for his change of allegiance and various political services, he was granted an annuity of fifty thousand francs by the Austrian government, in alleged compensation for a donation allotted to him by Napoleon I. The marshal had again got into serious financial difficulties, and the French government, which did not wish him to be publicly compromised, advised him to mortgage his Austrian annuity to Rothschild if the banker would put his affairs in order.

The duke did apply to Solomon Rothschild, but Solomon wanted first to make sure that the Austrian government would actually pay Marmont the annuity until he died. He therefore wrote to Metternich: "I would not have entered into any negotiations in this matter without having previously asked your Highness's consent, had I not done so at the suggestion of Count de Villèle. . . . I am therefore venturing to ask your Highness in this most humble private letter, whether the assumption of these negotiations or their continuance is in accordance with your Highness's wishes. Will your Highness please to be assured that on receipt of the slightest hint of the contrary being the case, all negotiations will immediately be broken off, and in such a way that neither Count de Villèle nor the Duke of Ragusa will discover the true reason of the change." [62]

Marmont also wrote to Metternich in order to get his support. [63] The chancellor replied cautiously. [64] He thought that the treasury would no doubt simply pay the annuity to Rothschild; but the finance minister would have to be asked for a special guarantee to that effect. Everything would be simple, "as long as the respective positions of the persons concerned remained the same."

This was rather a dangerous reply, and Solomon wanted to have various, and, as Marmont called them, "ridiculous" guarantees. [65] Rothschild, however, firmly adhered to the position that the Austrian government must give her full expressed consent to the arrangement, if he entered into it.

"I am fully aware," Marmont wrote, "that this requirement is not flattering to me, and that the only motive for making it is to obtain guarantees against the possibility of my *mauvaise foi*." But for fear of endangering the arrangement, he had to agree.

In November, 1825, the contract was submitted, constituting a speculation on the part of Rothschild that the marshal, who was fifty years old, would live a long time. Metternich, however, would not agree that Emperor Francis should give his express consent, as contemplated under the contract, because it was impossible to know in the case of a former marshal of Napoleon whether his political opinions would not undergo changes such as might cause Austria to cease her payments. If, however, these payments were mortgaged to Rothschild for the full term of the marshal's life, it would not be possible to discontinue them. The contract was therefore not concluded, and in order not to rebuff Villèle, James lent the marshal a small sum on the security of the next instalment of his pension.

On April 30, 1827, Solomon wrote the following letter to Metternich[66]: "Your Highness will perceive from the enclosed statement that Marshal de Marmont's affairs are in a state of the greatest confusion, and he is hard pressed by his creditors. He is bound to go bankrupt sooner or later, and in such a case our Paris branch would be a creditor to the extent of fifteen thousand francs, advanced to the marshal on the security of the personal annuity payable to him by the imperial government. There is only one way in which my firm can be secured against possible loss, and that is by impounding the two next instalments of this annuity. I therefore venture most humbly to request your Highness to issue the necessary authorization for the I. and R. Treasury to instruct the paymaster's office to accept a veto from me, in the usual form, upon the instalment of the pension now due and upon that due next quarter in so far as this may be necessary to cover our claim."

It was asking a good deal to expect the powerful Austrian chancellor to concern himself with securing a payment of 15,000 francs to the House of Rothschild. But Solomon was in a position to take this liberty, since Metternich himself was again negotiating a personal loan with the firm; and in fact on June 1, 1827, the prince received a loan of half a million gulden from the Rothschilds.

The failure of the conversion operation necessarily damped the Rothschilds' ardor with regard to any other ventures, the consequences of which could not be clearly foreseen. The situation in Spain was exceedingly critical, and the lack of money was being acutely felt. In ignorance of the way in which the conversion scheme was working out, the Rothschild representative at Madrid had been somewhat rash in making promises to the Spaniards.

"The financial problem [in Spain]," Vincent reported to Metternich,[67] "is now in the hands of the House of Rothschild, all of whose members are just now in London. It seems to me that M. Renevier, the manager of the Madrid branch, has gone rather too far in what he has said to the Spanish government. The House of Rothschild will not enter into business negotiations with Spain without having made previous inquiries in England, and assured themselves of the probable attitude of bankers there with regard to assistance rendered to Spain, for such a loan might damage the loans made to the South American governments which are in rebellion against that country."

When James Rothschild returned from London in the middle of September, 1825, after spending five weeks there with his four brothers, he was assailed by questions from all sides as to whether Spain had any prospect of securing a loan of 25 millions. Nathan had advised against it because for political reasons he did not wish the reactionary Spanish government to be supported. Metternich on the other hand would have been pleased by the granting of a loan, and desired it to go through.

"So far as I have been able to ascertain," Vincent reported to the chancellor,[68] "the House of Rothschild is not much inclined to have anything to do with a financial venture in Spain. They have little confidence in the guarantees offered by the government, and they are afraid of damaging themselves with English firms having interests opposed to those of Spain. Although the House of Rothschild may pretend that their sympathies are purely monarchistic, the recognition of the engagements entered into by the Cortes government, and the liberation of the Spanish colonies, would provide a far wider field for enterprise and political securities, the value of which they do not fail to appreciate."

The House of Rothschild could well be discriminating. Offers of business from governing circles flowed in on them from all quarters. Carl Rothschild had met Count Louis Philippe de Bombelles in connection with some payments which he was instructed by the Austrian government to make on the Neapolitan account for the passage of Austrian troops through Tuscany. Although large sums were involved the matter was promptly settled, and the Tuscan government gave him to understand that it would take the opportunity of demonstrating its satisfaction.

Grand Duke Leopold II, who had been ruler of Tuscany since 1824, was at that time considering a scheme of great benefit to his subjects, namely, to drain the Maremme, an area of marsh land in Tuscany embracing thousands of square miles. The grand duke proposed to Carl Rothschild through Bombelles that he should undertake a part of the drainage operation on his own account, subject to a suitable arrangement with the state of Tuscany. Such was the esteem in which the House was then held for its versatility and financial resources.

Carl Rothschild did not feel that he could undertake such a far-reaching scheme. "Would it not be better," he replied to Bombelles,[69] "if the Tuscan government, which has conceived such benevolent plans for their subjects, would itself supervise the carrying out of the scheme with the assistance of a loan to be taken up gradually as the work progressed? Such a method of procedure seems to me to be more advantageous than to entrust the work to foreigners who do not know the country, and who would be compelled at great expense first to find and engage workmen."

These discussions took place in August, 1825, a most unfavorable time for persuading the Rothschilds, who were uneasy at their losses, to agree to such a serious undertaking. The scheme nevertheless was carried through, and the firm took some part in financing it, although it had nothing to do with the work itself. It proved to be an inestimable boon to the country, although the work took very many years to carry out, and cost untold millions.

The relations of the House of Rothschild with Metternich had remained untroubled throughout the year 1825; and the Rothschilds actually ventured to intercede with the chancellor regarding the affairs of certain members of Napoleon's family. Toward these Metternich was in general anything but well disposed, and was always inclined to put the greatest difficulties in their way. Napoleon's mother, the aged Lætitia, who was then seventy-five years old, lived at Rome, and dearly wished to see again her eldest son Joseph, the former King of Spain, who was living in North America under the pseudonym of Count de Survilliers. Mother and son had not seen one another for ten years. Joseph had repeatedly attempted to get a passport, but the Austrian and French governments would not permit him to return to Europe. All entreaties had hitherto been in vain, and a friend of the family, Count Villeneuve, approached Solomon Rothschild, asking him to use his influence with Metternich, because the old lady was ill, and Joseph promised to return to America immediately after his visit. The world had indeed passed through great changes during the previous ten years when the son of a despised Frankfort tradesman was asked to intercede on behalf of the man who was once deemed all-powerful.[70]

Metternich, however, remained obdurate. To yield would not have been in accordance with the general principles of his policy. The House of Bonaparte was finished with, should remain finished with, and never be allowed to become dangerous to Metternich's system again. For this reason even the smallest favor was refused to the family; Rothschild was not listened to, and had to realize the limits of his influence. Although when interference with his policy was involved Metternich might remain absolutely firm, he often gave the House of Rothschild much too much rope in matters of finance; and in such instances he relied upon the finance minister and the treasury.

An accident has revealed the details of a transaction which clearly shows that Metternich and his assistants sometimes went too far in their reliance on the Rothschilds; and an examination of this incident offers an opportunity of noting the treasury's own comments on its mistakes and on the loss involved, which, it should be pointed out, was incurred under Count Stadion's successor.

Since the first Austrian occupation of Naples in 1815, the kingdom had had to pay a war indemnity. Since the end of 1818, it had been the duty of the Austrian ambassador at Naples, Prince Ludwig de Jablonovski, to receive the instalments as they were paid in each month, and, in connection with a banking syndicate controlled by the Neapolitan firm Dollfuss, to arrange for their transmission to Vienna. Everything went well at the start, but the bill for the second instalment was protested in Vienna, because the firm of Dollfuss was in difficulties.

Dollfuss reported this fact to Jablonovski in January, 1819, but the ambassador had already received the orders on the Neapolitan Treasury for the following instalments up to March and drawn these sums in advance. Jablonovski was now in danger of losing this money, and was forced to accept a very unfavorable settlement offered by the firm of Dollfuss, under which they handed him public securities, for the sum they held, at 87, the price at which they had bought them, although these securities had by then fallen to 78. Jablonovski hoped that they would appreciate again, so that he would avoid any loss.

"The power," Jablonovski remarked later, "which

autocratically governs quotations throughout Europe, so that the most careful calculations go astray, the autocratic power of the House of Rothschild was a factor of which I was not then aware."[71]

Jablonovski had miscalculated. The bonds continued to fall, and the prince was unable to make the payments to Vienna on the due dates, because he felt he could not sell the bonds at such a loss. He therefore mortgaged them at 60% in order to be able to send at any rate part of the money, and still hoped that they would appreciate. Later on, however, the remittances to Vienna ceased altogether. This greatly annoyed and worried Stadion, who needed the money. As an imperial ambassador, who was under Metternich's orders, was affected, Stadion complained to the chancellor, and Metternich had to try to think of a way out. Again he had recourse to the brothers Rothschild, a constant refuge in distress. It was in the summer of 1819, and James and Carl had just come to Vienna from Naples. They had informed themselves as to conditions there, reported to Prince Metternich and been commissioned by him[72] to undertake the transmission of Austria's outstanding claims in Naples.

Rothschild stated that he would be delighted to carry the matter through in collaboration with Gontard at the "most favorable possible rates," and asked for ½% commission and ½% brokerage. "You may be assured," his offer concluded,[73] "that we shall do everything in our power to carry out your commands with all the diligence and economy of which we are capable, so that we shall continue to justify the confidence which you place in us." The matter was accordingly entrusted to them.

Prince Jablonovski had not yet been told anything about the negotiations with Rothschild, and he was exceedingly upset when he was suddenly instructed to hand the business over. He expressed his astonishment, especially in view of the fact that he had meanwhile arranged a solution of the matter with the finance minister Medici by direct shipments of gold to Trieste.[74] "But," he wrote, "Herr James Rothschild was in Naples, and presumably heard of my unfortunate dealings with the firm of Dollfuss, and determined to turn them to his own advantage. Nothing else can explain how the House of Rothschild should have taken over such an unimportant business in a center with which they are not familiar, where the rate of exchange is constantly varying and unfavorable, or how they could have persuaded the I. and R. Treasury to renounce the advantages of transporting gold, and to bear the considerable loss of exchange."

In any case the matter was taken out of Jablonovski's hands, and his suggestion that further payments should be deferred until the Neapolitan bonds rose again was ignored. In January, 1820, Jablonovski received instructions to hand over all documents regarding the matter to a controller specially sent to Naples for this purpose. In July, 1820, the revolution broke out, and in the spring of 1821 the Austrian troops entered Naples. The immediate effect of these events upon the bonds was unfavorable, and they fell continuously until May, 1821. The result was that Stadion, who was always liable to sudden panics, hastily gave instructions that the bonds which had been mortgaged at 60% should be sold to Rothschild, and this was done in May, 1821, at the lowest point which they touched, namely 58⅛.

The following year saw an extraordinary rise in Neapolitan securities, so that it may be readily imagined that the House of Rothschild made an enormous profit out of this purchase. This became particularly apparent when in August, 1827, the new finance minister Count Nádasdy, after going through these accounts, declared that Prince Jablonovski was liable to make good an amount of 584,354.54 florins, and created a charge over his property at Rogozno for this amount.

The prince protested strongly with the result that an

imperial commission was appointed to investigate the matter. This investigation led to some lamentable revelations as far as Austrian public finances were concerned. The "most obedient loyal servant Count von Taaffe," president of the treasury, had some utterly devastating statements to make in his most submissive report [75] regarding the treasury's claims on the prince. He revealed that the transaction had been *most unprofitable* in every way, and declared that Prince Jablonovski's statement that it would have been better for him and for the treasury to have burned the certificates of the mortgage bonds, and rid himself of them completely, was correct, harsh though it sounded. For as the bonds [76] had been mortgaged for 60, and had later been transferred to Rothschild at 58⅛, the Austrian state had not merely failed to receive anything further, but had actually had to make up the difference. Jablonovski's proposal to hold the bonds, and wait until they improved in value before realizing them, had been a sound business speculation. Instead of this they had been handed over to the House of Rothschild, together with the interest payments for the first half of the year 1828.

On this memorandum an imperial instruction was issued, ordering the finance minister to examine the accounts again in collaboration with Prince Jablonovski, and if the results showed that any added compensation had to be paid, to take the necessary steps to collect the amount as speedily as possible. The fianance minister carried out these instructions; and the report on the matter concluded with the following words: "The assessor appointed for the investigation is of the opinion that, although there is in a general way . . . an obligation on the prince to make good the amount, the claim could be effectively resisted in the courts or otherwise. For we are not at all likely to succeed in replying to an order to show cause, such as will necessarily be granted if the charge created [on the prince's property] is not canceled."

The result of the further examination was that instead of being held liable for the amount of more than half a million florins, the prince was finally required to pay only 10,694 florins 34 kronen, in order that the complete failure of the treasury might be somewhat concealed from the outside world.

The facts which had thus been brought to light also gave the chancellor food for thought, and he afterwards observed a certain amount of caution in his relations with the House of Rothschild. They availed themselves of every occasion to make the sovereign and the leading statesmen forget such untoward occurrences, and endeavored to obliterate the bad impression by giving proof of their deepest devotion. This was especially the case when Emperor Francis fell ill in the spring of 1826, recovering only after many weeks of sickness. The whole of Europe had been in suspense, for the decease of the emperor would have involved profound political changes; and the news of his recovery offered an opportunity for the brothers Rothschild to send their congratulations to Metternich. It is true that they little guessed how cleverly he had provided for the continuance of his control of affairs, even in the event of Emperor Francis's death. It will suffice to quote the letter which Amschel wrote from Frankfort:

> I have by today's post received the news of the fortunate recovery of his Majesty our universally beloved emperor. Having suffered the greatest anxiety since the emperor fell sick it was one of the most joyful moments of my life when I heard the news.
>
> Heaven has heard our prayers in preserving the greatest and most virtuous of monarchs, and thus allowing the world to continue to enjoy a good fortune, the greatness of which I can but marvel at without venturing to appraise. It is impossible to describe the radiant joy that lights up all faces—only angels

could express in words our feelings of gratitude to Providence!

I cannot refrain from expressing to your Highness my congratulations on this blessed event. I would gladly make so bold as to lay my congratulations at the feet of his Majesty himself, our most benevolent emperor—so sincere and overwhelming are my feelings. May God preserve in full health this best father of mankind until the end of his days! And may it ever be my fortune in deepest reverence to call myself your Highness's most humble and most obedient servant,

AMSCHEL MEYER VON ROTHSCHILD.[77]

Now that the emperor had recovered, the fear that his death would deal a blow to Metternich's régime, and therefore also to the position which the brothers Rothschild had established in the I. and R. chancellor's office, was again remote. Solomon, who through Metternich and Gentz was constantly winning his way in Viennese court circles, was frequently invited to the chancellor's and also often entertained him in his own house.

One after another, families of the high aristocracy, requiring financial assistance, procured loans from the Frankfort banker who had settled at Vienna. In this way he placed many aristocrats under an obligation to himself, and whether they liked it or not they had to admit Solomon and his family to their exclusive salons. Thus both socially and in business Solomon climbed to dizzy heights at Vienna, and his commercial rivals began to become painfully aware of this, especially during the years of financial crisis of 1825 and 1826.

The firm Fries & Co., one of the four "monopolistic state bankers" which had come into prominence during the reign of Maria Theresa, had got into difficulties during the crisis of 1825. David Parish, a son of the well-known John Parish of Hamburg, and Rothschild's partner in numerous transactions, had entered the firm some time previously, and was now involved in its fall. Parish's extravagance and reckless speculation had caused him to be excluded from a partnership in his father's business, and he had set up on his own account. Being unable to meet his liabilities he had no other course open but to require his most powerful patrons such as Metternich and Gentz, who were at the same time his debtors, to repay their loans. He thus forfeited their favor, though he could not save his firm from ruin.

When he saw that the crash was inevitable Parish put an end to his life by jumping into the Danube; but before doing so he wrote two bitter letters expressing his resentment at the fact that the House of Rothschild had elbowed him out of many transactions. He blamed Metternich for having sacrificed him to the cupidity of a family who had succeeded better than he had in securing the chancellor's interest. He described the brothers Rothschild in a letter to Metternich as "heartless persons, only interested in their money-bags, who, standing under the special protection of Metternich, have behaved in a most ungrateful manner to him." [78]

Just before his death, Parish also wrote to Solomon Rothschild, reproaching him for having squeezed him out, although he had in 1817 introduced him to the big French and Austrian financial business. Now it has been ascertained that the Rothschilds would have succeeded in establishing this connection even without Parish, and that he invited them to join in several transactions simply because he was not sufficiently rich and powerful to carry through these great state financial operations alone.

On the other hand there is no doubt that the brothers Rothschild were entirely ruthless in competing with the firm of Fries and Parish, and that they succeeded as no one else did in consolidating their position with the public departments. In any case, Solomon neither desired nor expected that the rivalry should have such a tragic ending, and he was not a little shocked by it. He spent many hours discussing the tragedy with Metternich and Gentz, in its various aspects.

Two rivals had been disposed of, but life went on its course, and it appeared desirable to wipe out their memory, and to anticipate evil tongues by cleverly giving publicity to news regarding the fame, the business dealings, and the prestige of the House of Rothschild. The brothers had long recognized that good advertisement, which owing to the limitations of the time had to be of a literary nature, could be of the greatest value. Through their influence with the authorities, who were able to use the power of the censorship in order more or less to restrain press activities in all countries, they had little to fear from violent attacks in the press; and if any such occurred, they were almost always able to take effective countermeasures. Moreover, they had ample means at their disposal for influencing cowardly papers, and pressing the cleverest pens into their service.

First and foremost there was Gentz, the "Secretary of Europe." He had for a long time been writing propaganda articles for the Rothschilds in various papers, and exerting his influence—backed as it was by the powerful figure of Metternich looming behind him—upon the contemporary press in their favor. Gentz's growing intimacy with the House of Rothschild, which was marked by constant invitations to dinners and theatres, as well as by "highly welcome financial transactions with the excellent Rothschild," as faithfully recorded by Gentz,[79] gave a chance for carrying out a master-stroke of publicity.

In 1826 the Brockhaus publishing firm was just about to publish a new edition of its Conversational Encyclopedia, which had a very wide circulation at that time, and was regarded as an absolute gospel. The Rothschilds had not yet been featured in it, and it seemed to offer a convenient opportunity for describing the origin and progress of their House.

There was nobody better qualified to execute this, as regarded both manner and matter, than Gentz. Solomon Rothschild accordingly requested him in return for a princely fee, to undertake the task, explaining to him the points he wished to have emphasized. He was particularly anxious that the relationship with the Elector of Hesse should be described in such a way as to convey the impression that the whole of his enormous fortune had been entrusted to the management of the House of Rothschild; and that they had succeeded in saving it by risking all their possessions. Special emphasis was to be laid upon their integrity and disinterestedness, and the firm was to be described as more powerful than any contemporary firm, all the titles and dignities that the five brothers had acquired in the course of time being enumerated.

During the first week of April, 1826, Gentz wrote an essay entitled "Biographical Notes about the House of Rothschild," which was to serve as the basis of his article in the encyclopedia. The following extracts will give an idea of the way in which Gentz carried out his task. The essay was accepted at its face value by very large numbers of people, and after appearing in the Brockhaus publication was incorporated into similar foreign works, as for instance Encyclopédie des gens du monde. The article ran:

> The Rothschilds, at the present time the greatest of all business firms, are among those who have achieved greatness and prosperity simply through intelligently taking advantage of opportunities which were available for thousands of others, through a spirit of enterprise seasoned by calm judgment, and through their understanding of men and affairs, and their capacity to adjust themselves to the conditions of the time. Meyer Amschel Rothschild, the father of the five brothers, who are now living, was the founder of this firm. . . . In a short space of time his knowledge, his tireless industry, and his

straight dealing won for him the confidence of highly respected firms; he was given important orders, and his credit as well as his wealth increased. The relationship which Rothschild established with the Landgrave, afterwards Elector, of Hesse was a decisive factor in the enormous subsequent development of his business. The elector appointed him crown agent in 1801, having come to realize that he was as reliable as he was useful. When in 1806 the French occupied the elector's territories, and he himself was compelled to flee, he left the rescue of his private possessions to Rothschild, their value amounting to many million gulden. It was only by sacrificing the whole of his own property, and at considerable personal risk, that Rothschild contrived to save the property that had been entrusted to him.

The well-known fact that all Rothschild's possessions had been confiscated by the French led the exiled elector to believe that his own property had been lost too. In fact he does not appear to have thought it even worth while to make inquiries about it. When matters had settled down again Rothschild immediately proceeded to do business with the property he had saved. . . .

The brothers are most scrupulous in observing the injunction that their father laid upon them when he was dying, which was to collaborate in absolute brotherly harmony in all business matters. Indeed they treat the memory of their father with such piety that they refer to him in all important business matters, and Nathan generally applies to doubtful cases a rule his father recommended.

When the elector returned to his states in 1813, the House of Rothschild not merely offered immediately to return to him the capital sums with which it had been entrusted, it also undertook to pay the customary rate of interest from the day when it had received them. The elector, positively astonished by such an example of honesty and fair dealing, left the whole of his capital for several more years with the firm, and refused any interest payments for the earlier period, only accepting a small interest from the time of his return. Through recommending the House of Rothschild, especially at the Congress of Vienna, the elector certainly assisted greatly in extending their connections, until now as the result of the political developments since 1813 the House has, through an uninterrupted series of great transactions, attained the position it at present holds in the commercial and financial affairs of Europe, which are partly directed by it. . . .

Students of economics and politics have no doubt frequently wondered how the House of Rothschild has been able to achieve so much in so short a time. Leaving the effects of chance out of account, its success is attributable principally to the strictest observance of certain fundamental maxims, together with wise business management, and the exploitation of favorable opportunities. The principal maxim is harmonious collaboration in all business matters, to which reference has already been made.

After their father's death every offer, whatsoever its origin might be, was made the subject of joint discussion between the brothers; any transaction of any importance at all was carried through according to a concerted plan by their joint endeavors, and all the brothers had an equal share in the result. They continued to act in close agreement, in spite of the fact that they gradually settled in places far removed from one another. This circumstance, indeed, instead of interfering with their collaboration, has proved an actual advantage; it has enabled them to obtain the fullest information as to the state of affairs in the principal markets, so that each of them can from his own center the more effectively take the preliminary steps in any business. The firm as a whole then takes it over and carries it through.

Another of the principles which the Rothschilds have adopted is to keep moving, and not allow themselves to become enmeshed by circumstances. . . .

> Finally it should be noted that, apart from the reasonableness of their demands, the punctiliousness with which they carry out their duties, the simplicity and clarity of their schemes, and the intelligent way in which they are put into operation, the personal moral character of each of the five brothers has been a determining factor in the success of their undertakings.
>
> It is not difficult for those whose power enables them to attach large numbers to their interests, to secure the backing of a powerful party; but to unite the support of all parties and, in the popular phrase, to win the esteem of gentle and simple, implies the possession not merely of material resources, but also of spiritual qualities not always found in association with wealth and power. Ever ready to lend a helping hand, without distinction of person, to those who have come to them for assistance, all of the five brothers have achieved a real popularity. They have rendered the most important services in such a manner as to make them most acceptable, for they have been actuated not by considerations of policy but by natural benevolence and kindness..[80]

This eulogy of the Rothschilds was a masterpiece executed by a clever stylist; it was bound to raise the prestige of the House enormously, especially in the opinion of those who did not know how it came to be written. Then as now the great mass of the unthinking public accepted anything in print at its face value, and as the article, while containing statements that were untrue, did contain much that was the result of accurate observation, and attributed excellencies that were not fictitious, even the more critical were inclined to give credence to the description.

It was not signed by Gentz, although it is true he admitted to being the author, at any rate in conversation with his friends. Indeed he actually asked Adam Müller to express his opinion on it. "I should be glad," he wrote, [81] "if you would read the article on Rothschild in the supplement of the Conversational Encyclopedia. It is my work, and I have endeavored to give briefly a simple and I hope not infelicitous explanation of the greatness of that House. I shall greatly appreciate your opinion on this little article."

Gentz was proud of his work, and as he has noted in his diary, he read it to Rothschild's manager Wertheimstein, who naturally listened to it with "undisguised admiration." [82] Ten days later Gentz called on Rothschild and received his "actual" cash reward. [83]

Apart from the great advantage which its publication brought to the brothers Rothschild, his essay contained some shrewd observations which are of general interest. One passage in particular, although not included in the Conversational Encyclopedia, may be worth quoting. "There is a truth," Gentz remarks, "which, although not quite new, is generally not properly understood. The word *luck* as commonly used in the history of famous individuals or eminent families is bereft of all meaning, when we endeavor to dissociate it entirely from the personal and individual factors in each case. There are circumstances and events in life in which good or ill luck may be a determining although not an exclusive factor in human destiny. Lasting success, however, and constant failure are always, and to a much greater degree than is generally supposed, attributable to the personal deserts or the personal failings and shortcomings of those who are blessed by the one or damned by the other. Nevertheless the most outstanding personal qualities may sometimes require exceptional circumstances and world-shattering events to come to fruition. Thus have the founders of dynasties established their thrones, and thus has the House of Rothschild become great." [84]

The circumstances could not have been more aptly described, for the family Rothschild of that generation did undoubtedly bring mental forces into play in a definite direction, the results which they achieved being favored by the circumstances of the time.

CHAPTER VI

The House of Rothschild Rides the Storm

THE control of the business of the House of Rothschild, established as it was in five different centers in Europe, had become exceedingly difficult with the passage of time as a result of the enormous extension of its operations and their intimate interactions with the events of general European politics. It is true that Nathan quietly exerted an influence that tended to harmonize the often conflicting aims of the various branches; but on account of the primitive nature of the communication at that time, and the inadequate postal arrangements, it was impossible, in spite of all the efforts he made, for him to supervise everything.

The result was that each brother had a fairly wide scope within his own center, it being left entirely to his own judgment within certain limits to do what he considered best in the interests of the firm as a whole. Between Vienna, Frankfort, Paris, and London, these places being linked up on the main European routes, communication was easier. It was just the least gifted of the brothers, Carl, who was practically isolated from the others at Naples, and therefore often had to travel personally to Paris and London in order to get into touch with his brothers.

A final solution of the problem of the Austrian troops at Naples had become urgently necessary. Since the end of the year 1822, Neapolitan statesmen had been constantly protesting that the Austrian Army of Occupation should be reduced, in view of the enormous expense of maintaining it. Memorandum after memorandum, explaining the intolerable burden and the necessity of relieving the situation, was sent in.[1] The Congress of Vienna had decided that the occupying forces should be reduced to 35,000 men; but before this decision was put into effect (August, 1824) the Austrian government had already realized savings to the extent of about 6,500,000 florins out of the sums paid by Naples.[2] This fact naturally soon leaked out and caused great dissatisfaction in the kingdom,[3] especially as a rumor was abroad that the government would shortly reduce the pay of all those in its service.

The greater part of Naples public securities was held abroad. Of the annual interest, only about two million ducats remained in the country itself, while the balance constituted a tribute that Naples had to pay to foreign capitalists. The budget suffered from the malady of a constantly growing deficit, which rose to 3,800,000 ducats in 1825. This meant that the interest on foreign debt was only slightly less than the state's annual deficit.

Count Apponyi, afterwards ambassador in Paris, had been sent to Naples by Metternich to examine the situation on the spot. "Cavaliere de' Medici," he reported,[4] "regards the presence of our troops as nothing but an intolerable burden. As finance minister he trembles at the idea that the foreign occupation may last until after 1826, and by compelling him to take refuge in another loan, still more increase the state's terrifying deficit. This caused him to say to Rothschild a few days ago: 'If the Austrian troops remain here after the limit of time fixed by the convention, I am determined to hand in my resignation.' "

Fundamentally Carl Rothschild was absolutely on the side of the finance minister. It was not in accordance with his wishes that the expenses of the occupation should lead to the whole internal economy of the state being thrown into confusion, so that the loans handled and issued by the House of Rothschild would run the risk of declining seriously in value. He began, therefore, noticeably to adopt the Neapolitan point of view, and gradually to forget to consider the interests of Austria, although he owed his position in Naples to that country.

He too favored speedy evacuation, especially as the new king, who had succeeded to the throne in January, 1825, and on whom he wanted to make a good impression, cherished the same wish. At Vienna he was actually suspected of supporting the Neapolitan finance minister in his obstinate efforts to recover part of the moneys paid out to the Austrian troops on the ground that they were excessive. The Neapolitan government was claiming the repayment of 1,013,398 ducats as excess payments made only up to November, 1821, and proposed to retain 100,000 ducats each month from the moneys payable to the Austrian war account until the adjustment should have been fully effected. Austria offered only 650,000 gulden in satisfaction, and was contemplating making deductions even from this amount. However, she was afraid of any public dispute in the matter. The quartermaster-general himself admitted in a letter to Count Nádasdy that the estimate of 650,000 florins was too low. He said that in his view it would be better to agree to the amount demanded by the Neapolitan government as a lump sum, rather than to allow the matter to be discussed in detail, as that would be too damaging to Austria.[5]

Ficquelmont also expressed his fears[6] that innumerable claims might arise, the airing of which would be unpleasant for Austria. He offered to arrange for the settlement of the matter, "without publicity and without compromising the dignity of our government," asking only that the repayments should not be made out of the resources of the I. and R. war-chest at Naples, but through the House of Rothschild. For direct repayments through the war-chest would furnish proof that savings had been effected out of the lump sums paid by Naples.

"Looking at the matter coldly and impartially," he added, "we find that we are to refund only the portion of the excess payments attributable to the period between February 1 and November 30, 1821."

But Vienna was not prepared to refund the money so quickly, and hesitated about making it available. Medici urgently needed the money, and would not wait any longer. He therefore applied to Carl Rothschild, informing him that the royal treasury required 1,500,000 ducats in excess of its normal revenue. He asked Rothschild to advance this sum, offering as partial security the claim exceeding a million ducats which had been recognized by Austria.[7]

Carl Rothschild immediately sent Medici's letter to Vienna in order to ascertain the imperial government's attitude in the matter. As, however, it was not yet inclined to give way, in spite of Ficquelmont's representations, it simply put the letter by. Nevertheless, in return for special securities in the event of Austria failing to pay, Carl Rothschild advanced 1,200,000 ducats, because he attached great value to being on good terms with Medici and the new king.

This brought him into great favor in high quarters, a fact which Carl exploited to create a position for himself in society in Naples, as his brothers had done elsewhere. During the winter of 1826 many distinguished foreigners flocked to the beautiful city of the south; amongst them were Leopold of Saxe-Coburg—afterwards King Leopold I of Belgium[8]—the Duke of Lucca, and other princes, as well as several wealthy English families. "This greatly enlivens our social gatherings," Carl said in a private letter.[9] "Amateur companies perform French plays; there are balls and soirées—in a word, in spite of everything, life is very gay. . . ."

Meanwhile, as the result of representations made by Solomon to Metternich,[10] the House of Rothschild had been informed that there was no objection to crediting to the House of Rothschild the moneys which Austria would finally refund to Naples. Their total, however, remained undefined, and as it went very much against the grain to pay these amounts at all, Metternich was somewhat annoyed that the House of Rothschild should intervene in the matter.

At the end of December, 1826, Emperor Francis and Metternich decided finally to evacuate the Two Sicilies, although not without emphatically warning the king never to think of changing the form of government. On the occasion of the Austrians' leaving, General Frimont, the officer in command, had recommended various persons for decorations, including the finance minister Medici and Carl Rothschild. In view of the attitude adopted by both of these in the matter of the rebates, Vienna was not prepared to consider the suggestion. Metternich minuted on the proposal that Medici ought not to receive any distinction,[11] since he already possessed the Grand Cross of the Order of St. Stephen, and that Baron Rothschild should not receive one "because he is not qualified to receive the distinction suggested." This was, in effect, a reply to the new attitude which Carl Rothschild had assumed. People in Vienna were almost inclined to call him a traitor or a deserter.

The negotiations regarding the refund of the excessive payments made for the support of the army continued for some time. Austria maintained her resistance against paying in full the amount demanded, until the King of Naples finally yielded, in order not to upset the agreement arrived at. But he wished at least to receive the interest on the excess that had been paid.

A memorandum on the matter states: [12] "The king does not doubt that the difficult circumstances in which Naples has been forced to accept her onerous obligation to the

House of Rothschild will so far influence the noble heart of the emperor that he will without delay carry out at least this wish of the Court of Naples." The Austrian government was to arrange the method of payment with the House of Rothschild. This appeal, however, met with little success; Austria finally paid only 338,564 gulden, which Rothschild took over on account of his claim against Naples, and at the end of 1829 this settlement was accepted for the sake of peace.

Although, as in Carl's case, Metternich was sometimes not entirely in agreement with the attitude of the brothers Rothschild, he always came back to them again, in both public and personal matters. There was no other financier who controlled such large sums of money and such important international connections. Moreover, it had been the chancellor's experience that the strictest secrecy was observed and maintained by the Rothschilds in all transactions of a delicate nature. In that respect they were in marked contrast to most other bankers; and this was of special importance to a man in such a public position as Metternich.

Transactions constantly arose in which the financial interests of the imperial house, to which Metternich naturally always wished to prove his devotion, had to be made to harmonize with those of the state in such a way as to avoid any public criticism. The Rothschilds were particularly skilful in handling such cases, and they thereby made themselves indispensable to Austria's leading statesmen, in spite of any disagreements.

A striking example of this was furnished when Metternich had recourse to the services of the Rothschilds in connection with the financial affairs of Marie Louise, wife of Napoleon I and daughter of Emperor Francis. Although she was far superior to her husband in birth, this lady was in general character and in intellectual gifts no fit consort for the Corsican genius. She remained with him as long as fortune favored him; but when his

Marie Louise, Duchess of Parma
From a portrait in the Vienna National Library

collapse came she left him, with her son, and returned to her father without shedding a tear for her husband.

Notwithstanding Napoleon's entreaties, she never once expressed the wish to visit him at Elba, to say nothing of St. Helena, although it is true that if she had so wished, her father and, still more, Metternich would have opposed her. The chancellor wished Napoleon's memory to be completely obliterated, and he was particularly skilful in the case of Marie Louise in exploiting her weaknesses to that end. She was callous and pleasure-loving, and used to visit fashionable spas; she lived only for her own amusement and did not even trouble to answer Napoleon's letters.

In 1814, while the ex-empress was staying at Aix-les-Bains, Metternich allotted to her as courtier a man who not only played the part of courtier, but also had an important political rôle in Metternich's service. Adam Albert, Count von Neipperg, was a handsome man of thirty-nine; he had lost his eye through a sword-thrust in the war and wore a black eye-patch. He was a smart and elegant officer, and had the reputation of possessing unusual courage and exceptional intellectual and diplomatic gifts. It was his duty to obliterate all thoughts of Napoleon and the empire in Marie Louise's mind, and to keep her from all contact with any member of Napoleon's family or his supporters. He was to be only too successful.

The Congress of Vienna had decided that the dukedoms of Parma, Piacenza and Guastalla should belong to Marie Louise *"en toute souveraineté et propriété."* As long as she ruled in accordance with the principles of an absolute monarchy, without constitution or representative bodies, she thereby acquired a kind of private property in these territories, by the act of the congress, this being quite in accordance with the contemporary attitude of regarding a state as a patrimony. It had, however, been laid down by the Treaty of Paris of 1817 that these possessions should not be hereditary, but should pass to another prince on Marie Louise's death. Yet no provision had been made as to how the transfer should be effected, nor as to how the duchess's private property should be determined.

Marie Louise had entered Parma in 1816, Count Neipperg sitting with her in her carriage. He had in the meantime not merely obtained complete control over the duchess's actions, as Metternich had wanted—he had also won her heart. The man in gold-braided uniform, sitting next her in her carriage, as Marie Louise entered Parma, was already her lover, and Napoleon, the great emperor and general, her husband and the father of her child, had been completely forgotten.

The affair was no secret at Parma, and it proved useless to try to hush it up; it soon became publicly known that on May 1, 1817, a daughter had been born to Marie Louise and her courtier in the palace of the ruler of Parma. This child received the name Albertine at her christening. Two years later on August 8, 1819,[13] Marie Louise gave birth to a son, who received the names William Albert, Count of Montenuovo—this being the Italian equivalent to the name Neipperg (Neuberg).

Both children were therefore illegitimate, for Marie Louise's husband, from whom she never obtained a divorce, did not die until May 5, 1821, in his distant island prison at St. Helena, while the marriage between Neipperg and Marie Louise, who had been living constantly together for some years, was celebrated in secret in September, 1821.

As the Duke of Reichstadt was still alive, Neipperg feared that on the death of their parents, his children might be left unprovided for. He therefore begged Marie Louise, while there was still time, to extract from her small dominions some money that could be declared to be her private property so the children could be given portions out of it. Marie Louise too realized that something must be done for their future, since on her death her lands would pass to another prince. She knew that there was an intention to construct a dukedom out of some Bohemian estates for the son by her marriage with Napoleon, but nobody at Vienna knew anything about the Montenuovos.

Up to 1826 the annual income from the territories ruled by Marie Louise had never been completely absorbed in administration, and it had been possible to allot large sums to the building of castles and bridges, and to improvements in the ducal gardens, etc. The Castle of Piacenza had been built, and the palaces at Parma and Colorno had been magnificently refurnished; bridges had been constructed over the Taro and the Trebbia; a theater had also been built; and a survey had been made of the whole country. Neipperg argued that these outlays had been a drain on Marie Louise's personal income, since it could not be disputed that any balance left over in administering the state belonged to the ruler.[14] The expenditure in question amounted to 10,435,000 francs,[15] and he said that she should ask that at any rate a part of this sum should be refunded in cash and applied to forming a private estate for the duchess.

Neipperg fully realized how far his understanding with Metternich went, and that the chancellor would not be able to refuse his request. The general decided with Marie Louise that the matter should at first be dealt with without mentioning the Montenuovo children, but only the Duke of Reichstadt when necessary. The general then wrote to Metternich to say[16] that after all the sacrifices which Marie Louise had made for the peace and welfare of Europe, and in view of the enormous benefits which she had conferred on her subjects, the question of her personal and private property ought to be cleared up. It was obvious that the castles, etc., which had been built out of savings were her own private property, and in order to secure the furniture, pictures, library, horses, and jewels, all of which she wished to leave to her son, negotiations should be immediately entered into with her successors, so that there should not be any dispute in the event of her death.

Neipperg proposed that either all the powers should conclude a supplementary convention, or a loan should be issued whereby what was due to the duchess could be made immediately available. Neipperg pointed out in a memorandum [17] written in support of his contention that "nobody can protest that, according to the law of the land, the whole direct and indirect income of the state, of whatever kind it may be, is absolutely at the sovereign's disposal; and she may, after the expenses of the administration in all its branches have been met out of the annual budget, dispose of any sums saved or balances left over, entirely as she thinks fit."

Metternich wanted to keep the other powers out of the matter as far as possible, and advised as a "less compromising procedure" that a direct agreement should be reached [18] with the Duke of Lucca, Marie Louise's designated successor. He too was in favor of "the application of carefully designed measures in order to place her Majesty's property beyond the reach of foreign claims and, in so far as it cannot actually be taken out of the country, to secure its separation from the property of the state."

The issue of an "appropriate loan" seemed to him to furnish an easier way out. "In considering a loan," he wrote, "we have, it is true, to keep in mind the fact that her Majesty is herself the beneficiary of the dukedoms; but this does not constitute a reason for denying her power to contract loans on the country's security by virtue of her recognized sovereign rights." The justification for such a loan was to be found in the fact that Marie Louise "has made notable and extraordinary sacrifices in carrying through important works for the benefit of her subjects and the country; and in order to a certain extent to indemnify herself for these sacrifices without imposing new burdens upon her beloved subjects or exacting the taxes due with excessive severity, she has decided to have recourse to a loan."

Metternich stated emphatically that the questions of the Duke of Reichstadt's inheritance, of a civil list for Marie Louise, or of the distinction between private property and the public treasury should not be brought before the public. The only result of this would be to draw undue attention to the matter and to compromise oneself. Neither did he consider it necessary to go into any question of accounts with the public, excepting such as had reference to the amount and conditions of the loan.

After lengthy correspondence, Neipperg reported in a personal discussion of the matter with Metternich at Vienna that [19] "her Majesty the archduchess has decided to propose to her council that she shall apply one-sixth of the state property [*patrimonium*] which is valued at thirty millions to the formation of an allodial property, which would be hers to dispose of as she pleased, and to make a gift to her subjects of the rest of the sum that she had used in works for the benefit of the public weal, the cost of which amounted to 10,439,000 francs. Marie Louise wishes to leave it to the council to decide whether the public debt of Parma shall be increased from its present amount of four millions to nine millions, or whether steps shall be taken to sell some of the state lands."

Metternich felt it difficult to come to a decision. The problems involved were of a difficult and exceedingly delicate nature, such as were hardly suitable for official discussion. He therefore decided again to ask Solomon Rothschild for his advice. When the question became acute Metternich was staying on his Johannisberg estate on the Rhine. He first informed Marie Louise that he would ask Solomon Rothschild's advice on all these matters, and that he was certain that Solomon would have the most useful ideas as to the best way of carrying out her wishes. He then wrote a long letter to Solomon,[20] carefully explaining to him that the archduchess wished to have available a capital sum of from five to six million francs, and to assure herself of the right to spend the income derivable from it in such a manner as she should deem fit. There were political objections to Neipperg's proposal that state lands should be sold; while if she increased the public debt, the archduchess was afraid of losing popularity.

"In my humble opinion," Metternich wrote, "the following scheme might be suitable. The archduchess should state publicly to her council that she could just as well have applied the state revenues—used of her own free will in erecting buildings for public purposes, or about to be so used—for acquiring a private property, but that she does not intend to do this; that she is leaving for the benefit of the state what has already been spent, as well as what will be spent, but wishes to secure a sum of five to six million francs out of the whole amount for her free disposal.

"After making this declaration she should take up the sum as stated and deposit it in the form of bonds in her treasury. The transaction may be a fictitious one, for she does not need ready money; she could leave the securities in her treasury, or issue them in whole or in part. My idea is that only five per cent securities should be created."

Metternich wished to have Solomon's views as to how this scheme should be put into practice in detail; and on receipt of the chancellor's letter, Solomon hastened "to submit his suggestions for his Highness's wise consideration." [21]

"In my humble opinion," he replied, "the object which you have in view could best and most effectively be realized in the following way. The government of Parma should create for the total capital sum involved a general inscribed bond, made out in the name of our firm, which bond should be deposited at the government's option in the I. and R. Austrian National Bank at Vienna, or in the Bank of Milan. On the security of this general bond we should issue bearer certificates of varying amounts . . . the holders of which should be competent to change them at any time . . . for inscribed bonds registered in the Great Debt Book of the state."

Solomon submitted a three per cent rentes certificate, which the French government had privileged his House to issue. A sinking fund would furnish the necessary security, and punctual interest payments should place the business on a sound basis. Solomon certainly wished first to obtain information regarding Parma's outstanding loans, but he did not recommend sending anybody there yet.

"Perhaps," he concluded, "your Highness could obtain the documents relating to them direct from Parma. This would not arouse attention as would be the case if I did so. Finally, I assure your Highness that I shall most zealously use all my endeavors to deserve the satisfaction of her Majesty the Archduchess, as well as the gracious commendation of his Majesty the Emperor in this matter, since, as your Highness is aware, I always deem myself richly rewarded when I have the good fortune to contribute to the fulfilment of the lofty aims of the Imperial Court of Austria."

This was Solomon's official reply, for Metternich's use in dealing with Marie Louise. He sent also a covering confidential letter, intended for the chancellor alone.[22]

"I take the liberty, in accordance with your Highness's wish, of writing a few separate lines regarding the business dealt with in the enclosed business letter.

"I am pleased to say that I am confident of arranging this matter to the full satisfaction of her Majesty the Archduchess, and of H. M. the Emperor and King, and of achieving the desired results. As the financial considerations touch political questions at many points I venture to give it as my opinion that it is quite important for the archduchess to secure the capital in such a way that after her death the claims of her legal heirs cannot be disputed. The preparation of bearer bonds issued by an eminent banking firm, the holders of which will be constantly changing, seems to me to meet any possible eventuality. For if anyone attempted to seize such certificates . . . such action would ruin the credit of Parma for all time, consequently all governments who have an interest in maintaining an inviolable credit system would use their influence to prevent such a thing being done.

"In my opinion it would be better to fix the capital sum, not at six, but at ten millions, for as your Highness has yourself indicated, the state requires some millions for public institutes and buildings. In this way the bad impression which might, as the grand duchess fears, be produced by the issue of the loan would be largely counteracted by a consideration of the fact that the proceeds were to be adapted to purposes beneficial to the community and to the country. . . . If on my return to Vienna your Highness should feel convinced that my personal presence in Parma would assist in promoting the business, I should not hesitate for a moment to obey your Highness's wish—which for me is a command—and should immediately proceed thither.

"I shall count myself happy indeed, if my efforts are crowned with the success we desire, and if I carry through the business to your Highness's satisfaction, which I value above all else."

Metternich acted in accordance with Solomon's wishes, and obtained documents regarding Parma's former loans; these he forwarded to Solomon. They, however, did not sufficiently enlighten Solomon. He wrote to Metternich that he could not obtain a clear view of the situation from them, such as was absolutely necessary to enable him to draw a valid conclusion, applicable to such an important transaction as was involved. "I therefore venture to suggest that your Highness invite her Majesty the Archduchess of Parma to send to me a confidential man of business, furnished with the necessary powers, so that he can let me have any information I require, and I can negotiate the matter with him under the direction of your Highness. . . . It is with particular satisfaction that I am able constantly to assure your Highness that I count it the greatest honor to devote my best services to her Majesty the Archduchess of Parma, and to justify the confidence which that gracious lady reposes in me." [23]

Solomon's wish was granted, and Colonel von Werklein, who directly controlled the duchess's public purse, set off for Vienna, taking with him a letter from Marie Louise to her father, the emperor.

"My one desire this year," she wrote,[24] "is to have the great happiness of seeing you again, and I cherish the firm hope that this may be fulfilled. This letter will be brought by Colonel Werklein, whom I am sending to Prince Metternich in Vienna, in accordance with his wishes, so that he may give Rothschild all the explanations he needs in the financial matter which you know about. The loan itself, however, which is to clarify my claims on Parma, will be formally negotiated and concluded here, with the assistance of the finance president, and a plenipotentiary of Rothschild's. I will then be much more at ease regarding the future."

The main lines of the proposal to be submitted to Marie Louise were decided in long secret conferences between Metternich, Werklein, and Solomon.

Solomon Rothschild had brought with him a detailed memorandum [25] in which he showed that the commercial crisis had affected the credit of all states, so that public enthusiasm for investments of the kind in question had been considerably damped. Moreover, Parma's public debt was too small to arouse interest in any of the principal money-markets of Europe. These facts were mentioned in explanation of the rather unfavorable conditions which he was offering. He made it a *conditio sine qua non* that the consent of the Duke of Lucca, the presumptive successor, should be obtained. State lands of the value of twenty-five million would realize only twelve to fifteen millions at the outside, so that a loan was preferable; but Parma would have to undertake not to incur any further debt for a period of years.

"Finally," Solomon's memorandum concluded, "as his Highness Prince von Metternich is well aware, local conditions in Parma make it of the greatest importance that the government should be told most emphatically to maintain the strictest secrecy regarding the proposed business until the time comes for carrying it into effect. We must also bear in mind that the new loan will almost double the public debt of Parma, a fact which will have a far from good effect upon the country's securities, so that the loan cannot be issued at a very high price."

There was no fear that Metternich and Werklein would attempt to modify these conditions. They were far too well satisfied that the matter was being arranged so easily, to attempt to obtain better conditions. They therefore signed the draft agreement submitted by Rothschild and Mirabaud, under which a loan of 6,000,000 livres, bearing interest at 5 per cent was to be issued at 75 per cent on the security of the three dukedoms.

Both bankers undertook the sale of the bonds, stating explicitly in the contract [26] that it had been arranged "at the invitation of the government of Parma and under the auspices of his Highness Prince Metternich." The government of Parma also undertook for fifteen years not to issue any other loans, without the consent of Rothschild and Mirabaud, to reduce the present loan by 3 per cent per annum, and to obtain the requisite consent of the Court of Lucca. Metternich and Werklein agreed because they hoped easily to secure the other's agreement. "If he [the Duke of Lucca] should refuse," Metternich wrote,[27] "we should simply carry on and ignore him; that is, act against him."

Metternich expressed his satisfaction in a letter to Neipperg: "In settling the matter in this way every factor has been carefully considered. The best thing will be for your Majesty to sell your property to the House of Rothschild under a fictitious contract, and gradually . . . invest the funds skilfully. You will thus find in about twenty years that you have acquired the whole capital sum that you want without its having cost you a halfpenny, and you will also during the whole of the period have received 9 per cent interest upon it. . . . Unless I am very much mistaken you will then possess not merely six millions in cash but seven or eight."

The chancellor wrote a short letter to Marie Louise in which he expressed his satisfaction at the conclusion of such an excellent arrangement, which offered the prospect "of achieving the desired results in the simplest possible way. If on examining the contract," he added, "your Majesty shares my feelings, all my wishes will be completely satisfied." [28]

Marie Louise, who understood nothing of financial matters, but gathered that she would obtain the millions she wanted, agreed to everything, signed the contract, and rejoiced with Neipperg that the future of her children by the second marriage was now assured. She wrote to her father saying: [29] "I have accepted and ratified the fictitious loan of 300,000 francs annuities,[30] which Prince Metternich and Werklein have concluded at Vienna with Rothschild and Mirabaud. I should be glad if, when the Duke of Lucca is being asked to give his consent, everything affecting my private property and furniture could be cleared up at the same time, so that after my decease my son and those persons whom I wish to benefit will not become involved in actions and disputes with his successor."

Marie Louise, however, wished that Rothschild would

carry out the agreement, even if the duke's consent were not obtained. Metternich informed Solomon of this, assuring him that he would personally endeavor to secure the duke's consent. But Solomon was most unwilling to proceed without this security.

"I must honestly confess to your Highness," he replied,[31] "that I can see no prospect of this matter being satisfactorily settled in such a case. Her Majesty cannot flatter herself that it will be easy to double the country's indebtedness and to find a market for such a large quantity of bonds, without offering the public every kind of security." He therefore emphatically begged Metternich to use all his influence to secure the duke's consent. The chancellor concurred all the more readily in Rothschild's appeal, as he himself wished to secure this consent in view of possible further developments.[32]

Baron von Werklein accordingly went to see the Duke of Lucca with a letter from Marie Louise and Metternich. The duke unexpectedly made no difficulties. He authorized Werklein to write to Marie Louise and Metternich and say that it was a pleasure to him to be able to meet the wishes of the archduchess.[33] He also permitted Neipperg to have an inventory taken of Princess Marie Louise's personal effects. He stipulated only that the duchess should not arrange any further loan, that she should create a sinking fund and sell no property belonging to the state.

In the end all parties were satisfied, including the Austrian Treasury, which immediately recouped itself out of the loan to the extent of 400,000 francs disbursed on military expenditure and on the maintenance of Marie Louise during the years 1814 to 1816.

Metternich wrote a self-congratulatory letter to Marie Louise herself[34] in which he said: "The matter has so far worked out so entirely in accordance with my wishes that I cannot refrain from congratulating myself for having first conceived the idea of an arrangement that so extensively harmonizes your Majesty's interests with the principles of justice."

There were certain distinctions to be conferred in connection with this business. Metternich wrote to Neipperg:[35] "Werklein will have told you that Herr von Rothschild wants a little St. George for his managing clerk.[36] This indicates a certain amount of vanity, the Rothschilds, in spite of their millions and their generous loyalty, having a craving[37] for honors and distinctions. At the same time I feel that it is not in the best of taste to ask that such an order should be conferred upon a clerk, and I suggest that you reply to this request that the order of Constantine is a knightly order. It constitutes a genuine religious brotherhood, and is not simply a distinction, and as the (Jewish) religion forbids its adherents to take the statutory oath of the order, the chancellor of the order would not be able to confer the cross. Temper your refusal with appropriate expressions of your extreme regret, and the matter will be disposed of. Write to . . . Herr Solomon on these lines, but do not mention me, as nobody can take offense at a statutory provision, while a single personal remark can do untold mischief, and I myself have committed the great offense of making it impossible for all time[38] for the Rothschild family to obtain an Austrian decoration. If he thought I was implicated he would regard me as a positive cannibal."

Metternich certainly did leave Rothschild under the impression that he was prepared to use his influence in favor of securing a distinction for Leopold von Wertheimstein; but Solomon himself had been disingenuous in the matter. In putting his secretary forward he had himself in view, for if Wertheimstein were to be made a Companion, he himself was bound to be made at least a Commander. As he took Metternich's pleasant words at their face value, and had no suspicion of the correspondence quoted above, he wrote the following letter to Werklein at Parma:[39]

"I have just taken the opportunity of asking our most esteemed prince to lend his powerful support to my request, and the gracious reply which I have received from his Highness justifies me in anticipating that if you will only be so good as to make a suggestion in that quarter, his Highness will not be averse from . . . graciously acceding to it.

"I leave it to you to choose the most propitious moment for putting forward the proposal, having full confidence in your feelings of friendship for me, which I know how to value. I feel a correspondingly lively desire to find a suitable occasion for reciprocating them, and you will afford me the best possible proof of your friendship if you will give me an opportunity of being of use to you on the earliest possible occasion."

Leopold von Wertheimstein set off for Parma with full powers to conclude the business. He brought with him a secret letter from Metternich to Neipperg. "To my great satisfaction the matter has gone through," the letter ran,[40] "and something must be done for the bearer. He is Rothschild's right-hand man, and a splendid young fellow of first-rate intelligence. He hopes to get the minor cross; you know my views on that matter. Give him a nice present of a more useful kind."

The deeds were sealed, signed and delivered.[41] The two contracting firms underwrote 284,000 lire 5 per cent perpetual annuities representing a nominal capital of 5,680,000 lire at 75 per cent, i.e., 4,260,000 lire altogether were to be paid in monthly instalments of 355,000 lire. Rothschild and Mirabaud were if possible to sell the securities within six months, and they received as their commission 2 per cent of the nominal capital of the whole public debt of Parma, which amounted to 12,008,000 lire, so that they got 240,160 lire. Marie Louise informed her father[42] that they had now concluded the contract with Rothschild and Mirabaud which

Prince Metternich had prepared at Vienna, and that she was exceedingly relieved.

No sooner had the transaction been completed than Solomon Rothschild began to wonder how Marie Louise proposed to invest the sums of which she would become possessed. He meant to get this business for himself to the exclusion of his partner Mirabaud; and he proposed to Metternich that the duchess should purchase shares in the Austrian National Bank through the firm of Rothschild "at a fixed average price to be agreed," and deposit these shares in Vienna. Metternich supported Solomon's plan because he hoped that the money would thus certainly remain in Vienna, and would not, as the emperor feared, be dissipated by the duchess. He therefore used his influence with Marie Louise and Neipperg in support of Solomon's proposal, without considering that Solomon was hoping thus to derive further profit from the transaction.

While Wertheimstein was on his way to Parma, Metternich had accordingly written to the duchess in the following terms:[43] "Rothschild has some ideas regarding a transaction which is as easy as it should be advantageous for your Majesty, and which he would like to negotiate *discreetly* with someone who can be trusted. Monsieur Mirabaud will be in Parma, and Rothschild's authorized agent will not be able to discuss this matter in his presence. I know what Rothschild has in mind, and I guarantee that your Majesty cannot do better than to act in accordance with his suggestions."

Metternich wrote in the same sense to Neipperg and asked him to send Werklein to Vienna. Werklein brought with him a letter from Marie Louise to Metternich in which she said: "You have always given me such good advice that my interests cannot be in better hands, and I am entirely relieved with regard to my future."[44]

He also received a letter from Neipperg[45] stating:

"Herr von Wertheimstein has displayed as much zeal as he has understanding, and her Majesty has recommended that a ring with monogram of the value of 3,000 francs be given him."

Marie Louise also asked Metternich to let her know what would be a suitable present for Solomon, as the statutes of the Order of St. George made it quite impossible to admit him.

Metternich and Rothschild discussed the proposed investment of the money with Werklein at Vienna, and Werklein brought a detailed memorandum to Marie Louise [46] in which Rothschild showed that it would be to her advantage to sell the Parma bonds, and to invest the money thus made available in other suitable public securities. He pointed out that the Parma bonds did not constitute as good a security as those of larger states, since it was always the smaller states that were first endangered through political movements of any importance. He suggested that shares in the national bank would constitute an exceedingly good and safe investment.

Solomon Rothschild offered to carry through the business on the basis of the average purchase price of the shares during the years 1825 and 1826, this price to remain unaffected by any future changes, provided that he was granted a share in the dividends. Marie Louise accepted his offer, subject to the one condition that one-third of the share certificates should be sent to her at Parma, the others being deposited in the treasury at Vienna.[47]

Marie Louise maintained a constant business relationship with the House of Rothschild, even after the death of her second husband Neipperg. Everything connected both with the loan and with the budget of Parma went off sc well that in 1828 fully three million francs [48] were made available for Rothschild to apply in the purchase of 1,054 national bank shares. Marie Louise also en-

Karl Theodor Baron von Dalberg
Last Elector of Mainz

trusted Solomon with the settlement of the moneys due from her Bohemian estates, i.e., those of the Duke of Reichstadt; and Moritz Goldschmidt, a second secretary and confidential agent of Solomon, had to make several journeys to Parma.

When Marie Louise was staying in Vienna in July, 1828, Solomon had the great pleasure of being received in audience by her. At the end of 1829 Solomon sold Marie Louise's share, and the money received was divided into three parts. The amount of 484,824 gulden realized by 360 shares was put to a separate account "M," as a present to the children, William Albert and Albertine Montenuovo.[49] Two other accounts were opened for Marie Louise and for the Duke of Reichstadt. The money was first of all left with the Rothschilds to be invested in other securities at a suitable opportunity. The House of Rothschild had thus become the trustees of the property of the Montenuovo family, in which were merged the amounts standing in the accounts of the Duke of Reichstadt (who died early) and of Marie Louise on their respective deaths.

In view of the important position which the Princes Montenuovo came to occupy, owing to their relationship with the Imperial House of Austria, Rothschild's connection with the family was of great importance.

Gentz viewed with satisfaction the successes of his friend Solomon, for when his protégé later prospered, he was not left out in the cold. At such times Rothschild was easier in the matter of presents, and Gentz scarcely ever allowed the occasion of one of Rothschild's visits to pass without obtaining a loan he had no intention of repaying. In return Gentz used his influence with Metternich in Rothschild's favor.

On the occasion of one of these visits the conversation turned upon Goethe, who had requested the Austrian government to forbid the printing of one of his works in that country. Gentz asked whether the House of Rothschild had come into touch with the poet, who was also of Frankfort origin. They had in fact scarcely come into touch with each other at all, there having been only occasional and casual meetings between them. This was due primarily to the fact that Goethe did not stay at Frankfort at all during the period between 1796 and 1814, when the House of Rothschild was first coming to the front, and that in later years his visits to the town were always quite short; he was indeed not much attached to his native town, as is indicated by the fact that in 1817 he renounced Frankfort citizenship.

Nevertheless he, like the rest of the world, heard of the remarkable success of the family which had originated in the Jewish quarter of Frankfort. Born of patrician parents, Goethe had as a child, as he tells us in "Dichtung und Wahrheit," only rarely peered at the ghetto, as at a strange world.

From his earliest days he had been brought up in an atmosphere of hostility toward the Jews, and later when his intelligence matured he had scarcely developed any more friendly attitude toward them. These sentiments were often revealed in his conversation, and the efforts of the Jews to secure their emancipation would evoke harsh comments. The growing prominence of the Rothschilds, when he had reached an advanced age, often led to Goethe expressing his attitude on Jewish questions. The introduction at Frankfort on September 23, 1823, of a new law, permitting marriage between Christians and Jews, was the occasion of a passionate outburst in conversation with the Chancellor von Müller.

"This scandalous law," the poet exclaimed, "will undermine all family sense of morality, intimately associated with religion as it is. When this goes through, how can a Jewess be prevented from becoming principal Lady of the Bedchamber? Foreigners are bound to think that bribery has been at work to make such a law possible. I suspect the all-powerful Rothschilds are behind it." [50]

In 1823, therefore, Goethe was already referring to the Rothschilds as all-powerful, recognizing the fact that it was through their money and influence that the Jews had been enabled, with the support of foreign powers, to get their way against the senate and citizens of Frankfort. The poet also inferred quite rightly that the widely current myth that the Rothschilds had made all their money very easily, and practically at one stroke, was a pure fabrication.

On October 20, 1828, he was talking to Eckermann about the period required for cultural or any other great achievements and said: "Yes, my dear fellows, it all amounts to this; in order to do something you must *be* something. We think Dante great, but he had a civilization of centuries behind him; the House of Rothschild is rich, but it has required more than one generation to attain such wealth. Such things all lie deeper than one thinks." [51]

In any case this remark shows that Goethe found food for thought in the phenomenon of the rise of this family of fellow Frankforters. With the Bethmanns Goethe was more intimate, and he was interested in watching the rivalry between the two leading Frankfort banking firms; however, as he had little understanding for financial matters, he was amused rather than concerned about their rivalry, and enjoyed retailing good Frankfort jokes about Rothschild and Bethmann, and stories of the way in which they spoiled each other's game.[52]

It was only toward the end of his life that Goethe actually met any members of the Rothschild family. In his diaries we have only the short entry that on May 2, 1827, two young Rothschilds with their tutor John Darby called on Goethe. They were Nathan's two sons, Lionel and Anthony, who were twenty-three and twenty-one years old at the time. On August 7, 1831, Goethe noted: "Afterwards Frau von Rothschild, a young bright person." This may have been Betty, the wife of James

Rothschild of Paris, or more probably, perhaps, the wife of Solomon's son Anselm, who had married his cousin Charlotte, Nathan's twenty-four-year-old daughter.

The members of the Frankfort line are not mentioned by Goethe at all. The only other reference we find is to the effect that, a few days before his death, on March 14, 1832, Goethe was contemplating an oil painting, propped up on his easel, of the old bridge at Prague which was to go to "Baron Rothschild at Vienna." [53]

In view of these scanty references it is not unreasonable to assume that any personal intercourse during the latter years was of an exceedingly superficial nature, and that the colossus of intellect and the colossus of money, both originating from the same native city had had only the most casual intercourse, their knowledge of one another being derived practically from reading and hearsay.[54]

The Rothschild visitors referred to in the diaries were no doubt typical of the innumerable persons who called out of curiosity. Goethe had to receive many such, especially during the last years of his life. It had become a special honor to have seen the famous aged poet face to face, and this visit no doubt constituted a small step on the long road of social advancement.

James in Paris had had the best success, relatively, in making his way socially, since society in that city, having been convulsed by the changes of revolution and imperialism, did not hang together with the same consistency as in England and Austria. With few exceptions the most distinguished representatives of all parties and classes were to be found at James's house. At that time Metternich's son Victor,[55] who had already contracted a fatal disease of the lungs, was an attaché at the Austrian embassy in Paris. In accordance with his father's wish he had got into touch with James; and he told the chancellor of a *visite d'amitié* which he had paid to Rothschild.

"I paid a friendly visit," he wrote, "to Baron James yesterday morning. His office was positively like a magic lantern, for people of the most various appearance and every kind of expression were constantly coming in and out. On that particular day the coming and going was specially noticeable, as securities quoted on the Bourse were fluctuating violently. The great banker himself, who generally maintained an attitude of such dignified calm, betrayed a certain nervousness. Our conversation was frequently interrupted by Bourse agents reporting quotations to their chief. The Duke of Dalberg was there, too, indulging in outbursts of liberalism."

Prince Victor Metternich described other strange callers who would take James aside, and all of whom wanted much the same thing—money and more money. This description of the office of the Paris money king showed how the House was constantly extending its sphere of influence. In the course of time, however, an opposition party grew up both in Paris and in London which attempted to check the firm's growing power.

Nathan Rothschild had not acquired the Austrian title of Baron, as he would have had to complete certain formalities as a naturalized British subject. He also feared that it might be damaging to his recently acquired British citizenship if he made use of a foreign prefix. But he did not conceal from the Austrian ambassador Prince Esterházy that the title would have been welcome.[56] The ambassador asked Peel and Lord Aberdeen whether Nathan could be granted permission to use it, and they stated that they were aware of no objection, either legal or customary, to this being done. Nathan, however, decided to go no further in the matter, as he feared that his new fellow countrymen might regard him as a tool of the reactionary Metternich, and in general as a supporter of the system represented by the government of Austria.

Strong opposition against the Rothschilds made itself

felt when their friend Herries was suggested for the office of chancellor of the exchequer, on the reconstruction of the ministry consequent upon the death of Canning in 1827. The appointment of a Tory who would be so entirely amenable to the king aroused a storm of indignation amongst the Whigs. The appointment of Herries had actually been approved by the king, and he had been summoned to Windsor. Thereupon Lord Lansdowne and his party suddenly offered the strongest opposition and endeavored to persuade Herries to refuse office on the ground of ill health.

Herries refused to accede to their wishes, with the result that his opponents mobilized the press against him in order, if possible, to delay the appointment. The Times and the Morning Chronicle expressed the view that the appointment of Herries was out of the question, as he was closely associated with a big financier who controlled the European money-market. Other papers [57] took up the cry that this fact made it quite impossible to appoint Herries chancellor of the exchequer.

The conservative papers took up the issue, and for a week the whole British press was full of the relationship between Nathan and Herries. The First Lord of the Treasury actually felt called upon to intervene in the discussion with a public denial.

In the end, Herries was appointed, but he held office only for a few months. When the ministry, of which he was a member, was succeeded in January by a new government under Wellington, Herries had to resign the office of chancellor of the exchequer and content himself with the post of master of the mint. Nathan expressed his regret in a letter to Carl [58] written half in German and half in Yiddish, which was intercepted by the Austrian Police.

"Consols," he said, "have gone up because of our ministers. Our friend Herries is *broges* [slang for 'annoyed'] because he has been given a poor job—he is *broges* but

I cannot help him. He must be patient and perhaps he will get another job. Praise be to God that we have good news as Russia will wait, through Wellington everybody is for peace [*scholem*] which does not surprise me, for our king in his speeches is nothing but *scholem al leichem* [peace be unto you]."

In France, too, a new ministry had come to the helm in January, 1828. The harsh reactionary and clerical régime of Charles X had aroused such opposition in the country that in an election affecting 428 seats, only 125 supporters of the government were returned. Charles X was therefore forced to dismiss Villèle, and to send for Martignac to form a moderate ministry; but he cherished secret plans of revenge.

Although the state of things in France afforded the Rothschilds some ground for satisfaction, the general situation in Europe was anything but pleasant. The Greek problem was still unsolved, and the battle of Navarino, in which the Turko-Egyptian fleet was destroyed, produced a tense situation. This sought relief in open hostilities between Russia and Turkey. The Porte went so far as to declare that the tsar was the arch-enemy of the Turks.

In these circumstances Emperor Alexander's successor Nicholas began to think of war. Whereas Metternich still congratulated himself on having converted Alexander into an Ultra from being a Jacobin,[59] and on having attached him permanently to his system, Nicholas inclined to a Russo-Nationalist policy. But for this, and especially for war against Turkey, he needed money. The Russian government therefore inquired of the House of Rothschild in Paris, toward the end of March, 1828, whether it would place its services at the disposal of the Russian government for floating a large loan.

The bank fully appreciated the political nature of the question of financial assistance at such a time and for such a purpose. While on the one hand it was offered an opportunity of doing big business, it might on the other lose powerful patrons. The Rothschilds had struck their roots in Western and Central Europe. They had no considerable interests or connections in Russia, and their minds were oppressed by the ill treatment to which Jews were subjected in that country. It would, moreover, have been exceedingly dangerous to come to Russia's assistance without the chancellor's knowledge, at a time when Russian policy was starting out on a line hostile to Metternich.

James therefore decided to communicate the inquiry he had received to Metternich through his brother Solomon, asking the chancellor to express his opinion. Metternich naturally advised refusal, although his advice was clothed in soft words. Through a third person, probably Gentz, Solomon was shown a memorandum in reply, entirely in Metternich's handwriting, although composed in the third person. "The prince says," the memorandum ran, "that he entirely shares the opinions and sentiments of Solomon Rothschild. There are two questions that have especially to be considered in this matter. One is the purpose to which Russia is going to devote the money; and on this there can be no doubt. Russia is seeking money in order to pursue her plans, and these plans threaten the political peace of the world. In this case, therefore, the money would be applied to the most evil ends conceivable in the present dangerous condition of governments and of affairs generally.

"The other question is whether, if the House of Rothschild refuses to do the business, Russia will still find means for carrying through her plans. There is no one better qualified to answer this question than Herr Solomon Meyer Rothschild, for he alone can judge whether in the present state of credit there is a possibility of other firms being able to carry through such a considerable, if acceptable, business as Russia requires, without the assistance of the Rothschild bank. If the answer to this question be in the negative, the House of Rothschild would alone have to accept the moral responsibility for all the evil which would result from its acquiescence. If the answer be in the affirmative, it remains for the House of Rothschild to decide whether, merely to prevent others from securing the profit, they wish to take upon themselves such a heavy responsibility, and incidentally whether under prevailing conditions, and in view of the risks necessarily attendant upon the carrying out of Russia's plans, the entrepreneur would be reasonably certain of realizing his profit.

"All these are questions which Herr Rothschild is alone qualified to decide. If the prince be asked what he considers *sensible,* he feels he must declare *against* the business. In any case, he advises Herr S. M. Rothschild to discuss the matter quite frankly with Wellington, and ascertain his views. Indeed, he has no objection to the duke being informed of his (the prince's) views . . ."

England was fundamentally opposed to Russia's warlike operations against Turkey, and Nathan was therefore also against granting the loan. Metternich's memorandum, moreover, did not fail of its desired effect. For the Rothschilds, who had acquired their enormous fortune by taking advantage of the cross-currents of war, were now opposed to all wars, with their inevitable effect of shattering public credit. They were also able to claim approval from their coreligionists for their refusal as constituting a protest against the ill treatment of the Jews in Russia.

The Russian loan was frustrated, and Metternich ascribed this fact principally to *his* dominant influence. The chancellor deemed himself superior to everybody, including the Rothschilds; he credited them with a special knowledge of technical financial matters that he himself lacked, but it never for a moment occurred to him that they might be cleverer than he. Whenever the Rothschilds did, or omitted to do, anything from motives of personal interest, which happened to coincide with Metternich's wishes, they always conveyed the impression that it was Metternich who had won the day, and that they were making a sacrifice. Although not free from vanity themselves they recognized the great man's weakness very well, and exploited it cleverly.

It is true that their refusal did not prevent the Russo-Turkish war, for other financiers were found to provide the Russian government with the necessary cash. Solomon made great play with his refusal of Russia's request, to emphasize the extent to which the intentions of the Austrian government and Metternich's wishes were regarded as commands. Gentz especially had this dinned into him daily, so that he might be sure of retailing it to Metternich. In return, Wertheimstein industriously discounted Gentz's bills, greatly "facilitating his little financial transactions." The Rothschilds made extensive use of Gentz in other ways, too. He was paid to supply the banking firm with political information, the correspondence being carried on in the form of private letters.[60] This was an exceedingly important factor during such an unsettled period. Solomon, who was constantly traveling on business, was thus able to keep abreast of events. The written method of communication was, however, maintained, even when Solomon was staying in Vienna, as he sent the information on to his brothers.

Meanwhile the development of events in France was becoming more and more menacing. Although Charles X had at first seemed to yield, he demonstrated that he was unteachable by summoning on August 8, 1829, the ultra-royalist cabinet of Prince Polignac, whose slogan was "No more concessions."

Solomon, who was staying in Paris at the time, expected that the news of the change of ministry in France would exercise a marked influence on the Vienna bourse. He therefore sent a special courier with this news and appropriate financial instructions, to Wertheimstein at

Vienna. The letter was somewhat delayed, and when it arrived, Wertheimstein feared that he might not be the only person to have received the news, in which case he would be selling during a slump, and might sustain a loss.

"I had difficulty," he replied to Solomon, in the Hebraic language,[61] "in carrying out your instructions received by the post of the day before yesterday to sell 500 Métalliques and all our shares on the bourse. This was much increased by the fact that the postmaster of Sieghardskirchen, who brought us your letter himself, told us that another post had arrived at the same time as yours, which most probably also brought news of the change in the French ministry." The above letter was intercepted by the police, and a copy was laid before Metternich. It shows the manner in which the Rothschilds exploited political events, regarding which they always endeavored, through their own news and courier service, to have the earliest possible information.

The Russians had meanwhile been carrying on war against Turkey with varying success, and in August, 1829, they had advanced through the Balkans as far as Adrianople. Although their position was not by any means free from danger, their display of energy led the sultan to sign a treaty of peace at Adrianople on September 14, 1829, which, although it did not put Russia in possession of Constantinople, certainly secured her predominance in the East, improved her boundaries against Turkey, and offered great political and economic advantages.

The Danube Principalities served as a pledge for Russia. The Russians controlled the mouth of the river, and the straits were open to them. Turkey was to pay 11,500,000 Dutch ducats as war indemnity; in order to carry out this obligation, she applied to the principal European bankers, including Nathan Rothschild, for a loan.

Russia's successes gave little ground for satisfaction in England or Vienna. They had necessarily been achieved at the expense of England's influence; moreover, since the beginning of the war Russia had ignored all the protests made by England. Polignac was also disappointed, as he had hoped that European Turkey would be partitioned, and France would be indemnified by territorial acquisitions on the Rhine. Nathan sent a report on the situation to his brother Solomon in a letter written in Hebrew, of which Solomon made a personal, and therefore very poor, translation for Metternich's information.

"I am now going to tell you, my dear Solomon," the letter ran,[62] "all about how everything is here so far. There are some here who want to quarrel, and that with Lieven [63] . . . and want us to send angry notes, because Polignac is angry, too. Now I have spoken about the Turkish loan, and they said to me: 'Austria will do it, but it can't be done without us in England. Rothschild, speak to Wellington.'

"I must tell you Wellington and Peel would like to quarrel with Russia, but in the end we should have to go to war. I am not for demonstrations, and we must see to maintaining peace. What's the good of quarreling? The Russians have gone too far, and the world will be angry with us and will say: 'Why didn't you do it twelve months ago?' If England now says 'Yes, we are angry and want to go to war,' Austria and France will say: 'We will remain out.' They will leave us in the lurch, and we shall be involved alone.

"I went to Wellington and congratulated him on peace. He said: 'Peace is not yet. It is not yet ratified.' I spoke with him about Turkish loan as to whether he would give a guarantee. He replied, 'No, I cannot do so at the moment; you must get Austria to see to that.' Another minister said to me: 'I am afraid we shall make an enemy of Russia if we guarantee a loan.' The matter needs consideration. Perhaps the Turks will give the Island of Candia as guarantee.

"Wellington also said to me that many people had been to him who wanted a guarantee. There is dissatisfaction with the Russian Peace in every respect. The cabinet has now decided for the present to remain quite calm and not to write a word to Russia, to keep quiet and to let come what may. I shall certainly not leave you without news as soon as I hear anything further."

Political considerations alone prevented the Rothschilds from participating in a Russian loan before the war, or in a Turkish loan after the war, for they had not been severely hit by such few failures as they had suffered, and their wealth had increased enormously during the last few years. So that the "banking firm of the five brothers of Europe," as the House of Rothschild was called in several papers, had several million of cash available, for which it was seeking profitable employment. As a result of their happy knack in floating loans that almost immediately afterward were most favorably quoted, all countries wanted to have recourse to the Rothschilds for their loans, and a positively jealous rivalry developed to secure their favor.

While needy states were seeking opportunities for obtaining money on credit, the brothers Rothschild were looking for safe and profitable investments for their accumulated capital. The state of Prussia again entered into negotiations with the banking firm. The 5% interest payable on the £5,000,000 loan of 1818 was a heavy burden on the state budget. All states at that time were endeavoring to convert their public debt, and the Prussian finance minister, Motz, wished to reduce the interest payable on the state debt of 36,000,000 thalers from 5% to 4%.

The finance minister entrusted the preliminary negotiations to Christian Rother, an important treasury official and president of the Public Debt Administration, who had arranged the loan of 1818 with the Rothschilds. Rother asked [64] that he should not be hampered by detailed instructions, but that full confidence should be placed in him, as that was the only way in which he could be sure of success. From the start, Rother thought of no one but the Rothschilds. He went to Helgoland in July, 1829, where he met a confidential agent of Nathan's, and had a non-committal discussion with him about the business. He then went to Frankfort and negotiated with the house there. But he was offered conditions he could not accept.

"Gratuitous interference by business men here," Rother reported to his sovereign,[65] "has caused the Frankfort house to suspect the possibility of making large profits. In the course of our conversation conditions emerged, all of which I had to reject as being damaging to the interests of your Royal Majesty. I stated definitely that I would have to transact the business in question through the shipping interests, unless Solomon von Rothschild at Vienna would carry on the further negotiations, as I could not undertake a journey to London."

Rother thereupon decided to negotiate with Solomon, who, as he believed, had unlimited confidence in him. He met him at Troppau on December 24. They agreed—subject to Nathan's concurrence—"after two days' discussion, which was sometimes heated," [66] on a draft agreement which Rother declared to be "extraordinarily advantageous," adding that "the state could not have secured such conditions through other channels or with other firms."

Rother wrote: "I have succeeded in obtaining what we wanted throughout—and in some matters far beyond my expectations—through the good nature of Solomon von Rothschild, who is really an estimable person."

Under the agreement the state of Prussia was to issue a new loan of £3,860,400 in 4 per cent Prussian bonds, at 98½, through the House of Rothschild, the proceeds of which were to be devoted to redeeming a like amount of five per cent bonds of the 1818 loan within about two years. On signing the agreement Rother had to promise Solomon to indicate to his Royal Majesty that Solomon had not "done this business for financial gain, but regarded the whole affair as a matter of honor."

Benecke von Groeditzberg reported some details of the Troppau discussion to Berlin.[67] "Solomon Rothschild told me at the time," he wrote, "that in concluding this business—a highly profitable one for the State of Prussia, in my opinion—he had had the honor of his House particularly in view. He attached the greatest value to demonstrating to the royal government of Prussia that the consolidation of its public credit and the fulfilment of the assurances which his House had given in this matter were of more importance in his eyes than any considerations of private profit.

"While I do not wish to suggest that the least value should be attached to the unimportant part which I have played in this transaction, I consider it to be my duty in all humility to inform your Excellency of the sentiments expressed by Herr von Rothschild, which I believe to be sincere. We owe it entirely to him and to the efforts of Herr Rother that this business has been put through to the credit and profit of Prussia's finances."

Rother similarly reported [68] to the king that this extraordinarily favorable agreement had far exceeded anything that he had expected.

Nathan in London and his brother at Frankfort were less well satisfied. At first they turned the agreement down absolutely; but they had misgivings about disavowing their brother in Vienna, and Nathan contented himself with sending Solomon's son Anselm, who was then twenty-seven years old, to Berlin, to delay the signature of the agreement, and to secure improvements and alleviations. He was to agree only if better conditions were unobtainable.

Rother offered a stout resistance, and in the end, after some mutual concessions of minor importance, the matter was settled. The £3,809,400 in 5% debentures still outstanding with respect to the 1818 loan were to be fully exchanged for 4% bonds for the same amount, by October 1, 1832, in five half-yearly transactions. Rother himself was very high in praise of his own work. "This contract," he reported to his sovereign, "is purely advantageous to the state, and constitutes the first example of a financial operation by a great state for the reduction of interest on a large scale in which the nominal amount of the debt has not been increased, the interest payable on a debt of about 27,000,000 thalers being reduced from 5 to 4%. The commission of 1½% is quite negligible and scarcely covers the cost of such a transaction."

The king expressed his satisfaction with Rother, and wrote saying,[69] "I gladly assure you also that the conditions have led me to the conviction that Baron Solomon von Rothschild concluded the agreement with you in the interests of the state of Prussia, as a matter affecting the honor of his house, wherefore I particularly instruct you to convey to him my satisfaction."

It was all an affair of "disinterestedness and honor," and Rother was zealous in emphasizing this aspect to his royal master. It was a matter of satisfaction to him, too, that the business had gone through so well, and in praising Solomon, he was indirectly praising himself for getting such good terms out of an astute business man. Yet in normal circumstances Solomon might have been able to make the transaction a highly profitable one. All that he needed was a continuance of fair weather on the bourse and the absence of any violent external influences, while the operation affecting the millions of pounds' worth of Prussian securities was carried through. Such conditions apparently obtained at the time, for the Russo-Turkish war was over, the general situation in Europe

Moritz von Bethmann and Amschel Meyer Rothschild Driving Europa
Contemporary cartoons in the possession of the Frankfort Library

was tranquil, and there then seemed to be no risk in carrying through operations on the bourse.

Further loans immediately followed on that of Prussia. The Austrian government also wished gradually to proceed to the conversion of her 5% state debt to 4%, and the ministerial conference decided on the issue of a loan of from twenty to thirty million gulden 4% state debentures through the four native banking firms, in which Solomon Rothschild had come to be included, after the ruin of the Fries Bank.[70]

Count Kolowrat, who had been appointed head of the commission of the privy council to control the financial administration, had recommended this issue on the ground that[71] the interest rates obtaining in Germany, France, England, and Holland were lower than 4% and a reduction in those countries either had been or was about to be undertaken. It did not seem that there was any prospect of political complications for some time.

The loan was decided upon, and on April 3, the emperor expressed his special satisfaction with the conduct of the four banks on this occasion.

Rothschild certainly endeavored to get rid of the bonds as speedily as possible, and invested all the ready cash in the three accounts of Marie Louise of Parma in the new 4% Métalliques bonds, at the issue price (subject to a commission for his trouble), on the ground that they were a particularly safe investment.

Metternich had—to use Solomon's words—"in constant and zealous endeavor to be of service to her Majesty the Archduchess," made it clear to him that he must devote himself as much as possible to the interests of the Montenuovo family. . . .

"I have repeatedly endeavored to demonstrate," Rothschild replied,[72] "that I am filled with the same zeal. To show this to her Majesty again, and also to please your Highness, I will now undertake to forego the commission which her Majesty has allowed me in the past on the investments that I have effected in Austrian securities, as far as the capital of the Montenuovo family under my control is concerned; and I hereby declare that when the time comes, that family shall enter into the new bonds at their issue price, without my having derived any benefit from them."

Rothschild did in fact waive the commission on Account M. and reduced the commission on the two other accounts by one-half. He did this the more readily as he had already made a large profit out of the Parma business; but his sacrifice of the relatively trivial commission made a good impression. It was just such an occasion as Solomon would use for playing up to his reputation for "disinterestedness and honor." In any case Solomon was unable at once to find purchasers for the large volume of security issued in connection with the Austrian loan.

In addition to the Prussian and Austrian loans just described, they undertook an operation on a far larger scale, fraught with far more serious consequences, namely the underwriting of 80,000,000 francs of French rentes, needed by the French government to pay for the Algiers campaign on which it had just embarked. Several rival firms had stated that they were prepared to deal with it. Aguado offered [73] to underwrite it at 97.55%, a consortium headed by Mallet Frêres offered 98%, the Syndicat des Receveurs-Généraux offered 100%, and the Rothschilds—102.72½%. "The rivals perceived," wrote Capefigue, "that in future nobody would be able to stand against the Rothschilds."

Even these gigantic transactions left them unsatisfied. They suggested to Marie Louise that the public debt of Parma should be converted, and they also wanted to maneuver the House of Bethmann in Frankfort out of a connection it had recently established with Austria.

Solomon Rothschild had been informed by the finance minister Count Nádasdy that the Austrian administration was proposing to convert all its 5% securities to 4%. He promised on his journeys to ascertain foreign sentiment regarding this proposal, and to let Vienna know the result of his investigations. In June, 1830, he made his first report to Nádasdy;[74] it was sent from Frankfort and contained a proposal which in its essentials was directed against the House of Bethmann. His idea was that the 5% Bethmann bonds, which were still in circulation, should be redeemed at Frankfort by cash payments at par, through the Frankfort branch of the House.

"Your Excellency," he wrote, "is not unaware of my deep devotion to the Austrian state, which is shared by all my brothers and partners. I trust that you are convinced that we always have the best interests of the treasury in view, and that it must be our principal concern to fulfil your Excellency's wishes to the best of our ability."

The taking over of the Bethmann bonds was to serve "to secure and hasten the conversion operation as far as possible, and create enthusiasm abroad for the transaction." Not until he had delivered the 5% debentures did Solomon wish that his firm should receive 4% debentures at the rate of 105 florins for each hundred, or treasury notes, or money, or whatever else the authorities considered most convenient.

"Since my brothers and I," Solomon continued, "have no keener desire than constantly to furnish proofs to the Austrian state of our most disinterested service, unaffected by any private interests, we flatter ourselves that your Excellency will receive our most dutiful offer with your customary kindness." He hoped thereby to make the conversion more popular abroad.

"Your Excellency," he continued, "may be convinced it is neither pride nor self-interest that induces me to take this matter up. As I have already had the honor to prove to your Excellency, I always speak openly and sincerely; and I can absolutely assure you that if my suggestion be adopted the conversion will go through speedily and successfully. If therefore your Excellency is agreed that direct cash payments shall be made through my Frankfort house—which, I flatter myself, possesses the confidence of the public—we shall arrange for such payments to be made, not to Herr Bethmann here, but by us direct to the holders of the bonds."

The Austrian treasury thereupon asked the firm of Bethmann to submit a preliminary memorandum on the question of conversion. This was done, and the authorities forthwith sent this memorandum, which naturally differed in many respects from the Rothschilds' offers, to Amschel at Frankfort. He made some very sharp comments on Bethmann's document, ascribing its feebleness to that bank's lack of resources and knowledge.

"If that firm," he wrote,[75] "is really serious about the conversion, and means to throw itself heart and soul into the business, it is inconceivable that it should have neither the confidence nor the means to acquire the small quantity of six hundred 4% Métalliques bonds in advance. Smaller firms, without such a well-known name or such a position as the firm in question, would certainly have offered to do so."

The Rothschild memorandum described the reasons put forward by Bethmann as evasions, because that firm was not strong enough, and did not sufficiently possess the confidence of the public to carry out so great an operation. Amschel Meyer asked Solomon, who was about to make a journey to Paris, to come and see him at Frankfort in order to discuss the matter. The memorandum of the Frankfort Rothschild, written in grotesque German, ran:

"The same [Solomon] assured me on his honor that he was not actuated by the least resentment at the conversion having been entrusted to the House of Bethmann. He also asseverated that his house was devoted life and soul to the Austrian government, and that both his honor and his private interests were involved in carrying through the conversion. He had negotiated the French and the Prussian loan, 'all these things hanging upon one another and being interdependent,' and he did not propose to act against his own interest. His house held fifteen to sixteen million gulden of Austrian public securities, which he could produce on demand, whereas the House of Bethmann had neither the resources nor the knowledge of markets nor the influence that were necessary. Not one of its partners had the requisite energy to take control of such a business."

The memorandum went on to state: "It is possible and indeed probable that one or more banking firms and their supporters believe, if they directly or indirectly got fabricated articles into the papers, and spread unfounded rumors on several bourses, they could put the House of Rothschild in an unfavorable light to the Austrian government, and at the same time extend their own sphere of influence. We had expected such irresponsible newspaper articles as those that recently appeared in some French papers, attributing the fall in rentes to the action of the House of Rothschild, on the ground that we wanted to get rid of all our rentes at any price because we had taken over a Turkish loan of eighty million francs. They will not be the last, as they are not the first, of their kind."

The memorandum set forth that important firms dealing with governments would always have such fanciful stories attached to them. Truth and justice were, however, bound to prevail, and such lies would meet their own reward. By coming to the rescue with the greater part of its cash resources, the House of Rothschild had quite recently, in May, prevented a terrible crisis on the Frankfort bourse, which would have had serious consequences in other money-markets. Even now the political situation was far from satisfactory. In France nobody knew what was going to happen, while in England the king was ill and a change of ministry expected. The memorandum concluded on its original note, asking that the Rothschilds might convert the Bethmann debentures.

The finance minister Count Nádasdy [76] was, however, unshakable. He was not willing to offend the House of Bethmann by allowing the conversion to be carried through by a different firm from that which had originally negotiated the loan. The brothers Rothschild were then holding enormous quantities of state securities; in addition to their large Austrian investments they held millions of the newly issued French rentes as well as the bonds of the conversion loan of Prussia. The Rothschilds were therefore overstocked with bonds at a time when the general state of Europe might change from one of apparent calm to one of acute crisis.

While James did not feel that the political situation in France was wholly satisfactory, he did not realize how critical it really was. He gave balls, which were attended by princes such as the Duke of Chartres and the Duke of Brunswick. He supported French theatrical undertakings to give performances abroad, as in Vienna for instance. He was associating with princes and ministers and financiers. But the opinions that he heard were so various and so conflicting that he did not feel he could predict the future with any confidence.

James's own particular domain, the sensitive bourse, was already showing signs of the coming storm. On June 1 there was a severe slump, and several politicians implored Rothschild to use his power to prevent a collapse.[77] The Duke of Decazes wrote to him: "If you do not succeed in preventing the fall in values, everyone will believe that a coup d'état will occur such as you so rightly fear, for you may be sure that in such a case no creditor would be paid his debts." [78]

James Rothschild thereupon hastily went to see Polignac, as he had so often done before, and was again reassured by him. Anything of the kind was again out of the question; the bourse and the public were nervous, that was all.

Solomon, the chief of the Vienna house, had in the meantime also come from Frankfort to Paris. He had promised Metternich he would send an accurate report as to the state of affairs in France, and faithfully fulfilled his promise in spite of all difficulties.

His first report, dated June 19, 1830, reads as follows:[79]

> MOST EMINENT PRINCE:
>
> I hope that your Highness is enjoying perfect and constant well-being on your beautiful estate . . . I am taking the liberty of reporting to you my arrival here the day before yesterday. I am venturing already to avail myself of the permission accorded me by your Highness to inform you occasionally of political events here through other than the ordinary channels. So far as I have had the opportunity during my short stay here of ascertaining from conversations with well-informed persons of all parties and opinions, it seems that the spirit of opposition, which has grown so very much more embittered in the last month, is directed not against the sacred person of the king and the dynasty of the Bourbons, but only against the leaders of the present cabinet, Messieurs de Polignac and Peyronnet.

Solomon still hoped that peace might be maintained, but he viewed with dismay Polignac's intention of changing the electoral and press laws, to which he adhered in spite of the strongest representations. The whole tenor of Solomon's report revealed his uneasiness.

Shortly afterwards Solomon reported that the result of the new elections had been markedly unfavorable to the government. The generally prevailing spirit of opposition had infected everybody, with the result that elements hostile to the ministry had been returned to the chamber. In fact the elections had resulted in only 125 supporters of the ministry being returned for 428 seats. "The list is odious and contemptible," Count Apponyi reported to Vienna. The ministry was dismayed and shocked by the result. The idea of changing the electoral law was again being mooted.

"Such a step," Solomon wrote to Metternich, "might lead to the most unforeseen results. Meanwhile the king is firmly determined not to weaken his royal prerogative at any point, for he knows only too well from his own experience how quickly one concession leads to another, and how gravely the royal authority is endangered thereby."

The general situation was exceedingly unpleasant, although Solomon and James, especially James, still hoped that the storm would pass over. But at the end of June rumors were thickening to the effect that the king and Polignac meditated a coup d'état to rid themselves of the inconvenient liberal chamber before it met and to limit still further the rights of the people. Those who accepted these rumors, or whose actual knowledge confirmed them, secretly sold large holdings of bonds in the London market; and the House of Rothschild, being interested in maintaining their value, was forced to buy them.

James Rothschild, believing that as state banker [80] he must necessarily be in the confidence of the government, was convinced that before any such fatal decisions were made he would surely be consulted, or that at any rate he would be given a hint before any vital step was taken. He heard nothing, however; and the rumors of serious steps contemplated by the government increased. On Sunday, July 24, James accordingly decided to go to Monsieur Peyronnet, minister of the interior, and ask him what it all meant.[81] The minister expressed his astonishment that such an intelligent and well-informed man as James should attach any significance to such gossip, and pointed to his office desk, covered with letters summoning the newly elected delegates to the first session of the chamber.

In a reassured frame of mind, Rothschild went to dine at the country house of Madame de Thuret, where the whole diplomatic corps had been invited. People asked him anxiously about the situation. He told them about his call on the minister, and the letters summoning the delegates which he had seen, and his statements reassured the diplomats who were present.

Meanwhile the ministers were secretly framing the famous ordinances in which the king, on Polignac's advice, dissolved the hostile chamber before it had ever met, ordered new elections on a different electoral basis, and severely limited the freedom of the press.

Early on July 26, 1830, the ordinances were published, to the general astonishment. The secret had been most scrupulously kept. The whole capital was swept by indignation. Everyone said that this meant the end of all liberty, and the relapse of France into the darkest medievalism. The press was particularly vocal, and protested most vehemently, in spite of any ordinance.

The excitement in Paris was prodigious. High barricades were erected in the principal streets; the populace collected in groups, marching through the streets shouting menaces at the king; shops with weapons and military stores were plundered, and strong opposition was offered to the royal troops, who were completely unprepared, and were present only in small numbers under the command of Marshal Marmont, who was himself taken by surprise. Stones were thrown at the windows of Polignac's private house, and his carriage was almost smashed to pieces. By July 28 the rising was in full swing. The streets reechoed with shouts of "Down with the Bourbons!" "Down with the ministers!" The garrison consisted of only twelve thousand men, and large sections had gone over to the rebels. The remainder were far from being sufficient to hold down the indignant city.

By July 29 the revolt had extended to the whole of Paris. The royal troops were slowly forced back on Saint-Cloud, where the king anxiously awaited the development of events. He was now prepared to revoke the ordinances; but it was too late. Not only his position, but that of the whole of his House, had collapsed. The Louvre and the Tuileries, defended by Swiss troops, were stormed by the populace.

The revolution was victorious all along the line; on July 31 Charles X and his guilty ministers fled. Their dominion was at an end. If the monarchy was to be maintained, only one thing could make this possible: the old line of the Bourbons must be eliminated. Recourse would have to be had to the king's rival, Louis Philippe of Orléans, son of the notorious Philippe Égalité, of the days of the great revolution. This prince played his part very cleverly; he contrived to make the people feel that they were conferring the crown upon him. His liberal views, and his simple, unadorned appearance as he courageously showed himself to the angry mob, did not fail of its effect. The old royal house was finished, the Orléans followed it, and Louis Philippe became head of the state.

James and Solomon were both in Paris during this period, and were reduced to a state of the greatest anxiety as the revolution proceeded. They were not only afraid for their wealth. As foreigners who had been so closely associated with the hated king and his ministers, they went in fear of their lives. Holding, as they still did, such a large amount of paper from the state loan they had just taken over, they had watched with the greatest dismay the catastrophic fall in rentes, amounting to 20 to 30% during the first days of the revolution.

But this fear was for a moment kept in the background by their immediate bodily danger, although their nervousness in this respect proved to be unfounded. The revolution of July was a bourgeois revolution. The people, it is true, sacked a few royal châteaux, but the life and property of private persons were spared.

Nathan Rothschild appears to have been the first man in London—apparently by means of a carrier pigeon sent by his brother—to receive news of the great event. Even if this particular is unfounded, it is clear that he received news of events at Paris before the British government. Talleyrand once stated in a letter to Madame Adélaïde, the sister and adviser of King Louis Philippe: [82] "The English ministry is always informed of everything by Rothschild ten to twelve hours before Lord Stuart's dispatches [83] arrive. This is necessarily so because the vessels used by the Rothschild couriers belong to that House; they take no passengers and sail in all weathers."

On July 30, by which time peace had been restored in the capital after the "unexampled tumult and indescribable disturbances" of the previous three days, Solomon Rothschild remembered his promise to report to Metternich.

"We have been completely out of touch with the ministry for several days," he wrote,[84] "as we do not even know where the ministers are. We are also told that the king has left his residence today for the Vendée; the tricolor flag is flying on all public buildings, and the diplomatic corps here has ceased to function." Solomon's view was that the issue of events must be quietly awaited. He feared a civil war, and according to rumor the Duke of Orléans had accepted the crown. "Such is the state," he continued, "to which the self-confidence of three or four ministers has reduced France in three or four days."

Rothschild described how a new administration was being set up in the capital with the support of from thirty to forty thousand men, drawn from the dregs of the population, who had been "let loose against the king's troops." It could certainly not be denied that the people had behaved well, for apart from the king's property, no public or private property had been touched, even while the excitement was at its height. "It is satisfactory," Solomon admitted, "to see the uniforms of the regular citizen guard appearing at every corner; they are forty thousand strong, and often protected the city from pillage in 1814 and 1815."

The confirmation of the rumor that the Duke of Orléans had accepted the crown was a great relief to the brothers Rothschild. In spite of their connection with Charles X and his ministers, they had rendered financial services to the Duke of Orléans too, and had thus come into touch with his house. They felt that they had been in a sense betrayed by Charles X, as he had never informed them of the ordinances; and now that the duke's star was in the ascendant, they saw a profitable opportunity of changing their allegiance. They accordingly began to sympathize with the victorious revolution, and a letter from Solomon to a friend [85] clearly shows that they were preparing to play up to the new powers. In that letter Solomon spoke of the general indignation aroused by the ordinances.

"There was no armed force," he said, "that could have controlled a people beside themselves with rage, who felt that they were being led to the slaughter by their king's command. The nation would have let itself be cut in pieces before submitting again to the domination of the Bourbon family."

Solomon referred to the fears aroused by such a terrible explosion, but said that everything had fallen out in the most amazingly satisfactory manner. Private property had not been in danger for one moment; and in fact the people had refused money they had been offered. The troops and the people had fraternized everywhere; and all were forsaking the cause of Charles X and turning to Louis Philippe, who claimed to have been always devoted to liberty and to constitutional ideas. He was being received with the greatest enthusiasm wherever he appeared.

The Rothschilds' change of front was thus clearly stated; the revolution had triumphed, and the old powers were finished with, and the new man in whom they trusted seemed to be firmly in the saddle. They immediately adjusted their policy accordingly, and James offered his financial services to the new powers in the state, in spite of the losses incurred through the fall in the funds and the continuing uncertainty.

The news of the entirely unexpected revolution and the success it had gained in such a short time profoundly affected the whole of Europe. All governments saw with dismay how France—"Pandora's box," as Leopold of Coburg called her—was again spreading terror and unrest over Europe. There was a slump on all the bourses, while the hope of liberty ran high among the peoples; the consequences for Metternich's "peace of the world" seemed unpredictable.

It had been the worst possible blow for the chancellor and his system. At the time of the outbreak of the disturbances he was staying with Gentz at his country place Königswart in Bohemia, and he received the first news of these events through the Frankfort ambassador Baron von Münch-Bellinghausen, who had received the news from Rothschild. It is remarkable evidence of the efficiency of the Rothschild news service even during times of such disturbance, that both the British government and the powerful chancellor, who controlled the vast diplomatic machine of the Austrian Empire, should have received the first news of these important events from the House of Rothschild.

Münch-Bellinghausen's report, dated Frankfort, July 31,[86] was based on a letter from Solomon and James in Paris, which Meyer Amschel had received at Frankfort on the 30th, and upon a short report brought by a messenger. "Rothschild has just received through a courier who left Paris on the 28th," the report ran, "a short letter from his brothers, telling him not to worry about them, as they were well and hoped that things would improve within a few days. They could not write him any news, and the courier would tell them everything verbally. The courier's statement is to the effect that Paris is in a state of great commotion." There followed a description of the serious disturbances at the beginning of the revolution.

Metternich and Gentz were at first unwilling to believe the news. The chancellor had just expressed his great satisfaction at the issue of the ordinances. He was now quite terrified. He kept hoping that the news would not be substantiated.

"I confess to you," Gentz wrote to Pilat immediately after the first news was received,[87] "that I believe all this to be only partially true. The mysterious letter from a panic-stricken Rothschild and the stories of a courier are doubtful sources. But it is certain that things are not well."

Nevertheless the Rothschild courier was right; and liberals throughout Europe took courage from what had happened in Paris, and felt that freedom was in the air. The news of the revolution resulted in a catastrophic slump on the Frankfort bourse, and masses of securities were thrown on the market. While Meyer Amschel, being the first to receive the news, had made some provision for this, he had not been able to do much in the short time available, and the collapse of all public securities reduced him to a state of panic. He applied his efforts to keep the disaster within bounds.

When disturbances consequently broke out in several German cities, and it was feared that they might occur in Frankfort too, the senate called up the special constabulary, so as to be ready for possible attacks. Amschel, who as a result of the last settlement enjoyed the rights of citizenship, took up his duties as a special constable when his turn came. He had more reason than anyone else in Frankfort to fear for his possessions, and he heard with terror that outside the city walls the peasants were plundering country houses and driving landed proprietors from their estates.

He anxiously awaited his brother Solomon, who had just informed him that he would arrive from Paris early in September. He wanted to enlighten the head branch of the firm as to the present political situation in Paris, and to discuss the measures to be taken to meet the terrible losses which the House had incurred. In these hours of danger affecting the very existence of the House, the unity and harmonious collaboration of the brothers was particularly vital.

On his arrival at Frankfort, Solomon was able somewhat to reassure Amschel, at any rate as to the momentary position in Paris. After the abdication of the king, the funds had somewhat improved during the last few days, as compared with the lowest point which they had touched, and the proclamation of the Duke of Orléans had had a very good effect.

Solomon described that event as a particularly fortunate one for the House of Rothschild. Their difficulties consisted in their large holdings of securities. They would not be able at the moment to get rid of the enormous stock of French rentes except at very heavy loss. The conversion loan with the Prussian government, arranged during a boom period, would also prove to be a ruinous business. Austrian securities were still the best, but these too had suffered somewhat. The solution was: Get out of all engagements! Have loan agreements rescinded wherever possible; and especially the new Prussian loan.

Amschel promised to put out feelers in that direction, and especially to try to secure Rother's support. After the most pressing matters had been agreed upon, Solomon immediately returned to Paris, where his presence was urgently required. The news of the July revolution had already begun to produce disturbances in all the states of Europe, and there was the danger of fresh complications in the form of military intervention by the absolutist conservative powers, whose peace was threatened.

There was still a possibility that the danger to the House of Rothschild arising out of the July revolution might be averted. But if a European war were to break out, securities would continue to fall in value and the very existence of the House would be imperiled. The brothers' slogan therefore was: Avert war at any price.

It was in their favor that the new king feared a campaign against his usurped powers, and was anxious at all costs to avoid external complications. He was at pains to show the powers that if he had not stepped into the breach, France must have fared far worse, and that possibly it would even have come to the establishment of a republic.

In order to put this view to Metternich more particularly, the king made use of James Rothschild. In the middle of August, as a member of the Société des Antiquités, James was one of a deputation to congratulate Louis Philippe on ascending the throne. As the deputation was leaving, the king signaled to James to remain behind, and made the following remarks to him:

"Having seen the happiness that I enjoyed in the bosom of my family, such as accorded with my peaceful and entirely unambitious disposition, you know me too well to be deceived for a moment as to the state of mind in which I am approaching my present task. . . . In giving up such a pleasant and carefree existence in order to mount to a throne set with dangers and difficulties, I have made an enormous sacrifice for my country. . . . France was heading straight for a republic. She would have ruined herself and perhaps the whole of Europe with her. . . . The monarchist principle has triumphed over anarchy. . . . My most ardent desires are centered upon the peace of Europe, and I hope that the states will resume their former friendly relations with France, and come to have confidence in France's new government."[88]

James saw to it that this was accurately conveyed to Metternich at Vienna, and that the call to peace was properly emphasized.

Meanwhile there were occurrences in Paris that threatened further risings in various states of Europe. Countless emigrants from the period of the Neapolitan and Spanish revolutions thought that the moment had come for resuming their revolutionary activities. The Rothschilds knew some of these people and heard of their plans, and they did everything possible to induce the new authorities in Paris to refrain from supporting their efforts. What, for instance, would be the fate of Neapolitan bonds, which had already slumped heavily, if General Pepe, who was staying in Paris, were, as Solomon put it,[89] "again to arouse the spirit of the Carbonari"?

A rising was expected hourly in Spain. The Rothschilds immediately informed the newly constituted French government of everything that they heard of these activities, and through a common friend they also put Metternich in possession of such information.

"Count de Molé,"[90] Solomon wrote to Vienna,[91] "is well aware of all these activities, and has been enlightened as to the importance of suppressing them in the general interests of peace and of the tranquillity of France. He fully shares our convictions in this matter, and is applying all the means at his disposal to frustrate these unscrupulous schemes. I hope, my dear friend, that you will observe the strictest confidence in the use you make of this communication. It was made to me under the seal of the strictest secrecy . . . it would be exceedingly unpleasant for me if there were the slightest suspicion that I had breathed a word about it. For this reason I am not signing this letter."

Owing to their excellent connections, the Rothschilds were thus receiving the most important and confidential information in spite of the complete change in affairs. The new king, Louis Philippe, and the bourgeois ministers who now received the seals of office had the greatest interest themselves in seeing that peace was maintained, that law and order was restored, and that private property was not interfered with. The aims of the Rothschilds were identical and they were to learn Louis Philippe's intentions from the best possible source, namely, the king himself.

On September 7, 1830, James was received by Louis Philippe in private audience, and discussed the general situation with him. "My brother," Solomon reported thereon to Vienna,[92] "yesterday had the opportunity of a leisured discussion with the King of France. The king said with regard to Austria, which was strengthening her forces in the Italian provinces, that she should not go too far with her military preparations, as this alone would automatically lead to war in the end. My brother represented to the king that he was not dealing firmly enough with the activities of the Spanish and Neapolitan exiles in the heart of the capital itself, and that such laxity might produce the most pernicious results. The king replied that he was using every means in his power to frustrate the agitators' schemes, but that his mandate as a constitutional monarch involved limitations which he could not legally exceed.

"The king assured me that he was opposing revolutionaries in all countries as far as his position as a constitutional monarch allowed him to do, but he stated that he was compelled to show a certain regard for liberal aspirations.

"'I should be exceedingly glad,' he said to James, 'if you could possibly be the means of communicating my views to his Highness Prince von Metternich, and request him in his wisdom to make urgent representations to the court of Naples, so that it may be moved to make a few concessions in the general interests of the country, and in accordance with the progress of contemporary ideas.' "

Solomon skilfully incorporated in this letter, which he intended Metternich to read, a few flattering remarks about the chancellor, attributed to Louis Philippe. The letter concluded with the following words: "Such, my dear friend, are the essential points mentioned in my brother's conversation with the king. With the exception of certain highly placed persons, observe the strictest secrecy in regard to it, and accept again the assurance of my most friendly sentiments."

The fears that the revolutionary movement might spread prove to be well founded. The July revolution produced repercussions throughout Europe. Apart from minor disturbances in Germany, Italy and Spain, there were serious risings leading to important results. The peoples of the kingdom of the United Netherlands, which had been welded together in 1815 without any consideration of the diverse populations of Belgium and Holland living within its boundaries, had long been restive. On August 25, 1830, revolution broke out in Brussels, as the result of which a change in the form of government, separation from the dynasty of Orange, and indeed the severance of Belgium from Holland were demanded and soon afterwards achieved. This produced a severe crisis in the commercial world, and increased the fears of a general European war, for news was received from both Vienna and St. Petersburg that the authorities were not merely determined to suppress these revolutionary uprisings individually, but also proposing to use military force against the new régime in France, as the breeding-place of all these dangerous movements.

Meanwhile Solomon had returned from Paris on a most important mission. His brothers had urged him to bring all his influence to bear upon Metternich—to restrain his warlike zeal from embarking on such an adventure, which—quite otherwise than in the case of Naples—would be fraught with the gravest consequences, such as nobody could foresee, for Europe in general and for the House of Rothschild in particular. Solomon was to do what he could in the way of direct written and verbal communications with the chancellor, and also to bring pressure to bear upon Gentz daily, while enlisting the influence of third persons whom he had placed under financial obligations. His brothers in London and Paris unceasingly urged him in their letters not to flag in his efforts.

James wrote on November 24, 1830: [93]

MY DEAR BROTHER:

An Austrian courier will be passing through Frankfort, so I am taking this opportunity of writing to you. I hope that as Uncle [Metternich] will be back in Vienna, you will know more about what is happening. You know that Count Sebastiani, minister for foreign affairs, has given me permission to call on him every morning. I am on the most friendly terms with him, a fact which is not likely to be displeasing to Uncle, as it enables me often to let you have advance news. He said to me, "My dear Rothschild, the one question is, are the foreign powers seeking an excuse to declare war on the king? It will be a murderous one if they are, and God knows when and how it will end. We will leave nothing undone to preserve peace. We will do *everything possible;* and the king sent a man to Brussels yesterday to beg that the Nassau dynasty should not be excluded, and to say that if it behaved foolishly it was at its own risk, as France would not interfere."

Talleyrand has been written to in London to try and settle the question between Holland and Luxembourg. Sebastiani told me that the king had had a very long conversation with Apponyi and *had no other wish than to preserve peace.* Therefore, my

Louis Philippe, Duke of Orléans, King of France
From a portrait by François Gérard
in the Vienna National Library

dear Solomon, do try to find out the position, for even though we are not carrying out any transaction in rentes, we have a holding of 900,000 rentes (i.e., 18 million francs nominal). If peace is preserved they will be worth 75%, while in case of war they will drop to 45. We should not be certain of dropping 25 to 30%, and I should say that we better go straight and secure ourselves.

You have no idea what the position is here with regard to actual rentes. People are selling every day in England, and today I sold 25,000 francs again in London; but I see no real sellers, and in spite of all the military preparations, the rentiers are not getting nervous, because it is not consistent with sanity that the powers should now undermine industry, trade, and public credit through a war.

Meanwhile, my dear Solomon, the whole world is arming, and this fact alarms me. They are already telling us here that they are going to station a defense force of 300,000 men on the frontiers. Now experience unfortunately teaches us that military preparations very easily lead to war, and if anybody wants war we shall have it. Believe me, I feel sure that it depends now on the prince alone, and he can use the opportunity to influence France as he wishes. If Uncle wants peace and convinces our government that he does, we shall have peace; and he will certainly have a firmer control over affairs here than he had in Polignac's time. For neither the ministry nor the chambers are, as has been supposed, ultra-liberal; indeed their views have been modified so much that they are much more inclined to royalism than in Polignac's time. You can see a proof of this in their way of dealing with the Spanish revolutionaries; there are no more clubs or popular gatherings. Each day we have new laws for maintaining peace; there are no posters or tub-thumpers; the revolutionary papers are being suppressed.

Sebastiani also said to me: "The one person for whom I have unbounded admiration in all the ministries is Prince Metternich, and he will find me a straight man to deal with. I want to maintain the existing agreements, but if he means to declare war on us we must conclude an agreement with England, but believe that I am making every effort to maintain peace. . . . As far as I can see the issue of peace or war depends entirely upon your prince."

Stuart [94] believes that peace will be maintained; that peace and war are being discussed a great deal, but that peace will prevail. I beg you, if there is any news, send somebody to Strassburg, or send a special courier here, because it makes a great difference. We have been cautious enough to consolidate our position by realizing a large holding of rentes at a loss, and I am convinced that if peace is maintained, rentes will improve in three months by at least ten percent, since there is a shortage of actual rentes on the market, and the bear speculators require millions to cover. And it would be a very good thing to recover part of their ill-gotten gains from these wretched people, and this is just the moment for doing so. You yourself will see, my dear brother, how exceedingly important it is that I should have the earliest possible news of what we are to expect. People are for war here today because of an article in the Journal des Débats. Everybody here is very pleased with Apponyi. I assure you one nearly loses one's head here, because common sense is in favor of peace, but warlike ideas are getting the upper hand. I am hoping to have full news from you at an early date, and am your very affectionate brother [no signature].

This effusion was followed three days later by a second letter:

MY DEAR BROTHERS: [95]

The news that the Belgians have dethroned the Orange dynasty has shocked everybody deeply. Rentes fell to 60.25, but closed at 61.19, and the five per cents at 91.15 while ducats were 65.40. As the Bourse was closing it was stated that Laffitte[96] would make a speech on Monday demanding 500,000 men; not that France should intervene in Belgian affairs, but only for her own security. I spent a long time with Laffitte and Sebastiani. I have *never* known them so moderate. They said to me, "We sent somebody to Brussels and they did not listen to us. Are we to set Europe ablaze in order to put Monsieur Mérode on the Belgian throne? The powers are arming and we must do the same; we have bought 100,000 muskets in Hamburg; we have also bought munitions at Frankfort, as we must take precautions, and the interests of the powers are identical with ours." They said that they definitely believed that there would be no war; but the Belgian affair complicates everything very much.

Good news is supposed to have been received from Russia. I shall probably send you a courier on Monday night or on Tuesday with the speech, if it is important and likely to be helpful. The moderates, such as Périer and all the rest are wild, and are screaming against Russia, saying that the publication of Emperor Nicholas's letter was an insult to the nation. You have no idea of the war spirit among these people; but it is clear that none of those in real authority wants war.

Do tell the prince these things, my dear Solomon. The massing of troops exasperates them, hence these great preparations. Be assured, however, that it depends entirely on the prince, whether we have peace or war. If we have war I see the whole of France putting up barricades, and I assure you I tremble for Germany. The people are like a lion; and it is not well to rouse such a strong and powerful nation.

This all amounted to the fact that Sebastiani wished to warn Austria through Rothschild not to prompt Russia to make war or to arm herself. While such developments might prove embarrassing to the new government in France, they might also produce results disastrous to all absolute governments.[97]

On receipt of these letters Solomon went to see the prince and Gentz, and gave them copies. He tried to read the mind of the chancellor, and if possible to influence him. Metternich repeated his well-worn phrases, and realizing that his reply would be conveyed to the French government through James, just as that government's views had been conveyed to him by Solomon, he uttered an emphatic warning that Louis Philippe should render no assistance to revolutionaries, in any country, if he was concerned for the continuance of his rule and the maintenance of peace.

Solomon thereupon replied to James:[98]

> MY DEAR BROTHER:
>
> I have received your valued communication of November, and conveyed its contents to the prince. One may now infer that the French government must be principally concerned to secure its own position, and will therefore have no use for mere adventurers like Molé and Broglie.[99]

On behalf of the prince, Solomon conveyed an assurance that he also desired peace, but that he would strike a blow in Italy, not against a power but against the revolution which had to be fought everywhere in the interests of peace and order. If France permitted this, it would not be troubled, and peace would be maintained; but if not, there would be war, in which case Austria would certainly not stand alone, for it would be in the interests of all governments to support the state which desired nothing but peace and order.

"I have also informed the prince of your inquiry," Solomon continued. "If General Sebastiani wishes to say anything to him as man to man it is perfectly open to him to do so, either through you or through any particular person in whom he has confidence."

Metternich thus appointed the Rothschilds over the head of his Paris ambassador as the channel of communication between him and the French cabinet. This implied extensive confidence in them, and was a priceless advantage to the Rothschilds, for it meant that during those dangerous times they would receive news of the most important decisions before anyone else. However, they continued to be in a state of great anxiety as to whether peace would be maintained. Their losses already amounted to millions; in accordance with their own estimate, perhaps deliberately somewhat exaggerated, they had irrevocably lost about 17 million gulden at one blow through the July revolution.[100] A war might cause further losses, and perhaps occasion the collapse of their House. Even the tame extracts from the Rothschild Paris letter made for Prince Metternich's benefit still sounded exceedingly menacing.

"We have received your valued letter of the tenth of this month," one of these letters ran,[101] "and regret to learn that your securities are falling as badly as ours. Yesterday things got a great deal worse. War is on everybody's lips; there are those who want war for its own sake, and those who want it to take the public's mind off the proceedings against the ministers.[102] Sebastiani remarked today that it would be better for the public to have something else to think of now than these proceedings, and that after the action things would be much better.

"Others, such as our friend Stuart, are of a different opinion, and think that after the action things will be much worse, and that we shall have nothing but war to think about then, and that the present ministers are not strong enough to adopt an unpopular line. Rentes remain at 58.50, and from today all the *gardes nationaux* must wear uniforms, so that you will see nothing but soldiers. On the Bourse were several soldiers in uniform. This does not look like peace.

"Last night Laffitte said that war was less likely now than ever, and that everything possible will be done to avoid it. He hopes that Prince Metternich will seriously think of means for settling matters before all the powers have their armies equipped, and everything is ready for war. For as soon as the young French are ready, and anything happens to set them off, the devil himself won't stop them. . . . Frankness and mutual forbearance are more than ever necessary.

"I read out to General Sebastiani what you told me about Uncle. He said that he was pleased with everything I had heard from the good gentleman; I assure you that he actually used the word 'good.' He went on to say, 'I am doing everything possible for peace . . . and I do not see what we should go to war about. I have given orders in Italy to be accommodating to Austria in all matters. If, however, which God forbid, anything should happen there, I do ask for God's sake not to let troops march into any other country, for that might produce war.'

"You see, my dear brother, that the issue of war and peace really does hang on a thread today; God grant that everything may remain peaceful in Italy, for if God does not maintain peace, He alone can say what will become of Europe."

James might have added "and of us" after "Europe." It is exceedingly probable that the original letter did contain some such phrase, for the passage quoted was only a carefully selected extract made for the benefit of the chancellor.

And indeed, when, in the last days of November, a rising broke out in Poland against Russian rule, the danger of hostilities against France, which stood before the world as the originator of all these revolutionary troubles, became particularly acute. The future destinies of the House of Rothschild largely depended upon whether the decision should be for peace or for war. They redoubled their efforts to win the statesmen and persons in power for the cause of peace. The three brothers in Paris, London, and Vienna rivaled one another in their feverish efforts to influence their countries' policies.

Amschel Meyer at Frankfort had meanwhile been allotted the task of relieving the House of Rothschild from as many of its financial agreements and obligations as he possibly could. Carl stayed with him in order to help in this labor of Sisyphus, involved in dealing with the enormous ramifications of businesses that were mostly in a bad way. The great question continued to be, war or peace?

NOTES

CHAPTER I

(1) For further details see *Geschichte von Frankfurt am Main in ausgewählten Darstellungen,* Kriegk (Frankfort-on-the-Main, 1871). (2) *"Meyer Amschel Rothschild," der Gründer des Rothschildschen Bankhauses,* Berghoeffer (Frankfort-on-the-Main, 1923) p. 5. (3) The usual story, which is given in all publications except Berghoeffer's, and according to which Rothschild was announced to the prince as he and Estorff were playing chess, is a myth. On the other hand we may take it as proved that General von Estorff effected the introduction, relying on the family connections between him and Hesse. (4) Published in full by Berghoeffer; see above, p. 7. (5) The original catalogues are in the Municipal Library at Frankfort. The reproductions here given of a title-page and a portion of the text are taken from one of these. (6) Dr. Philipp Losch, *Kurfürst Wilhelm I., Landgraf von Hessen,* (Marburg, 1923), p. 71. (7) Vehse in his *Geschichte der deutschen Höfe* (pp. 27 and 266) declares that there were seventy-four illegitimate children in existence. Others put the number even higher. For further details see appendix to Losch's book referred to above. (8) Losch, as above, p. 43. (9) The family later received the name "von Carlshausen" as also did the estate which remains in their possession. The family is still flourishing, but now only bears the name of Barons von Carlshausen, without Buderus. (10) Losch, see above, p. 158. (11) *Der Soldatenhandel deutscher Fürsten nach Amerika, 1775-1783,* Friedrich Kapp (Berlin, 1864), p. 57. (12) Berghoeffer, as above; p. 20. (13) Carlshausen archives: accounts entry dated Nov. 9, 1790. *Laubtaler* ("leaf" thaler) were silver coins, so called from the foliage which formed part of the design. They were worth one Prussian thaler, fifteen silver groats. (14) The "green" shield has given rise to a good deal of error. The name is in fact derived from the earlier house with the red shield. (15) The illustration gives an excellent idea of the Rothschild house in its original condition. The Schiffs' old-clothes shop can also be seen. The descendants of this family have also achieved great things, particularly in America where they have made a huge fortune. (16) Reichsgulden; the Convention-gulden—so called because, in accordance with a Convention, 20 gulden (in 20 florin measure) or 24 gulden (in 24 florin measure) were coined out of 1 mark (16 *loth*) of fine silver—was worth rather more. One florin Convention coin in 24 florin measure was worth about 1⅕ reichsgulden. (17) The Landgrave of Hesse-Cassel to Francis of Aus-

tria, Weissenstein, Apr. 30, 1792, State Archives, Vienna. (18) Francis of Austria to the Landgrave of Hesse-Cassel, May 10, 1792, State Archives, Vienna. (19) *Die Fugger, Rothschild, Krupp,* Richard Ehrenberg (Jena, 1925) p. 136. (20) Emperor Francis to the Landgrave of Hesse-Cassel (Baden, September 8, 1797) Draft in the State Archives, Vienna. (21) The eldest son's actual name was Amschel Meyer, but he later adopted the name of Anselm.

CHAPTER II

(1) Ehrenberg; see former ref., p. 50. (2) Berghoeffer; see former ref., page 75. (3) Lawaetz to Buderus (Altona, Feb. 2, 1805), Carlshausen Archives. (4) See Scherb, *Geschichte des Hauses Rothschild* (Berlin, 1872), p. 27. (5) Berghoeffer; see former ref., p. 35. (6) Losch; see former ref. p. 151. (7) Wilhelm Kurfürst of Hesse to His Majesty the Roman Emperor and Hereditary Emperor of Austria, Cassel, Jan. 11, 1805, State Archives, Vienna. (8) Baron von Wessenberg to Count Stadion, State Archives, Vienna. (9) Baron von Wessenberg to Count Colloredo, in September, 1805, State Archives, Vienna. (10) *Correspondance de Napoleon I* (Paris, 1863). (11) Berghoeffer, p. 37. (12) Baron von Wessenberg to Count Stadion, Cassel, Jan. 10, 1808, very secret special dossier. State Archives, Vienna. (13) Buderus to Lorentz, Hessian Chargé d'Affaires in London; from Schleswig, Nov. 17, 1806. Carlshausen Archives. (14) The passage in the memoirs of General Baron de Marbot (Paris, 1891), Vol. I, pp. 309-311, from which the possible presence of Rothschild at Cassel might be inferred, will not bear serious examination, for it was not Marshal Augereau, but Mortier, who occupied Cassel, and the domiciliary search of the Rothschild house, as well as the cross-examination of the members of the family, occurred much later, at Frankfort, and not, in 1806, at Cassel. In publishing these "Memoirs," which appeared more than eighty years later, the writer was obviously influenced by the old and widely current legend regarding the rescue of the electoral property by the Rothschild family, the modest facts regarding which Berghoeffer was the first to bring to light. (15) *Correspondance de Napoleon I,* XIII, p. 588. (16) From Buderus in Schleswig to Lorentz in London, Nov. 17, 1806. Carlshausen Archives. (17) From Meyer Amschel Rothschild to William of Hesse, Dec. 15, 1806. Berghoeffer, p. 70. (18) Buderus to the elector, Hanau, Mar. 8, 1807. Carlshausen Archives. (19) Buderus to the elector, Hanau, Mar. 10, 1807. Carlshausen Archives. (20) Berghoeffer, p. 64. (21) Elector William of Hesse to King Frederick William III of Prussia, Rendsburg, Mar. 8, 1807. Prussian Secret State Archives, Berlin. (22) Elector William of Hesse to Emperor Francis, Rendsburg, Mar. 23, 1807. State Archives, Vienna. (23) Prince Wittgenstein to Frederick William III of Prussia, Altona, Mar. 31, 1807, Prussian Secret State Archives, Berlin. (24) For further details see Berghoeffer, p. 79. (25) Berg-

hoeffer, p. 78. (26) Berghoeffer, p. 132. (27) Emperor Francis to the Elector of Hesse, Vienna, Jan. 22, 1808, State Archives, Vienna. (28) Berghoeffer, p. 109. (29) An anonymous correspondent to Emperor Francis, June, 1808, Treasury Archives, Vienna. (30) Emperor Francis to Count Zichy, Mar.-July, 1808, Treasury Archives, Vienna. (31) Secret Police Report from Prague, Sept. 9, 1808, Treasury Archives, Vienna. (32) Autograph letter from Emperor Francis to Count O'Donnell, dated Sept. 13, 1808, Treasury Archives, Vienna. (33) Most humble ministerial address from Count O'Donnell, Sept. 14, 1808, Treasury Archives, Vienna. (34) Emperor Francis to Count O'Donnell, Oct. 6, 1808, Treasury Archives, Vienna. (35) Stein to Wittgenstein, Königsberg, Aug. 15, 1808. Published in the *Monitor* of Sept. 8, 1808. (36) Memorandum from Wittgenstein to Metternich, Hamburg, Mar. 20, 1809, State Archives, Vienna. (37) Berghoeffer, p. 123. (38) Vienna Police Report, Feb. 25, 1809, Police Archives, Vienna. (39) Report of the Prague Chief of Police, Mar. 12, 1809, Police Archives, Vienna. (40) Berghoeffer, p. 112 and following pages. (41) Agreement between Buderus and Meyer Amschel Rothschild, Frankfort, Feb. 17, 1809. Copy in the Carlshausen Archives. (42) Elector William of Hesse to Emperor Francis, Prague, Mar. 6, 1809, State Archives, Vienna. (43) Berghoeffer, p. 173. (44) *Les Rothschild, une famille de financiers juifs au XIXième siècle* (Paris, 1896) and in *Les Rothschilds* by a "petit porteur de fonds russes," who has used Démachy's distorted book and his documents in a manner showing extreme malice toward the Rothschild family.—Police Report of the French Imperial Police of Jan. 17, 1812, and Dec. 23, 1813, National Archives, Paris. *Les Rothschild,* p. 139 and following pages, and p. 158 and following pages. (45) Elector William of Hesse to Count Stadion, Prague, Nov. 4, 1809, State Archives, Vienna. (46) See the Police Report from the French National Archives, published in *Les Rothschild,* as above, p. 151. (47) William of Hesse to Count Metternich, Prague, Feb. 20, 1810, State Archives, Vienna. (48) Elector William of Hesse to Barbier, Prague, Aug. 31, 1810, Treasury Archives, Vienna. (49) The Treasury to the Elector of Hesse, Sept. 25, 1810, Treasury Archives, Vienna. (50) Baron von Hügel to Count Stadion, Frankfort, Aug. 20, 1810, and Apr. 15, 1812, State Archives, Vienna. (51) The fifteen articles, from the Municipal Archives of Frankfort-on-the-Main, are published in full by Berghoeffer, p. 195 and following pages. (52) Ehrenberg: see former ref., p. 56. (53) Buderus to the elector, Nov. 12, 1810, Carlshausen Archives. (54) Buderus to the elector, Carlshausen, Nov. 2, 1810, Carlshausen Archives. (55) Baron von Hügel to Count Stadion, Frankfort, Feb. 16, 1812. There is a list attached to this report in which Meyer Amschel features under No. 41. State Archives, Vienna. (56) The elector to Buderus, Prague, Dec. 6, 1810, Carlshausen Archives. (57) *Archives Nationales,* Paris. Mainz, Mar. 3, 1812. Published in *Les Rothschild,* see former ref., p. 121. (58) Buderus to the elector, Hanau, Apr. 7, 1811, Carlshausen Archives.

(59) The elector to Buderus, Prague, May 20, 1811. (60) Buderus to the elector, undated, Carlshausen Archives. (61) The elector to Buderus, Prague, Aug. 28, 1811, Carlshausen Archives. (62) The elector to Buderus, Prague, Aug. 28, 1811, Carlshausen Archives. (63) Buderus to the elector, Carlshausen, Sept. 21, 1811, Carlshausen Archives. (64) Buderus to the elector, Carlshausen, Sept. 21, 1811. Carlshausen Archives. (65) Buderus to the elector, Carlshausen, Sept. 25, 1811, Carlshausen Archives. (66) Buderus to the elector, Hanau, Feb. 24, 1812, Carlshausen Archives. (67) The elector to Buderus, May 24, 1812. Carlshausen Archives. (68) An extract is published in translation in *Les Rothschild,* p. 132 and following pages. (69) *Les Rothschild,* p. 135. (70) Bacher to Savary, Feb. 17, 1812. *Les Rothschild,* p. 144. (71) *Les Rothschild,* p. 153. (72) Israel Jacobsohn, Privy Revenue Councilor. Most respectful plea to his Highness, the Prince President of the Confederation of the Rhine, concerning his new settlement and regulation for the protection of the Jews in Frankfort-on-the-Main. Brunswick, 1808. (73) Meyer Amschel Rothschild to a Land Registrar, Frankfort, Jan. 29, 1811. See facsimile in the Frankfort Municipal Library. (74) Dispatch from Weyland to Emperor Francis, Vienna, Oct. 27, 1814. Police Archives. (75) A copy was enclosed in Hügel's report to Metternich. Frankfort, Jan. 22, 1815. State Archives, Vienna. (76) Decree of the Grand Duke Carl Dalberg. Fulda, Oct. 17, 1812. (77) The Will, which is in the Municipal Archives of Frankfort-on-the-Main, is published in Berghoeffer, p. 201 and following pages.

CHAPTER III

(1) In 1834, on the occasion of a dinner to a friend, Nathan spoke about his career in England. This is described in the *Memoirs of Sir Thomas Fowell Buxton, Bart.,* edited by his son Charles Buxton, Esq. (London, 1848), pp. 333 and foll. It has been often quoted and reprinted, but we should bear in mind that an account given by Nathan during a good dinner should not be taken too literally, and that it also had the object of increasing the prestige of the House of Rothschild. Critically regarded, the account is worthy of consideration. (2) See Démachy and *Les Rothschild,* p. 168. (3) Mollien to Napoleon, Mar. 26, 1811. See *Histoire financière de la France depuis 1715,* Marion (Paris, 1914), IV, p. 358. (4) Marion; see above, p. 358. (5) Wellington to R. H. J. Villiers, Ciomba, May 25, 1809. *The Dispatches of Field Marshal the Duke of Wellington During His Various Campaigns, from 1799 to 1811,* IV, p. 374. (6) Wellington to Huskisson, Corticada, July 28, 1809. Wellington Dispatches, IV, p. 473. (7) Wellington to the Earl of Liverpool, from Sanct Marinca, Mar. 23, 1811. Wellington Dispatches, VII, p. 392. (8) Wellington to Earl Bathurst. Madrid, Aug. 18, 1812. Dispatches, IX, p. 368. (9) In the somewhat boastful dinner conversation in 1834 with

Sir Thomas Buxton, Nathan estimated the value of this gold at £800,000. (10) James Rothschild to Nathan Rothschild, Paris, Apr. 6, 1812, *Les Rothschild,* p. 183. (11) Report of the Chief of Police in Hamburg of Jan. 24, 1812, *Les Rothschild,* p. 106. (12) Marshal Davoust, Duke of Auerstädt, to Emperor Napoleon, Hamburg, Feb. 13, 1812, *Les Rothschild,* p. 108 and following pages. (13) From Hubert, the Commissioner of Police in Mainz, to Desmarets in Paris, Mainz, Mar. 3, 1812. *Les Rothschild,* p. 117. (14) Count von Réal, dispatch to Paris, Feb. 6, 1812, *Les Rothschild,* p. 77 and following pages. (15) James Rothschild to Nathan, Mar. 28, 1812, *Les Rothschild,* p. 181 and following pages. (16) Marion, see former ref., IV, p. 359. (17) The elector to Emperor Francis, July 14, 1813, State Archives, Vienna. (18) *Die Judenfrage auf dem Wiener Kongress,* Baron (Vienna and Berlin, 1920), p. 32. (19) Herries, Memoirs, p. 86. (20) Buxton, see former ref., p. 343. (21) *Metternich, der Staatsmann und der Mensch,* Srbik, I, p. 130. (22) As in 1808, when Metternich was ambassador in Paris, 80,000 francs, and in September, 1813, 43,000 gulden for his personal expenses. These advances were made out of state money, and the emperor's action was to be kept strictly secret. Autograph letters from Emperor Francis, Dec., 1808, and Sept., 1813. Instructions from Count Stadion, Treasury Archives, Vienna. (23) Humboldt to Goethe, Jan. 10, 1797. *Goethes Briefwechsel mit den Gebrüdern von Humboldt,* Bratranek, p. 24 and following pages. (24) Count Ugarte to Count von Metternich, Memorandum dated Sept. 15, 1813, State Archives, Vienna. (25) Baron von Wessenberg to Count von Metternich, London, Oct. 30, 1813, Court Archives, Vienna. (26) Emperor Francis to Count Ugarte, Dec. 12, 1813, Court Archives, Vienna. (27) Count Ugarte to the emperor, Dec. 24, 1813, Count Archives, Vienna. (28) Imperial Order from Freiburg, dated Jan. 11, 1814, Court Archives, Vienna. (29) The elector to Emperor Francis, Cassel, Apr. 14, 1814, State Archives, Vienna. (30) Barbier to Count Ugarte, Frankfort, July 28, 1814, Court Archives, Vienna. (31) Meyer Amschel Rothschild and Sons to Barbier, Frankfort, July 28, 1814, Court Archives, Vienna. (32) Meyer Amschel Rothschild and Sons to Barbier, Frankfort, Aug. 1, 1814, Court Archives, Vienna. (33) Barbier to Count Ugarte, July 28, 1814, Court Archives, Vienna. (34) Barbier to Count Ugarte, Frankfort, Aug. 6, 1814, Court Archives, Vienna. (35) Meyer Amschel Rothschild and Sons to Barbier, Frankfort, Aug. 8, 1814, Court Archives, Vienna. (36) Barbier to Ugarte, Frankfort, Aug. 18, 1814, Court Archives, Vienna. (37) Count Ugarte to Barbier, Vienna, Aug. 11, 1814, Court Archives, Vienna. (38) Meyer Amschel Rothschild and Sons to Barbier (written by Amschel), Aug. 22, 1814, Court Archives, Vienna. (39) Barbier to Count Ugarte, Aug. 29, 1814, Court Archives, Vienna. (40) Meyer Amschel Rothschild and Sons to Barbier, Frankfort, Aug. 8, 1814, Court Archives, Vienna. (41) Barbier to Ugarte, Aug. 9, 1814, Court Archives, Vienna. (42) Barbier to Ugarte, July 13, 1814, Court Archives, Vienna. (43) Meyer

Amschel Rothschild and Sons to Barbier, July 29, 1814, from Frankfort, Court Archives, Vienna. (44) Count Ugarte to Barbier, Aug. 17, 1814, Treasury Archives, Vienna. (45) Baron von Hügel in Frankfort to Metternich, Jan. 11, 1815, State Archives, Vienna. (46) Ehrenberg; see former ref., p. 65. (47) *Histoire des grandes opérations financières,* M. Capefigue (Paris, 1858), III, pp. 5 and 49. (48) Herries; see former ref., p. 92 and following pp. (49) Buderus to Lorentz, Cassel, May 13, 1814, Carlshausen Archives. (50) Baron von Hügel to Baron von Stein, Frankfort, Aug. 31, 1814, State Archives, Vienna. (51) Metternich to the attorney, Dr. Buchholz, Vienna, June 9, 1815, State Archives, Vienna. (52) For particulars see Ehrenberg, pp. 68-69. (53) *Selbstbiographie und Bildnisse,* Grillparzer (Vienna, 1923), p. 143. (54) *Ibid.,* p. 118. (55) *Ibid.,* p. 132. (56) Stadion to Prince Metternich, Vienna, Apr. 22, 1815, State Archives, Vienna. (57) Privy Council office to Count Stadion, May 4, 1815, State Archives, Vienna. (58) See Chapter II. (59) From Neumann, Counselor of Legation in London, to Baron von Hügel at Frankfort, London, May 22, 1815. State Archives, Vienna. (60) See *National Biography,* Vol. XLIX, p. 307. (61) Neumann to Schwinner, London, May 5, 1815, State Archives, Vienna. (62) Schwinner to Neumann, Frankfort, Nov. 13, 1815, State Archives, Vienna. (63) Limburger to Schwinner, Frankfort, Sept. 2, 1815, State Archives, Vienna. (64) Solomon and Carl Rothschild to Hardenberg, from Paris (undated; from its position in the files, was probably written in the summer of 1815), Prussian Secret State Archives, Berlin. (65) Meyer Amschel Rothschild and Sons to Hardenberg and Metternich, Paris, Aug. 29, 1815, Prussian Secret State Archives, Berlin. (66) Hardenberg to Metternich, Paris, Oct. 12, 1815. Above source. (67) Buol to Metternich, Frankfort, Dec. 5, 1815, State Archives, Vienna. (68) Barbier to Count Stadion, Paris, Nov. 10, 1815, Treasury Archives, Vienna. (69) Barbier to Count Stadion, Paris, Jan. 10, 1816, Treasury Archives, Vienna. (70) Meyer Amschel Rothschild and Gontard to Barbier, Paris, Jan. 6, 1816, Treasury Archives, Vienna. (71) Baron Frimont to the vice-president of the treasury Count von Herberstein, Colmar, Apr. 29, 1816, State Archives, Vienna. (72) Thus three million francs on Jan. 31, 1816. Barbier to Stadion, Jan. 1, 1816, Treasury Archives, Vienna. (73) Herries, see former ref., p. 108. (74) Mr. Herries's memorandum to Lord Liverpool and Vansittart, July 12, 1816. Herries, former ref., p. 247. (75) Mr. Herries's memorandum to Lord Liverpool and Vansittart, July 12, 1816. Herries, former ref., pp. 86-87. (76) Count Stadion to Barbier, Mar. 2, 1816, Treasury Archives, Vienna. (77) Report of the finance minister Count Stadion of July 18, 1816, State Archives, Vienna. (78) Report of the finance minister, Count Stadion of July 30, 1816, State Archives, Vienna. (79) Advice of Baron von Lederer, Aug. 6, 1816, State Archives, Vienna. (80) Note by Count Zichy (known as "Zuputz" among his colleagues) on Baron von Lederer's advice, State Archives, Vienna. (81) Emperor Francis to Metternich, undated, State Archives,

Vienna. (82) Emperor Francis to Ugarte, Vienna, Sept. 25, 1816, Old Gratz Registry, Vienna. (83) Emperor Francis to Ugarte, Vienna, Oct. 21, 1816, Old Gratz Registry, Vienna. (84) Count Stadion to Count Ugarte, Vienna, Sept. 30, 1816, Old Gratz Registry, Vienna. (85) Design for the Rothschild coat-of-arms, Old Gratz Registry, Vienna. (86) Escutcheon Inspector von Holza. Most Obedient Report, Vienna, Jan. 28, 1817, Old Gratz Registry, Vienna. (87) James Rothschild to Barbier, July 2, 1817, from Paris, Treasury Archives, Vienna. (88) Meyer Amschel Rothschild and Sons and J. Friedrich Gontard and Sons to Barbier, from Paris, July 8, 1817, Treasury Archives, Vienna. It is not my intention, and it is in any case impossible to give a full account of the money transactions of the House of Rothschild; I have given as examples those which helped it to attain its unique position. (89) Barbier to Stadion, July 9, 1817, Treasury Archives, Vienna. (90) Stadion to Barbier, Vienna, Aug. 3, 1817, Treasury Archives, Vienna. (91) Meyer Amschel Rothschild and Sons and J. F. Gontard and Sons to Barbier, Paris, July 8, 1817, Treasury Archives, Vienna. (92) Ehrenberg, see former ref., p. 81. (93) Jordan to Buol, Berlin, Nov. 8, 1816, Prussian Secret State Archives. (94) Amschel Rothschild to Metternich, Frankfort, November, 1817, State Archives, Vienna. (95) Amschel Rothschild to Stadion, Frankfort, November, 1817, State Archives, Vienna. (96) Carl Rothschild to Count Zichy, Berlin, Nov. 5, 1817, State Archives, Vienna. (97) Count Zichy to Metternich, Berlin, Nov. 23, 1817, State Archives, Vienna.

CHAPTER IV

(1) *Les hommes de mon temps,* Ignotus (Paris, 1889), p. 289. (2) Amschel Meyer to Hardenberg, Frankfort, Jan. 16, 1818, Prussian Secret State Archives, Berlin. (3) King Frederick William III of Prussia to Prince Hardenberg, Berlin, Nov. 25, 1817, Prussian Secret State Archives, Berlin. (4) Hardenberg's notes on the above. (5) *Simon Moritz von Bethmann und seine Vorfahren* (Frankfort-on-the-Main, 1898), p. 227. (6) Rother to King Frederick William III, Berlin, Mar. 9, 1830, Prussian Secret State Archives, Berlin. (7) Prince Hardenberg to Rother, Feb. 10, 1818, Prussian Secret State Archives, Berlin. (8) This report of Humboldt has often been printed, as in Ehrenberg, p. 86, and Balla, *Die Rothschilds,* p. 96. The Prussian loan of 1818 in England is dealt with only shortly here, as Ehrenberg's work, referred to above, deals with the matter exhaustively and admirably. (9) Rother to King Frederick William III, Berlin, Mar. 9, 1830, Prussian Secret State Archives, Berlin. (10) Ehrenberg, see former ref., p. 9. (11) *Wilhelm und Caroline von Humboldt in ihren Briefen, 1815-1817,* Vol. VI, p. 320. (12) Meyer Amschel Rothschild and Sons to the Elector of Hesse, Frankfort, July 10, 1818, Carlshausen Archives. (13) The Elector of Hesse to Buderus, Cassel, July 26, 1808, Carlshausen Archives. (14) Buderus

to the elector, Hanau, Aug. 4, 1818, Carlshausen Archives. (15) The elector to Buderus, Cassel, Aug. 12, 1818, Carlshausen Archives. (16) Buderus to the elector, Hanau, Aug. 15, 1818. Carlshausen Archives. (17) Concluding letter, dated Oct. 15, 1818, Carlshausen Archives. (18) The Elector of Hesse to Buderus, Feb. 6, 1819. Carlshausen Archives. (19) The Elector of Hesse to Carlshausen, Feb. 9, 1819, same source. (20) Meyer Amschel von Rothschild and Sons to Carlshausen, Frankfort, Mar. 10, 1819, Carlshausen Archives. (21) *Tagebücher von Friedrich Gentz* (Leipzig, 1874), Vol. I, pp. 365 and 430; Vol. II, pp. 27, 37, 39 and following. (22) Gentz, see above, Vol. II, p. 280. (23) *Die Judenfrage auf dem Wiener Kongress,* Baron (Vienna, 1920), pp. 191 and 192. (24) Meyer Amschel von Rothschild and Sons to Hardenberg, Frankfort, Sept. 11, 1818, Prussian Secret State Archives, Berlin. (25) *Geschichte der Freien Stadt Frankfurt a. M.,* Schwemer (Frankfort, 1910), Vol. II, p. 138. (26) Gentz, see former ref., Vol. II, p. 277. (27) Gentz, Vol. II, p. 280. (28) *Briefwechsel zwischen Friedrich Gentz und Adam Heinrich Müller, 1800-1829,* Gentz (Stuttgart, 1857), p. 267. (29) *Briefwechsel Gentz an Müller,* as above, p. 267, Munich, Dec. 12, 1818. (30) Baron von Handel to Prince Metternich, Darmstadt, Dec. 12, 1818, State Archives, Vienna. (31) Will of Carl Frederick Buderus von Carlshausen, Hanau, Aug. 2, 1818, Carlshausen Archives. (32) Police report from Frankfort, dated June 19, 1819, Police Archives, Vienna. (33) A reference to the raising of the family to the nobility. (34) *Deutsche Geschichte im 19. Jahrhundert,* Heinrich von Treitschke (Leigzig, 1897), Vol. III, p. 756. (35) A derisive cry dating from the medieval hatred of the Jews. The term appears to have been derived from the sound which a goat makes, having reference to the traditional appearance of the Jews, with their goatee beards. (36) Le Monnier, secretary of the legation, to the president of the police Count Sedlnitzky, Frankfort, Aug. 6, 1819, Police Archives, Vienna. (37) Himly to the Frankfort Senate, Aug. 11, 1819, Prussian Secret State Archives, Berlin. (38) Burgomasters Metzler and Usemer to Himly, Aug. 11, 1819, Prussian Secret State Archives, Berlin. (39) Extract from a letter from James Meyer von Rothschild to David Parish, in Carlsbad, Paris, Aug. 18, 1819, State Archives, Vienna. (40) Baron von Handel to Metternich, Frankfort, Sept. 3, 1819, State Archives, Vienna. (41) The Treasury to the Commercial Department, Sept. 16, 1819, State Archives, Vienna. (42) Ritter von Stahl to Count Stadion, Vienna, Sept. 27, 1819, State Archives, Vienna. (43) Count Stadion to Count Saurau, Vienna, Sept. 26, 1819, State Archives, Vienna. (44) Count Saurau to Ritter von Stahl, Vienna, Sept. 29, 1819, State Archives, Vienna. (45) Police Report of Le Monnier, from Frankfort, Oct. 8, 1819, Police Archives, Vienna. (46) Barbier to Count Saurau, Paris, Oct. 8, 1819, Treasury Archives, Vienna. (47) Barbier to Stadion, Paris, Sept. 23, 1819, Treasury Archives, Vienna. (48) Meyer Amschel Rothschild and Sons to Count Stadion, Dec. 20, 1819, Treasury Archives, Vienna. (49) See "*Kaiser Franz und Metternich;" ein nachgelassenes Fragment,* Hormayr (Leipzig, 1848). (50) *Tagebücher des Karl Friedrich Freiherrn Kübeck von Kübau* (Vienna, 1909), Vol. I, Part 2, p. 319. (51) Simon Moritz von Bethmann, see former ref. (52) Handel to Metternich, Feb. 19, 1820, State Archives, Vienna. (53) Handel to Metternich, Frankfort, Nov. 28, 1819, State Archives, Vienna. (54) Le Monnier to the director of the Secret Service Dept., Vienna, Frankfort, Feb. 22, 1821, State Archives, Vienna. (55) Schwemer, see former ref., II, p. 33. (56) Stahl to Metternich, Vienna, Apr. 4, 1820, Archives of the Ministry of the Interior. (57) Metternich to Esterházy, May 31, 1820, State Archives, Vienna. (58) The chancellor to Stahl, Vienna, May 27, 1820, State Archives, Vienna. (59) See Handel to Metternich, in the files of the period between the 6th and the 11th Nov., 1819, State Archives, Vienna. (60) Police Report dated May 1, 1820. Police Archives, Vienna. (61) See story by Siegfried Loewy, "Hotel Rothschild," in the *Neues Wiener Journal* of Apr. 29, 1927. (62) Metternich to Barbier, Vienna, Oct. 6, 1820, Treasury Archives, Vienna. (63) Private letter from Barbier to Buol, Paris, July 11, 1820, Treasury Archives, Vienna. (64) Memorandum on the discussion between Tsar Alexander and Metternich of Jan. 13, 1821, State Archives, Vienna. (65) Private letter from Count Stadion to Metternich, Jan. 29, 1821, State Archives, Vienna. (66) Solomon Rothschild to Count Nesselrode, Vienna, Jan. 29, 1821, State Archives, Vienna. (67) Stadion to Metternich, Feb. 18, 1821, State Archives, Vienna. (68) Solomon Rothschild to Metternich, Vienna, Feb. 3, 1821, State Archives, Vienna. (69) Stadion to Metternich, Feb. 18, 1821, State Archives, Vienna. (70) Stadion to Metternich, Vienna, Feb. 15, 1821, State Archives, Vienna. (71) Stadion to Metternich, Feb. 20, 1821, State Archives, Vienna. (72) Stadion to Metternich, Vienna, Mar. 2, 1821, State Archives, Vienna. (73) Stadion to Metternich, Vienna, Mar. 6, 1821, State Archives, Vienna. (74) Count Sedlnitzky to Metternich, Vienna, Mar. 3, 1821, State Archives, Vienna. (75) Count Stadion to Metternich, Vienna, Mar. 8, 1821, State Archives, Vienna. (76) Stadion to Metternich, a few days after Mar. 8, 1821, no nearer date being given, State Archives, Vienna. (77) Metternich to Field Marshal Count Bubna, Laibach, Mar. 10, 1821, State Archives, Vienna. (78) Carl Rothschild to Metternich, Laibach, Mar. 13, 1821, State Archives, Vienna. (79) Count Ficquelmont to Metternich, Rome, Mar. 13, 1821, State Archives, Vienna. (80) *Tagebücher von Friedrich von Gentz,* see former ref., Vol. II, p. 297. (81) Stadion to Metternich, Vienna, Mar. 22, 1821, State Archives, Vienna. (82) Stadion to Metternich, second letter of Mar. 22, 1821, State Archives, Vienna. (83) Metternich to Baron Vincent, Austrian Ambassador in Florence, Mar. 19, 1821, State Archives, Vienna. (84) Metternich to Baron Vincent, Laibach, Jan. 1, 1821, State Archives, Vienna. (85) Metternich to Baron Vincent, Laibach, Mar. 22, 1821, State Archives, Vienna. (86) Vincent to Metternich, Florence, Apr. 2, 1821, State Archives, Vienna. (87) Vincent to

Metternich, Florence, Apr. 5, 1821, State Archives, Vienna. (88) Vincent to Metternich, Florence, Apr. 5 and 8, 1821, State Archives, Vienna. (89) Vincent to Metternich, Florence, Apr. 8, 1821, State Archives, Vienna. (90) Carl Rothschild's offer of a loan to the Neapolitan Government, Apr. 19, 1821, State Archives, Vienna. (91) Count Ficquelmont to Metternich, Naples, Apr. 19, 1821, State Archives, Vienna. (92) Count Ficquelmont to Metternich, Naples, Apr. 19, 1821, State Archives, Vienna. (93) Carl Rothschild to Metternich, Naples, Apr. 28, 1821, State Archives, Vienna. (94) Losch, see former ref., p. 368. (95) President of the Commercial Department Ritter von Stahl to Emperor Francis, Vienna, Mar. 4, 1821, State Archives, Vienna. (96) Count Stadion to Emperor Francis, Mar. 6, 1821, State Archives, Vienna. (97) Baron von Lederer's note on Stadion's report, Apr. 14, 1821, State Archives, Vienna. (98) Count Stadion to Emperor Francis, Vienna, Apr. 11, 1821, State Archives, Vienna. (99) *Histoire des grandes opérations financières*, M. Capefigue (Paris, 1858), Vol. III, p. 103. (100) Ritter von Stahl to Count Stadion, Vienna, Apr. 23, 1821, State Archives, Vienna. (101) Metternich to Ritter von Stahl, Vienna, July 10, 1821. (102) Metternich to Ficquelmont, July 4, 1821, State Archives, Vienna. (103) Project for Naples Convention, Aug. 4, 1821, State Archives, Vienna. (104) Metternich to Count Ficquelmont, Vienna, July 21, 1821, State Archives, Vienna. (105) Carl Meyer Rothschild to Ficquelmont, Naples, Sept. 10, 1821, State Archives, Vienna. (106) Marquis d'Andrea, Finance Minister, to Ficquelmont, Naples, Sept. 5, 1821. (107) Marquis d'Andrea to Carl Rothschild, Naples, Oct. 27, 1821, copy in the State Archives, Vienna. (108) Carl Rothschild to Ficquelmont, Naples, Nov. 17, 1821, State Archives, Vienna. (109) Marquis d'Andrea to Carl Rothschild, Naples, Jan. 31, 1822, State Archives, Vienna. (110) Schwemer, see former ref., Vol. II, p. 138 and following pp. (111) Schwemer, Aug. 30, 1820, see former ref., II, p. 149. (112) Deed of Surety with respect to Barbaia's obligations, Archives of the Ministry of the Interior, Vienna. (113) Amschel Meyer Rothschild to Metternich, Frankfort, Nov. 3, 1821, State Archives, Vienna. (114) From the publishing firm of J. G. Cotta, of Stuttgart, which kindly put its archives at the author's disposal. (115) *Die Allgemeine Zeitung, 1798-1898,* Heyck (Munich, 1898), p. 252 and following pp. (116) See Gentz's Diary for June 7, 1821. Gentz, former ref., Vol. II, p. 431. (117) The same, Vol. II, p. 432. (118) The same, Vol. II, p. 438. (119) The same, Vol. II, p. 439. (120) For several years Gentz had written political letters to the Princes of Moldavia and Wallachia, for pay. (121) Gentz's Diary for Dec. 22, 1821. See former ref., Vol. II, p. 484. (122) Abstract of the Cash Payments of the Neapolitan State Treasury for the Royal Imperial Treasury, Appendix to Report of Ficquelmont to Metternich, Naples, Dec. 5, 1824, Vienna, State Archives. (123) Count Mentz to Metternich, Naples, Feb. 16, 1824, State Archives, Vienna. (124) Count Ficquelmont to Metternich, Naples, Dec. 5, 1824, State Archives,

Vienna. (125) Stadion's memorandum to the emperor and Metternich, January, 1822, State Archives, Vienna. (126) Bethmann, see former ref., p. 228. (127) Memorandum by Pillersdorff, Vienna, Apr. 12, 1822, Treasury Archives, Vienna. (128) Meyer Amschel Rothschild and Sons to Pillersdorff, Vienna, Apr. 12, 1822, Treasury Archives, Vienna. (129) Meyer Amschel Rothschild and Sons and Parish to Pillersdorff, Vienna, Apr. 12, 1822, Treasury Archives, Vienna. (130) Gentz's Diaries, see former ref., Vol. III, p. 34.

CHAPTER V

(1) Solomon Rothschild to Metternich, Verona, Oct. 22, 1822, State Archives, Vienna. (2) Gentz's Diaries, see former ref., Vol. III, p. 97. (3) *Briefe von Friedrich von Gentz an Pilat* (Leipzig, 1868), Vol. II, p. 105. (4) An anonymous correspondent to Montmorency, Paris, Nov. 12, 1822, State Archives, Vienna. (5) *Mémoires et Correspondances du Comte de Villèle* (Paris, 1888), Villèle to Montmorency, Feb. 18, 1822, Vol. III, p. 219. (6) Meyer Amschel Rothschild and Sons to the Chancellor's Office at Vienna, Vienna, Jan. 22, 1823, State Archives, Vienna. (7) Nathan Rothschild to the Commercial Commission, London, Sept. 3, 1822, State Archives, Vienna. (8) Bertran de Lis to the brothers Rothschild in Paris, Madrid, Feb. 20, 1823, copy in the State Archives, Vienna. Underneath is written in a different handwriting the words: "We beg that these lines may be kept secret, as we should not like them to be seen in the papers." (9) Bertran de Lis to the brothers Rothschild, via H. Belin in Bayonne, copy from the State Archives, Vienna. (10) Gentz's Diaries, see former ref., Vol. III, p. 155. (11) Villèle to the Duke of Angoulême, Paris, May 11, 1823. See *Mémoires et correspondances,* Villèle, Vol. III, p. 366 and following pp. (12) Villèle, see above, Vol. IV, p. 90. (13) Villèle, see above, Vol. IV, p. 51. Letter dated June 26, 1823. (14) Villèle, see former ref., Vol. III, p. 335. Letter dated May 30, 1823. (15) Villèle, see former ref., Vol. IV, p. 212. Letter from Villèle to Angoulême, July 10, 1823. (16) Villèle, see former ref., Vol. IV, p. 228. Letter from Villèle to Angoulême, July 11, 1823. (17) Villèle; see former ref., Vol. IV, p. 244, Villèle to Angoulême, July 19, 1823. (18) Villèle, see former ref., Vol. IV, p. 276, Villèle to Angoulême, July 31, 1823. (19) Francis Baring, John Irving, and James Rothschild to Villèle, one letter undated, and another dated Dec. 28, 1823. (20) Villèle to Baring, Irving, and Rothschild, Paris, Dec. 25, 1823, copy in the State Archives, Vienna. (21) Gentz's Diaries, see former ref., Vol. III, p. 39. (22) Münch-Bellinghausen to Metternich, Frankfort, Mar. 15, 1823, State Archives, Vienna. (23) Schwemer, see former ref., Vol. II, p. 157. (24) Schwemer, see former ref., Vol. II, p. 161. (25) Protocol dated Apr. 13, 1822, State Archives, Vienna. (26) Rescript of Emperor Francis, dated May 22, 1822, State Archives, Vienna. (27) Report from Stadion, dated Apr.

29, 1823, State Archives, Vienna. (28) *Österreichische Staatsverträge,* Alfred Francis Pribram (Vienna, 1913), p. 454 and following pp. (29) The same, p. 558. (30) Solomon to Nathan, undated, 1823, State Archives, Vienna. (31) Baring, Rothschild and Irving to Stadion, Oct. 15, 1823, State Archives, Vienna. (32) Solomon Rothschild to Metternich, Vienna, Oct. 31, 1823, State Archives, Vienna. (33) Count Zichy's Memorandum, Jan. 28, 1824, State Archives, Vienna. (34) Written in the Emperor Francis's hand, dated Feb. 18, 1824, State Archives, Vienna. (35) Pribram, see former ref., p. 573. From Neumann's report from London, dated Apr. 9, 1824. (36) Anton Schnapper to Emperor Francis, July 7, 1823, State Archives, Vienna. (37) Anton Schnapper to Solomon Rothschild, Vienna, Nov. 9, 1823, State Archives, Vienna. (38) Solomon Rothschild to Metternich, Vienna, Nov. 11, 1823, State Archives, Vienna. (39) Report of the finance minister, Count Stadion, dated Feb. 20, 1824, State Archives, Vienna. (40) Villèle to James Rothschild in Paris, undated copy in the Vienna State Archives for 1824. (41) Nathan to James, London, Mar. 6, 1824, copy in State Archives, Vienna. (42) Vincent to Metternich, Paris, Mar. 25, 1824. Information supplied by Count Senft. State Archives, Vienna. (43) *Ouvrard, Mémoires de, sur sa vie et ses diverses opérations financières* (Paris, 1826), Vol. III, p. 289. See Ehrenberg, former ref., pp. 110 and 111. (44) *Briefe von und an Friedrich von Gentz* (Berlin, 1909), Vol. II, Part II, p. 206. (45) Ficquelmont to Prince Metternich, Naples, Apr. 21, 1824, State Archives, Vienna. (46) Ficquelmont to Metternich, Naples, Aug. 17, 1824, State Archives, Vienna. (47) Ficquelmont to Metternich, Naples, July 19, 1824, State Archives, Vienna. (48) Postmaster Berger, from Milan, Mar. 24, 1825, Police Archives, Vienna. (49) Instructions to the Chief of Police in Milan, dated July 13, 1825, Police Archives, Vienna. (50) *Kaiser Franz und Metternich,* Hormayr (Leipzig, 1848), p. 80. (50a) A reference to the money for building fortresses which had been entrusted to Rothschild. See Chapter IV. (51) *The Migration of British Capital to 1875,* Leland Hamilton Jenks (New York-London, 1927). (52) Nathan Rothschild to Prince Metternich, London, Apr. 16, 1825, State Archives, Vienna. (53) *Aus Metternichs nachgelassenen Papieren,* Richard, Prince Metternich (Vienna, 1880), Vol. IV, p. 174. Private letter from Metternich to Gentz, dated June 30, 1825. (54) Vincent to Metternich, Paris, May 5, 1825, State Archives, Vienna. (55) Vincent to Metternich, Paris, June 8, 1825, State Archives, Vienna. (56) Vincent to Metternich, Paris, June 9, 1825. *Lettre particulière.* State Archives, Vienna. (57) Metternich, see former ref., Vol. IV, p. 174. Private letter from Metternich to Gentz, June 30, 1825. (58) Solomon Rothschild to Metternich, Paris, June 18, 1825, State Archives, Vienna. (59) Metternich, see former ref., p. 474. (60) Vincent to Metternich, Paris, Aug. 14, 1825, State Archives, Vienna. (61) Communication from Schärding, Commissioner of Frontier Police, Linz, July 5, 1825, Police Archives, Vienna.

(62) Solomon Rothschild to Metternich, Paris, June 18, 1825, State Archives, Vienna. (63) Marmont to Metternich, May 20, 1825. Same source. (64) Metternich to Rothschild, Milan, June 28, 1825. (65) Marmont to Metternich, Paris, Nov. 6, 1825, State Archives, Vienna. (66) Solomon Rothschild to Metternich, Vienna, Apr. 30, 1827, State Archives, Vienna. (67) Vincent to Metternich, Paris, Aug. 26, 1825, State Archives, Vienna. (68) Vincent to Metternich, Paris, Sept. 14, 1825, State Archives, Vienna. (69) Carl Rothschild to Louis Philippe of Bombelles, Paris, Sept. 12, 1825, State Archives, Vienna. (70) Count Villeneuve to Metternich, through the medium of James Rothschild, Paris, Oct. 20, 1825, State Archives, Vienna. (71) Jablonovski's Statement, Mar., 1827, Treasury Archives, Vienna. (72) Barbier to Stadion, Paris, June 16, 1819, Treasury Archives, Vienna. (73) Meyer Amschel Rothschild and Sons and J. F. Gontard and Sons to Baron Barbier, Paris, June 16, 1819, Treasury Archives, Vienna. (74) Jablonovski's report of June 20, 1819, Treasury Archives, Vienna. (75) Vienna, Sept. 30, 1827, Treasury Archives, Vienna. (76) A total of 300,485 florins. (77) Amschel (Anselm) Meyer von Rothschild to Metternich, Frankfort, Mar. 20, 1826, State Archives, Vienna. (78) Ehrenberg, see former ref., p. 117. (79) Gentz's Diaries, see former ref., Vol. III, pp. 231 and 247. (80) *Allgemeine deutsche Realenzyklopädie für die gebildeten Stände,* F. A. Brockhaus (Leipzig, 1826), Vol. IX, article on Rothschild. (81) Letters between Gentz and Müller, see former ref., p. 406. (82) Gentz's Diaries, see former ref., Vol. IV, p. 61. (83) Gentz's Diaries, see former ref., Vol. IV, p. 164. (84) "Biographische Nachrichten über das Haus Rothschild," printed in Schlesier's *Ungedruckte Denkschriften, Tagebücher und Briefe von Gentz* (Mannheim, 1840).

CHAPTER VI

(1) Ficquelmont to Metternich, Nov. 21, 1822, State Archives, Vienna. (2) Ficquelmont to Metternich, Aug. 17, 1824, State Archives, Vienna. (3) Ficquelmont to the general-commander Count Frimont, Naples, Sept. 27, 1824, State Archives, Vienna. (4) Count Apponyi to Metternich, Naples, Feb. 22, 1825, State Archives, Vienna. (5) Baron von Koller to Nádasdy, Naples, Sept. 20, 1825, State Archives, Vienna. (6) Koller to Nádasdy, Naples, Dec. 10, 1825, State Archives, Vienna. (7) De' Medici to Carl Rothschild, Naples, May 30, 1826, State Archives, Vienna. (8) See the author's biography of Leopold I of Belgium (Vienna, London, and Brussels). (9) Carl Rothschild to Count Louis Philippe of Bombelles, Naples, Jan. 20, 1827, State Archives, Vienna. (10) Solomon Rothschild to Metternich, Vienna, Jan. 21, 1827, State Archives, Vienna. (11) Metternich's note on a report of Ficquelmont's dated Feb. 20, 1827, State Archives, Vienna. (12) Memorandum by the Neapolitan Embassy in Vienna, Aug. 11, 1827, State Archives, Vienna. (13) The dates of the births

of the Montenuovo children have been obtained from a letter of Empress Marie Louise to Metternich, dated Mar. 17, 1829 (State Archives, Vienna) in which, to use her own expression, she "confesses" these dates to the prince. Hitherto she had pretended, even to her own father, Emperor Francis, that the Montenuovo children had not been born until after Napoleon's death, and after her marriage with Neipperg. In Gotha (1914), however, William Montenuovo's birthday is wrongly given as August 9, 1821. (14) Neipperg to Metternich, Parma, Dec. 16, 1825, State Archives, Vienna. (15) See statement in the imperial family papers, State Archives, Vienna. (16) Count Neipperg to Metternich, Parma, Dec. 16, 1825. (17) Memorandum from Neipperg dated Dec. 16, 1825, State Archives, Vienna. (18) Metternich to Neipperg, Jan. 14, 1826, State Archives, Vienna. (19) Memorandum from Neipperg, dated June 26, 1826, State Archives, Vienna. (20) Metternich to Solomon Rothschild, Johannisberg, Aug. 28, 1826, State Archives, Vienna. (21) Solomon Rothschild to Metternich, Paris, Nov. 1, 1826, State Archives, Vienna. (22) Enclosure in letter from Solomon to Metternich, dated Sept. 1, 1826, State Archives, Vienna. (23) Solomon Rothschild to Metternich, Vienna, Nov. 27, 1826, State Archives, Vienna. (24) Marie Louise to Emperor Francis, Parma, Jan. 13, 1827, State Archives, Vienna. (25) Remarks on the projected loan to her Highness the Duchess of Parma, signed by Solomon Rothschild, Vienna, Jan. 31, 1827, State Archives, Vienna. (26) Agreement dated Feb. 4, 1827, signed by Metternich, Werklein, Solomon Rothschild, and Mirabaud and Co. (27) Metternich to Neipperg, Vienna, Feb. 4, 1827, State Archives, Vienna. (28) Metternich to Marie Louise, Feb. 4, 1827, State Archives, Vienna. (29) A capital sum, therefore, of six million francs. (30) Marie Louise to Emperor Francis, June 7, 1827, State Archives, Vienna. (31) Solomon Rothschild to Metternich, Vienna, Mar. 2, 1827, State Archives, Vienna. (32) Metternich to Count Neipperg, Vienna, Mar. 6, 1827, State Archives, Vienna. (33) Werklein in Lucca, to Count Neipperg, May 13, 1827, State Archives, Vienna. (34) Metternich to Marie Louise, Vienna, June 3, 1827, State Archives, Vienna. (35) Metternich to Neipperg, Vienna, Apr. 18, 1827, State Archives, Vienna. (36) Wertheimstein. (37) This word is difficult to decipher in the original. Author's note. (38) Metternich subsequently denied the permanent validity of his decision. (39) Solomon Rothschild to Werklein, undated, State Archives, Vienna. (40) Metternich to Neipperg, Vienna, June 3, 1827, State Archives, Vienna. (41) Decree, beginning *"Noi Maria Luigia,"* etc., Parma, June 18, 1826, original in the State Archives, Vienna. (42) Marie Louise to Emperor Francis, June 17, 1827, State Archives, Vienna. (43) Metternich to Marie Louise, Vienna, May 3, 1827, State Archives, Vienna. (44) Marie Louise to Metternich, June 17, 1827, State Archives, Vienna. (45) Neipperg to Metternich, Parma, June 17, 1827, State Archives, Vienna. (46) Memorandum by Solomon Rothschild, Vienna, June 30, 1827, State Archives, Vienna. (47) Marie Louise's dowry dispositions,

Casino dei Boschi, July 9, 1827. (48) Solomon Rothschild to Werklein, Vienna, Feb. 2, 1828, State Archives, Vienna. (49) Deed of gift, dated Jan. 1, 1829, State Archives, Vienna. (50) Goethe to Chancellor von Müller, Sept. 23, 1823. (51) Goethe to Eckermann, Oct. 20, 1828. (52) Eckermann, Apr. 11, 1829. (53) Eckermann, Mar. 14, 1832. (54) My efforts to discover dates of possible relations between Goethe and the Rothschilds yielded poor results. The keeper of the Goethe and Schiller archives at Weimar informed me that there were no letters or other documents that mentioned any connections between Goethe and the House of Rothschild. Tewele's *Goethe und die Juden,* as well as Bab's essay under the same title, mention only the passages which I have quoted. Dr. Max Maurenbrecher's *Goethe und die Juden* (Munich, 1921) introduces further material bearing on the poet's general attitude toward the Jews, but fails to furnish any other dates relative to the problem of Goethe and the Rothschild family. (55) By the marriage between Metternich and Eleonore Kaunitz; like his brothers and sister he died prematurely at Naples in 1829. (56) Prince Esterházy to Metternich, London, Apr. 24, 1829, State Archives, Vienna. (57) See for instance the *Morning Chronicle* of Aug. 28, 1827. (58) Extract from a German-Hebraic communication from Nathan Rothschild to Carl, London, Jan. 19, 1828, Police Archives, Vienna. (59) Srbik's *Metternich,* see former ref., Vol. I, p. 628. (60) *Aus dem Nachlasse Friedrichs von Gentz* (Vienna, 1867), Vol. I, p. 9. The letters cover the period from October, 1828, to December, 1831. (61) Wertheimstein to Rothschild in Paris, from the Hebrew, Vienna, Aug. 13, 1829, Police Archives, Vienna. (62) Extract from a letter from Nathan to Solomon, Oct. 12, 1829, State Archives, Vienna. (63) Russian Ambassador in London. (64) Rother to von Motz, Apr. 14, 1829, Prussian Secret State Archives. (65) Rother to Frederick William III, Berlin, Mar. 9, 1830, Prussian Secret State Archives. (66) Rother to the privy councilor Count von Lottum, and to Motz, Jan. 9, 1830, Prussian Secret State Archives, Berlin. (67) Benecke to Count von Lottum, Rome, Jan. 14, 1830, Prussian Secret State Archives, Berlin. (68) Rother to the king, Berlin, Mar. 9, 1830. Prussian Secret State Archives, Berlin. (69) King Frederick William III to Rother, Mar. 17, 1830, Prussian Secret State Archives, Berlin. (70) The four Houses were Arnstein and Eskeles, Geymüller and Co., S. G. Sina, and M. A. Rothschild and Sons. (71) Count Kolowrat to Emperor Francis, Feb. 18, 1830, State Archives, Vienna. (72) Rothschild to Metternich, Vienna, Feb. 17, 1830, State Archives, Vienna. (73) *Historie des grandes opérations financières,* Capefigue (Paris, 1858), Vol. III, p. 158. (74) Solomon Rothschild to Count Nádasdy, Mainz, June 14, 1830, State Archives, Vienna. (75) Memorandum from the Frankfort branch of the House of Rothschild, June, 1830, State Archives, Vienna. (76) Nádasdy to Kolowrat. Memorandum dated Aug. 5, 1830, State Archives, Vienna. (77) *La révolution de juillet en 1830 et l'Europe,* Guichen (Paris, 1907). (78) Apponyi to Metternich, June 2, 1830, State Archives, Vienna. (79)

Solomon Rothschild to Prince Metternich, Paris, June 19, 1830, State Archives, Vienna. (80) Capefigue; see former ref., Vol. III, p. 312. (81) *Mémoires de la Princesse de Boigne,* Charles Nicoullaud (Paris, 1908), Vol. III, p. 312. (82) Talleyrand to Mme. Adélaïde, London, Oct. 15, 1830, *Mémoires du Prince Talleyrand* (Paris, 1892), Vol. III, p. 456. (83) British ambassador in Paris. (84) Solomon Rothschild to Metternich, Paris, July 30, 1830. Because the letter might have fallen into the hands of the revolutionaries, it lacks the usual formal beginning and ending. State Archives, Vienna. (85) Probably Wertheimstein. Report from Solomon in Paris, dated July 31, 1830, State Archives, Vienna. (86) State Archives, Vienna. (87) *Briefe von Friedrich von Gentz an Pilat* (Leipzig, 1868), Vol. II, p. 288. (88) Apponyi to Metternich, Paris, Aug. 16, 1830, State Archives, Vienna. (89) Solomon Rothschild to a friend, Paris, September, 1830, State Archives, Vienna. (90) Minister of foreign affairs in Louis Philippe's new ministry. (91) Solomon Rothschild "to a friend," Paris, September, 1830, State Archives, Vienna. (92) Solomon Rothschild to a friend (in this case possibly Gentz), Paris, Sept. 9, 1830, State Archives, Vienna. (93) James to Solomon, Paris, Nov. 24, 1830, State Archives, Vienna. (94) British ambassador in Paris. (95) James to Solomon, Paris, Nov. 27, 1830, State Archives, Vienna. (96) France's new finance minister. (97) Also from a communication from Solomon to Baron von Kübeck. See *Tagebücher des Karl Friedrich Freiherrn Kübeck von Kübau* (Vienna, 1909), Vol. I, Part II, p. 302. (98) Solomon to James, Vienna, Dec. 3, 1830, State Archives, Vienna. (99) Duke of Broglie, in the first Ministry of Aug. 11, 1830, when Molé was minister for foreign affairs. (100) Estimate of Rother in a report to King Frederick William III, based on a letter from Rothschild, Mar. 30, 1831, Prussian Secret State Archives, Berlin. (101) Extract from Rothschild's Paris letters dated Dec. 10 and 14, 1830, which Solomon handed to Metternich on Dec. 22, 1830, "for his gracious perusal," waiting upon Metternich personally later. State Archives, Vienna. (102) The intention was to take legal proceedings against Polignac, as being the originator of the ordinances, and against several of his fellow ministers.

BIOGRAPHICAL NOTES

on the principal persons mentioned

Bethmann, Simon Moritz von: Born 1768. Head of the Frankfort banking firm. Ennobled by Emperor Francis. Appointed consul-general and counselor by the Tsar. A patron of science and the arts. On his march through Frankfort, Napoleon I stopped at the Villa Bethmann in 1813. Died 1826.

Buderus von Carlshausen, Carl Friedrich: Born 1759. Son of a schoolmaster. Became principal revenue officer of Hesse and soon afterwards administrator of William of Hesse's estates, and his financial adviser. Later he became president of the Hessian Treasury at Hanau, minister plenipotentiary and envoy extraordinary to the German Diet at Frankfort, and to the grand-ducal court at Darmstadt, as well as electoral privy councilor. Died 1819.

Dalberg, Karl Theodor, Baron von: Born 1744. Last Elector of Mainz, and electoral high chancellor. In 1806 he was the presiding prince of the Confederation of the Rhine, his residence being at Frankfort. In 1810 made Grand Duke of Frankfort. The fall of Napoleon brought about the end of his rule. Died at Regensburg, 1817.

Gentz, Friedrich von: Born 1764 in Breslau. Was first in the Prussian, and later in the Austrian service. Was a publicist and secretary to Metternich. Was councilor in the chancellor's office, and became his most trusted adviser. Died at Vienna, 1832.

Hardenberg, Karl August, Prince von: Born 1750. Prussian statesman. Minister of Foreign Affairs, 1803, 1806 and during part of 1807. Appointed chancellor and head of the government after Stein's retirement in 1810. Died at Genoa, 1822.

Herries, John Charles: Born 1778. Private secretary to Vansittart, Chancellor of the Exchequer. Commissary-in-chief for financing the British and Allied forces on the Continent from Oct. 1, 1811, to Oct. 24, 1816. Appointed chancellor of the exchequer in 1827, but had to retire shortly afterwards.

Louis Philippe of Orléans, King of France: Born 1773. Joined the National Guard on the outbreak of the revolution, and served in the Republican army until 1793. After his father's execution he emigrated to Switzerland, and during the Napoleonic period he lived in America, England, Sicily, and Spain, not returning to France until the restoration of the elder line of the Bourbons. Having been placed on the throne after the July Revolution of

1830, he ruled until the February Revolution of 1848, and then went to England, where he died in 1850.

Marie Louise: Born 1791. Eldest daughter of Emperor Francis. Married Napoleon 1810, and bore him a son 1811, the King of Rome, afterwards Duke of Reichstadt. Left her husband on his abdication. Assumed the government of Parma, Piacenza, and Guastalla in 1816. After Napoleon's death, in 1822 married Count Neipperg morganatically, and after his death, Count Bombelles. Died 1847 at Vienna.

Marmont, Auguste Frédéric de, Duke of Ragusa, Marshal of France: Born 1774. Regarded as an exceptionally fine general by Napoleon. Appointed administrator of the Illyrian Provinces. One of the first to desert Napoleon in 1814 and submit to the Bourbons. Commanded the household troops of King Louis XVIII and Charles X, but failed to suppress the revolution in 1830. Left Paris and accompanied Charles X abroad. Died at Venice, 1852.

Metternich, Clemens Lothar, Prince von: Born 1773. Married Princess Marie Eleonore Kaunitz in 1795. In Austrian diplomatic service until 1809. Appointed minister of foreign affairs October 8, 1809. Chancellor and secretary of state 1821. Appointed president of ministerial conference for internal affairs 1826. Fled from Austria on account of the revolution in 1848. Did not return to Vienna until 1851. Died there 1859. Metternich's second wife was Baroness von Leykam. Third wife (1831) Melanie, Countess Zichy-Ferraris.

Neipperg, Adam Adalbert, Count von: Born 1775. General in the Austrian service. Concluded an alliance with Murat at Naples in 1814. Intervened again in the military affairs of that town in 1815. Became majordomo to Marie Louise in Parma, and her morganatic husband in 1822. Died Feb. 22, 1829 at Parma.

Parish, David, Baron von Senftenberg: Son of a Hamburg banker. Set up on his own, and later became a partner of the Vienna banking firm Fries and Co., in whose fall he was involved. Committed suicide at Vienna in April, 1826.

Rother, Christian von: Born 1778. Prussian Treasury official. Principal accountant to Hardenberg, who entrusted him with most important business. Director of the merchant service 1819. Reorganized the financial department 1820. Minister of state 1836. Died 1849.

Rothschild, Meyer Amschel: Born at Frankfort-on-the-Main 1743. Founder of the firm. Married Gutli Schnapper on Aug. 29, 1770. Died at Frankfort 1812.

Rothschild, Amschel Meyer: Eldest son of the above. Born June 12, 1773. Married Eva Hanau Nov. 16, 1796. Head of the Frankfort Bank. Died Dec. 6, 1855.

Rothschild, Salomon Meyer: Eldest son of the above. Born Sept. 9, 1774. Married Caroline Stern Nov. 26, 1800. Head of the Vienna Bank. Died July 27, 1855.

Rothschild, Nathan Meyer: Brother of the above. Born Sept. 16, 1777. Married Oct. 22, 1806, Hannah Barent Cohen. Head of the London Bank. Died July 28, 1836.

Rothschild, Carl Meyer: Brother of the above. Born Apr. 24, 1788. Married Adelheid Hertz Sept. 16, 1818. Head of the Naples Bank. Died Mar. 10, 1855.

Rothschild, James Meyer: Brother of the above. Born May 15, 1792. Married daughter of Salomon Rothschild on July 11, 1824. Head of the Paris Bank. Died Nov. 15, 1868.

Stadion, Johann Philipp, Count von: Born 1763. Entered Austrian diplomatic service. Minister of foreign affairs 1805-1809. After 1812, sometimes employed diplomatically and was appointed president of the treasury and finance minister. Died at Baden, near Vienna, 1824.

Villèle, Joseph, Count: Born 1773. French statesman. Member of the Chamber from 1815, and leader of the royalist ultras. Finance minister 1821. Prime minister 1822 to 1828. Died 1854.

Wellington, Arthur Wellesley, Duke of, Prince of Waterloo: Born 1769. Fought in East Indies and Denmark. Commanded British Expedition to Portugal 1808. Commander-in-chief against the French in Spain and Portugal until Napoleon's fall in 1814. Won the battle of Waterloo June 18, 1815. Took part in politics and represented England at Aix-la-Chapelle in 1818, and at the Congress of Verona in 1822. Commander-in-chief of the British forces on land in 1827. Member of the House of Lords. Tory. Prime minister 1828. After the July Revolution resigned, on William IV coming to the throne in November, 1830. Secretary of state for foreign affairs 1834-1835, under Peel. Died 1852 at Dover.

Wilhelm von Hesse: Born 1743. Ruled as Landgrave Wilhelm IX from 1785-1803, then as Elector Wilhelm I. Died at Cassel, 1821.

BIBLIOGRAPHY

Anonymous, *Les Rothschild* (Paris, 1925).
Ayer, Jules, *A Century of Finance, 1804 to 1904* (The London House of Rothschild).
Balla, Ignatz, *Die Rothschilds* (Berlin, 1912).
Baron, Dr. Salo. *Die Judenfrage auf dem Wiener Kongress* (Vienna and Berlin, 1920).
Beaulieu-Marconnay, Karl, Baron von, *Karl von Dalberg und seiner Zeit* (Weimar, 1879).
Beer, *Die österreichische Handelspolitik im 19. Jahrhundert* (Vienna, 1891).
Beer, Adolf, *Die Finanzen Österreichs im 19. Jahrhundert* (Prague, 1877).
Berghoeffer, Chr. W., *Meyer Amschel Rothschild* (Frankfort-on-the-Main, 1923).
Bethmann, Simon Moritz von, und seine Vorfahren (Frankfort-on-the-Main, 1898).
Bianchini, Cav. Lodovico, *Della storia delle finance del regno di Napoli libri sette* (Palermo, 1839).
Biographie, Allgemeine deutsche.
Biographie générale, Nouvelle (Paris, 1863).
Biography and Obituary, The Annual, 1857, Vol. XXI.
Boigne, Mémoires de la Comtesse de (Paris, 1907).
Bounatian, Dr. Mentor, *Geschichte der Handelskrisen in England 1640—1840* (Munich, 1908).
Brialmont, A., *Histoire du Duc de Wellington* (Paris, 1856).
Brunner, Dr. Hugo, *General Lagrange* (Cassel, 1897).
Buxton, Charles, ed., *Memoirs of Sir Thomas Fowell Buxton, Baronet* (London, 1848).
Capefigue, M., *Histoire des grandes opérations financières* (Paris, 1858), Vol. III.
Castelli, I. F. *Memoiren meines Lebens* (Munich, 1914).
Cussy, Souvenirs du chevalier de, 1795–1866 (Paris, 1909).
Démachy, Edouard, *Les Rothschild, une famille de financiers juifs au XIXe siècle* (Paris, 1896).
Despatches, Correspondence and Memoranda of Field Marshal Arthur, Duke of Wellington, edited by his son, the Duke of Wellington (London, 1867).
Dietz, Dr. Alex, *Frankfurter Handelsgeschichte* (Frankfort-on-the-Main, 1921 to 1925). This excellent and comprehensive five-volume work, in those pages devoted to Rothschild, points out the necessity of "reading between the lines" of Berghoeffer's work.

Drumont, Edouard, *La France juive* (Paris).
Ehrenberg, Dr. Richard, *Die Fugger, Rothschild, Krupp,* 3rd ed. (Jena, 1925).
Ehrenberg, Dr. Richard, *Das Haus Parish in Hamburg* (Jena, 1905).
Elking, Max von, *Die deutschen Hilfstruppen im nordamerikanischen Befreiungskriege 1776-1783.*
Enzyklopädie für die gebildeten Stände, Allgemeine deutsche Real. . . .
Faber, *Herr von Hormayr und die Lebensbilder aus dem Befreiungskriege* (Leipzig, 1844).
Fournier, *Napoleon I* (Vienna, 1822).
Frankfurter Zeitung, Geschichte der (Frankfort-on-the-Main, 1911).
Gentz, *Briefwechsel zwischen Friedrich Gentz und Adam Müller 1800 bis 1829* (Stuttgart, 1857).
Gentz, *Aus dem Nachlass Friedrich von Gentz* (Vienna, 1867).
Gentz, *Briefe von Friedrich von Gentz an Pilat* (Leipzig, 1868).
Gentz, *Tagebücher von Friedrich von Gentz aus dem Nachlass Varnhagens von Ense* (Leipzig, 1874).
Gentz, *Briefe von und an Friedrich von Gentz* (Vienna, 1867).
Grillparzer, *Selbstbiographie und Bildnisse* (Vienna, 1923).
Guichen, *La révolution de juillet en 1830 et l'Europe* (Paris, 1917).
Herries, Edward, *Memoirs of the Public Life of the Right Hon. John Charles Herries in the Reigns of George III, George IV, William IV, and Victoria* (London, 1880).
Heyck, *Die Allgemeine Zeitung* (Munich, 1898).
Heyden, *Galerie berühmter und merkwüralger Frankfurter* (Frankfort-on-the-Main, 1861).
(Hormayr zu Hartenburg), *Kaiser Franz und Metternich* (Leipzig, 1848).
Humboldt, Wilhelm und Caroline von, in ihren Briefen 1815-1817 (Berlin, 1912).
Jakobson, Israel, *Unterthänigste Vorstellung an S.H. den Fürstprimas der Rheinkonföderation über dessen neue Stättigkeitsschutzordnung für die Judenschaft in Frankfurt a. Main* (Braunschweig, 1808).
Jost, *Neuere Geschichte der Israeliten 1815-1845* (Berlin, 1846).
Kapp, Friedrich, *Der Soldatenhandel deutscher Fürsten nach Amerika 1775-1783* (Berlin, 1864).
Kohout, Dr. Adolph, *Finanzgrössen und grosse Finanzen* (Berlin, 1909).
Kralik, *Geschichte der neuesten Zeit von 1815 bis zur Gegenwart* (Vienna and Graz, 1820).
Kriegk, G. L., *Geschichte von Frankfurt a. M. in ausgewählten Darstellungen* (Frankfort-on-the-Main, 1871).
Kübeck von Kübau, *Tagebücher des Carl Friedrich, Frh. v* (Vienna, 1909).
Kübeck von Kübau, *Metternich und Kübeck—Ein Briefwechsel* (Vienna, 1910).
Lee, Sidney, *Dictionary of National Biography* (London, 1897).
Losch, Dr. Philipp, *Kurfürst Wilhelm I* (Marburg, 1923).
Marbot, Mémoires du général baron de (Paris, 1891)

Marion, Marcel, *Histoire financière de la France depuis 1715* (Paris, 1914).
Matrac, *Les Rothschild, leur origine, Waterloo, leur fortune* (Paris, 1909).
Metternich, Richard, Prince, *Aus Metternichs nachgelassenen Papieren* (Vienna, 1880).
Nervo, Baron de, *Les finances françaises sous la restauration 1814-1830* (Paris, 1867).
Nicoullaud, Charles, *Mémoires de la Comtesse de Boigne* (Paris, 1908).
Ouvrard, G. I., *Mémoires de, sur sa vie et ses diverses opérations financières* (Paris, 1926).
Picciotto, James, *Sketches of Anglo-Jewish History* (London, 1875).
Pribram, Alfred Francis, *Österreichische Staatsverträge* (Vienna, 1913).
Rabinowics, Dr. I. M., *La famille de Rothschild* (1882).
Reeves, John, *The Rothschilds—The Financial Rulers of Nations* (London, 1887).
Rother, Christian von, Obituary Notice. Special edition of the Preussischer Staatsanzeiger of Dec. 15 and 16, 1849 (Berlin, 1849).
Scharf von Scharffenstein, *Das geheime Treiben, der Einfluss und die Macht des Judentums in Frankreich seit 100 Jahren (1771-1871)* (Stuttgart, 1872).
Scherb, von, *Geschichte des Hauses Rothschild* (Berlin, 1872).
Schlesier, Gustav von, *Ungedruckte Denkschriften, Tagebücher und Briefe von Gentz* (Mannheim, 1840).
Schmidt-Weissenfels, E., *Geschichte des modernen Reichtums* (Berlin, 1893).
Schmidt-Weissenfels, E., *Friedrich Gentz* (Prague, 1859).
Schwemer, *Geschichte der freien Stadt Frankfurt a. M. 1814-1856* (Frankfort-on-the-Main, 1910).
Smidt, Johann, *Ein Gedenkbuch zur Säcularfeier seines Geburtstags* (Bremen, 1878).
Srbik, Heinrich von, *Metternich, der Staatsmann und der Mensch* (Munich, 1925).
Statistical review of all coin, exchange and bond values between the years 1796-1832, State Archives, Vienna.
Steinmann, Fr., *Das Haus Rothschild. Seine Geschichte und seine Geschäfte* (Prague and Leipzig, 1857).
Strobl von Ravelsberg, *Metternich und seine Zeit 1773-1859* (Vienna and Leipzig, 1907).
Talleyrand, *Mémoires du Prince, publiés par le Duc de Broglie* (Paris, 1892).
Treskow, A. von, *Biographische Notizen über Nathan Meyer Rothschild* (Quedlinburg, 1837).
Übersicht der Lage und der rechtlichen Gesuche der Fuldaischen und Hanauischen Domänenkäufer (Frankfort-on-the-Main, 1814).
Vehse, *Geschichte der deutschen Höfe.*
Verschner, O. C., Baron von, *Die deutschen Hilfstruppen im amerikanischen Revolutionskriege* (Brunswick, 1901).

Verschner, O. C., Baron von, *Die Hessen und die anderen deutschen Hilfstruppen im Kriege Grossbritanniens gegen Amerika 1776-1783* (Brunswick and Leipzig, 1901).
Villèle, Mémoires et correspondances du Comte de (Paris, 1888).
Wachstein, *Die Inschriften des alten Judenfriedhofes in Wien* (Vienna, 1912).
Walpole, Spencer, *History of France from the Conclusion of the Great War in 1815* (London, 1878).
Ward and Gooch, *The Cambridge History of British Foreign Policy, 1783-1919.*
Webster, *The Foreign Policy of Castlereagh, 1815–1822* (London, 1925).
Weil, *Les dessous du Congrès de Vienne* (Paris, 1917).
Weill, *Rothschild und die europäischen Staaten* (Stuttgart, 1844).
Wellington, *The Dispatches of Field Marshal the Duke of, During his Various Campaigns, from 1799 to 1848* (London, 1837).
Wirth, Max, *Geschichte der Handelskrisen* (Frankfort-on-the-Main, 1883).
Zichy, *Gróf Széchényi István* (Budapest, 1896).

Why Businessmen Need a Philosophy of Capitalism

Capitalism has built the modern world. Although there are some who would dispute that claim, it is clear, at least for those who examine the facts without bias or political intent, that economies based on capitalism are stronger and expand at a faster rate than other economic systems. This fact has been well established throughout history.

At its simplest and purest, capitalism is an economic system in which private individuals and companies produce and exchange goods and services through free markets. Ideally, capitalism is not hindered by governmental controls; in reality, however, there are many shades and nuances of capitalism that result in economic systems that are often described as a *mixed economy.* In some lands, capitalism is restrained by laws and governmental regulations; the degree determined by political and social objectives. Many political leaders hope to influence their people via the economy, they may attempt to protect domestic business from foreign competition, or they may try to increase revenue with tariffs or export duties. That these types of objectives usually only hinder economic activity over the long term is frequently ignored, lost in the rhetoric about social considerations and goals.

Of the many factors that can affect how the capitalist spirit develops in a country, one which is often overlooked is that of entrepreneurship. In lands where capitalism is unfettered by unnecessary regulation and where entrepreneurship is dynamic, impressive economic gains and advancements can be expected. Entrepreneurship is perhaps one of the greatest driving forces of capitalism. Indeed, the two are inseparable.

Capitalism is an economic system in which the means of production and distribution are privately owned and operated, and an entrepreneur is an individual who undertakes to start and conduct a business. Entrepreneurs propel capitalism forward. The bottom line here is quite clear: if a person is restricted in his ownership of a business through governmental regulations or social constraints, why should he or she risk starting any economic enterprise? Conversely, if an individual perceives that his or her efforts will be the overall deciding factor in economic gain or loss, he or she is more likely to risk investment in a business venture.

The world has seen many different economic systems throughout history. With its origins deep in the mists of ancient societies, barter was one of the first economies in which individuals and groups exchanged goods and services, paying for one commodity with another. Rudimentary forms of capitalism were not far behind and their origins are likewise obscure. Capitalism is generally thought to have arisen in various places around the world, gained prominence in old Europe centuries ago where it developed slowly and gradually spread through most of the world, reaching its zenith during the 19th century and remaining dominant until World War I. For a time during the 20th century, communism, a system in which the state plays a major role in economic ownership, regulation, and intervention, challenged capitalism's dominance, particularly in the Eastern Hemisphere, but as the century ended, capitalism, in one form of another, has re-emerged as the world's premier economic system.

The effect of capitalism extends far beyond economics, however, for capitalism is a major factor in the evolution of nations. Virtually every great nation through history has been a potent economic power as well. An excellent example of this in the 20th century is the ascendance of the Soviet Union as a world power after World War II. For a time the Soviet Union, founded on communism, seemed ready to challenge the United States for world military, cultural, and economic supremacy, but their threat was short-lived. While some observers of the world scene argue that it was American President Ronald Reagan's hard-line military stance against the Soviet Union that led to the eventual breakup and dissolution of that communist state, it was American economic power, based on capitalism, that provided Reagan with the foundation on which he could make his stand. Communism could not keep pace with America's economic strength. Reagan's policies also have led to the People's Republic of China slowly but steadily turning to capitalism to enhance their economy. Mainland China's appreciation of capitalism is well illustrated with the reversion of Hong Kong – one of the world's greatest free-market success stories – to Mainland control and the pledge of the Chinese government not to tamper with Hong Kong's economy, a promise the Chinese have honored.

The resurgence of capitalism at the end of the 20th century has been driven by a powerful tide of entrepreneurship in the technology sector, most apparent in the explosive growth of the Internet, and has led to spectacular economic gains. E-commerce (electronic commerce) is without question changing the way the world does business, and it can easily be termed E-capitalism.

We are in a period in which economic opportunity has seldom been greater. As technology and the Internet continue to advance, every business or enterprise that can benefit from them has the opportunity to advance as well. Ten years ago, few of the top Internet companies had even been imagined. Ten years ago, we were only on the verge of the new capitalist economy that, while built on the old principles of capitalism, is immeasurably enhanced by technological know-how. Ten years ago, traditional businesses were still the norm. And now, new ideas are giving rise to new companies every day. The businesses, services, and companies that may dominate the economic landscape ten years from now are still in the formulation stages of their creators. The opportunities for entrepreneurs are perhaps greater than ever.

Certainly we are witnessing the coming of a new economic age in which those individuals and companies that produce the goods and services that satisfy the needs of a modern, fast-paced world will be the most successful. Technology permits customers to buy the items or services they desire with a mere click of a mouse. Individuals who embrace the spirit of the entrepreneur and who are able to ascertain the needs of potential customers stand to benefit handsomely.

After all, entrepreneurs have been creating and running businesses since primitive times. Going back to the earliest societies, farmers, fisherman, and merchants traded their goods and services. Every business that exists today at one time was the dream and ambition of an entrepreneur. The entrepreneur is the visionary, the man or woman with the better idea, the innovator, the doer. It is the entrepreneur who creates the original product, acquires the facilities and materials, obtains the capital, assembles the workforce, and brings the finished product to market. It is also the entrepreneur who reaps the profits of a successful venture. In the case of failure, the entrepreneur stands to take the major loss.

Capitalism and entrepreneurship are closely linked. Capitalism is the economic system most conducive to entrepreneurship, and entrepreneurship provides the innovation and energy of capitalism. Each sustains and gains strength from the other, together forming a solid bedrock for economic activity.

While opportunity for entrepreneurs is present in the most advanced economies, clearly developing economies offer the greatest opportunities because of their nature, which usually includes a rapidly growing middle class with a strong desire for consumer products. As companies attempt to meet the needs of these new consumers, entrepreneurs are likely to find countless opportunities. In advanced nations new products and services are typically brought to market by major corporations that maintain huge staffs, whose primary purpose is the design and creation of new products. In smaller, developing nations, however, niche markets and special needs present an environment that is ripe for innovation. In many of these nations, governments may actively support entrepreneurs through a variety of special programs, including tax incentives, special trade status, and an assortment of grants, to encourage investment and economic activity. The leaders of such governments are aware that entrepreneurs energize capitalism, which in turn leads to economic growth.

As the global economy continues to expand, world trade will undoubtedly increase. At the same time, because of the growing role of technology, boundaries between nations and markets will shrink, providing entrepreneurs will marvelous opportunities, limited only by their own imaginations. The world is entering a rare and wonderful environment for the entrepreneur.

An extensive library of articles on capitalism and free-markets is at http://www.libertyhaven.com

Afterword by Adam Starchild

Over the past 25 years, Adam Starchild has been the author of over two dozen books, and hundreds of magazine articles, primarily on business and finance. His articles have appeared in a wide range of publications around the world — including Business Credit, Euromoney, Finance, The Financial Planner, International Living, Offshore Financial Review, Reason, Tax Planning International, The Bull & Bear, Trust & Estates, and many more.

Now semi-retired, he was the president of an international consulting group specializing in banking, finance and the development of new businesses, and director of a trust company.

Although this formidable testimony to expertise in his field, plus his current preoccupation with other books-in-progress, would not seem to leave time for a well-rounded existence, Starchild has won two Presidential Sports Awards and written several cookbooks, and is currently involved in a number of personal charitable projects.

His personal website is at http://www.cyberhaven.com/starchild/

www.ingramcontent.com/pod-product-compliance
Lightning Source LLC
Chambersburg PA
CBHW021544210326
41599CB00010B/304
* 9 7 8 0 8 9 4 9 9 0 5 8 8 *